Borgo Literary Guides
Number One
ISSN 0891-9623

Reginald's Science Fiction and Fantasy Awards

A Comprehensive Guide to the
Awards and Their Winners

*Third Edition,
Revised and Expanded*

by
Daryl F. Mallett
and Robert Reginald

THE BORGO PRESS
Publishers Since 1975
Post Office Box 2845
San Bernardino, CA 92406
United States of America

* * * * * * * *

Copyright © 1979, 1981 by Robert Reginald
Copyright © 1991, 1993 by Robert Reginald & Daryl F. Mallett

All rights reserved.
No part of this book may be reproduced in any
form without the expressed written consent of the publisher. Printed in the United States of America by Van
Volumes, Ltd. Cover design by Highpoint Type & Graphics.

Library of Congress Cataloging-in-Publication Data

Reginald, R.
 Reginald's science fiction and fantasy awards : a comprehensive guide to the awards and their winners / by Daryl F. Mallett and Robert Reginald. — 3rd ed., rev. and expanded.
  p. cm. (Borgo literary guides, ISSN 0891-9623 ; no. 1)
 Includes bibliographical references and index.
  ISBN 0-8095-0200-3 (cloth). — ISBN 0-8095-1200-9 (pbk.)
  1. Science fiction—Awards. 2. Fantastic literature—Awards. I. Mallett, Daryl F. (Daryl Furumi), 1969- . II. Title. III. Series.
P96.S34R4 1993   92-24445
808.83'876'079—dc20   CIP

THIRD EDITION

CONTENTS

Introduction 9
How to Use This Book 11
About the Authors 12

I. GENRE AWARDS

1. A. Bertram Chandler Award 14
2. Aëlita Award 14
3. Aisling Gheal Award 14
4. Alkor Poll Award 15
5. Alvar Appletofft Memorial Award 16
6. Andre Norton Award 16
7. Andre Norton Fantasy/SF Short Story Award 16
8. Arthur C. Clarke Award 17
9. Atlanta Fantasy Faire Award 18
10. Atorox Award 18
11. Balrog Award 18
12. Boomerang Award 20
13. Boris Strugatsky Prize 21
14. Bram Stoker Award 21
15. British Fantasy Award 22
16. British Science Fiction Association Award 25
17. Casper and Aurora Awards [Canadian SF and Fantasy Achievement Award] 27
18. Chesley Award 28
19. China SF Constellation/Galaxy Award 30
20. China SF Milky Way Award/Forest Cup 31
21. *Chronic Rift* Roundtable Award 31
22. Chumatski Shlyah Award 31
23. Clampett Humanitarian Award 32
24. Clarion Award 32
25. Clark Darlton Prize 32
26. Collectors Award 32
27. Compton N. Crook/Stephen Tall Memorial Award 33
28. Count Dracula Society Award 34
29. Daedalus Award 37
30. Dasa Award 37
31. Davis and Dell Readers Awards 37
32. Deutscher Fantasy Preis 39
33. Ditmar Award [Australian SF and Fantasy Achievement Award] 39
34. Doc Weir Award 43
35. E. E. Evans/Paul Frehafer Award 43
36. E. Everett Evans "Big Heart" Award 44
37. Early Universe Award 45

38. Eastcon Award 45
39. Edmond Hamilton/Leigh Brackett Memorial Award 45
40. Eurocon Award 45
41. Fantastyka Award 46
42. *Fear* Fiction Award 47
43. Festival Fantastique d'Avoriaz Award 47
44. Festival Internazionale del Film di Fantascienza Award 47
45. First Fandom Hall of Fame Award 51
46. Fond Fantastiki Prize 51
47. Forry Award 51
48. Frank R. Paul Award 52
49. Galaxy/Dell Science Fiction Novel Contest 52
50. Georges Méliès Award 53
51. Gernsback Award 53
52. Golden Duck Award 53
53. Golden Lion Award 54
54. Gollancz/BBC Radio 4 *Bookshelf* First Fantasy Novel Award 54
55. Grand Prix de la Science-Fiction Française 54
56. Grand Prix Logidec 56
57. Graviton Award 56
58. Gray Mouser Award 56
59. Grimmy Award [Horror Hall of Fame Award] 57
60. Gryphon Award 57
61. HOMer Award 57
62. Hugo Award [Science Fiction Achievement Award] 58
63. *IAM* Award 67
64. Inkpot Award 67
65. International Association for the Fantastic in the Arts Award 69
66. International Fantasy Award 70
67. Invisible Little Man Award 71
68. J. Lloyd Eaton Memorial Award 71
69. Jack Gaughan Memorial Award 72
70. James Tiptree Jr. Memorial Award 72
71. Japan Fantasy Novel Award 72
72. Jerónimo Montiero Contest 73
73. Jerry Oltion's Really Good Story Award 73
74. John W. Campbell Jr. Memorial & Theodore Sturgeon Memorial Awards ... 73
75. Jules Verne Award 75
76. Jupiter Award 75
77. Karel Award [World Science Fiction Award] 76
78. Karel Capek Award 77
79. Ken McIntyre Award 78
80. King Kong Award 79
81. Kurd Lasswitz Award [German SF and Fantasy Achievement Award] 79
82. L. Ron Hubbard's Writers of the Future/Illustrators of the Future Awards ... 81
83. Lambda Literary Award [SF categories only] 85
84. Lazar Komarcic Award [Yugoslavian SF and Fantasy Achievement Award] . 86
85. *Locus* Award 87
86. Ludvik Soucek Award [Czechoslovak SF & Fantasy Achievement Award] ... 92
87. Mannesmann-Tally Award 93
88. Más Alla Award [Argentinian SF and Fantasy Achievement Award] 93
89. Milford Award 94

90. Minnesota Fantasy Award..94
91. Mythopoeic Society Fantasy Award 94
92. N3F Amateur Short Story Contest 95
93. Nebula Award...96
94. Nihon Science Fiction Taisho 99
95. Nova Award..100
96. Philip K. Dick Memorial Award...100
97. Phoenix & Rebel Awards..101
98. Pilgrim & Pioneer Awards..101
99. Polish Science Fiction and Fantasy Achievement Award 102
100. Pong Award 103
101. Premios Cometa d'Argento 103
102. Premios Gilgamés de Narrativa Fantastica 104
103. Premios Italiano di Fantascienza 107
104. *Prisoners of Gravity* Reality 1 Commendation Award................109
105. Prix Apollo 109
106. Prix Boréal..110
107. Prix Cosmos 2000 110
108. Prix Jules Verne 111
109. Prix Julia Verlanger 111
110. Prix Rosny-Aîné..111
111. Prix Rotary 112
112. Prometheus Award 112
113. Pyramid Books/*F&SF*/Kent Productions Science Fiction Novel Contest.....113
114. Readercon Small Press Science Fiction Award 113
115. Reuben Award 115
116. Rhysling Award...116
117. Robbie Award [Australian Science Fiction Media Award]...........117
118. Russ Manning Award..117
119. Saturn Award [Science Fiction, Fantasy, and Horror Film Award]...........118
120. Saturn Award (II)...124
121. Science Fiction & Fantasy Workshop Award 125
122. Science Fiction Book Club Award 125
123. *Science Fiction Chronicle* Award 125
124. Science Fiction Club Deutschland Award 128
125. Science Fiction Games of the Year Award 129
126. Science Fiction Writers of Earth Short Story Contest 129
127. Seiun Taisho..130
128. Shasta Publishers/Pocket Books Contest......................................132
129. Skylark Award 132
130. Soccon Award 133
131. Southpaw Award...133
132. Svenska SF Priset [Swedish SF and Fantasy Achievement Award]............133
133. Turner Tomorrow Award 134
134. Twilight Dimension Award 134
135. Wetzlar Fantastik Preis 134
136. Will Eisner Comic Industry Award...135
137. World Fantasy Award..137
138. Writers of the Past Award...140
139. Zauber Zeit Award 140

5

II. NON-GENRE AWARDS

140. Academy of Family Films and Family Television Award 142
141. A.D.E.-M.L.A. Distinguished Teaching Award 142
142. Aerospace Communications Award 142
143. American and National Book Awards 142
144. American Mystery Award 143
145. American Studies Book Prize 143
146. Antonius Prize of Danish Society for Mental Hygiene 143
147. Arts and Letters Award 143
148. Athenaeum Literary Award 143
149. AWA Writing Award 143
150. Award of Merit Medal 144
151. Benson Medal 144
152. Bess Hokin Prize 144
153. *Boston Globe* Horn Book Award 144
154. British Critics Award 144
155. Brown University/Academy of American Poets Prize 145
156. Buenos Aires City Hall Literary Prize 145
157. Caldecott Medal 145
158. California Writers Award 145
159. Carnegie Medal 145
160. Catholic Library Association Reginal Medal 145
161. Children's Book Award 145
162 Cleveland Critics Award 146
163. Daroff Memorial Fiction Award 146
164. Duodecimal Society Award 146
165. Edgar (Allen Poe) Award [American Mystery Writers Award] 146
166. Emmy Award 146
167. Empire State Award for Excellence in Literature 148
168. Eunice Tietjens Memorial Award 148
169. Freedom Foundation at Valley Forge Honor Medal 148
170. Golden Globe Award 148
171. Governor General's Literary Award 148
172. Hall of Fame Colonnade 148
173. Hans Christian Andersen International Medal 149
174. Harold V. Dursell Memorial Award 149
175. Heinemann Award 149
176. Image Award 149
177. International Forum for Neurological Organization Award 149
178. Jack I. & Lillian L. Poses/Brandeis University Creative Arts Award 149
179. James J. Strebig Award 150
180. James Tait Black Memorial Prize 150
181. Jerusalem Prize 150
182. John Llewelyn Rhys Memorial Prize 150
183. John Masefield Award 150
184. Knighthood of Mark Twain 150
185. Lenin Peace Prize 151
186. Levinson Prize 151
187. Macmillan Cock Robin Award 151
188. *Manchester Guardian* Fiction Prize 151
189. Mary Lyons Award 151

190. Medicis Prize..151
191. Melville Cane Award 151
192. Morton Dauwen Zabel Award..152
193. NASA Headquarters Exceptional Performance Award 152
194. NCR Book Award for Nonfiction..152
195. New York Critics Award..152
196. Newbery Nedal 152
197. Nobel Prize..152
198. Oklahoma Professional Writers Hall of Fame..152
199. Oscar Award...153
200. Patsy Award 156
201. Peabody Award 157
202. *Playboy* Writing Award 157
203. Presidential Medal of Freedom..157
204. Prix du Meilleur Roman Etranger 157
205. Prix Sylla Monsegur 157
206. Pulitzer Prize..158
207. Robert S. Ball Memorial Award 158
208. Sidney Howard Memorial Award 158
209. Somerset Maugham Award...158
210. Southwest Book Award..158
211. Spur Award...158
212. Theresa Helburn Memorial Award..159
213. Top Hands Award 159
214. U.S. Air Force Academy Special Achievement Award..........................159
215. U.S. Industrial Film and Video Festival Award.....................................159
216. U.S.S.R. Writers' Union Award..159
217. Union League Arts & Civic Foundation Poetry Prize 159
218. University of Chicago Professional Achievement Award 160
219. University of Michigan/Avery Hopwood Drama Award........................160
220. University of Oklahoma/Dwight V. Swain Award.................................160
221. University of Texas/Carl Hertzog Award...160
222. ViRA Award 160
223. W. H. Smith Illustration Award..160
224. Waldo Award..161
225. Western Heritage Award 161
226. Whitbread Prize..161
227. William Allen White Children's Book Award 161
228. Writers Guild of America, West Award 161

APPENDICES

1. Officers of the Science Fiction and Fantasy Writers of America, Inc. 163
2. Officers of the Science Fiction Research Association............................167
3. Officers of the Horror Writers of America 170
4. World Science Fiction Conventions 171
5. World Fantasy Conventions..173
6. World Horror Conventions 174

Author Index...175
Index to Award Names..245

DEDICATION

*For Annette:
The Golden Lion,
Winner of my heart*

*And for Hal W. Hall:
Whose trust inspires loyalty,
And creates winners*

—D.F.M.

*To Jack Dann,
Always a Winner*

—R.R.

INTRODUCTION

This version of *Reginald's Science Fiction and Fantasy Awards* is the third edition of a comprehensive guide to the major and minor awards presented in the related fields of science fiction, fantasy, and horror literature and film. The book emphasizes English-language awards, although information on foreign accolades is included when known. The second edition was expanded by more than three times over the 1981 version, itself the most comprehensive listing of such honors ever published, and this third edition adds even more awards, and rearranges the basic data into two sections: Genre Awards and Non-Genre Awards. Future editions will be issued at intervals of roughly two years, and will continue to add further accolades, as well as providing more details about the awards already listed.

Any project of this type inevitably follows in the footsteps of previous scholarship. Very special thanks to: George Slusser and Mary Burgess, who helped create a monster; to Jerry & Debbie Hewett and Arthur Loy Holcomb for providing computers and hardware/software support as well as encouragement; to Gladys Murphy and Karen Madokoro (the staff of the Eaton Collection at UCR) for materials.

For moral support, thanks to: Gavan Albright, Maureen "Mouse" Cline, Justin Cluer, Eric Curry, April Dancer, James & JoLynn Huff, Bill and Masuko Mallett, Luella Mallett, Stacie and Briana Mallett, Kathleen Mayo, Michelle Montano, Miriam Pace, Roger Palmer, Janice Replogle, Leonard & Teddy Replogle, Michele Riddle, Alison Saylor, Danielle Slusser, Jennifer Stilson, Shoshona Stocking, Clint Zehner; and Annette, the Golden Lion, for all her love and encouragement.

And for assistance in all areas: Forrest J Ackerman; Paul Alkon; Ian & Betty Ballantine; Greg Bear; Gregory Benford; David Brin; Charles N. Brown; Algis Budrys; Zayra Cabot; Elizabeth Chater; Rob Chilson; John Clute; Robert Collins; Bill Contento; Chris Curry; Ginger Curry; Charles de Lint; Rachel Denk; Fae Desmond; Harlan & Susan Ellison; Jackie Estrada; Dennis Etchison; Sheila Finch; Kelly & Laura Freas; Diana G. Gallagher; Dale & Liz Gibbons; Jaq Greenspon; James Gunn; Jon Gustafson; Hal Hall; Fred Harris; Christopher Hinz; L. Dean James; Roy Lavender; Barry & Sally Levin; Gary Louie; Peter Lowentrout; Faren Miller; Elizabeth Moon; Marianne O. Nielsen; Andre Norton; Jerry Oltion; Ron & Val Ontell; Andy Porter; Robert Runté; Charles C. Ryan; Brendan & Helen Ryder; Robert J. Sawyer; Charles Sheffield; Robert Silverberg; Rick Sternbach; Jefferson P. Swycaffer; Michael D. Toman; A. E. & Lydia van Vogt; Jack & Norma Vance; Scott Welch; William F. Wu.

Thanks too to the following organizations and libraries for assistance: Author Services Inc.; Bridge Publications Inc.; The Dragon's Lair Bookstore, Riverside, CA; The Golden Lion Library, Riverside, CA; The Horror Writers of America (HWA); The International Association for the Fantastic in the Arts (IAFA); The Irish Science Fiction Association (ISFA); The J. Lloyd Eaton Collection of Science Fiction and Fantasy Literature, Tomás Rivera Library, University of California, Riverside; The John M. Pfau Library, California State University, San

Bernardino; L. Ron Hubbard's Writers & Illustrators of the Future Contest; Los Angeles Science Fantasy Society (LASFS); Paramount Pictures (*Star Trek*; *Star Trek: The Next Generation*); San Diego ComiCon; The Science Fiction Poetry Association (SFPA); The Science Fiction Research Association (SFRA); The Science Fiction & Fantasy Writers of America, Inc. (SFFWA); and The Unicorn Library, San Bernardino, CA.

Comments, corrections, and additions are welcome, and should be sent to the editors care of The Borgo Press, P.O. Box 2845, San Bernardino, CA 92406.

—Daryl F. Mallett
Robert Reginald
6 January 1993

HOW TO USE THIS BOOK

Those English-language awards unique to the fields of science fiction, fantasy, or horror are arranged alphabetically in the main section by award name, then chronologically by year (the first year listed represents the period for which the work or person was honored; the second date [in parentheses] is the year of actual presentation). Achievements which are customarily broken into two or more categories are listed under each year in the order by which they are typically organized by the issuing agency—usually in descending order by size of the work being honored. Thus, novel-length winners are typically listed first, followed by novellas, novelettes, short stories, dramatic works, in that order, plus miscellaneous awards.

The second section of the book includes those awards not specifically limited to fantastic literature, but which have occasionally honored SF and fantasy writers or filmmakers. The appendices provide lists of the officers of The Science Fiction and Fantasy Writers of America, Inc. (SFWA), The Horror Writers of America (HWA), and The Science Fiction Research Association (SFRA), a complete record of World Science Fiction Conventions, World Fantasy Conventions, and World Horror Conventions and their guests of honor, and statistical tables showing all-time winners of each of the major awards.

End matter includes: a complete index to the individuals honored, giving names of winners, award names, and categories and years of award; eight statistical tables; and an index to award names and the pages on which each award is listed.

ABOUT THE AUTHORS

DARYL F. MALLETT was born at Los Angeles in 1969, and is currently an editor at The Borgo Press, a freelance writer, an actor, and editor of *The SFRA Review*. In addition to compiling the second incarnation of this book (with Robert Reginald), he has also edited an anthology of verse (*Full Frontal Poetry*) with Chaelyn L. Hakim and Frances McConnel, and was Associate Editor (with Mary A. Burgess) on Reginald's massive bibliography of fantastic literature, *Science Fiction and Fantasy Literature* (Gale Research, 1992). Soon to be published are *The Work of Jack Vance* (with Jerry Hewett) and *The Work of Elizabeth Chater* (with Annette Mallett). He and collaborators Arthur Loy Holcomb and Barbra Wallace recently sold a premise to *Star Trek: The Next Generation* which appeared as the two-part episode "Birthright."

Screen appearances include: *Cannibal Women in the Avocado Jungle of Death*, *Star Trek: The Next Generation*, and *Star Trek VI: The Undiscovered Country*, all in categories for which there is no Oscar. He, his wife Annette, and their small family of two cats make their home in Riverside, CA, where he attempts to write as much as possible.

ROBERT REGINALD (Professor Michael Burgess) is the author of sixty-five books, including the 1500-page bibliography, *Science Fiction and Fantasy Literature, 1975-1991* (Gale Research, 1992), and *Reference Guide to Science Fiction, Fantasy, and Horror* (Libraries Unlimited, 1992). His next major work will be the Second Edition of *Lords Temporal and Lord Spiritual*, a chronological checklist and history of the popes, patriarchs, and catholicoi of the autocephalous Orthodox churches, to be published by The Borgo Press in 1993.

PART ONE

GENRE

AWARDS

1. THE A. BERTRAM CHANDLER AWARD
(AUSTRALIA)

The A(rthur) Bertram Chandler Award, named for the well-known Australian science fiction writer (1912-1984), is presented by the Australian Science Fiction Foundation for outstanding achievement in Australian science fiction. A jury selects the award annually.

THE A. BERTRAM CHANDLER AWARDS

1992—Van Ikin

2. THE AELITA AWARD
(USSR/RUSSIA)

The Aëlita Award, sponsored by the Soviet Writers Union and *Uralsky Sledopyt* (a Russian science fiction magazine), was established in 1981. The award is named for the heroine of Aleksei Tolstoi's SF novel, *Aëlita*, and consists of a crystal globe perched upon a helix of two intertwining strips of metal on a raw quartz base, costing roughly 2,000 rubles each. The Ivan Yefremov Award recognizes contributions to the development of Soviet science fiction. The Great Ring Award is given by Soviet fandom for their favorite novel, and physically resembles the American Hugo Award. The Start Award was added in 1989 as a runnerup prize to the Aëlita.

THE AELITA AWARDS

1980 (1981)—(tie) A. Kazantsev; Arkady and Boris Strugatsky
1981 (1982)—*The Children of the Blue Flamingo*, by Vladislav Krapivin
1982 (1983)—Zinovi Yuriev; **Great Ring Award**—*And We'll Talk It Over*, by Vladimir Mikhalikov
1983 (1984)—*The Moon Rainbow*, by Sergei Pavlov
1984 (1985)—*Men Like Gods*, by Sergei Snegov
1985 (1986)—No awards
1986 (1987)—*Sonata of the Sea*, by Olga Larionova; **Yefremov Award**—Georgi Gurevich
1987 (1988)—Viktor Kolupayev for lifetime achievement; **Yefremov Award**—(tie) Dmitri Bilenkin; Vitaly Bugrov, for editing *Uralsky Sledopyt*

1988 (1989)

Aëlita—*Instinct?*, by Sever Gansovskii
Yefremov Award—Georgii Grechko, for helping popularize SF
Start—*Whose is the Planet?*, by Boris Shtern
Fan Award (Novel)—*Time of Rain* (aka *The Ugly Swans*), by Arkady and Boris Strugatsky
Fan Award (Short Story)—"The Industrial Story #1," by Boris Shtern
Fan Award (Translation)—*The Futurological Congress*, by Stanislaw Lem

1989 (1990)

Aëlita—*Na Vostok ot Polunochi* (*Eastward from Midnight*), by Oleg Korabel'nikov
Yefremov Award—Viktor Babenko, for best SF propaganda
New Author—Andry Stolyarov

3. THE AISLING GHEAL AWARD
(IRELAND)

The Aisling Gheal Award (Gaelic for Bright Vision) was presented by the Irish Science Fiction Association (ISFA) in the late 1970s and early '80s to encourage new writers of science fiction and fantasy in Ireland. Between twenty and thirty stories were submitted each year to ISFA, which then reduced the list to seven or eight finalists. Winners were selected by

James White, Anne McCaffrey, and Harry Harrison. The award consisted of a bronze, amulet-like trophy of Celtic design, plus a cash prize of twenty-five Irish punts. Second and third place winners received fifteen and ten punts, respectively. The association became inactive in 1981, but has revived recently, and reportedly plans to present the awards again.

THE AISLING GHEAL AWARDS

1978 (1979)
1st—"A Vector of Vacuum," by John McCarthy
2nd—"Museum," by Martin Hayes
3rd—"Harp Uppermost," by Gerry McCarthy

1979 (1980)
1st—"The ParaPresent," by Graham Andrews
2nd—"Child of the Age," by Donal Hurley
3rd—"Icemice," by Hugo Duffy

Awards suspended.

4. THE ALKOR POLL AWARDS
(USSR/RUSSIA)

Voted upon by the members of the Alkor SF Club for the best published SF works of the previous year.

THE ALKOR POLL AWARDS

1988 (1989)
Novel—*Time of Pain* (a.k.a. *The Ugly Swans*), by Arkady & Boris Strugatsky
Short Story—"Khimiya i Zhizn #1" ("The Industrial Story #1"), by Boris Shtern
Translated Novel—*The Futurological Congress*, by Stanislaw Lem

1989 (1990)
Novel—*Snail on a Slope*, by Arkady & Boris Strugatsky; *Burdened by Evil, or Forty Years Later*, by Arkady & Boris Strugatsky; *Zvezdochka-vol-bu* (*Stars on My Mind*), by Olga Larionova; *The Settlement*, by Kir Bulychev
Short Story—"Izgnanie Besa" ("The Demon's Exile"), by A. Stolyarovwon; "Invitation to the Night Hunt," by V. Mikhalikov
Translated Novel—*The Status Civilization*, by Robert Sheckley; *Peace on Earth*, by Stanislaw Lem; *Damnation Alley*, by Roger Zelazny; *The Mist*, by Stephen King; *Animal Farm*, by George Orwell; *Sirens of Titan*, by Kurt Vonnegut; *The Star Kings*, by Edmond Hamilton; *Brave New World*, by Aldous Huxley; *Childhood's End*, by Arthur C. Clarke; *Professor Donda*, by Stanislaw Lem; *Ballad of the Flexible Bullet*, by Stephen King; *The Castle*, by Franz Kafka; *Memo*, by A. Rouellan
Translated Short Story—"Long Jaunt," by Stephen King; "Grotto of the Dancing Deer," by Clifford D. Simak; "Cosmic Crises DDD," by Harry Harrison; "Sexquake," by Stanislaw Lem; "By the Hand of the Lord," by Robert Silverberg; "The Ones Who Walk Away from Omelas," by Ursula K. Le Guin; "The Taste Beware the Wabe," by Philip K. Dick; "I'm All Crying Inside," by Clifford D. Simak; "Nightmare World," by Robert Sheckley; "That Damned Computer," by E. Loren; "Neutron Star," by Larry Niven; "The Tenth Day of Birth," by Frederik Pohl; "The Night He Cried," by Fritz Leiber

5. THE ALVAR APPLETOFFT MEMORIAL AWARD
(SWEDEN)

This accolade was established by the Alvar Appletofft Memorial Foundation through a grant from the parents of a legendary Swedish science fiction fan of the 1950s. The awards are presented annually for best fanzine, fan writer, or fan activity in Sweden during the previous year, and consist of a cash prize of roughly $200, plus an inscribed diploma. Early winners were chosen by the Foundation Board, but since 1982 have been selected through the votes of Swedish SF fans who have been active for at least two years. Voting rules are similar to those used by TAFF.

THE ALVAN APPLETOFFT MEMORIAL AWARDS

1977 (1978)—Alvar Appletofft
1978 (1979)—Ahrvid Engholm
1979 (1980)—Erik Andersson
1980 (1981)—David Nessle
1981 (1982)—Mika Henry Tenhovaara
1982 (1983)—Kaj Harju
1983 (1984)—Maths Claesson
1985 (1986)—LarsArne Karlsson
1986 (1987)—Michael Svensson
1987 (1988)—Martin and Malte Andreasson
1988 (1989)—Holger Eliasson

6. THE ANDRE NORTON AWARD
(UNITED STATES)

The Andre Norton Award was created in 1978 at OrangeCon, Orlando, Florida, to honor the contributions of women to science fiction. It was administered by Oasis, the Orlando SF Association. Only one award year is known.

THE ANDRE NORTON AWARDS

1978—Andre Norton

Awards discontinued?

7. THE ANDRE NORTON FANTASY/SF SHORT STORY AWARD
(UNITED STATES)

Named for the prolific science fiction and fantasy author, this award is part of a Florida state writing contest started in 1989 (1990). The 1988 (1989) awards were a precursor to the Norton Award, and were originally just a "science fiction and fantasy" category. The award is presented at the Florida Freelance Writers Conference in Orlando. About fifteen manuscripts are selected by Ginger Curry and others, and sent to the revolving judge (a professional writer) who chooses the winners. Judges have included Frederik Pohl, Joseph Green, and Jean Lorrah. From 1989 (1990), first prize is $150, second is $75, third is $50, and the top award is sponsored by Andre Norton.

THE ANDRE NORTON FANTASY/SF SHORT STORY AWARDS

1988 (1989)

1st—"The Last Gift," by Eleanora Sabin
2nd—"There's Something Trying to Get Out," by Joseph Straub
3rd—"Final Custody," by Lucy Taylor

1989 (1990)
1st—"Correction Day," by Joseph Straub
2nd—No award
3rd—No award

1990 (1991)
1st—"Warriors of the Gentle Dream," by Karen Rigley & Ann Miller
2nd—"Taken for Granite," by Andrea I. Alton
3rd—"Reject," by Helen Fried

1991 (1992)
1st—"The Milk of the Unicorn," by Barbara Martin
2nd—"The Bloodletting," by Cleo Kokol
3rd—"The Paths of the Dead," by Eleanora Sabin

8. THE ARTHUR C. CLARKE AWARD
(UNITED KINGDOM)

The Clarke Award honors the best science fiction novel published in the United Kingdom in the previous year. Selections are made by a panel of judges, including elected representatives from the British Science Fiction Association, the International Science Policy Foundation, and the Science Fiction Foundation. The presentation consists of a prize of £1,000, donated by Clarke.

This prize should not be confused with several other accolades bearing the Clarke name: The Arthur C. Clarke Award for Space Education is given by Students for the Exploration and Development of Space (SEDS), and consists of a black monolith (much like TMA1) inscribed with the words, "Arthur C. Clarke Award." The Arthur C. Clarke Award for Technology, given by the Arthur C. Clarke Center for Modern Technologies (ACCCMT), consists of a brass monolith etched with a constellation and three satellites. The Arthur C. Clarke Trophy is given annually by ACCCMT to the best Astronomy and Space Quiz team (similar to Academic Decathlon teams in America) in Sri Lanka (Ceylon), as voted upon by members of the Young Astronomer's Association of Sri Lanka and the Interact Club (Rotary Junior Wing) of Nalanda Vidyalaya; it consists of a golden urn surmounted by a NASA-type symbol.

THE ARTHUR C. CLARKE AWARDS

1986 (1987)—*The Handmaid's Tale*, by Margaret Atwood

1987 (1988)
Winner—*The Sea and Summer*, by George Turner
2nd—*Fiasco*, by Stanislaw Lem
3rd—*Aegypt*, by John Crowley

1988 (1989)
Winner—*Unquenchable Fire*, by Rachel Pollack
2nd—*The Empire of Fear*, by Brian Stableford
3rd—*Rumours of Spring*, by Richard Grant

1989 (1990)
Winner—*The Child Garden*, by Geoff Ryman
2nd—*A Child Across the Sky*, by Jonathan Carroll
3rd—(tie) *A Mask for the General*, by Lisa Goldstein; *Desolation Road*, by Ian McDonald

1990 (1991)
Winner—*Take Back Plenty*, by Colin Greenland
2nd—*Rats and Gargoyles*, by Mary Gentle
3rd—*The City, Not Long After*, by Pat Murphy

1991 (1992)
Winner—*Synners*, by Pat Cadigan
2nd—*Eternal Light*, by Paul McAuley
3rd—*The Hyperion Cantos*, by Dan Simmons

9. THE ATLANTA FANTASY FAIRE AWARD
(UNITED STATES)

The Atlanta Fantasy Faire (AFF) Award is presented annually by the AFF committee at the Faire, for lifetime achievement in the fields of science fiction, fantasy, horror, comics, and related fields, in any medium. Winners must be present to claim the award, or it passes to the second or third choice, etc. The award was established in 1982. The prize consists of a statuette of Miss Fantasy Faire, sculpted in sterling silver by Edward Knox. Miss Fantasy Faire has an elaborate headdress with a diamond in one eye.

THE ATLANTA FANTASY FAIRE AWARDS

1982—Forrest J Ackerman
1983—Chuck Jones
1984—Robert Bloch
1985—Will Eisner
1986—Stan Lee
1987—Tom Savini
1988—Julius Schwartz
1989—George Perez
1990—unknown
1991—Greg Bear

10. THE ATOROX AWARD
(FINLAND)

The Atorox Award honors the robot hero of Finnish science fiction writer, Aarne Haapakoski (1904-1961), and is presented annually for the best science fiction or fantasy short story published in Finland during the previous year. The physical prize consists of a diploma and a statue of Atorox, and is chosen by the Turku Science Fiction Society (established 1976), the oldest SF group in Finland.

THE ATOROX AWARDS

1984 (1985)—Johanna Sinisalo
1987 (1988)—"Keskiyon Mato Ikaalisissa" ("The Worm of Midnight at Ikaalinen"), by S. Albert Kivinen
1988 (1989)—"Hanna," by Johanna Sinisalo
1989 (1990)—"Matkalla Nurin Kaannettyyn Avaruuteen" ("En Route to the Inverted Universe"), by Ari Tervonen

11. THE BALROG AWARD
(UNITED STATES)

The Balrog Award was named for the grotesque creature from J. R. R. Tolkien's *Lord of the Rings* trilogy, and consisted of a balrog statuette. The award was discontinued in 1985.

Reginald's Science Fiction & Fantasy Awards, Third Edition

THE BALROG AWARDS

1978 (1979)
Novel—*Blind Voices*, by Tom Reamy
Short Fiction—"Death From Exposure," by Pat Cadigan
Collection/Anthology—*Born to Exile*, by Phyllis Eisenstein
Poet—Ray Bradbury
Artist—Tim Kirk
Amateur Publication—*Shayol*, Pat Cadigan and Arnold Fenner, eds.
Professional Publication—*Age of Dreams*, Alicia Austin, ed.
Outstanding Amateur Achievement—Paul C. Allen, for *Fantasy Newsletter* and "Of Swords and Sorcery"
Judges' Choice—Andre Norton, for lifetime achievement
Judges' Choice—Jonathan Bacon, for *Fantasy Crossroads*

1979 (1980)
Novel—*Dragondrums*, by Anne McCaffrey
Short Fiction—"The Last Defender of Camelot," by Roger Zelazny
Collection/Anthology—*Night Shift*, by Stephen King
Poet—H. Warner Munn
Artist—Michael Whelan
Amateur Publication—*Fantasy Newsletter*, Paul C. Allen, ed.
Professional Publication—*Omni*, Ben Bova, ed.
Science Fiction Film—(tie) *Star Wars*, George Lucas, Writer; *2001: A Space Odyssey*, Arthur C. Clarke and Stanley Kubrick, writers
Fantasy Film—*Fantasia* (Disney Studios)
Outstanding Amateur Achievement—Paul C. Allen, for *Fantasy Newsletter*
Outstanding Professional Achievement—Anne McCaffrey
Special Award—Ian and Betty Ballantine

1980 (1981)
Novel—*The Wounded Land*, by Stephen R. Donaldson
Short Fiction—"The Web of the Magi," by Richard Cowper
Collection/Anthology—*Unfinished Tales*, by J. R. R. Tolkien
Poet—H. Warner Munn
Artist—Frank Frazetta
Amateur Publication—*Fantasy Newsletter*, Paul C. Allen and Susan Allen, eds.
Professional Publication—*The Magazine of Fantasy & Science Fiction*, Edward L. Ferman, ed.
Outstanding Amateur Achievement—Paul C. Allen and Susan Allen, for *Fantasy Newsletter*
Outstanding Professional Achievement—George Lucas, for *Star Wars*
Fantasy Film Hall of Fame Inductee—*The Wizard of Oz* (1939), Noel Langley, writer
Science Fiction Hall of Fame Inductee—*The Empire Strikes Back* (1980), George Lucas, Leigh Brackett, Lawrence Kasdan, writers
Special Award—Jorge Luis Borges
Special Award—Fritz Leiber

1981 (1982)
Novel—*Camber the Heretic*, by Katherine Kurtz
Short Fiction—"A Thief in Korianth," by C. J. Cherryh
Collection/Anthology—*Shadows of Sanctuary*, by Robert Asprin
Poet—Frederick J. Mayer
Artist—Real Musgrave
Amateur Publication—*Eldritch Tales*, Crispin Burnham, ed.
Professional Publication—*Omni*, Ben Bova and Bob Guccione, eds.
Amateur Achievement—Robert Collins and Florida Atlantic University, for saving *Fantasy Newsletter*
Professional Achievement—George Lucas and Steven Spielberg, for filmmaking
Science Fiction Film Hall of Fame Inductee—*Forbidden Planet* (1956), Cyril Hume, writer

Fantasy Film Hall of Fame Inductee—*King Kong* (1933), Edgar Wallace, Ruth Rose, James A. Creelman, writers

1982 (1983)

Novel—*The One Tree*, by Stephen R. Donaldson
Short Fiction—"All of Us Are Dying," by George Clayton Johnson
Collection/Anthology—*Storm Season*, by Robert Asprin
Poet—Frederick J. Mayer
Artist—Tim Hildebrandt
Amateur Publication—*Shayol*, Pat Cadigan and Arnold Fenner, eds.
Professional Publication—*The Magazine of Fantasy & Science Fiction*, Edward L. Ferman, ed.
Amateur Achievement—Alan Bechtold
Professional Achievement—Ben Bova
Science Fiction Film Hall of Fame Inductee—*The Day the Earth Stood Still* (1951), Edmund North, writer
Fantasy Film Hall of Fame Inductee—*The Dark Crystal* (1982), Jim Henson and David Odell, writers
Special Award—Kirby McCauley, for his encouragement of new talent

1983 (1984)

Novel—*Armageddon Rag*, by George R. R. Martin
Short Fiction—"Wizard Goes A-Courtin'," by John Morressy
Collection/Anthology—*Unicorn Variations*, by Roger Zelazny
Poet—Frederick J. Mayer
Artist—Real Musgrave
Amateur Publication—*Fantasy Newsletter*, Robert Collins, ed.
Professional Publication—*The Magazine of Fantasy & Science Fiction*, Edward L. Ferman, ed.
Amateur Achievement—Stan Gardner, for saving the Balrog Awards
Professional Achievement—The Pendragon Gallery, for promoting science fiction, fantasy, and horror artwork
Special Award—Mercer Mayer, for educating children in the field of fantasy art

1984 (1985)

Novel—*The Practice Effect*, by David Brin
Short Fiction—"A Troll and Two Roses," by Patricia McKillip
Collection/Anthology—*Daughter of Regals*, by Stephen R. Donaldson
Poet—Ardath Mayhar
Artist—Wendy and Richard Pini
Amateur Publication—*Eldritch Tales*, Crispin Burnham, ed.
Professional Publication—*Masques*, J. N. Williamson, ed.
Amateur Achievement—David B. Silva, for *The Horror Show*
Professional Achievement—Hap Henriksen, for the National Science Fiction and Fantasy Hall of Fame
Science Fiction Film Hall of Fame Inductee—(tie) *E.T., the Extraterrestrial* (1982), Steven Spielberg and Melissa Mathison, writers; *Starman* (1984), Bruce A. Evans and Raynold Gideon, writers
Fantasy Film Hall of Fame Inductee—*Raiders of the Lost Ark* (1981), Lawrence Kasdan, writer
Special Award—Lester del Rey

Awards discontinued.

12. THE BOOMERANG AWARD
(UNITED STATES)

The Boomerang Award is a readers' award similar to the Davis Readers' Awards, voted upon by subscribers to the magazine *Aboriginal Science Fiction*, and is restricted to works appearing only in *Aboriginal*. Recipients receive a wooden boomerang with the category and winner's name engraved on its side.

THE BOOMERANG AWARDS

1988 (1989)
Short Story—"Cat Scratch," by Emily Davenport
Artist—Cortney Skinner, for "The Darkness Beyond"
Poem—(tie) "Against the Ebon Rush of Night," by Bruce D. Boston; "From a New World," by Bonita Kale

1989 (1990)
Short Story—"In the Shadow of Bones," by Robert A. Metzger
Artist—Carol Heyer, for "JimBob and the Alien," by Vivian Vande Velde and T. Serio
Poem—"Imprinting," by Terry McGarry

1990 (1991)
Short Story—"U.F.O," by Michael Swanwick
Artist—Bob Eggleton, for "A View of Neptune from Triton"
Poem—"To an Android Lover," by Holly Lisle

13. THE BORIS STRUGATSKY PRIZE
(RUSSIA)

The Boris Strugatsky Prizes were begun in 1991 to honor works published during the previous year (4 years in the first instance) in Russia. The winners are chosen by Boris Strugatsky and receive a certificate and monetary award.

THE BORIS STRUGATSKY PRIZES

1986-1990 (1991)
Fiction—"Doverie" ("Trust"), by Vyacheslav Rybakov
Critical Study—"The Quiet Decade Before the Hurricane," by Sergey Pereslagin
Essay—"In Search of Memory," by Vladimir Vasil'ev
Fiction by a New Writer—"Okno v Zhestokj Mir" ("Window Onto the Cruel World"), by Gennadij Mel'nikov
Fan Article—"Fandom Gets Its Voice," by Vladimir Shelukhin

14. THE BRAM STOKER AWARD
(UNITED STATES)

The Bram Stoker Award was the first modern American award to recognize outstanding achievement in horror and dark fantasy. The Stoker Awards are chosen annually by active members of The Horror Writers of America (HWA). Each participant votes for two winners in each category, designating "first" and "second" on the ballot. The votes are then counted by an outside agency. The physical prize, designed by Stephen M. Kirk, brother of science fiction artist Tim Kirk, consists of a miniature gothic mansion eight inches high, decorated with gargoyles, skeletons, and creeping vines. The front door of the mansion opens to reveal the winner's name and category.

THE BRAM STOKER AWARDS

1987 (1988)
Novel—(tie) *Misery*, by Stephen King; *Swan Song*, by Robert McCammon
First Novel—*The Manse*, by Lisa Cantrell

Novelette—(tie) "The Pear-Shaped Man," by George R. R. Martin; "The Boy Who Came Back from the Dead," by Alan Rodgers
Short Story—"The Deep End," by Robert McCammon
Collection—*The Essential Ellison*, by Harlan Ellison
Nonfiction—*Mary Shelley*, by Muriel Spark
Life Achievement—Fritz Leiber, Frank Belknap Long, Clifford D. Simak

1988 (1989)

Novel—*The Silence of the Lambs*, by Thomas Harris
First Novel—*The Suiting*, by Kelley Wilde
Novelette—"Orange Is for Anguish, Blue for Insanity," by David Morrell
Short Story—"The Night They Missed the Horror Show," by Joe R. Lansdale
Collection—*Charles Beaumont: Selected Stories*, by Charles Beaumont, edited by Roger Anker
Life Achievement—Ray Bradbury; Ronald Chetwynd-Hayes

1989 (1990)

Novel—*Carrion Comfort*, by Dan Simmons
First Novel—*Sunglasses After Dark*, by Nancy Collins
Novella/Novelette—"On the Far Side of the Cadillac Desert with Dead Folks," by Joe R. Lansdale
Short Story—"Eat Me," by Robert R. McCammon
Collection—*Richard Matheson: Collected Stories*, by Richard Matheson
Nonfiction—(tie) *Harlan Ellison's Watching*, by Harlan Ellison; *Horror: The 100 Best Books*, edited by Stephen Jones and Kim Newman

1990 (1991)

Novel—*Mine*, by Robert R. McCammon
First Novel—*The Revelation*, by Bentley Little
Novella/Novelette—"Stephen," by Elizabeth Massie
Short Story—"The Calling," by David B. Silva
Collection—*Four Past Midnight*, by Stephen King
Nonfiction—*Dark Dreamers: Conversations with the Masters of Horror*, by Stanley Wiater
Life Achievement—Hugh B. Cave; Richard Matheson

1991 (1992)

Novel—*Boy's Life*, by Robert R. McCammon
First Novel—(tie) *The Cipher*, by Kathe Koja; *Prodigal*, by Melanie Tem
Novelette—"The Beautiful Uncut Hair of Graves," by David Morrell
Short Story—"Lady Madonna," by Nancy Holder
Collection—*Prayers to Broken Stones*, by Dan Simmons
Nonfiction—*Shadows in Eden*, by Stephen Jones
Life Achievement—Gahan Wilson

15. THE BRITISH FANTASY AWARD
(UNITED KINGDOM)

The British Fantasy Awards are presented annually by the British Fantasy Society to honor the best fantasy works of the year. The prize was established in 1971 in memory of August Derleth, the well-known writer, editor, and publisher of Arkham House. The physical award consists of a statuette of the Lovecraftian god Cthulhu, fashioned of white ivory on a wood base. Associational awards in various categories take the same physical form as the novel award. The Icarus Award, given each year to the most promising newcomer to the field (the British equivalent of the John W. Campbell Award), was established in 1987 (1988).

Reginald's Science Fiction & Fantasy Awards, Third Edition

THE BRITISH FANTASY AWARDS

1972 (1973)
August Derleth Award—*The Knight of the Swords*, by Michael Moorcock

1973 (1974)
August Derleth Award—*The King of the Swords*, by Michael Moorcock

1974 (1975)
August Derleth Award—*Hrolf Kraki's Saga*, by Poul Anderson
Short Story—"Sticks," by Karl Edward Wagner
Film—*The Exorcist*, William Peter Blatty, writer

1975 (1976)
August Derleth Award—*The Hollow Lands*, by Michael Moorcock

1976 (1977)
August Derleth Award—*The Dragon and the George*, by Gordon R. Dickson
Short Story—"Two Suns Setting," by Karl Edward Wagner
Film—*The Omen*, David Seltzer, Writer
Artist—Michael William Kaluta, for *The Sacrifice*
Small Press Magazine—*Andurile*
Comics—*Howard the Duck #3*

1977 (1978)
August Derleth Award—*A Spell for Chameleon*, by Piers Anthony
Short Story—"In the Bag," by Ramsey Campbell

1978 (1979)
August Derleth Award—*The Chronicles of Thomas Covenant the Unbeliever*, by Stephen R. Donaldson
Short Story—"Jeffty Is Five," by Harlan Ellison
Film—*Close Encounters of the Third Kind*, Steven Spielberg, writer
Artist—Boris Vallejo, for *The Amazon Princess and Her Pet*
Small Press Magazine—*Fantasy Tales #2*, Stephen Jones and David Sutton, eds.
Comics—"The Scarlet Citadel" in *Savage Sword of Conan #30*, by Roy Thomas and Frank Brunner

1979 (1980)
August Derleth Award—*Death's Master*, by Tanith Lee
Short Story—"The Button Molder," by Fritz Leiber
Film—*Alien*, Dan O'Bannon and Ronald Shusett, writers
Artist—Stephen Fabian
Small Press Magazine—*Fantasy Tales #5*, Stephen Jones and David Sutton, eds.
Comics—*Heavy Metal*

1980 (1981)
August Derleth Award—*To Wake the Dead*, by Ramsey Campbell
Short Story—"Stains," by Robert Aickman
Film—*The Empire Strikes Back*, George Lucas, Leigh Brackett, Lawrence Kasdan, writers
Artist—Dave Carson
Small Press Magazine—*Airgedlamh*, David McFerran, Stephen Jones, David Sutton, eds.
Special Award—Stephen King, for outstanding contributions to the genre

1981 (1982)
August Derleth Award—*Cujo*, by Stephen King
Short Story—"The Dark Country," by Dennis Etchison
Film—*Raiders of the Lost Ark*, Lawrence Kasdan, writer
Artist—Dave Carson
Small Press Magazine—*Fantasy Tales*, Stephen Jones and David Sutton, eds.

1982 (1983)
August Derleth Award—*The Sword of the Lictor*, by Gene Wolfe
Short Story—"Breathing Method," by Stephen King
Film—*Blade Runner*, Hampton Fancher and David Peoples, writers
Artist—Dave Carson
Small Press Magazine—*Fantasy Tales*, Stephen Jones and David Sutton, eds.
Special Award—Karl Edward Wagner

1983 (1984)
August Derleth Award—*Floating Dragons*, by Peter Straub
Short Story—"Neither Brute Nor Human," by Karl Edward Wagner
Film—*Videodrome*, David Cronenberg, writer
Artist—Rowena Morrill
Small Press Magazine—*Ghosts and Scholars*, Rosemary Pardoe, ed.
Special Award—Donald and Elsie Wollheim

1984 (1985)
August Derleth Award—*The Ceremonies*, by T. E. D. Klein
Short Story—"The Forbidden," by Clive Barker
Film—*A Nightmare on Elm Street*, Wes Craven, writer
Artist—J. K. Potter
Small Press Magazine—*Fantasy Tales*, Stephen Jones and David Sutton, eds.
Special Award—Leslie Flood

1985 (1986)
August Derleth Award—*The Ragged Astronauts*, by Bob Shaw
Short Story—"Kaeti and the Hangman," by Keith Roberts
Film—unknown
Artist—Keith Roberts, for *Kaeti and the Hangman*
Special Award—Manly Wade Wellman

1986 (1987)
August Derleth Award—*It*, by Stephen King
Short Story—"The Olympic Runner," by Dennis Etchison
Film—*Aliens*, James Cameron, writer
Artist—J. K. Potter
Small Press Magazine—*Fantasy Tales*, Stephen Jones and David Sutton, eds.
Special Award—Charles L. Grant

1987 (1988)
August Derleth Award—*The Hungry Moon*, by Ramsey Campbell
Short Story—"Leaks," by Steve Rasnic Tem
Film—*Hellraiser*, Clive Barker, writer
Artist—J. K. Potter
Small Press Magazine—*Dagon*, Carl Ford, ed.
Icarus Award—Carl Ford

1988 (1989)
August Derleth Award—*The Influence*, by Ramsey Campbell
Short Story—"Fruiting Bodies," by Brian Lumley
Artist—Dave Carson
Small Press Magazine—*Dagon*, Carl Ford, ed.
Special Award—R. Chetwynd-Hayes
Icarus Award—John Gilbert

1989 (1990)
August Derleth Award—*Carrion Comfort*, by Dan Simmons
Short Fiction—"On the Far Side of the Cadillac Desert with Dead Folks," by Joe R. Lansdale

Film—*Indiana Jones and the Last Crusade*, screenplay by Jeffrey Boam based on a story by George Lucas
Artist—Dave Carson
Special Award—Peter Coleborn

1990 (1991)

August Derleth Award—*Midnight Sun*, by Ramsey Campbell
Short Fiction—"The Man Who Drew Cats," by Michael Marshall Smith
Artist—Les Edwards
Small Press Magazine—*Dark Dreams*, David Cowperthwaite & Jeff Dempsey, eds.
Anthology/Collection—*Best New Horror*, Ramsey Campbell & Stephen Jones, eds.
Special Award—Dorothy Lumley
Icarus Award—Michael Marshall Smith

1991 (1992)

August Derleth Award—*Outside the Dog Museum*, by Jonathan Carroll
Short Fiction—"The Dark Land," by Michael Marshall Smith
Artist—Jim Pitts
Small Press Magazine—*Peeping Tom*
Anthology/Collection—*Darklands*, Nicholas Royle, ed.
Icarus Award—Melanie Tem

16. THE BRITISH SCIENCE FICTION ASSOCIATION AWARD (UNITED KINGDOM)

The BSFA Awards are nominated by members of the British Science Fiction Association (BSFA). A panel of judges from the BFSA, International Science Policy Foundation, and Science Fiction Foundation make the final decision. Presentations are made annually at England's National Science Fiction Convention, held usually in April. The physical award is an engraved plaque on a wooden shield. When the awards were first established in 1969, they were presented only for best novel. After being reorganized in 1979, they now recognize the best SF works in four categories: novel, short fiction, media presentation, and artist, for works first published or presented in the United Kingdom during the preceding calendar year.

THE BRITISH SCIENCE FICTION ASSOCIATION AWARDS

1969 (1970)—*Stand on Zanzibar*, by John Brunner; **Special Award**—Brian W. Aldiss, as Britain's Most Popular Author of SF
1970 (1971)—*The Jagged Orbit*, by John Brunner
1971 (1972)—*The Moment of Eclipse*, by Brian W. Aldiss
1972 (1973)—No award
1973 (1974)—*Rendezvous with Rama*, by Arthur C. Clarke; **Special Award**—*Billion Year Spree*, by Brian W. Aldiss
1974 (1975)—*Orbitsville*, by Bob Shaw
1976 (1977)—*Brontomek!*, by Michael G. Coney; **Special Award**—*A Pictorial History of Science Fiction*, by David A. Kyle
1977 (1978)—*The Jonah Kit*, by Ian Watson
1978 (1979)—No award

1979 (1980)

Novel—*The Unlimited Dream Company*, by J. G. Ballard
Short Fiction—"Palely Loitering," by Christopher Priest
Media Presentation—*The Hitchhiker's Guide to the Galaxy*, by Douglas Adams
Artist—Jim Burns

1980 (1981)

Novel—*Timescape*, by Gregory Benford

Short Fiction—"The Brave Little Toaster," by Thomas M. Disch
Media Presentation—*The Hitchhiker's Guide to the Galaxy, Second Series*, Douglas Adams, writer
Artist—Peter Jones

1981 (1982)

Novel—*The Shadow of the Torturer*, by Gene Wolfe
Short Fiction—"Mythago Wood," by Robert Holdstock
Media Presentation—*Time Bandits*, Terry Gilliam and Michael Palin, writers
Artist—Bruce Pennington

1982 (1983)

Novel—*Helliconia: Spring*, by Brian W. Aldiss
Short Fiction—"Kitemaster," by Keith Roberts
Media Presentation—*Blade Runner*, Hampton Fancher and David Peoples, writers
Artist—Tim White

1983 (1984)

Novel—*TikTok*, by John Sladek
Short Fiction—"After Images," by Malcolm Edwards
Media Presentation—*Android*, James Reigle and Don Opper, writers
Artist—Bruce Pennington

1984 (1985)

Novel—*Mythago Wood*, by Robert Holdstock
Short Fiction—"Unconquered Country," by Geoff Ryman
Media Presentation—unknown
Artist—Jim Burns

1985 (1986)

Novel—*Helliconia: Winter*, by Brian W. Aldiss
Short Fiction—"Cube Root," by Dave Langford
Media Presentation—*Brazil*, Terry Gilliam, writer
Artist—Jim Burns

1986 (1987)

Novel—*The Ragged Astronauts*, by Bob Shaw
Short Fiction—"Kaeti and the Hangman," by Keith Roberts
Media Presentation—*Aliens*, James Cameron, writer
Artist—Keith Roberts

1987 (1988)

Novel—*Gráinne*, by Keith Roberts
Short Fiction—"Love Sickness," by Geoff Ryman
Media Presentation—*Star Cops*
Artist—Jim Burns

1989 (1990)

Novel—*Pyramids*, by Terry Pratchett
Short Fiction—"In Translation," by Lisa Tuttle
Media Presentation—*Red Dwarf*, Rob Grant and Doug Naylor, writers
Artist—Jim Burns, for *Other Edens III*

1990 (1991)

Novel—*Take Back Plenty*, by Colin Greenland
Short Fiction—"The Original Dr. Shade," by Kim Newman
Media Presentation—*Twin Peaks*, David Lynch, writer
Artist—Ian Miller, for *The Difference Engine* (cover of *Interzone 40*)

1991 (1992)
Novel—*The Fall of Hyperion*, by Dan Simmons
Short Fiction—"Bad Timing," by Molly Brown
Media Presentation—*Terminator 2: Judgment Day*, James Cameron, writer
Artist—Mark Harrison, for cover of *Interzone* 48

17. THE CASPER AND AURORA AWARDS
[THE CANADIAN SCIENCE FICTION AND FANTASY ACHIEVEMENT AWARD]
(CANADA)

The Casper Awards (the Canadian Hugos) were created in 1980, and are awarded annually at CanVention, the Canadian National Science Fiction Convention, to recognize achievements by Canadian writers. The award is chosen by a mail vote of the convention's attending and supporting membership. Nomination forms and ballots are distributed by the CanVention committee through the national science fiction newsletter, *MLR*, fanzines, clubs, amateur press associations, and other conventions. The awards began with a single presentation, usually for lifetime contribution, but were reorganized in 1984 to honor best novel, short fiction, and other categories. The prize takes the form of a statuette of Coeurl, the alien creature from Canadian SF author A. E. van Vogt's story, "Black Destroyer," and was created by Michael Spencer. In 1991 the awards were renamed the Aurora Awards.

THE CASPER AWARDS

1980—A. E. van Vogt, for lifetime contributions to science fiction
1981—Susan Wood, for lifetime contributions to science fiction (posthumous)
1982—*Judgment of Dragons*, by Phyllis Gotlieb
1983—Judith Merril, for lifetime contributions to science fiction
1984—No awards
1984 (1985)—*Journey to Apriloth*, by Eileen Kernaghan

1985 (1986)
Novel—*Maple Leaf Rag*, by Garth Spencer (Yves Frémion)
Short Fiction—"Yadjine et la Mort," by Daniel Sermine
Special Award—Judith Merril, for lifetime contributions to science fiction

1986 (1987)
Novel—*The Wandering Fire*, by Guy Gavriel Kay
Short Fiction—"La Carte du Tendre," by Elisabeth Vonarburg
Special Award—Elisabeth Vonarburg, for *Solaris* and improving Francophone/Anglophone communications

1987 (1988)
Novel—*Jack the Giant Killer*, by Charles de Lint
Short Fiction—"Les Crabes des Venus," by Alain Bergeron
Special Award—Michael Skeet, for *MLR*

1988 (1989)
English Long Form—*Mona Lisa Overdrive*, by William Gibson
English Short Form—"Sleeping in a Box," by Candas Jane Dorsey
English Work (Other)—Gerry Truscott, editor at Porcépic/Tesseract Books
French Long Form—*Temps Mort*, by Charles Montpetit
French Short Form—"Survie sur Mars," by Joel Champetier
French Work (Other)—*Solaris*, Luc Pomerleau, ed.
Fan Achievement (Organizational)—Paul Valcour, PineKone I Treasurer and Steering Committee Chair
Fan Achievement (Fanzine)—*MLR*, Michael Skeet, ed.

Fan Achievement (Other)—*NCF Guide to Canadian Science Fiction Fandom, 3rd Edition*, Robert Runte, ed.

1989 (1990)

English Long Form—*West of January*, by Dave Duncan
English Short Form—"Carpe Diem," by Eileen Kernaghan
English Work (Other)—*On Spec*, Marianne O. Nielsen, ed.
French Long Form—*L'Oiseau de Feu*, by Jacques Brossard
French Short Form—"Cogito," by Elisabeth Vonarburg
French Work (Other)—*Solaris*, Luc Pomerleau, ed.
Fan Achievement (Organizational)—The Alberta Speculative Fiction Association (TASFA), for the Edmonton Convention (Context '89) to organize the formation of the Speculative Writers Association of Canada
Fan Achievement (Fanzine)—*MLR*, Michael Skeet, ed.
Fan Achievement (Other)—Robert Runté for promoting Canadian SF writing

THE AURORA AWARDS

1990 (1991)

English Long Form—*Tigana*, by Guy Gavriel Kay
English Short Form—"Muffin Explains Technology to the World at Large," by James Alan Gardner
English Work (Other)—*On Spec*, Marianne O. Nielsen, ed.
French Long Form—*Histoire de la Princesse et du Dragon*, by Elisabeth Vonarburg
French Short Form—"Ici, des Tigres," by Elisabeth Vonarburg
French Work (Other)—*Solaris*, Luc Pomerleau, ed.
Artistic Achievement—Lynne Taylor Fahnestalk, for the cover of *On Spec* (Fall 1990)
Fan Achievement (Organizational)—Dave Panchyk, for services as President of the Saskewatchen Speculative Fiction Society and Chair of Conbine 0
Fan Achievement (Fanzine)—*Neology*, Catherine Girczyc, ed.
Fan Achievement (Other)—Al Betz, for "Ask Mr. Science" column in *BCSFanzine*.

1991 (1992)

English Long Form—*Golden Fleece*, by Robert J. Sawyer
English Short Form—(tie) "Breaking Ball," by Michael Skeet; "A Niche," by Peter Watts
English Work (Other)—*Prisoners of Gravity* TV show, TV Ontario
French Long Form—*Ailleurs et au Japon*, by Elisabeth Vonarburg
French Short Form—"L'Enfant des mondes assoupis," by Yves Meynard
French Work (Other)—*Solaris*, Luc Pomerleau, ed.
Artistic Achievement—Martin Springett, for covers of *On Spec* magazine and novel *Strandis*
Fan Achievement (Organizational)—John Mansfield, for chairing the Winnipeg in '94 Worldcon Bid Committee
Fan Achievement (Fanzine)—*SOL Rising: The Newsletter of the Friends of the Merril Collection of Science Fiction, Speculation, and Fantasy*, D. Larry Hancock, ed.
Fan Achievement (Other)—David W. New, for editing *Horizons SF*.

18. THE CHESLEY AWARD
(UNITED STATES)

The Chesley Award is presented annually by the Association of Science Fiction Artists (ASFA) to honor the memory of the late science fiction illustrator, Chesley Bonestell. These are the only awards in the field (outside of the art Hugos and various other awards within awards) which specifically recognize the best science fiction and fantasy art of the previous year, in multiple categories.

Reginald's Science Fiction & Fantasy Awards, Third Edition

THE CHESLEY AWARDS

1984 (1985)

Paperback Cover—Carl Lundgren, for *Day of the Dinosaurs*, by Alan Dean Foster
Hardback Cover—Michael Whelan, for *The Integral Trees*, by Larry Niven
Magazine Cover—Bob Walters, for *Promises to Keep (Isaac Asimov's Science Fiction Magazine)*
Interior Illustrator—Dell Harris, for an illustration in *Analog* (March 1985)
Unpublished Color—Dawn Wilson, for *Winter's King*
Unpublished Monochrome—Suzanna Griffin, for *Can I Keep Him, Mom?*
3D Art—Hap Henriksen, for *Merchant of Dreams*
Artistic Achievement—Carl Lundgren, for founding the Studio of Illustration and Fine Art
Special Award—Michele Lundgren, for *ASFA Newsletter*

1986 (1987)

Paperback Cover—Michael Whelan, for *The Cat Who Walks Through Walls*, by Robert A. Heinlein
Hardback Cover—David A. Cherry, for *Chanur's Homecoming*, by C. J. Cherryh
Magazine Cover—Bob Eggleton, for *Isaac Asimov's Science Fiction Magazine* (January 1987)
Interior Illustration—(tie) Dell Harris, for an illustration in *Analog*; Bob Walters, for *Vacuum Flowers* in *Isaac Asimov's Science Fiction Magazine*
Unpublished Color—(tie) Michael Whelan, for *Sentinels*; David A. Cherry
3D Art—Butch and Susan Honeck, for *Magic Mountain*
Artistic Achievement—Alex Schomburg
Special Award—Matt Fertig, for *ASFA Newsletter and Quarterly*

1987 (1988)

Paperback Cover—Don Maitz, for *Wizard War*
Hardback Cover—James Gurney, for *On Stranger Tides*, by Tim Powers
Magazine Cover—Terry Lee, for *Amazing Stories* (January 1988)
Interior Illustration—Janet Aulisio, for an untitled illustration in *Amazing Stories* (May 1987, p. 41)
Unpublished Color—Don Maitz, for *Conjure Maitz*
Unpublished Monochrome—Dawn Wilson, for *Queen of the Snows*
3D Art—John Longendorfer, for *Hawk Mountain*
Artistic Achievement—Frank Frazetta

1988 (1989)

Unpublished Monochrome—Brad Foster, for *Night Flyer*
Unpublished Color—James Gurney, for *The Waterfall City*
Interior Illustration—Alan Lee, for *Merlin Dreams*, by Peter Dickinson
Cover Illustration (Magazine)—Bob Eggleton, for *Isaac Asimov's Science Fiction Magazine* (July 1988)
Cover Illustration (Paperback)—Jody Lee, for *The Oathbound*, by Mercedes Lackey
Cover Illustration (Hardback)—Don Maitz, for *Cyteen*, by C. J. Cherryh
3D Art—John A. Morrison, for *Metropolis*
Artistic Achievement—Don Maitz, for *First Maitz*
Special Award—David A. Cherry, for contributions to ASFA

1989 (1990)

Cover Illustration (Hardback)—Keith Parkinson, for *Rusalka* by C. J. Cherryh
Cover Illustration (Paperback)—Stephen Hickman, for *Gryphon*
Cover Illustration (Magazine)—Frank Kelly Freas and Laura Brodian Freas, for *Marion Zimmer Bradley's Fantasy Magazine* (Autumn 1989)
Interior Illustration—Todd Cameron Hamilton, for *Dragonlover's Guide to Pern*, by Anne McCaffrey and Jody Lynn Nye
Unpublished Color—Tom Kidd, for *Windsor McKay City*
Unpublished Monochrome—Ruth Thompson, for *The Guardian*
3D Art—Arlin Robins, for *Wave Born* [bronze]

Artistic Achievement—Don Maitz, for the body of his work
Special Award—David A. Cherry, for contributions to ASFA
Art Direction—Betsy Wollheim and Sheila Gilbert (DAW Books)

1990 (1991)

Cover Illustration (Hardback)—Keith Parkinson, for *Chernovog*, by C. J. Cherryh
Cover Illustration (Paperback)—(tie) Don Maitz, for *Magic Casement*, by Dave Duncan; Michael Whelan, for *The Madness Season*, by C. S. Friedman
Cover Illustration (Magazine)—Bob Eggleton, for *Aboriginal Science Fiction* (January 1990)
Interior Illustration—Val Lakey Lindahn, for "The Flowers"
Unpublished Color—Dean Morrissey, for *Charting the Skies*
3D Art—James C. Christensen, for *The Fishwalker* [bronze]
Artistic Achievement—Michael Whelan, for the body of his work
Special Award—Erin McKee & Bettyann Guarino, for chairmanship & coordination of the Chesley Awards
Art Direction—Don Munson (Ballantine Books)

1991 (1992)

Cover Illustration (Hardback)—Michael Whelan, for *The Summer Queen*, by Joan D. Vinge
Cover Illustration (Paperback)—David A. Cherry, for *Sword and Sorceress VIII*, ed. by Andre Norton
Cover Illustration (Magazine)—David Mattingly, for *Amazing Stories* (September 1991)
Interior Illustration—Bob Walters, for "It Grows On You" (Summer 1991 *Weird Tales*)
Unpublished Color—David A. Cherry, for *Filea Mea*
Unpublished Monochrome—Michael Whelan, for *Study for All the Weyrs of Pern*, by Anne McCaffrey
3D Art—Clayburn Moore, for *Celestial Jade*
Artistic Achievement—James Gurney, for the body of his work
Special Award—Jan Sherrell Gephardt, for her service to ASFA; Richard Kelly, for financial assistance to ASFA
Art Direction—Betsy Wollheim & Sheila Gilbert (DAW Books)

---

19. CHINA SF CONSTELLATION/GALAXY AWARD
(CHINA)

The China SF Constellation/Galaxy Award is presented by the Chinese National Culture Ministry, The Chinese Popular Science Writers Association (CPSWA), and fourteen national magazines to the best short stories and novelettes of the previous year. Eleven writers, editors, and critics serve as the judges. Eighty-six short stories and novelettes are awarded 200 (Yan) R.M.B., approximately $37 US. The top winners are awarded the Aries Gold Medal.

THE CHINA SF CONSTELLATION/GALAXY AWARDS

1985 (1986)

"The Lost Navigation Line," Liu Xingshi
"Idiot," Wu Yan
"Warrior Breaks Through Hurricanes," Wu Xiankui
"Don't Ask Me Where I Come From," Miushi
"One Who Steals Youth," Kong Liang
"A Guest From Afar," Wei Yahua
And seventeen others

1990 (1991)

"The Legend of the Misty Mountain," by Liu Xingshi
"OutWindows," by Wu Yan
"Weaving a Piece of a Beautiful Dream," by Chi Fang

"A Spy Case Outside the World Football Championship," by Wang Heping
"The Annoying Computer," by Qi Lin
"The Country of UnDeath," by Zhang Jinsong

20. CHINA SF MILKY WAY AWARD/FOREST CUP
(CHINA)

The China SF Milky Way Award, also known as the Forest Cup, is presented by *SF World Magazine* and the Guangzhou Forest A/V Factory. Winners receive 1,000 (Yan) R.M.B., approximately $187 US.

THE CHINA SF MILKY WAY AWARD/FOREST CUP

1990 (1991)

1st—"Space Conveny," by Tan Li & Tan Kai
2nd—(tie) "The Legend of the Misty Mountain," by Liu Xingshi; "A Story of an Old Man in 1888," by Jiang Yunshen
3rd—(3-way tie) "Nu Va's Love," by Zhang Jin; "In the Day Six: Life or Death?" by Wu Yan; "Hard to Leave Home," by Jin Ping

21. THE *CHRONIC RIFT* ROUNDTABLE AWARD
(UNITED STATES)

Given by *The Chronic Rift* cable science fiction talk show for best novel of the previous year. Hall of Fame Inductees are also chosen on the basis of merit for career contributions to the field.

THE CHRONIC RIFT ROUNDTABLE AWARDS

1990 (1991)

Novel—*The Dark Half*, by Stephen King
Hall of Fame Inductee—William Gibson

1991 (1992)

Novel—*Beauty*, by Sheri S. Tepper
Short Story—"Silver or Gold," by Emma Bull
Hall of Fame Inductee—Gene Roddenberry

22. THE CHUMATSKI SHLYAH AWARD
(USSR/RUSSIA)

This award is given for best fantastic books of the previous year in Russia. The physical award consists of a "glittering glass" base connected to a glass globe on top.

THE CHUMATSKI SHLYAH AWARDS

1988 (1989)—(tie) Vladimir Savchenko; *Whose is the Planet?* by Boris Shtern

23. THE CLAMPETT HUMANITARIAN AWARD
(UNITED STATES)

The Clampett Humanitarian Award is given in the memory of animator Bob Clampett, who was best known for his zany Warner Brothers cartoons and his *Beany and Cecil* TV series. The award is given annually by the San Diego ComicCon, where Clampett was a regular attendee.

THE CLAMPETT AWARDS

1984—Forrest J Ackerman
1985—Robert A. Heinlein
1986—Berni Wrightson; Jim Starlin
1987—Ray Bradbury
1988—June Foray
1989—Phil Yeh
1990—Sergio Aragonés
1991—The Comic Book Legal Defense Fund
1992—Archie Goodwin

24. THE CLARION AWARD
(UNITED STATES)

The Clarion Award appears to have been presented just once, in 1984, to honor graduates of the 1977-1983 Clarion Science Fiction Workshop who had had no professional stories published as of July 19, 1982. The panel of judges included: Kate Wilhelm, Algis Budrys, Marta Randall, Orson Scott Card, Pat LoBrutto, and Terrence Rafferty. First Place was $200, second was $150, and third was $100.

THE CLARION AWARDS

1984

1st—"The Etheric Transmitter," by Lucius Shepard
2nd—"The Coming of the Goonga," by Gary W. Shockley
3rd—"Pursuit of Excellence," by Rena Yount
         Awards discontinued.

25. THE CLARK DARLTON PRIZE
(GERMANY)

The Clark Darlton Prize is given by Der Deutscher SF Club for the best foreign novel published in Germany of the previous year. Only one winner is known.

THE CLARK DARLTON PRIZES

1983 (1984)—*The Ceres Solution*, by Bob Shaw

26. THE COLLECTORS AWARD
(UNITED STATES)

The Collectors Award is given by SF book dealer Barry R. Levin for the "Most Collectible" Author and Book of the year, based on a combination of book sales and requested items. The physical award has a twenty-two-inch lucite base with a solid, travertine sphere, five inches in diameter (resembling a ringed planet). Different colored spheres are used each year. With the 1989 (1990) awards, a new category of "Most Collectible over Lifetime" was added. The physical award has the same shape as in the other categories, except the sphere is made of obsidian, "to represent a black hole"—Sally Levin. All the awards have brass plaques attached to the front.

THE COLLECTORS AWARDS

1988 (1989)

Author—Dean R. Koontz
Book—Alex Berman (Phantasia Press), for the deluxe lettered edition of *The Uplift War*, by David Brin

1989 (1990)

Author—Salman Rushdie
Book—May Castleberry (Whitney Museum of American Art), for the limited first edition of *My Pretty Pony*, by Stephen King; illustrated by Barbara Kruger
Lifetime—Harlan Ellison

1990 (1991)

Author—Stephen King
Book—Doubleday Books, for the limited edition of *The Stand: The Complete & Uncut Edition*, by Stephen King
Lifetime—Lloyd Arthur Eshbach

1991 (1992)

Author—Dan Simmons
Book—Tracy Cocoman and Joe Stefko (Charnal House), for the lettered edition of *The New Neighbor*, by Ray Garton
Lifetime—Isaac Asimov

27. THE COMPTON N. CROOK/ STEPHEN TALL MEMORIAL AWARD
(UNITED STATES)

The Compton N. Crook/Stephen Tall Memorial Award is voted upon and given by the Baltimore Science Fiction Society (Baltimore SFS), for the best first novel of science fiction from the previous year. The name honors the memory of late SF writer Compton Newby Crook (1908-1981), who wrote under the name Stephen Tall. The prize consists of $500 and a certificate presented annually at Balticon.

THE COMPTON N. CROOK/STEPHEN TALL MEMORIAL AWARDS

1982 (1983)—*Courtship Rite*, by Donald Kingsbury
1983 (1984)—*The War for Eternity*, by Christopher Rowley
1984 (1985)—*Emergence*, by David R. Palmer
1985 (1986)—*Infinity's Web*, by Sheila Finch
1986 (1987)—*The Doomsday Effect*, by Thomas Wren (Thomas T. Thomas)
1987 (1988)—*Liege-Killer*, by Christopher Hinz
1988 (1989)—*Sheepfarmer's Daughter*, by Elizabeth Moon
1989 (1990)—*The Shining Falcon*, by Josepha Sherman
1990 (1991)—*In the Country of the Blind*, by Michael F. Flynn
1991 (1992)—*Reefsong*, by Carol Severance

28. THE COUNT DRACULA SOCIETY AWARD
(UNITED STATES)

The Count Dracula Awards are given by the Count Dracula Society (CDS), "a nonprofit association devoted to the serious study of horror films and gothic literature, founded in 1962 by Dr. Donald A. Reed." Categories include: the Dr. Frank H. Cunningham International Cinema Award (usually called the Cunningham Award), a Dracula statuette given annually for outstanding recognition in the film industry; the Virgil and Inez Fauria Award, which recognizes outstanding services to the CDS; the President's Award, which honors unselfish service to CDS (it also is a Dracula figurine). The Reverend Dr. Montague Summers Memorial Award honors an individual for outstanding achievements in the area of horror films and gothic literature; it consists of a gold trophy. The Horace Walpole Gold Medal recognizes achievement in science fiction, fantasy, or horror, in any medium; the prize includes the aforementioned medal and a Dracula statuette.

The remaining categories, known collectively as the Mrs. Ann Radcliffe Awards, honor the Eighteenth-century gothic writer, and are presented for outstanding achievements in television, cinema, and literature in the fields of science fiction, fantasy, and horror. The award consists of a scroll. The awards may have been discontinued in 1980.

THE COUNT DRACULA SOCIETY AWARDS

1962 (1963)

Literature—Forrest J Ackerman
Cinema—Boris Karloff
Television—Station KTLA, for *Shock Theatre*

1963 (1964)

Literature—Russell Kirk and Donald A. Reed
Cinema—Herman Cohen and Peter Lorre
Television—No award

1964 (1965)

Literature—Ray Bradbury
Cinema—Vincent Price
Television—Alfred Hitchcock
Special Award—Brocard Sewell, for his *Montague Summers*

1965 (1966)

Literature—Forrest J Ackerman
Cinema—Lon Chaney, Jr.
Television—Robert Bloch
Special Award—Milt Larsen, for *The Magic Castle*
Fauria Award—Virgil and Inez Fauria

1966 (1967)

Literature—August Derleth
Cinema—Christopher Lee
Television—*Star Trek*
Special Award—Karl Freund
Fauria Award—Dion O'Donnol

1967 (1968)

Literature—A. E. van Vogt
Cinema—Curtis Harrington
Television—Rod Serling
Special Award—George Pal
Special Award—James Michael Martin, for his championship of Tod Slaughter
Special Award—Gordon R. Guy, for *Count Dracula Society Quarterly*
Special Award—Devendra P. Varma
Fauria Award—Forrest J Ackerman and Walter J. Daugherty

Reginald's Science Fiction & Fantasy Awards, Third Edition

Walpole Medal—Donald A. Reed

1968 (1969)

Literature—Robert Bloch
Cinema—John Carradine
Television—Jonathan Frid
Special Award—Bud Abbott
Special Award—Boris Karloff
Special Award—Walter J. Daugherty
Special Award—*Journey to the Unknown*
Fauria Award—Frank Cunningham
Walpole Medal—Vincent Price
Summers Award—Donald A. Reed

1969 (1970)

Literature—Fritz Leiber
Cinema—Fritz Lang
Television—Dan Curtis
Special Award—Morris Scott Dollens
Special Award—Peter Cushing
Special Award—Katherine Stubergh Keller, for waxworks
Fauria Award—Rolf Flinga and Sir Alvin Germeshausen
Walpole Medal—Devendra P. Varma and Rouben Mamoulian
Summers Award—Frank Cunningham

1970 (1971)

Literature—Ray Bradbury
Cinema—Roger Corman
Television—KHJ-TV, for *Fright Night with Seymour*
Special Award—Ray Harryhausen
Special Award—Tom and Terri Pinckard, for their literary salon
Special Award—Roddy McDowell
Special Award—Merian C. Cooper
Fauria Award—Henry Eichner and Alan White
Walpole Award—George Pal and Barbara Steele
Summers Award—Devendra P. Varma

1971 (1972)

Literature—Henry Eichner
Cinema—Robert Quarry
Television—Francis Lederer
Special Award—Glenn Strange
Special Award—Ray Milland
Special Award—Richard Matheson
Fauria Award—Rich Correll and Richard Harmetz
Walpole Medal—Rod Serling and Christopher Lee
Summers Award—William Crawford
Cunningham Award—Sol Fried

1972 (1973)

Literature—No award
Cinema—Robert Wise
Television—Barry Atwater
Special Award—William Marshall
Special Award—The Simonton Family
Special Award—Rock Hudson
Fauria Award—Ron Somers
Walpole Medal—Raymond McNally and Radu Florescu
Summers Award—Bob Clampett
Cunningham Award—Fay Wray

1973 (1974)

Literature—Thomas Tryon
Cinema—William Marshall
Television—Dan Curtis, Jack Palance, Richard Matheson
Special Award—Helen Gahagan Douglas
Special Award—John Newland
Fauria Award—Linda and Kris Vosburgh
Walpole Medal—W. S. Lewis and Manuel Weltman
Summers Award—E. B. Murray
Cunningham Award—Elsa Lanchester

1974 (1975)

Literature—Arthur Lenning
Cinema—William Castle
Television—Darren McGavin
Special Award—E. G. Marshall
Special Award—Jim Rumph
Special Award—Hi Brown
Special Award—Larry "Seymour" Vincent
Fauria Award—Barbara Elder and Joseph R. Mass
Walpole Medal—Devendra P. Varma
Summers Award—Raymond McNelly
Cunningham Award—Forrest J Ackerman

1975 (1976)

Literature—Leonard Wolf
Cinema—Jay Robinson
Television—Gene Roddenberry
Special Award—Jim Rumph
Special Award—Radu Florescu
Special Award—Don Johnson
Fauria Award—Seid Mahdavi, David Hall, Natalie Harris, Ron Somers
Walpole Medal—Margaret L. Carter
Summers Award—Donald F. Glut
Cunningham Award—Frank R. Saletri

1976 (1977)

Literature—Robert Cremer
Cinema—Ida Lupino
Television—Jay Robinson
Special Award—Robert "Grimsley" Foster
Fauria Award—Donald Lindsey
Walpole Medal—Devendra P. Varma
Summers Award—Stephen Kaplan
Cunningham Award—Christopher Lee

1977 (1978)

Literature—C. L. Moore
Cinema—George Pal
Television—Louis Jordan and Donald A. Reed
Fauria Award—Christine MacIntyre
Walpole Medal—Frank Langella
Summers Award—Edward Ansara
Cunningham Award—Ray Harryhausen

1978 (1979)

Literature—Raymond McNelly and Leonard Wolf
Cinema—George Hamilton
Television—Michael Nouri
Special Award—Frank Langella

Special Award—Michael Ansara
Special Award—Mike Mazurki
Fauria Award—Donald A. Reed
Walpole Medal—Christopher Lee
Summers Award—Bramwell Young
Cunningham Award—Delphine Seyrig

1979 (1980)

Literature—Nicholas Meyer
Cinema—Susan St. James
Television—Eric Greene
Special Award—Richard Donner
Special Award—Richard Kiel
Special Award—Charles Gray
Fauria Award—Jeff and Gloria Greene

Awards discontinued?

29. THE DAEDALUS AWARD
(INTERNATIONAL)

The Daedalus Award is given by the Daedalus Society to honor creative influence upon the science fiction field. Only one award year is known.

THE DAEDALUS AWARDS

1986 (1987)

Life Achievement—Andre Norton
Horror Short Story—Steve Rasnic Tem
Fantasy Short Story—Jane Yolen
Science Fiction Short Story—Tim Sullivan
Horror Novel—*It*, by Stephen King
Fantasy Novel—*The Shattered Horse*, by S. P. Somtow
Science Fiction Novel—*Radio Free Albemuth*, by Philip K. Dick
Zeus Award—Gardner Dozois

Awards discontinued?

30. THE DASA AWARD
(GERMANY)

Presented by SF magazine, *Dasa*, for best SF and fantasy novels of the year.

THE DASA AWARDS

1990 (1991)

SF Novel—*Mona Lisa Overdrive*, by William Gibson (United States)
Fantasy Novel—*The DragonLance Chronicles, Volume 1*, by Margaret Weis and Tracy Hickman (United States)

31. THE DAVIS AND DELL READERS AWARDS
(UNITED STATES)

The Davis Readers Awards are given annually by *Analog Science Fiction/Science Fact Magazine*, and *Isaac Asimov's Science Fiction Magazine (IASFM)*, both issued by Davis Publications, through polls taken of those publications' readers. The physical prize consists of $200 and a certificate. After the magazines were sold in 1992 to Dell Publishing Co., the awards were renamed The Dell Readers Awards.

THE DAVIS READERS AWARDS

1986 (1987)

ANALOG

Novelette—"Eifelheim," by Michael F. Flynn
Short Story—"Phreak Encounter," by Roger MacBride Allen
Science Fact Article—"The Long Stern Case: A Speculative Exercise," by Rick Cook
Cover Artist—Tom Kidd, for *Marooned in Realtime*, by Vernor Vinge

IASFM

Novella—"Spice Pogrom," by Connie Willis
Novelette—"Prisoner of Chillon," by James Patrick Kelly
Short Story—"Robot Dreams," by Isaac Asimov

1987 (1988)

ANALOG

Novelette—"The Gift," by Pat Forde
Short Story—"The Love Song of Laura Morrison," by Jerry Oltion
Science Fact Article—"Nanotechnology," by Chris Peterson
Cover Artist—Vincent DiFate, for *The Smoke Ring*, by Larry Niven

IASFM

Novella—"Mother Goddess of the World," by Kim Stanley Robinson
Novelette—"Rachel In Love," by Pat Murphy
Short Story—"Why I Left Harry's All-Night Hamburgers," by Lawrence Watt-Evans
Cover Artist—Bob Eggleton
Interior Artist—J. K. Potter
Poem—"The Famous Hospitality of Dao'i," by J. J. Hunt

1988 (1989)

ANALOG

Novelette—"Sanctuary," by James White
Short Story—"The Circus Horse," by Amy Bechtel
Science Fact Article—"An Introduction to Psychohistory," by Michael F. Flynn
Cover Artist—Vincent DiFate, for *Falling Free*, by Lois McMaster Bujold

IASFM

Novella—"The Last of the Winnebagos," by Connie Willis
Novelette—"Dowser," by Orson Scott Card
Short Story—"A Midwinter's Tale," by Michael Swanwick
Cover Artist—Hisaki Yasuda
Interior Artist—Laura Lakey

1989 (1990)

ANALOG

Novella/Novelette—"Labyrinth," by Lois McMaster Bujold
Short Story—"The Happy Dead," by Amy Bechtel
Science Fact Article—"The Ape-Man Within Us," by L. Sprague de Camp
Cover Artist—Todd Cameron Hamilton, for *The Gentle Seduction*

IASFM

Novella—"A Touch of Lavender," by Megan Lindholm
Novelette—"The Loch Moose Monster," by Janet Kagan

Short Story—"Windwagon Smith and the Martians," by Lawrence Watt-Evans
Poem—"Old Robots Are the Worst," by Bruce D. Boston
Cover Artist—Keith Parkinson
Interior Artist—Janet Aulisio

1990 (1991)

ANALOG
Novella/Novelette—"Weatherman," by Lois McMaster Bujold
Short Story—"VRM547," by W. R. Thompson
Science Fact Article—"Sixty Astounding Years," by Michael F. Flynn
Cover Artist—Vincent DiFate, for *Glorystar*

IASFM
Novella—"Mr. Boy," by James Patrick Kelly
Novelette—"Getting the Bugs Out," by Janet Kagan
Short Story—"Bears Discover Fire," by Terry Bisson
Poem—"A Dragon's Yuletide Shopping List," by Robert Frazier and James Patrick Kelly
Cover Artist—Michael Whelan
Interior Artist—Janet Aulisio

1991 (1992)

ANALOG
Novella/Novelette—"Ode to Joy," by Dean McLaughlin
Short Story—"The Cold Solution," by Don Sakers
Fact Article—"The Mote in NASA's Eye," by Charles Sheffield
Cover Artist—(tie) Nicholas Jainschigg; Frank Kelly Freas

IASFM
Novella—"Beggars in Spain," by Nancy Kress
Novelette—"Understand," by Ted Chiang
Short Story—"A Walk in the Sun," by Geoffrey A. Landis
Poem—"Angels Fly Because They Take Themselves Lightly," by Jane Yolen
Cover Artist—(tie) Bob Eggleton; Gary Freeman
Interior Artist—Laura Lakey

32. THE DEUTSCHER FANTASY PREIS
(GERMANY)

The Deutscher Fantasy Preis (German Fantasy Award) is presented annually by Erster Deutscher (First German) Fantasy Club to honor fan contributions in Germany.

THE DEUTSCHER FANTASY PREIS

1990 (1991)

1990 (1991)—Thomas Le Blanc, founder of the *Wetzlaer Tage der Phantastik* and the *Phantastische Bibliothek Wetzlar*.

33. THE DITMAR AWARD
[THE AUSTRALIAN SCIENCE FICTION AND FANTASY ACHIEVEMENT AWARD]
(AUSTRALIA)

The Ditmars (the Australian equivalent of the Hugos) were created in 1969 by Dick Jensen, Terry Dowling, Merv Binns, and others on the committee of that year's Australian National

Science Fiction Convention. After much argument over the name of the award, Jensen suggested the Scandinavian form of his own name, Ditmar, as a joke; much to his astonishment, the name was adopted. Jensen then put up the money to make the first trophies. The award is administered by the organizing committee of each annual Australian National SF Convention. Theoretically, all works nominated should have first become available in Australia in the year prior to the awards ceremony, but in reality, works have been nominated up to ten years after their first appearance there; also, some of the nominated works have been only marginally fantastic. Categories have changed frequently from convention to convention.

The William Atheling, Jr. Award (referred to below as the Atheling Award) is given for best nonfiction work in science fiction and fantasy fields. Atheling was the pseudonym used on his criticism by the late SF writer, James Blish (1921-1975).

THE DITMAR AWARDS

1968 (1969)
Australian Fiction—*False Fatherland*, by A. Bertram Chandler
International Fiction—*Camp Concentration*, by Thomas M. Disch (United States)
Contemporary Author—Brian W. Aldiss (United Kingdom)
Australian Fanzine—*Australian Science Fiction Review*, John Bangsund, ed.

1969 (1970)
Australian Fiction—*Dancing Gerontius*, by Lee Harding
International Fiction—*Cosmicomics*, by Italo Calvino (Italy)
Professional Magazine—*Vision of Tomorrow*, Ron Graham, ed.
Australian Fanzine—*The Journal of Omphalistic Epistemology*, John Foyster, ed.

1970 (1971)
Australian Fiction—"The Bitter Pill," by A. Bertram Chandler
International Fiction—No award
Australian Fanzine—*The Somerset Gazette*, Noel Kerr, ed.
Special Award—John Baxter, for *Science Fiction in the Cinema*
Special Award—Ron Graham, for *Vision of Tomorrow*

1971 (1972)
Australian Fiction—*Fallen Spaceman*, by Lee Harding
International Fiction—*Ringworld*, by Larry Niven (United States)
Australian Fanzine—*SF Commentary*, Bruce Gillespie, ed.

1972 (1973)
Australian Fiction—*Let It Ring*, by John Foyster
International Fiction—*The Gods Themselves*, by Isaac Asimov (United States)
Australian Fanzine—*SF Commentary*, Bruce Gillespie, ed.
Dramatic Presentation—*Aussiefan*

1973 (1974)
No awards

1974 (1975)
Australian Fiction—*The Bitter Pill*, by A. Bertram Chandler
International Fiction—*Protector*, by Larry Niven (United States)
Australian Fanzine—*Osiris*, Del and Dennis Stocks, eds.

1975 (1976)
Australian Fiction—*The Big Black Mark*, by A. Bertram Chandler
International Fiction—*The Forever War*, by Joe Haldeman (United States)
Australian Fanzine—*Fanew Sletter*, Leigh Edmonds, ed.
Atheling Award—"Paradigm and Pattern: Form and Meaning in *The Dispossessed*," by George Turner

1976 (1977)
Australian Fiction—*Walkers on the Sky*, by David Lake
International Fiction—*The Space Machine*, by Christopher Priest (United Kingdom)
Australian Fanzine—*SF Commentary*, Bruce Gillespie, ed.
Atheling Award—"Review of *The Jonah Kit*," by George Turner
Special Award—Philippa Maddern, for "The Ins and Outs of the Hadya City-State"

1977 (1978)
Australian Novel—*The Luck of Brin's Five*, by Cherry Wilder
Australian Short Fiction—"Albert's Bellyful," by Francis Payne
International Fiction—*The Silmarillion*, by J. R. R. Tolkien (United Kingdom)
Australian Fanzine—*Enigma*, Van Ikin, ed.
Atheling Award—"The Novels of D. G. Compton," by Andrew Whitmore

1978 (1979)
Australian Fiction—*Beloved Son*, by George Turner
International Fiction—*The White Dragon*, by Anne McCaffrey (Ireland)
Australian Fanzine—*Chunder!*, John Foyster, ed.
Australian Fan Writer—Marc Ortlieb
Atheling Award—"Women and Science Fiction," by Susan Wood

1979 (1980)
Australian Fiction—*Australian Gnomes*, by Robert Ingpen
International Fiction—*The Hitchhiker's Guide to the Galaxy*, by Douglas Adams (United Kingdom)
Australian Fanzine—*SF Commentary*, Bruce Gillespie, ed.
Australian Fan Writer—Leanne Frahm
Australian Artist—Marilyn Pride
Atheling Award—"Paradox as Paradigm: A Review of *The Chronicles of Thomas Covenant the Unbeliever*," by Jack R. Herman
Pat Terry Award—Douglas Adams

1980 (1981)
Australian Novel—*The Dreaming Dragons*, by Damien Broderick
Australian Short Fiction—"Deus Ex Corporus," by Leanne Frahm
International Fiction—*Timescape*, by Gregory Benford (United States)
Australian Fanzine—*Q36*, Marc Ortlieb, ed.
Australian Fan Writer—Marc Ortlieb
Australian Artist—Marilyn Pride
Atheling Award—"Frederik Pohl as a Creator of Future Societies," and "Samuel R. Delany: Victim of Great Applause," both by George Turner
Pat Terry Award—Walt Willis

1981 (1982)
Australian Novel—*The Man Who Loved Morlocks*, by David Lake
Australian Short Fiction—"Where Silence Rules," by Keith Taylor
International Fiction—*The Affirmation*, by Christopher Priest (United Kingdom)
Australian Fanzine—*Q36*, Marc Ortlieb, ed.
Australian Fan Writer—Marc Ortlieb
Australian Artist—Marilyn Pride
Atheling Award—"Sing a Song of Daniel," by Bruce Gillespie
Pat Terry Award—Randall Garrett

1982 (1983)
Australian SF/Fantasy—*The Man Who Walks Away Behind the Eyes*, by Terry Dowling
International SF/Fantasy—*Riddley Walker*, by Russell Hoban (United Kingdom)
Australian Fanzine—*Q36*, Marc Ortlieb, ed.
Australian Fan Writer—Marc Ortlieb
Australian SF/Fantasy Artist—Marilyn Pride
Australian SF/Fantasy Cartoonist—John Packer

Australian SF/Fantasy Editor—Van Ikin
Atheling Award—"Kirth Gersen: The Other Demon Prince," by Terry Dowling
Special Award—Robin Johnson, for contributions to fandom

1983 (1984)
Long Australian SF/Fantasy—*Yesterday's Men*, by George Turner
Short Australian SF/Fantasy—"Above Atlas His Shoulders," by Andrew Whitmore
International SF/Fantasy—No award
Australian Fanzine—*Rataplan/Ornithopter*, Leigh Edmonds, ed.
Australian Fan Writer—Leigh Edmonds
Australian SF/Fantasy Artist—Nick Stathopoulos
Australian SF/Fantasy Cartoonist—John Packer
Australian SF/Fantasy Editor—Van Ikin
Atheling Award—No award

1984 (1985)
Long Australian SF/Fantasy—*Beast of Heaven*, by Victor Kelleher
Short Australian SF/Fantasy—"The Terrarium," by Terry Dowling
International SF/Fantasy—*Neuromancer*, by William Gibson (Canada)
Australian Fanzine—*Australian SF News*, Merv Binns, ed.
Australian Fan Writer—Leigh Edmonds
Australian SF/Fantasy Artist, Cartoonist or Illustrator—Nick Stathopoulos
Australian SF/Fantasy Editor—Bruce Gillespie
Australian SF/Fantasy Dramatic Presentation—*Kindred Spirits* (ABC Telemovie)
Atheling Award—"In the Heart or In the Head," by George Turner

1985 (1986)
Australian Novel—*Illywacker*, by Peter Carey
Australian Short Fiction—"The Bullet That Grows in the Gun," by Terry Dowling
International Fiction—*Compass Rose*, by Ursula K. Le Guin (United States)
Australian Fanzine—*The Metaphysical Review*, Bruce Gillespie, ed.
Australian Fan Writer—Leigh Edmonds
Australian Artist—Nick Stathopoulos
Atheling Award—"*Neuromancer*," and others by George Turner

1986 (1987)
Australian SF/Fantasy Novel—*Bard III: The Wild Sea*, by Keith Taylor
Australian SF/Fantasy Short Fiction—"The Man Who Lost Red," by Terry Dowling
Australian Fanzine—*Thyme*, Roger Weddall and Peter Burns, eds.
Australian SF/Fantasy Artist—Craig Hilton
Outstanding Contribution to Australian Fandom—Carey Handfield, T.R.O.
Atheling Award—"Debased and Lascivious," by Russell Blackford

1987 (1988)
Australian Long Fiction—*For As Long As You Burn*, by Terry Dowling
Australian Short Fiction—"The Last Elephant," by Terry Dowling
Australian Fanzine—*Science Fiction*, Van Ikin, ed.
Australian Fan Writer—Perry Middlemiss
Australian Fan Artist—Lewis Morley
Atheling Award—"Mirror Reversals and the Tolkien Writing Game," by Van Ikin

1988 (1989)
Australian Long Fiction—*Striped Holes*, by Damien Broderick
Australian Short Fiction—"My Lady Tongue," by Lucy Sussex
International Fiction—*Seventh Son*, by Orson Scott Card (United States)
Fanzine—*Get Stuffed*, Jacob Blake, ed.
Fan Writer—Bruce Gillespie
Fan Artist—Ian Gunn
Atheling Award—Russell Blackford, for articles in *Australian Science Fiction Review*

1990 (1991)
Australian Long Fiction/Anthology—*Rhynosseros*, by Terry Dowling
Australian Short Story—"While the Gate Is Open," by Sean McMullen
Fanzine—*Australian SF Review (Second Series)*, SF Collective, eds.
Fan Writer—Bruce Gillespie
Fan Artist—Ian Gunn
Fannish Cat—"Typo," owned by Roger Weddall
Atheling Award—Bruce Gillespie, for "The Non-SF Novels of Philip K. Dick"

34. THE DOC WEIR AWARD
(UNITED KINGDOM)

The Doc Weir Awards honor contributions to science fiction fandom in the United Kingdom. They are voted upon by fans in the English science fiction community, and are awarded at Eastercon, the annual British National SF convention.

THE DOC WEIR AWARDS

1988—No award
1989—unknown
1990—Roger Perkins
1991—Pat Brown
1992—Roger Robinson

35. E. E. EVANS/PAUL FREHAFER AWARD
(UNITED STATES)

The Evans/Frehafer Award is presented by and to members of the Los Angeles Science Fiction Society (LASFS) for outstanding contributions to LASFS and science fiction in general. The winner is selected by the jury comprised of the last three recipients, and the award presented at the annual LosCon convention.

THE E. E. EVANS/PAUL FREHAFER AWARDS

1959—Al Lewis
1960—Rick Sneary
1961—John Trimble
1962—Virginia Mill
1963—Leland Sapiro
1964—Paul Turner
1965—Fred Patten
1966—Bruce Pelz
1967—No award
1968—Chuck Crayne
1969—Bruce Pelz
1970—Don Fitch
1971—Milt Stevens
1972—No award; retrospective 1946 Award—Forrest J Ackerman
1973—Bill Warren
1974—Lee Gold
1975—Tom Digby
1976—Craig Miller
1977—Jerry Pournelle
1978—Jim Glass
1979—Louis Gray
1980—Elayne Pelz

1981—Bob Null
1982—Marilyn "Fuzzy Pink" Niven
1983—Marjii Ellers
1984—Gavin Claypool
1985—Susan J. Haseltine
1986—Mike Frank
1987—Galen Tripp
1988—Charles Lee Jackson II
1989—Robbie Cantor
1990—Gary Louie
1991—George Mulligan

36. THE E. EVERETT EVANS "BIG HEART" AWARD
(UNITED STATES)

The E. Everett Evans Award, often called the "Big Heart" Award, was founded by agent and editor Forrest J Ackerman to honor outstanding service and generosity to the science fiction field by individuals not previously recognized for such contributions, and for "typifying the spirit of [the late sf writer] Evans (1893-1958)." The award consists of a plaque inscribed with the name of the winner, and is presented at the World Science Fiction Convention as part of its awards ceremony. It is sponsored by Ackerman, Walter J. Daugherty, and The Order of St. Fantony. Many award years remain unverified.

THE BIG HEART AWARDS

19??—Edward Elmer Smith
19??—David H. Keller
19??—Georges Gallet
19??—Herbert Haeussler
19??—Walter Ernsting
19??—Donald H. Tuck
19??—Ron Graham
19??—Tom & Terri Pinckard
19??—Rick Sneary
19??—Elaine Wojciechowski
19??—David A. Kyle
19??—Stan Woolston
19??—Tetsu Yano & Takumi Shibano

1959—Robert Bloch
1967—Janie Lamb
1968—Walter J. Daugherty
1978—William Rotsler
1980—Lou Tabakow
1981—Walt Liebscher
1982—Darrell Richardson
1983—Peggy Rae Pavlat
1985—William L. Crawford
1986—Rusty Hevelin
1988—Andre Norton
1989—Arthur L. Widner, Jr.
1990—J. K. Klein
1991—Julius Schwartz
1992—Samanda Jeudé

37. THE EARLY UNIVERSE AWARD
(UNITED STATES)

This one-shot, $1,000 prize was created by physicist Frank Wilczak and SF writer Gregory Benford to promote excellence in science fiction writing postulated on real scientific backgrounds. Any University of California undergraduate student was eligible to submit a story to a panel of judges. The prize was awarded at the 1983 J. Lloyd Eaton Conference of Science Fiction and Fantasy Literature.

THE EARLY UNIVERSE AWARD

1983—"Gargoyles," by Kari Llewellyn Leigh (UC San Diego)
Awards discontinued.

38. EASTCON AWARD
(UNITED KINGDOM)

The Eastcon Award is given at EasterCon, the British National SF Convention, held each Easter in Liverpool, England. Only one award year is known.

THE EASTCON AWARDS

1989 (1990)
Long Text—*The Wooden Spaceships*, by Bob Shaw
Short Text—"Dark Night in Toyland," by Bob Shaw
Artist—Sue Mason, for *The Drunken Drabble Project*
Dramatic Presentation—*Horizon Voyager Programs*

39. EDMOND HAMILTON/LEIGH BRACKETT MEMORIAL AWARD
(UNITED STATES)

The Hamilton/Brackett Memorial Award is given by the Spellbinders Foundation in Sonoma County, California, and is awarded annually at the Octocon convention, having been voted upon by attending members. Only two award dates are known.

THE EDMOND HAMILTON/LEIGH BRACKETT MEMORIAL AWARDS

1980—Jack Chalker
1986—*The Peace War*, by Vernor Vinge

40. EUROCON AWARD
(INTERNATIONAL)

Awarded annually at Eurocon for best SF authors, publishers, and magazines around the world.

THE EUROCON AWARDS

1990 (1991)
Author—Stanislaw Lem (Poland)
Artist—Kaja Saudek (Czechoslovakia)
Publisher—Unwin/Hyman (United Kingdom)

41. THE FANTASTYKA AWARD
(POLAND)

The Fantastyka Awards are presented by Poland's only science fiction magazine, *Fantastyka*, the final selections being made by the publication's editorial staff. The physical award consists of a certificate plus cash. In 1986, due to the many "no award" categories, *Fantastyka* announced that it would present the awards biennially thereafter.

THE FANTASTYKA AWARDS

1983 (1984)

Novel—No award; honorable mentions to *Pierwszy Ziemianin*, by Bohdan Petecki; *Wyjscie z Cienia*, by Janusz A. Zajdel
Short Fiction—"Karlgoro Godz, 18.00," by Marek Baraniecki
New Author—Jerzy Grundkowski
Nonfiction—(3-way tie) Andrzej Stoff, for his books reviewing Stanislaw Lem; Leszek Bugajski, for his volume of essays on science fiction; Marek Oramus, for his reviews of SF books in magazines
Fandom Award—The Polish Science Fiction Association
Fandom Award—The editors of *Kwazar* (fanzine)

1984 (1985)

Novel—No award
Short Fiction—No award
New Author—No award
Nonfiction—*Conversations with Stanislaw Lem*, by Stanislaw Beres
Grand Master—Janusz A. Zajdel
Fandom Award—The Warsaw Branch of the Polish Science Fiction Association

1985 (1986)

Novel—No award; honorable mentions to *Arsenal*, by Marek Oramus; *Imago*, by Wiktor Zwikiewicz
Short Fiction—No award
New Author—Grzegorz Drukarczyk
Nonfiction—(3-way tie) *H. G. Wells' The Time Machine*, by Juliusz K. Palczewski; Agnieszka Cwikiel, for a book of SF as a media type; Boleslaw Holdys, for a book presenting new SF films
Fandom Award—No award

1986/1987 (1988)

Novel—No award
Short Fiction—No award
New Author—Wlodzimierz Rozycki
Nonfiction—*Seans z Wampirem*, by Andrzej Kolodynski
Special Award for International Cooperation in the Exchange of SF Material and Rights—Hanna and Franz Rottensteiner (Austria); Vadim Dunin (USSR)
Special Award for the Best Catalog of Translations—Wiktor Bukato (Poland); Marek Nowowiejeski (Poland)

42. *FEAR* FICTION AWARD
(UNITED STATES)

Presented by the magazine for the best short stories published during the previous year in *Fear.*

FEAR FICTION AWARDS

1989 (1990)

Established Author—Brian Lumley
Newcomer—Mark Chadborn

1990 (1991)

Established Author—Jeff VanderMeer
Newcomer—Rick Cadger

---

43. FESTIVAL FANTASTIQUE D'AVORIAZ AWARDS
(FRANCE)

The Avoriaz Film Awards are given by the Avoriaz International Festival of Fantasy and Science Fiction Films to recognize the best fantasy and science fiction motion picture of the year. The prizes include the following categories: The Grand Prize, The Special Jury Prize, and The Critics Prize. Paintings or prints of famous artists are presented each January or February at the Festival held in Avoriaz, twenty miles from Lake Geneva. The awards may have been discontinued in 1983.

THE AVORIAZ FILM FESTIVAL AWARDS

1973—*Duel*, Steven Spielberg (United States), director; Richard Matheson (United States), writer
1974—*Soylent Green*, Richard Fleischer (United States), director; Stanley Greenberg, writer
1975—*Phantom of the Paradise*, Brian De Palma (United States), director and writer
1976—No award; special Jury Prizes awarded to *The Bedsitting Room*, Richard Lester (United Kingdom), director; Spike Milligan and John Antrobus, writers; and *The Final Programme (The Last Days of Man on Earth)*, Robert Fuest (United Kingdom), director and writer
1977—*Carrie*, Brian De Palma (United States), director; Stephen King (United States), writer
1978—*Full Circle (The Haunting of Julia)*, Richard Loncraine (United Kingdom), director; Peter Straub (United States), writer
1979—*Patrick*, Richard Franklin (Australia), director; Everett De Roche, writer
1980—*Time After Time*, Nicholas Meyer (United States), director and writer
1981—*The Elephant Man*, David Lynch (United Kingdom), director; Christopher De Vore and Eric Bergren (United Kingdom), writers
1982—*Mad Max II (The Road Warrior)*, George Miller (Australia), director
1983—*The Dark Crystal*, Jim Henson (United States) and David Odell (United Kingdom), writers

Awards discontinued?

---

44. FESTIVAL INTERNAZIONALE DEL FILM DI FANTASCIENZA AWARD
(ITALY)

These awards were presented by the Trieste Festival of Fantastic Films in Trieste, Italy, to recognize the best science fiction films of the year, judged on the basis of scientific, imaginative, technological, and philosophical achievements. The following categories were honored: the Golden Asteroid Award, for best full-length film; and the Silver Asteroid, for second place. The Golden Seal of the City of Trieste was given for best short film, and the Silver Seal for second place. Silver Asteroids were also presented to the Best Actor and Actress in an SF film. The Gold Medal of the President of the Festival and the Gold Medal of the Gruppo Giornalisti Cinematografici del Friuli-Venezia Guilia were sometimes given by the President of the Festival and the Journalist/Cinematographer Guild of Friuli-Venezia, respectively. The awards were distributed annually in July. They were discontinued in 1985.

THE INTERNATIONAL FANTASY FILM FESTIVAL AWARDS

1962 (1963)
Golden Asteroid—(tie) *Ikaria XB1*, Indrik Polack (Czechoslovakia), director; *La Jetée*, Chris Marker (France), director
Silver Asteroid—*L'Uomo Anfibio*, Kanancey Tserjentjev (USSR), director
Golden Seal—*Kiberneticka Babicka*, Jiri Trnka (Czechoslovakia), director
Silver Seal—*Little Island*, Richard Williams (United Kingdom), director

1963 (1964)
Golden Asteroid—*The Damned (These Are the Damned)*, Joseph Losey (United Kingdom), director; Evan Jones, writer
Golden Seal—*Popletema Planeta*, Pavel Prochazha (Czechoslovakia), director

1964 (1965)
Golden Asteroid—*Alphaville*, Jean-Luc Goddard (France), director and writer
Golden Seal—*Invasions*, Camillo Bazzonni (Italy), director

1965 (1966)
Golden Asteroid—*Kdo Chce Zabit Jessil? (Who Wants to Kill Jessie?)*, Vaclav Vorlicek (Czechoslovakia), director
Golden Seal—*Luna*, Pyotr Kluscjantsev (USSR), director
Silver Seal—*Les Escargots*, Topor and René Laloux (France), directors

1966 (1967)
Golden Seal—*The Machine Stops*, Philip Saville (United Kingdom), director
Silver Seal—(tie) *Muha*, Aleksandr Marks and Vladimir Jutrisa (Yugoslavia), directors; *What on Earth?*, Les Drew and Kaj Pindal (Canada), directors

1967 (1968)
Golden Asteroid—*The Sorcerers*, Michael Reeves (United Kingdom), director; John Burke, writer
Silver Asteroid (Actor)—Oleg Strizhenov (USSR), in *Eto Svat' Robert*, I. Olscvangher (USSR), director
Silver Asteroid (Actress)—Catherine Lacey (United Kingdom), in *The Sorcerers*, Michael Reeves (United Kingdom), director
Golden Seal—*Sinteticna Komika*, Ort Skodlar (Yugoslavia), director
Gold Medal (President)—Boris Karloff (United States), for his role in *The Sorcerers*, Michael Reeves (United Kingdom), director
Gold Medal (Gruppo)—*Ne Jouex pas avec les Martiens*, Henri Lance (France), director
Special Award—*Tummanost' Andromedy*, Eugenii Shertobytov (USSR), director, for special effects and photography
Special Award—*Ya, Spravedlnost*, Zbynek Brynych (Czechoslovakia), director, for unusual theme
Scroll of Honor—*Poem Field #1* (United States), for the fantastic and original use of a computer as a cinematographic technique

1968 (1969)
Golden Asteroid—*Le Dernier Homme (The Last Man)*, Charles Bitsch (France), director
Silver Asteroid (Actor)—Tobias Engel (France), in *Tu Imagines Robinson*, Jean-Daniel Polet (France), director

Reginald's Science Fiction & Fantasy Awards, Third Edition

Silver Asteroid (Actress)—Ritva Vepsa (Finland), in *Ruusujen*, Risto Jarva (Finland), director
Golden Seal—*Cosmic Zoom*, Eva Szasz (Canada), director
Silver Seal—*Why Man Creates*, Saul Bass (United States), director
Special Award—*Ruusujen*, Risto Jarva (Finland), director

1969 (1970)
Golden Asteroid—*The Gladiators*, Peter Watkins (Sweden), director
Golden Seal—*Arena*, Judit Vas (Hungary), director
Silver Seal—(tie) *Pauk*, Aleksandr Marks (Yugoslavia), director; *Computer Film Program*, by Bell Telephone Laboratories (United States)
Certificate of Honor—*Demon with a Glass Hand*, Harlan Ellison, writer (United States)

1970 (1971)
Golden Asteroid—*Hauser's Memory*, Boris Segal (United States), director; Curt Siodmak, writer (United States)
Silver Asteroid (Actor)—Roberto Antonelli (Italy), in *La Ragazza di Latta*, Marcello Aliprandi (Italy), director
Silver Asteroid (Actress)—Iva Janzurova (Czechoslovakia), in *Pane, Vi Jste Vdova*, Vaclav Vorlicek (Czechoslovakia), director
Golden Seal—*Ljubitelji Cviieca*, Boris Dovnikovic (Yugoslavia), director
Special Award—*Le Temps du Mourir*, Andre Farwagi (France), director
Special Award—*Ténèbres*, Claude Loubarie (France), director

1971 (1972)
Golden Asteroid—*Silent Running*, Douglas Trumbull (United States), director and writer
Silver Asteroid (Actor)—Mitia Nikolayev (USSR), in *Shag a Kryshi*, Rado Bogodine (USSR), director
Silver Asteroid (Actress)—Dominique Erlanger (France), in *Le Seuil du Vide*, Jean-François Davy (France), director
Golden Seal—*Het Laatste Oordel*, Guido Henderickx (Belgium), director
Special Award—*Beware the Blob*, Larry Hagman (United States), director; Jack Woods and Anthony Harris, writers (United States)
Special Award—*Divka na Kosteti*, Vaclav Vorlicek (Czechoslovakia), director
Special Award—*Ecce Homo*, Mas Massimino Gardnier (Italy) and Aleksandr Marks (Yugoslavia), directors

1972 (1973)
Golden Asteroid—*Schlock*, John Landis (United States), director
Silver Asteroid (Actor)—John Steiner (United Kingdom), in *Rada 1001*, Giorgio Treves (Italy), director
Silver Asteroid (Actress)—Susan Hampshire (United Kingdom), in *Malpertius*, Harry Kuemel (Belgium), director
Golden Seal—*Korytarz*, Jerzy Kopozynski (Poland), director
Special Award—*La Planète Sauvage*, René Laloux (France), director
Special Award—*Tup-Tup*, Reginald Raparelli (Italy) and Nedeljiko Dragic (Yugoslavia), directors

1973 (1974)
Golden Asteroid—*Sanatorium pod Klepsydra (The Sand Glass)*, Wojonisch J. Has (Poland), director
Silver Asteroid (Actor)—John Ryan (United States), in *It's Alive*, Larry Cohen (United States), director and writer
Silver Asteroid (Actress)—Jana Bolotova (USSR), in *Molcianie Doktora Ivensa*, Budimir Metalnicov (USSR), director
Golden Seal—*The Making of Silent Running*, Chuck Barbee (United States), director
Special Award—*Molcianie Doktora Ivensa*, Budimir Metalnicov (USSR), director
Special Award—*Slenca Golem*, Jaroslav Balik (Czechoslovakia), director

1974 (1975)

Golden Asteroid—*Phase IV*, Saul Bass (United Kingdom), director
Silver Asteroid (Actor)—Henk van Ulsen (Belgium), in *Golden Ophelia*, Marcel Martin (Belgium), director
Golden Seal—*Il Computer de l'Enigma Leonardo*, Boris Zagriajski (USSR), director
Special Award—*Cassiopeia*, Rikiard Victorov (USSR), director
Special Award—*Jasszunk Istent*, Felix Bodrossy (Hungary), director

1975 (1976)

Golden Asteroid—*Hu-Man*, Jerome Laperrousaz (France), director and writer
Silver Asteroid (Actor)—Terrence Stamp (France), in *Hu-Man*, Jerome Laperrousaz (France), director
Silver Asteroid (Actress)—Helina Gryglaszewska (Poland), in *Bielszy niz Snieg* (Poland)
Golden Seal—*Avaria*, Krzysztof Kiwerski (Poland), director
Special Award—*Otraki vo Vselennoi*, Rikiard Viktorov (USSR), director

1976 (1977)

Golden Asteroid—*Izbaviteli* (*The Rat Saviour*), Krsto Papic (Yugoslavia), director
Silver Asteroid (Actor)—David Rodigan (United Kingdom), in *The Worp Reaction* (United Kingdom)
Silver Asteroid (Actress)—Kate Reid (Canada), in *The Ugly Little Boy*, Don Thompson (Canada) and Barry Morse (Canada), directors
Golden Seal—*Fantabiblical*, Guido Manuli (Italy), director
Special Award—*La Fuga del Signor McKinley*, Mikhail Schweitzer (USSR), director
Special Award—*Babfilm*, Otto Foky (Hungary), director

1977 (1978)

Golden Asteroid—*Operation Ganymed* (*Operation Ganymede*), Rainer Erler (West Germany), director
Silver Asteroid (Actor/Actress)—The extraterrestrial actors in *Laserblast*, Michael Rae (United States), director, for best interpretation
Golden Seal—*Oczy Uroczne*, Piotr Szulkin (Poland), director
Special Award—*Spaceborne*, Dauber, Valens and McKechnie (United States), directors
Special Award—*L'Intelleto dell'Universo*, Victor Milioti (USSR), director

1978 (1979)

Golden Asteroid—*Test Pilota Pirxa* (*Test Pilot Pirx*), Marek Piestrak (Poland), director
Silver Asteroid (Actor)—Johnson Yap (Phillipines), in *The Bionic Boy*, Leody Diaz (United Kingdom), director
Silver Asteroid (TV Film)—*Plutonium*, Rainer Erler (West Germany), director
Golden Seal—*S.O.S.*, Guido Manuli (Italy), director
Special Award—*Koumani*, V. Tarassov (USSR), director
Special Award—*Powers of Ten*, Charles and Ray Eames (United States). directors
Special Award—*Infinity's Child*, Charles Barnett (United States), director

1979 (1980)

Golden Asteroid—*La Mort en Direct* (*Death Head-On*), Bertrand Tavernier (France), director
Silver Asteroid (Actor/Actress)—Entire cast of *The Fortress* (Hungary)
Silver Asteroid (TV Film)—*Hollywood's Wild Angel: Roger Corman*, Christian Blackwood (United States), director
Golden Seal—*Giallo Automatico*, Bruno Bozzetto (Italy), director
Special Award—*The Hotel of the Lost Alpinist*, Grigori Kromanov (USSR), director
Special Award—*The Quatermass Conclusion*, Piers Haggard (United Kingdom), director

1980 (1981)

Golden Asteroid—*Possession*, Andrzej Zulawski (Poland), director

1981 (1982)
Golden Asteroid—*The Survivor*, David Hemmings (Australia), director; James Herbert, writer
Silver Asteroid (Actor)—[unknown male Lead], in *War of the Worlds: The Next Century*
Silver Asteroid (Actress)—Elena Metiolkina (USSR), in *To the Stars by Hard Ways* (USSR)
Awards discontinued.

45. THE FIRST FANDOM HALL OF FAME AWARD
(UNITED STATES)

The physical form of the First Fandom Award changes each year. The first two years it consisted of a wooden base with a clock and penholder, surmounted by a metal moebius strip. The award is usually presented by Forrest J Ackerman. Many award years are missing.

THE FIRST FANDOM AWARDS

19??—Forrest J Ackerman

1964—E. E. "Doc" Smith
1968—Jack Williamson
1974—Sam Moskowitz
1980—George O. Smith
1981—Stanton A. Coblentz
1982—William L. Crawford
1985—Robert Bloch, Wilson Tucker
1986—Julius Schwartz, Donald Wandrei
1988—Lloyd Arthur Eshbach, Charles D. Hornig, David A. Kyle, Neil R. Jones
1989—L. Sprague de Camp, Donald Grant, Frederik Pohl
1990—Robert Madle, Edd Cartier, Alex Schomburg
1991—Robert A. W. "Doc" Lowndes
1992—J. Harvey Haggard

46. THE FOND FANTASTIKI PRIZE
(RUSSIA)

Established in 1990 (1991), this prize honors the Best Russian Fanzine of the year.

THE FOND FANTASTIKI PRIZES

1990 (1991)
Fiction Fanzine—*Sizif*, Andrej Nikolaev, ed.
Small-Circ. Fanzine—*Oversun-Inform*, Sergey Berezhnoy, ed.

47. THE FORRY AWARD
(UNITED STATES)

The Forry Award is presented by the President of the Los Angeles Science Fantasy Society (LASFS) for lifetime achievement in the fields of science fiction, fantasy, or horror. It is voted upon by the membership of LASFS and is given at LosCon. It is named in honor of Forrest J Ackerman.

THE FORRY AWARDS

1966—Ray Bradbury
1967—Fritz Leiber
1968—Poul Anderson
1969—Larry Niven
1970—Harlan Ellison
1971—Theodore Sturgeon
1972—A. E. van Vogt
1973—C. L. Moore
1974—Robert Bloch
1975—Kris Neville
1976—Marion Zimmer Bradley
1977—L. Sprague de Camp
1978—Leigh Brackett
1979—Jerry Pournelle
1980—Robert A. Heinlein
1981—Horace Gold
1982—Arthur C. Clarke
1983—Frank Kelly Freas
1984—Julius Schwartz
1985—Robert Silverberg
1986—Jack Williamson
1987—Donald A. Wollheim
1988—Ursula K. Le Guin
1989—Andre Norton
1990—Isaac Asimov
1991—Curt Siodmak
1992—Hal Clement

48. THE FRANK R. PAUL AWARD
(UNITED STATES)

This award is named in honor of the late SF artist, Frank R. Paul (1884-1963). Only one award is known.

THE FRANK R. PAUL AWARDS

19??—Forrest J Ackerman

                    Awards discontinued?

49. THE GALAXY/DELL SCIENCE FICTION NOVEL CONTEST
(UNITED STATES)

Galaxy magazine and Dell Books sponsored this one-time contest for best original science fiction novel of the year.

THE GALAXY/DELL SCIENCE FICTION NOVEL CONTEST WINNER

1955—*Preferred Risk*, by EDSON MCCANN (pseud. of Frederik Pohl & Lester del Rey)

50. THE GEORGES MELIES AWARD
(UNITED STATES)

The Méliès Award is given for Outstanding Cinematic Achivement in science fiction television. Only two award years are known; the accolade may have been discontinued in 1973.

THE GEORGES MELIES AWARDS

1972—"Demon With a Glass Hand" episode of *The Outer Limits*, teleplay by Harlan Ellison
1973—"City on the Edge of Forever" episode of *Star Trek*, teleplay by Harlan Ellison
Awards discontinued?

51. THE GERNSBACK AWARD
(UNITED STATES)

The Gernsback Awards were created by Forrest J Ackerman and sponsored by Tom and Sylvia Woods of Triton Books, as a kind of retrospective Hugo Award for SF works published prior to 1953 (when the Hugos were first issued). They were chosen by surviving members of First Fandom (fans and professionals active in science fiction before 1939) as the best fiction published in specific years. The award consisted of a metal hand holding a spark-emitting torch on a wooden base, and were presented just once (in 1983) for the year 1926. First Fandom also voted winners for 1936 and 1946, and although they were not actually presented, the honorees are also listed here. The stories selected for 1926 were featured in a special anthology, *The Gernsback Awards 1926*, edited by Ackerman.

THE GERNSBACK AWARDS

1926 (1983)
Novel—*The Moon Maid*, by Edgar Rice Burroughs
Editor—Hugo Gernsback
Magazine—*Amazing Stories*
Special Pioneer Award—"The Eggs from Lake Tanganyika," by Curt Siodmak

1936 (1983)
Novel—*The Incredible Invasion*, by Murray Leinster
Editor—F. Orlin Tremaine
Artist—Frank R. Paul

1946 (1983)
Novel—*Pattern For Conquest*, by George O. Smith
Magazine—*Astounding Science Fiction*
Short Fiction—"Vintage Season," by Lawrence O'Donnell (Henry Kuttner and C. L. Moore)

Awards discontinued.

52. GOLDEN DUCK AWARD
(UNITED STATES)

The Golden Duck Awards were started in 1992 to promote excellence in children's science fiction. The award is sponsored by Duckon, an SF convention held in Du Page County, Illinois, and the first year's awards were given at MagicCon, the 1992 World SF Convention. Winners are presented a $200 cash prize and certificate. Anyone may nominate books for this award, the winners being chosen by a committee of authors.

THE GOLDEN DUCK AWARDS

1991 (1992)
Children's Science Fiction Book—*My Teacher Glows in the Dark*, by Bruce Coville
Children's Science Fiction Picture Book—*Time Train*, by Paul Fleischman, illustrated by Claire Ewart

53. THE GOLDEN LION AWARD
(UNITED STATES)

The Golden Lion Award is given by The Burroughs Bibliophiles to honor works furthering the reputation of the well-known fantasy writer, Edgar Rice Burroughs. The award consists of a bronze plaque of Tarzan and the Golden Lion, adapted from the famous painting by J. Allen St. John, illustrator of many Burroughs's books. Only two award years are known.

THE GOLDEN LION AWARDS

1981—Michael Whelan
1983—Donald A. Wollheim

54. GOLLANCZ/BBC RADIO 4 *BOOKSHELF* FIRST FANTASY NOVEL AWARD
(UNITED KINGDOM)

Victor Gollancz Ltd. in association with BBC Radio 4 awarded £2,000 for the first-place prize winner in this one-shot fantasy novel contest.

THE GOLLANCZ/BBC RADIO 4 *BOOKSHELF* AWARDS

1990 (1991)
1st—*A Dangerous Energy*, by John Whitborn
2nd—*Red Adam*, by Nick Black
3rd—*Merlin and the Last Trump*, by Colin Webber

55. GRAND PRIX DE LA SCIENCE FICTION FRANÇAISE
(FRANCE)

The Grand Prix was created in 1974 by Jean-Pierre Fontana at the Clermont-Ferrand French National Science Fiction Convention, to honor original French language works published in France during the preceeding calendar year. Originally, only Best Novel and Short Story were featured, but other categories have since been added. The awards are chosen by a panel of judges. There is no physical award as such, but beginning in 1989, 40,000 French francs were awarded annually by the city of Clermont-Ferrand to be divided among the winners: 20,000 F. for best novel, 5,000 F. each for the other categories.

GRAND PRIX DE LA SCIENCE FICTION FRANÇAISE

1973 (1974)
Novel—*Le Temps Incertain*, by Michel Jeury
Novelette—"Réhabilitation," by Gérard Klein

1974 (1975)
Novel—*L'Homme à Rebours*, by Philippe Curval
Novelette—"Thomas," by Dominique Douay

1975 (1976)
Novel—No award
Novelette—No award
Special Award—*Urm le Fou*, by Philippe Oruillet

1976 (1977)
Novel—*Les Galaxiales*, by Michel Demuth
Novelette—"Retour à la Terre Definitif," by Philip Goy
Special Award—Yves Dermeze

1977 (1978)
Novel—*Délirium Circus*, by Pierre Pelot
Novelette—"Petite Mort, Petite Anie," by Yves Frémion

1978 (1979)
Novel—*La Maison du Cygne*, by Yves and Ada Rémy
Novelette—"Funnyway," by Serge Brussolo
Special Award—*L'Art Fantastique*, by Siudmak

1979 (1980)
Novel—*L'Épouvante*, by Daniel Walther
Novelette—"Les Hautes Claimes," by Pierre Giuliani
Special Award—*Civilisation et Civications*, by Louis-Vincent Thomas
Special Award—*Major Fatal*, by Moëbius [art]

1980 (1981)
Novel—*Vue en Coup d'une Ville Malade*, by Serge Brussolo
Novelette—"La Femme-Escargot Allant au Bout du Morde," by Bruno Lacigne
Juvenile—*La Fée et le Géomète*, by Jean-Pierre Andrevon
Special Award—*Le Cycle des Glaces*, by G. J. Arnaud

1981 (1982)
Novel—*L'Enfant du Cinquième Nord*, by Pierre Billon
Novelette—"Papier," by Jacques Mondoloni
Juvenile—*Le Tyran d'Axylane*, by Michel Grimaud
Special Award—*Le Bunker de la Dernière Rafale*, by Caro and Jeunet

1982 (1983)
Novel—*Le Champ du Rêveur*, by Jean-Pierre Hubert
Short Fiction—"Les Nageurs de Sable" ("The Sand Swimmers"), by Jean-Claude Dunyach
Juvenile—*Le Naviluk*, by Thérèse Roche
Special Award—H. Delmas and A. Julian, for *Le Rayon SF* (*The SF Shelf*)

1983 (1984)
Novel—*Memo*, by André Ruellan
Short Fiction—"Un Fils de Promethée" ("A Child of Prometheus"), by René Sussan
Juvenile—*L'Enfant qui Venait de l'Espace*, by Robert Escarpit
Special Award—Gérard Cordesse, for *La Nouvelle SF Américaine*

1984 (1985)
Novel—*Les Vatours*, by Joël Houssin
Short Fiction—*Le Commerce des Mondes*, by Charles Dobynski [collection]

1985 (1986)
Novel—*Rituel du Mépris*, by Antoine Volodine
Short Fiction—"Memoire Vive, Memoire Morte," by Gérard Klein
Special Award—Emmanuel Carrère, for "Le Détroit de Behring" ("The Behring Strait")

1986 (1987)
Novel—*Operation Serrures Carnivores*, by Serge Brussolo

Short Fiction—*Le Parc Zoönirique* (Collection), Jacques Barberi, Francis Berthelot, Lionel Evrard, Emmanuel Jouanne, Frédéric Serva, Jean-Pierre Vernay, and Antoine Volodine, eds.

1987 (1988)
Novel—*Le Créateur Chimerique*, by Joëlle Wintrebert
Short Fiction—"Etoile," by Richard Canal
Juvenile—*Le Coeur en Abîme*, by Christian Grenier
Special Award—Dominique Douay and Maly, for *Les Voyages Ordinaires d'un Amateur de Tableux*
Nonfiction—(tie) *Fiction Philosophique et Science Fiction*, by Guy Lardreau; *Ecrits sur la Science Fiction*, by Norbert Spehner

1989 (1990)
Novel—*Rivage des Intouchables*, by Francis Berthelot
Short Fiction—"ExtraMuros," by Raymond Milési
Juvenile—*Temps sans Frontière*, by Liliane Korb
Nonfiction—*Le Prisonnier*, by Hélène Oswald and Alain Carrazé

56. THE GRAND PRIX LOGIDEC
(CANADA)

The Grand Prix Logidec is given for best SF and fantasy published in Québec. The prize consists of a check for C$2,000.

THE GRAND PRIX LOGIDEC

(1990) 1991—*L'Espace du Diamant* (*The Diamond Space*), by Esther Rochon

57. THE GRAVITON AWARD
(BULGARIA)

The Graviton Award was established by the Bulgarian SF Society to honor Bulgarian SF, fantasy, and horror, and is sponsored by Lyuben Dilov, the father of Bulgarian SF.

THE GRAVITON AWARDS

1989 (1990)
Writer—Agop Melkonyan
Illustrator—Tekla Aleksieva

1990 (1991)
Writer—Velitchka Nasstradinova
Illustrator—Boyan Penev

58. THE GRAY MOUSER AWARD
(UNITED STATES)

The Gray Mouser Award is given at the Annual Fantasy Faire in honor of Fritz Leiber, creator of the character, The Gray Mouser. Only three award years are known.

THE GRAY MOUSER AWARDS

1981—Marion Zimmer Bradley

1983—Andre Norton
1984—Poul Anderson

59. THE GRIMMY AWARD
[THE HORROR HALL OF FAME AWARD]
(UNITED STATES)

The Grimmy Award is given to professionals in the field of horror. Only four awards are known.

THE GRIMMY AWARDS

19??—Boris Karloff
19??—Vincent Price
19??—Alfred Hitchcock

1990—Forrest J Ackerman

60. THE GRYPHON AWARD
(UNITED STATES)

The Gryphon Award was created by Andre Norton in 1989 to honor works by women SF writers who have not yet made more than two professional sales. Fantasy manuscripts of at least 80,000 words in length are submitted to Andre Norton by July of the year in which the award is presented. The winner each year serves as a judge for the following year. The first year's prize was awarded and chosen by Andre Norton. The physical award consists of an etched plastic artifact in the form of a sitting (and writing) gryphon with a halo of stars about its head (designed by fantasy artist Mary Hansen-Roberts), accompanied by a $500 prize given by Norton.

THE GRYPHON AWARDS

1988 (1989)—*Changing Fate* (originally *Acila*), by Elisabeth Waters
1989 (1990)—*A Dream of Drunken Hollow*, by Lee Barwood
1990 (1991)—No award
1991 (1992)—*A School for Sorcery*, by Eleanora Sabin

61. THE HOMer AWARD
(UNITED STATES)

Presented by CompuServe Science Fiction and Fantasy Forum, an electronic bulletin board service for on-line pros and fans, the HOMers are voted upon by the membership.

THE HOMER AWARDS

1990 (1991)
SF Novel—*Redshift Rendezvous*, by John E. Stith
Fantasy Novel—*Servant of the Empire*, by Raymond E. Feist & Janny Wurts
Horror/Dark Fantasy Novel—*Moon Dance*, by S. P. Somtow
First Novel—*Golden Fleece*, by Robert J. Sawyer
Novella—"Naught for Hire," by John E. Stith
Novelette—"The Manamouki," by Mike Resnick
Short Story—"Designated Hitter," by Harry Turtledove

62. THE HUGO AWARD
[THE SCIENCE FICTION ACHIEVEMENT AWARD]
(UNITED STATES)

Originally called the Science Fiction Achievement Awards, these second oldest and most popular of all the SF accolades quickly became known as the Hugos in honor of Hugo Gernsback (1884-1967), founder of the first professional SF magazine. The Hugos were first presented at the Philadelphia World Science Fiction Convention in 1953 (Philcon 2), dropped the following year, and restored permanently in 1955. The awards are decided by a mail vote of attending and supporting members of each World Science Fiction Convention (Worldcon), in a double-ballot (nominations and final ballot) system. Prior to 1959 there were no nominating ballots. The early conventions also varied considerably in the categories they honored; gradually, however, the awards were standardized into their present-day categories, with each convention being allowed to issue one or more special awards at its discretion.

Adjunct awards have included: the John W. Campbell, Jr. Award, created to honor the best new author in the SF field (not to be confused with the John W. Campbell, Jr. Memorial Award, presented by the Science Fiction Research Association [q.v.]); and the Gandalf Award, created by Lin Carter to honor fantasy writers (now defunct). The physical award has always consisted of a rocket-shaped statue in various permutations. In 1953 the Hugo was a stubby, delta-winged rocket with no name plate. In 1955 Ben Jason and Jack McKnight redesigned the award as a silver, needle-pointed rocket twelve inches tall. Today's Hugo consists of a thirteen-inch black rocket mounted on a thirteen-inch black ceramic pillar of flame, itself mounted on a marble base weighing about twelve pounds.

The 1985 (1986) award for Best Professional Editor, given posthumously to Judy-Lynn del Rey, was refused by her husband, Lester del Rey, on the grounds that she received the accolade only because of her death. This is the only instance to date of a Hugo being refused. In 1958 (1959), "No Award" received the most votes for New Author; Brian W. Aldiss received a plaque as runner-up. In 1983 (1984) Larry Niven presented Jerry Pournelle with a mock "Chocolate Hugo" in response to his lamentation that "a Hugo will tide you over when there's no money and money will tide you over when there's no Hugos." Larry stated that the chocolate Hugo would "tide him over when there was no money and no Hugo."

THE HUGO AWARDS

1952 (1953)
Number One Fan Personality—Forrest J Ackerman
Novel—*The Demolished Man*, by Alfred Bester
Professional Magazine—(tie) *Galaxy Science Fiction*, Horace L. Gold, ed.; *Astounding Science Fiction*, John W. Campbell, Jr., ed.
Cover Artist—(tie) Ed Emshwiller; Hannes Bok
New Author/Artist—Philip José Farmer
Interior Illustrator—Virgil Finlay
Excellence in Fact Articles—Willy Ley

1953 (1954)
No awards

1954 (1955)
Novel—*They'd Rather Be Right*, by Frank Riley and Mark Clifton
Novelette—"The Darfstellar," by Walter M. Miller, Jr.
Short Story—"Allamagoosa," by Eric Frank Russell
Professional Magazine—*Astounding Science Fiction*, John W. Campbell, Jr., ed.
Illustrator—Frank Kelly Freas
Amateur Publication—*Fantasy Times*, James V. Taurasi and Ray van Houten, eds.
Special Plaque—Sam Moskowitz for *The Immortal Storm*
Best Unpublished Story—"Sven," by Lou Tabakow

1955 (1956)
Novel—*Double Star*, by Robert A. Heinlein
Novelette—"Exploration Team," by Murray Leinster
Short Story—"The Star," by Arthur C. Clarke
Feature Writer—Willy Ley
Professional Magazine—*Astounding Science Fiction*, John W. Campbell, Jr., ed.
Illustrator—Frank Kelly Freas
New Author—Robert Silverberg
Amateur Publication—*Inside and Science Fiction Advertiser*, Ron Smith, ed.
Critic—Damon Knight

1956 (1957)
American Professional Magazine—*Astounding Science Fiction*, John W. Campbell, Jr., ed.
British Professional Magazine—*New Worlds*, Edward J. Carnell, ed.
Amateur Publication—*Science Fiction Times*, James V. Taurasi, Ray van Houten, Frank Prieto, eds.

1957 (1958)
Novel—*The Big Time*, by Fritz Leiber
Short Story—"Or All the Seas With Oysters," by Avram Davidson
Professional Magazine—*The Magazine of Fantasy & Science Fiction*, Anthony Boucher, ed.
Illustrator—Frank Kelly Freas
Motion Picture—*The Incredible Shrinking Man*, Richard Matheson, writer
Most Outstanding Actifan—Walter A. Willis
Special Plaque—Brian W. Aldiss, as Most Promising New Author of the Year

1958 (1959)
Novel—*A Case of Conscience*, by James Blish
Novelette—"The Big Front Yard," by Clifford D. Simak
Short Story—"The Hell-Bound Train," by Robert Bloch
Illustrator—Frank Kelly Freas
Professional Magazine—*The Magazine of Fantasy & Science Fiction*, Anthony Boucher and Robert P. Mills, eds.
Amateur Publication—*Fanac*, Terry Carr and Ron Ellik, eds.
New Author—No award; Brian W. Aldiss received a plaque as runner-up

1959 (1960)
Novel—*Starship Troopers*, by Robert A. Heinlein
Short Fiction—"Flowers for Algernon," by Daniel Keyes
Professional Magazine—*The Magazine of Fantasy & Science Fiction*, Robert P. Mills, ed.
Amateur Publication—*Cry of the Nameless*, F. M. Busby, ed.
Illustrator—Ed Emshwiller
Dramatic Presentation—*The Twilight Zone*, created [and mostly written] by Rod Serling
Special Award—Hugo Gernsback, as "The Father of Magazine Science Fiction"

1960 (1961)
Novel—*A Canticle for Leibowitz*, by Walter M. Miller, Jr.
Short Story—"The Longest Voyage," by Poul Anderson
Professional Magazine—*Analog Science Fiction/Science Fact*, John W. Campbell, Jr., ed.
Amateur Publication—*Who Killed Science Fiction?* Earl Kemp, ed.
Illustrator—Ed Emshwiller
Dramatic Presentation—*The Twilight Zone*, created by Rod Serling

1961 (1962)
Novel—*Stranger in a Strange Land*, by Robert A. Heinlein
Short Fiction—The "Hothouse" series, by Brian W. Aldiss
Professional Magazine—*Analog Science Fiction/Science Fact*, John W. Campbell, Jr., ed.
Amateur Magazine—*Warhoon*, Richard Bergeron, ed.
Professional Artist—Ed Emshwiller

Dramatic Presentation—*The Twilight Zone*, created by Rod Serling
Special Plaque—Cele Goldsmith, for editing *Amazing Stories* and *Fantastic Stories*
Special Plaque—Donald Tuck, for *The Handbook of Science Fiction*

1962 (1963)

Novel—*The Man in the High Castle*, by Philip K. Dick
Short Fiction—"The Dragon Masters," by Jack Vance
Dramatic Presentation—No award
Professional Magazine—*The Magazine of Fantasy & Science Fiction*, Robert P. Mills and Avram Davidson, eds.
Amateur Magazine—*Xero*, Richard Lupoff, ed.
Professional Artist—Roy G. Krenkel
Special Plaque—P. Schuyler Miller, for "The Reference Library" column in *Analog Science Fiction/Science Fact*
Special Plaque—Isaac Asimov, for distinguished contributions to the field of science fiction

1963 (1964)

Novel—*Here Gather the Stars*, by Clifford D. Simak [book title: *Way Station*]
Short Fiction—"No Truce With Kings," by Poul Anderson
Professional Magazine—*Analog Science Fiction/Science Fact*, John W. Campbell, Jr., ed.
Professional Artist—Ed Emshwiller
Publisher—Ace Books, Donald A. Wollheim, ed.
Amateur Publication—*Amra*, George Scithers, ed.

1964 (1965)

Novel—*The Wanderer*, by Fritz Leiber
Short Fiction—"Soldier, Ask Not," by Gordon R. Dickson
Professional Magazine—*Analog Science Fiction/Science Fact*, John W. Campbell, Jr., ed.
Professional Artist—John Schoenherr
Publisher—Ballantine Books, Ian and Betty Ballantine, eds.
Amateur Publication—*Yandro*, Robert and Juanita Coulson, eds.
Dramatic Presentation—*Doctor Strangelove*, Stanley Kubrick and Peter George, writers

1965 (1966)

Novel—(tie) *And Call Me Conrad* [book title: *The Dream Master*], by Roger Zelazny; *Dune*, by Frank Herbert
Short Fiction—"'Repent, Harlequin,' said the Ticktockman," by Harlan Ellison
Professional Magazine—*Worlds of If*, Frederik Pohl, ed.
Professional Artist—Frank Frazetta
Amateur Magazine—*ERB-dom*, Camille Cazadessus, ed.
Best All-Time Series—*The Foundation Trilogy*, by Isaac Asimov

1966 (1967)

Novel—*The Moon Is a Harsh Mistress*, by Robert A. Heinlein
Novelette—"The Last Castle," by Jack Vance
Short Story—"Neutron Star," by Larry Niven
Professional Magazine—*Worlds of If*, Frederik Pohl, ed.
Professional Artist—Jack Gaughan
Dramatic Presentation—"The Menagerie" episode of *Star Trek*, Gene Roddenberry, writer
Amateur Publication—*Niekas*, Ed Meskys and Felice Rolfe, eds.
Fan Artist—Jack Gaughan
Fan Writer—Alexei Panshin
Special Plaque—CBS-TV, for *The 21st Century*

1967 (1968)

Novel—*Lord of Light*, by Roger Zelazny
Novella—(tie) "Weyr Search," by Anne McCaffrey; "Riders of the Purple Wage," by Philip José Farmer
Novelette—"Gonna Roll Them Bones," by Fritz Leiber
Short Story—"I Have No Mouth, and I Must Scream," by Harlan Ellison

Reginald's Science Fiction & Fantasy Awards, Third Edition

Dramatic Presentation—"The City on the Edge of Forever" episode of *Star Trek*, Harlan Ellison, writer
Professional Magazine—*Worlds of If*, Frederik Pohl, ed.
Amateur Publication—*Amra*, George Scithers, ed.
Professional Artist—Jack Gaughan
Fan Writer—George Barr
Fan Artist—Ted White
Special Plaque—Harlan Ellison, for *Dangerous Visions*
Special Plaque—Gene Roddenberry, for *Star Trek*

1968 (1969)

Novel—*Stand on Zanzibar*, by John Brunner
Novella—"Nightwings," by Robert Silverberg
Novelette—"The Sharing of Flesh," by Poul Anderson
Short Story—"The Beast That Shouted Love at the Heart of the World," by Harlan Ellison
Dramatic Presentation—*2001: A Space Odyssey*, Arthur C. Clarke and Stanley Kubrick, writers
Professional Magazine—*The Magazine of Fantasy & Science Fiction*, Edward L. Ferman, ed.
Professional Artist—Jack Gaughan
Amateur Publication—*Psychotic* [aka *Science Fiction Review*], Richard E. Geis, ed.
Fan Writer—Harry Warner, Jr.
Fan Artist—Vaughn Bodé
Special Award—Neil Armstrong, Edwin Aldrin, Michael Collins, for "The Best Moon Landing Ever"

1969 (1970)

Novel—*The Left Hand of Darkness*, by Ursula K. Le Guin
Novella—"Ship of Shadows," by Fritz Leiber
Short Story—"Time Considered as a Helix of Semi-Precious Stones," by Samuel R. Delany
Dramatic Presentation—TV coverage of the Apollo XI flight
Professional Magazine—*The Magazine of Fantasy & Science Fiction*, Edward L. Ferman, ed.
Professional Artist—Frank Kelly Freas
Amateur Magazine—*Science Fiction Review*, Richard E. Geis, ed.
Fan Writer—Wilson Tucker
Fan Artist—Tim Kirk

1970 (1971)

Novel—*Ringworld*, by Larry Niven
Novella—"Ill Met in Lankhmar," by Fritz Leiber
Short Story—"Slow Sculpture," by Theodore Sturgeon
Dramatic Presentation—No award
Professional Artist—Leo and Diane Dillon
Professional Magazine—*The Magazine of Fantasy & Science Fiction*, Edward L. Ferman, ed.
Amateur Magazine—*Locus*, Charles and Dena Brown, eds.
Fan Writer—Richard E. Geis
Fan Artist—Alicia Austin

1971 (1972)

Novel—*To Your Scattered Bodies Go*, by Philip José Farmer
Novella—"The Queen of Air and Darkness," by Poul Anderson
Short Story—"Inconstant Moon," by Larry Niven
Dramatic Presentation—*A Clockwork Orange*, Anthony Burgess and Stanley Kubrick, writers
Amateur Magazine—*Locus*, Charles and Dena Brown, eds.
Professional Magazine—*The Magazine of Fantasy & Science Fiction*, Edward L. Ferman, ed.
Professional Artist—Frank Kelly Freas

Fan Writer—Harry Warner, Jr.
Fan Artist—Tim Kirk
Special Plaque—Club du Livre d'Anticipation (France), for excellence in book production
Special Plaque—Harlan Ellison, for *Again, Dangerous Visions*
Special Plaque—*Nueva Dimensión* (Spain), for excellence in magazine production

1972 (1973)
Novel—*The Gods Themselves*, by Isaac Asimov
Novella—"The Word for World Is Forest," by Ursula K. Le Guin
Novelette—"Goat Song," by Poul Anderson
Short Story—(tie) "Eurema's Dam," by R. A. Lafferty; "The Meeting," by Frederik Pohl and C. M. Kornbluth
Dramatic Presentation—*Slaughterhouse 5*, Kurt Vonnegut, Jr., writer
Professional Artist—Frank Kelly Freas
Professional Editor—Ben Bova
Fanzine—*Energumen*, Michael and Susan Glicksohn, eds.
Fan Writer—Terry Carr
Fan Artist—Tim Kirk
Special Plaque—Pierre Versins, for *Encyclopédie de l'Utopie et de la Science Fiction*
Campbell Award—Jerry Pournelle

1973 (1974)
Novel—*Rendezvous with Rama*, by Arthur C. Clarke
Novella—"The Girl Who Was Plugged in," by James Tiptree, Jr.
Short Story—"The Ones Who Walk Away from Omelas," by Ursula K. Le Guin
Professional Editor—Ben Bova
Professional Artist—Frank Kelly Freas
Dramatic Presentation—*Sleeper*, screenplay by Woody Allen
Fanzine—(tie) *Algol*, Andrew Porter, ed.; *Alien Critic*, Richard E. Geis, ed.
Fan Writer—Susan Wood
Fan Artist—Tim Kirk
Special Hugo—Chesley Bonestell
Campbell Award—(tie) Spider Robinson; Lisa Tuttle
Gandalf Award (Grand Master)—J. R. R. Tolkien

1974 (1975)
Novel—*The Dispossessed*, by Ursula K. Le Guin
Novella—"A Song for Lya," by George R. R. Martin
Novelette—"Adrift, Just Off the Islets of Langerhans...," by Harlan Ellison
Short Story—"The Hole Man," by Larry Niven
Professional Editor—Ben Bova
Professional Artist—Frank Kelly Freas
Dramatic Presentation—*Young Frankenstein*, Mel Brooks and Gene Wilder, writers
Fanzine—*Alien Critic*, Richard E. Geis, ed.
Fan Writer—Richard E. Geis
Fan Artist—William Rotsler
Special Plaque—Donald A. Wollheim, as "The Fan Who Has Done Everything"
Special Plaque—Walt Lee, for *The Reference Guide to Fantastic Films*
Campbell Award—P. J. Plauger
Gandalf Award (Grand Master)—Fritz Leiber

1975 (1976)
Novel—*The Forever War*, by Joe Haldeman
Novella—"Home Is the Hangman," by Roger Zelazny
Novelette—"Borderland of Sol," by Larry Niven
Short Story—"Catch That Zeppelin," by Fritz Leiber
Dramatic Presentation—*A Boy and His Dog*, L. Q. Jones, writer, based on a story by Harlan Ellison
Fanzine—*Locus*, Charles and Dena Brown, eds.
Professional Editor—Ben Bova

Reginald's Science Fiction & Fantasy Awards, Third Edition

Professional Artist—Frank Kelly Freas
Fan Writer—Richard E. Geis
Fan Artist—Tim Kirk
Campbell Award—Tom Reamy
Gandalf Award (Grand Master)—L. Sprague de Camp

1976 (1977)
Novel—*Where Late the Sweet Birds Sang*, by Kate Wilhelm
Novella—(tie) "Houston, Houston, Do You Read?" by James Tiptree, Jr.; "By Any Other Name," by Spider Robinson
Novelette—"The Bicentennial Man," by Isaac Asimov
Short Story—"Tricentennial," by Joe Haldeman
Dramatic Presentation—No award
Fanzine—*Science Fiction Review*, Richard E. Geis, ed.
Professional Artist—Rick Sternbach
Professional Editor—Ben Bova
Fan Writer—(tie) Susan Wood; Richard E. Geis
Fan Artist—Phil Foglio
Special Plaque—George Lucas, for *Star Wars*
Campbell Award—C. J. Cherryh
Gandalf Award (Grand Master)—Andre Norton

1977 (1978)
Novel—*Gateway*, by Frederik Pohl
Novella—"Stardance," by Spider and Jeanne Robinson
Novelette—"Eyes of Amber," by Joan D. Vinge
Short Story—"Jeffty Is Five," by Harlan Ellison
Dramatic Presentation—*Star Wars*, screenplay by George Lucas
Professional Artist—Rick Sternbach
Professional Editor—George Scithers
Fanzine—*Locus*, Charles and Dena Brown, eds.
Fan Writer—Richard E. Geis
Fan Artist—Phil Foglio
Campbell Award—Orson Scott Card
Gandalf Award (Grand Master)—Poul Anderson
Gandalf Award (Fantasy Novel)—*The Silmarillion*, by J. R. R. Tolkien

1978 (1979)
Novel—*Dreamsnake*, by Vonda N. McIntyre
Novella—"The Persistence of Vision," by John Varley
Novelette—"Hunter's Moon," by Poul Anderson
Short Story—"Cassandra," by C. J. Cherryh
Dramatic Presentation—*Superman*, Mario Puzo, David Newman, Leslie Newman, Robert Benton, writers
Professional Artist—Vincent DiFate
Professional Editor—Ben Bova
Fanzine—*Science Fiction Review*, Richard E. Geis, ed.
Fan Writer—Bob Shaw
Fan Artist—William Rotsler
Campbell Award—Stephen R. Donaldson
Gandalf Award (Grand Master)—Ursula K. Le Guin
Gandalf Award (Fantasy Novel)—*The White Dragon*, by Anne McCaffrey

1979 (1980)
Novel—*The Fountains of Paradise*, by Arthur C. Clarke
Novella—"Enemy Mine," by Barry B. Longyear
Novelette—"Sandkings," by George R. R. Martin
Short Story—"The Way of Cross and Dragon," by George R. R. Martin
Nonfiction—*The Science Fiction Encyclopedia*, Peter Nicholls and John Clute, eds.
Dramatic Presentation—*Alien*, Dan O'Bannon and Ronald Shusett, writers

Professional Artist—Michael Whelan
Professional Editor—George Scithers
Fanzine—*Locus*, Charles N. Brown, ed.
Fan Writer—Bob Shaw
Fan Artist—Alexis Gilliland
Campbell Award—Barry B. Longyear
Gandalf Award (Grand Master)—Ray Bradbury

1980 (1981)

Novel—*The Snow Queen*, by Joan D. Vinge
Novella—"Lost Dorsai," by Gordon R. Dickson
Novelette—"The Cloak and the Staff," by Gordon R. Dickson
Short Story—"Grotto of the Dancing Deer," by Clifford D. Simak
Nonfiction—*Cosmos*, by Carl Sagan
Professional Editor—Edward L. Ferman
Professional Artist—Michael Whelan
Fanzine—*Locus*, Charles N. Brown, ed.
Fan Writer—Susan Wood [posthumous]
Fan Artist—Victoria Poyser
Dramatic Presentation—*The Empire Strikes Back*, Leigh Brackett and Lawrence Kasdan, writers, based on a story by George Lucas
Campbell Award—Somtow Sucharitkul (S. P. Somtow)
Gandalf Award (Grand Master)—C. L. Moore

1981 (1982)

Novel—*Downbelow Station*, by C. J. Cherryh
Novella—"The Saturn Game," by Poul Anderson
Novelette—"Unicorn Variation," by Roger Zelazny
Short Story—"The Pusher," by John Varley
Nonfiction—*Danse Macabre*, by Stephen King
Dramatic Presentation—*Raiders of the Lost Ark*, Lawrence Kasdan, writer
Professional Editor—Edward L. Ferman
Professional Artist—Michael Whelan
Fanzine—*Locus*, Charles N. Brown, ed.
Fan Writer—Richard E. Geis
Fan Artist—Victoria Poyser
Campbell Award—Alexis Gilliland
Special Award—Mike Glyer, for "Keeping the fan in fanzine publishing"

1982 (1983)

Novel—*Foundation's Edge*, by Isaac Asimov
Novella—"Souls," by Joanna Russ
Novelette—"Fire Watch," by Connie Willis
Short Story—"Melancholy Elephants," by Spider Robinson
Nonfiction—*Isaac Asimov: The Foundations of Science Fiction*, by James E. Gunn
Dramatic Presentation—*Blade Runner*, Hampton Fancher and David Peoples, writers
Professional Editor—Edward L. Ferman
Professional Artist—Michael Whelan
Fanzine—*Locus*, Charles N. Brown, ed.
Fan Writer—Richard E. Geis
Fan Artist—Alexis Gilliland
Campbell Award—Paul O. Williams

1983 (1984)

Novel—*Startide Rising*, by David Brin
Novella—"Cascade Point," by Timothy Zahn
Novelette—"Blood Music," by Greg Bear
Short Story—"Speech Sounds," by Octavia E. Butler
Nonfiction—*Encyclopedia of Science Fiction and Fantasy, Vol. 3*, by Donald Tuck
Dramatic Presentation—*Return of the Jedi*, George Lucas and Lawrence Kasdan, writers

Professional Editor—Shawna McCarthy
Professional Artist—Michael Whelan
Semiprozine—*Locus*, Charles N. Brown, ed.
Fanzine—*File 770*, Mike Glyer, ed.
Fan Writer—Mike Glyer
Fan Artist—Alexis Gilliland
Campbell Award—R. A. MacAvoy
Special Award—Robert Bloch
Special Award—Larry Shaw

1984 (1985)

Novel—*Neuromancer*, by William Gibson
Novella—"Press ENTER ■," by John Varley
Novelette—"Bloodchild," by Octavia E. Butler
Short Story—"The Crystal Spheres," by David Brin
Nonfiction—*Wonder's Child: My Life in Science Fiction*, by Jack Williamson
Dramatic Presentation—*2010*, Arthur C. Clarke, writer
Professional Editor—Terry Carr
Professional Artist—Michael Whelan
Semiprozine—*Locus*, Charles N. Brown, ed.
Fanzine—*File 770*, Mike Glyer, ed.
Fan Writer—Dave Langford
Fan Artist—Alexis Gilliland
Campbell Award—Lucius Shepard

1985 (1986)

Novel—*Ender's Game*, by Orson Scott Card
Novella—"Twenty-Four Views of Mt. Fuji, by Hokusai," by Roger Zelazny
Novelette—"Paladin of the Lost Hour," by Harlan Ellison
Short Story—"Fermi and Frost," by Frederik Pohl
Nonfiction—*Science Made Stupid*, by Tom Weller
Dramatic Presentation—*Back to the Future*, Robert Zemeckis and Bob Gale, writers
Professional Editor—Judy-Lynn del Rey [posthumous; refused by Lester del Rey]
Professional Artist—Michael Whelan
Semiprozine—*Locus*, Charles N. Brown, ed.
Fanzine—*Lan's Lantern*, George Laskowski, ed.
Fan Writer—Mike Glyer
Fan Artist—Joan Hanke-Woods
Campbell Award—Melissa Scott

1986 (1987)

Novel—*Speaker for the Dead*, by Orson Scott Card
Novella—"Gilgamesh in the Outback," by Robert Silverberg
Novelette—"Permafrost," by Roger Zelazny
Short Story—"Tangents," by Greg Bear
Nonfiction—*Trillion Year Spree*, by Brian W. Aldiss
Dramatic Presentation—*Aliens*, James Cameron, writer
Professional Editor—Terry Carr [posthumous]
Professional Artist—Jim Burns
Semiprozine—*Locus*, Charles N. Brown, ed.
Fanzine—*Ansible*, Dave Langford, ed.
Fan Writer—Dave Langford
Fan Artist—Brad Foster
Campbell Award—Karen Joy Fowler

1987 (1988)

Novel—*The Uplift War*, by David Brin
Novella—"Eye for Eye," by Orson Scott Card
Novelette—"Buffalo Gals, Won't You Come Out Tonight," by Ursula K. Le Guin
Short Story—"Why I Left Harry's All-Night Hamburgers," by Lawrence Watt-Evans

Nonfiction—*Michael Whelan's Works of Wonder*, by Michael Whelan
Semiprozine—*Locus*, Charles N. Brown, ed.
Other Forms—*Watchmen*, by Alan Moore and Dave Gibbons
Dramatic Presentation—*The Princess Bride*, William Goldman, writer
Professional Artist—Michael Whelan
Professional Editor—Gardner Dozois
Fanzine—*Texas SF Inquirer*, Pat Mueller, ed.
Fan Writer—Mike Glyer
Fan Artist—Brad Foster
Campbell Award—Judith Moffett
Special Award—The SF Oral History Association

1988 (1989)

Novel—*Cyteen*, by C. J. Cherryh
Novella—"The Last of the Winnebagos," by Connie Willis
Novelette—"Schrödinger's Kitten," by George Alec Effinger
Short Story—"Kirinyaga," by Mike Resnick
Nonfiction—*The Motion of Light in Water*, by Samuel R. Delany
Dramatic Presentation—*Who Framed Roger Rabbit?*, Jeffrey Price and Peter S. Seaman, writers
Semiprozine—*Locus*, Charles N. Brown, ed.
Professional Editor—Gardner Dozois
Professional Artist—Michael Whelan
Fanzine—*File 770*, Mike Glyer, ed.
Fan Writer—David Langford
Fan Artist—(tie) Diana Gallagher Wu; Brad Foster
Campbell Award—Michaela Roessner
Special Award—SF Lovers Digest (Computer Network)
Special Award—Alex Schomburg

1989 (1990)

Novel—*Hyperion*, by Dan Simmons
Novella—"The Mountains of Mourning," by Lois McMaster Bujold
Novelette—"Enter a Soldier. Later: Enter Another," by Robert Silverberg
Short Story—"Boobs," by Suzy McKee Charnas
Dramatic Presentation—*Indiana Jones and the Last Crusade*, Jeffrey Boam, writer, based on a story by George Lucas
Nonfiction—*The World Beyond the Hill*, by Alexei and Cory Panshin
Professional Editor—Gardner Dozois
Professional Artist—Don Maitz
Semiprozine—*Locus*, Charles N. Brown, ed.
Fan Writer—Dave Langford
Fan Artist—Stu Shiffman
Fanzine—*The Mad 3 Party*, Leslie Turek, ed.
Campbell Award—Kristine Kathryn Rusch
Original Artwork [not a Hugo Award]—Don Maitz, for *Rimrunners*, by C. J. Cherryh

1990 (1991)

Novel—*The Vor Game*, by Lois McMaster Bujold
Novella—"The Hemingway Hoax," by Joe Haldeman
Novelette—"The Manamouki," by Mike Resnick
Short Story—"Bears Discover Fire," by Terry Bisson
Dramatic Presentation—*Edward Scissorhands*
Nonfiction—*How to Write Science Fiction and Fantasy*, by Orson Scott Card
Professional Editor—Gardner Dozois
Professional Artist—Michael Whelan
Semiprozine—*Locus*, Charles N. Brown, ed.
Fan Writer—Dave Langford
Fan Artist—Teddy Harvia
Fanzine—*Lan's Lantern*, George "Lan" Laskowski, ed.

Campbell Award—Julia Ecklar
Special Award—Elst Weinstein, as best hoax for keeping humor alive in fandom [a blank Hugo base]
Special Award—Andrew Porter, for excellence in editing *Science Fiction Chronicle*

1991 (1992)

Novel—*Barrayar*, by Lois McMaster Bujold
Novella—"Beggars in Spain," by Nancy Kress
Novelette—"Gold," by Isaac Asimov
Short Story—"A Walk in the Sun," by Geoffrey Landis
Dramatic Presentation—*Terminator 2*, James Cameron, writer
Nonfiction—*The World of Charles Addams*, by Charles Addams
Professional Editor—Gardner Dozois
Professional Artist—Michael Whelan
Semiprozine—*Locus*, Charles N. Brown, ed.
Fan Writer—Dave Langford
Fan Artist—Brad Foster
Fanzine—*Mimosa*, Dick and Nicki Lynch, eds.
Campbell Award—Ted Chiang
Original Artwork—Michael Whelan, for *The Summer Queen*, by Joan D. Vinge

63. THE *IAM* AWARD
(BRAZIL)

The *IAM* Award is given by the Brazilian edition of *Isaac Asimov's Science Fiction Magazine* for stories published in that magazine in Brazil, and is voted upon by its readership.

THE *IAM* AWARDS

Novella—"Waiting for the Olympians," by Frederik Pohl
Novelette—"Dogwalker," by Orson Scott Card
Short Story—"Ripples in the Dirac Sea," by Geoffrey A. Landis

64. THE INKPOT AWARD
(UNITED STATES)

The Inkpot Award is given annually at the San Diego ComicCon for achievement in comic arts, animation, film/TV, science fiction/fantasy, and fandom service; there are no set number of winners per year. The award consists of a plaque with a statue mounted on it. Awards are listed alphabetically below, year by year.

THE INKPOT AWARDS

1974—Forrest J Ackerman, Kirk Alyn, Ray Bradbury, Milton Caniff, Frank Capra, Bob Clampett, June Foray, Eric Hoffman, Chuck Jones, Jack Kirby, Stan Lee, Bill Lund, Russ Manning, Russell Myers, Charles Schulz, Phil Seuling, Roy Thomas, Bjo Trimble
1975—Barry Alfonso, Brad Anderson, Robert Bloch, Vaughn Bodé, Edgar Rice Burroughs, Daws Butler, Richard Butner, Shel Dorf, Will Eisner, Mark Evanier, Gil Kane, Alan Light, Dick Moores, George Pal, Rod Serling, Joe Shuster, Jerry Siegel, Barry Winsor-Smith, Jim Starlin, Jim Steranko, Theodore Sturgeon, Larry "Seymour" Vincent
1976—Neal Adams, Sergio Aragonés, Mel Blanc, Frank Brunner, Rick Griffin, Johnny Hart, George Clayton Johnson, Vicky Kelso, Mell Lazarus, Sheldon Mayer, Dale Messick, Alex Nino, Don Rico, Noel Sickles, Don Thompson, Maggie Thompson
1977—Alfredo Alcala, Carl Barks, C. C. Beck, Howard Chaykin, Lester Dent, Jackie Estrada, Hal Foster, Walter Gibson, Jim Harmon, Robert A. Heinlein, Gene Henderson, Michael Kaluta, Joe Kubert, Harvey Kurtzman, George Lucas, Stan Lynde, Byron

Preiss, Trina Robbins, Stanley Ralph Ross, Bill Scott, David Scroggy, Jay Ward, Len Wein

1978—John Buscema, Al Capp, Gene Colan, Gil Fox, Tom French, Steve Gerber, Chester Gould, Burne Hogarth, Bob Kane, Ken Krueger, Bernie Lansky, Gray Morrow, Clarence Nash, Grim Natwick, William Rotsler, Mike Royer, Gilbert Shelton, Dave Sheridan, Bil Stout, Frank Thorne, Boris Vallejo, Mort Weisinger, Elmer Woggon

1979—Craig Anderson, Steve Englehart, Dale Enzenbacher, Frank Kelly Freas, Virginia French, H. R. Giger, Gene Hazelton, Carl Macek, Victor Moscoso, Larry Niven, Dan O'Neill, Virgil Partch, Jerry Pournelle, Nestor Redondo, Marshall Rogers, John Romita Sr., Bill Spicer, Mort Walker, Marv Wolfman

1980—Terry Austin, Murray Bishoff, Pat Boyette, John Byrne, Canadian Film Board, Ernie Chan, Chris Claremont, Shary Flenniken, Mike Friedrich, Rick Geary, Donald F. Glut, S. Gross, Al Hartley, B. Kliban, Jerry Muller, George Olshevsky, Joe Orlando, Fred Patten, Don Phelps, Richard Pini, Wendy Pini, David Raskin, Scott Shaw, Jim Shooter, John Stanley, B. K. Taylor, Osamu Tezuka, Adam West, Wally Wood

1981—Jerry Bails, L. B. Cole, Jim Fitzpatrick, Dick Giordano, Dave Graue, Mary Henderson, Karl Hubenthal, Bil Keane, Frank Miller, Doug Moench, Monkey Punch, Dennis O'Neil, Gary Owens, Richard Rockwell, Allen Saunders, Julius Schwartz, Mike Sekowsky, Bill Sienkiewicz, Dave Sim, Alex Toth, Morrie Turner, Bill Woggon

1982—Bob Bindig, Brian Bolland, Russ Cochran, David Cockrum, Max Allen Collins, Chase Craig, Archie Goodwin, Mike Grell, Bruce Hamilton, Jack Katz, Howard Kazanjian, Hank Ketcham, Walter Koenig, Richard Kyle, Lee Marrs, Frank Marshall, John Pound, Tony Raiola, Steven Spielberg, Leonard Starr, Robert Williams

1983—Douglas Adams, Maeheah Alzmann, Don Bluth, Floyd Gottfredson, Norman Maurer, George Perez, Arn Saba, Dan Spiegel, Joe Staton, James Van Hise, cat yronwode

1984—Murphy Anderson, Ramon Arambola, Greg Bear, Fae (Gates) Desmond, Stan Drake, John Field, Rick Hoberg, Greg Jein, Ollie Johnson, Brant Parker, Robert Shayne, Curt Swan, Frank Thomas, Jim Valentino, Al Williamson

1985—Brent Anderson, Ben Bova, David Brin, Jack Cummings, Jack Davis, Alan Moore, Dan O'Bannon, Tome Orzechowski, John Rogers, Alex Schomburg, Walt Simonson

1986—Poul Anderson, Marion Zimmer Bradley, Dave Gibbons, Jean "Moebius" Giraud, Gilbert Hernandez, Jaime Hernandez, Denis Kitchen, Steve Leialoha, Marty Nodell, Harvey Pekar, Mark Stadler, Dave Stevens

1987—Harlan Ellison, Larry Geeck, Ward Kimball, Deni Loubert, Bill Messner-Loebs, Mike Peters, Bill Schanes, Steve Schanes, Robert Silverberg, Art Spiegelman, Berni Wrightson, Ray Zone

1988—Robert Asprin, Mike Baron, Lynda Barry, John Bolton, Jules Feiffer, Raymond E. Feist, Matt Groening, Gary Groth, George R. R. Martin, Mike Pasqua, Steve Rude, John Severin, Marie Severin, Rick Sternbach, Matt Wagner

1989—Richard Alf, R. Crumb, Howard Cruse, Tom DeFalco, Kevin Eastman, Lee Falk, Ron Goulart, Walt Kelly, Peter Laird, Syd Mead, Andre Norton, Jerry Robinson, Diana Schutz, Janet Tait, Ron Turner, Gahan Wilson

1990—Karen Berger, Bob Burden, William Gaines, Jim Henson, Jean-Marc Lofficier, Randi Lofficier, Grant Morrison, Bob Overstreet, Mary Reynante, Bob Schreck, Ken Steacy, Rick Sternbach, Charles Vess

1991—Alicia Austin, Clive Barker, Dan Barry, Dan DeCarlo, Neil Gaiman, Ted ("Dr. Seuss") Geisel, Keith Giffen, Heorge Gladir, Joe Haldeman, Lynn Johnston, Carol Kalish, Don Maitz, Sheldon Moldoff, Steve Oliff, Julie Roloff, Stan Sakai

1992—Carina Burns-Chenelle, Bob Chapman, Francis Ford Coppola, Robin Doig-Colls, Creig Flessel, Alan Grant, Bill Griffith, Ray Harryhausen, Marc Hempel, Jim Lee, Milo Manara, Scott McCloud, Todd McFarlane, Rowena Morrill, Diane Noomin, Louise Simonson, Dick Sprang, Vernor Vinge, Mark Wheatley

65. THE INTERNATIONAL ASSOCIATION FOR THE FANTASTIC IN THE ARTS AWARD
(INTERNATIONAL)

Presented by the International Association of the Fantastic in the Arts, these awards include several separately-named categories: The William L. Crawford Memorial Award is given for the best first fantasy novel of the previous eighteen months, as chosen by a panel of judges from the International Association for the Fantastic in the Arts (IAFA). The award honors the late fan, writer, and publisher, William L. Crawford (1911-1984), and consists of a cash prize of $100, sponsored by Andre Norton.

The Robert A. Collins Award, the Distinguished Scholarship Award, and the Graduate Scholarship Award, consist of bronze trophies designed by SF sculptor and artist Hap Henriksen. The Collins Award is given for outstanding service to IAFA. The Distinguished Scholarship Award includes, in addition to the plaque, an honorarium of $1,000.

THE IAFA AWARDS

1984 (1985)
Crawford Award—*Moonheart*, by Charles de Lint

1985 (1986)
Crawford Award—*Things Invisible to See*, by Nancy Willard
Distinguished Scholarship Award—Brian W. Aldiss
Collins Award—Roger C. Schlobin

1986 (1987)
Crawford Award—*The Hound and the Falcon* Trilogy, by Judith Tarr
Distinguished Scholarship Award—Brian M. Stableford
Graduate Scholarship Award—Veronica Hollinger

1987 (1988)
Crawford Award—*Reindeer Moon*, by Elisabeth Marshall Thomas
Distinguished Scholarship Award—Kathryn Hume
Graduate Scholarship Award—Sally Ann Bartlett, for "Fantasy and Mimesis in *Dr. Faustus*"

1988 (1989)
Crawford Award—*Walkabout Woman*, by Michaela Rossner-Herman
Distinguished Scholarship Award—Colin N. Manlove
Graduate Scholarship Award—Michael J. Collings, for "The Body of the Work of the Body: Physio-Textuality in Contemporary Horror"
Collins Award—Marshall B. Tymn

1989 (1990)
Crawford Award—*Silk Road*, by Jeanne Larsen
Distinguished Scholarship Award—H. Bruce Franklin
Graduate Scholarship Award—Jianjiong Zhu, for "Reality, Fiction, and Satori in *The Man in the High Castle*"

1990 (1991)
Crawford Award—*The Winter of the World* Trilogy, by Michael Scott Rohan
Distinguished Scholarship Award—Brian Attebery
Graduate Scholarship Award—Rob Latham, for "Collage as Critique and Invention in the Fiction of W. S. Burroughs and Kathy Acker"
Collins Award—Donald E. Morse

1991 (1992)
Crawford Award—*Moonwise*, by Greer Ilene Gilman
Distinguished Scholarship Award—Jack Zipes

Graduate Scholarship Award—(tie) Marcelaine Rovano, for "The Angel as a Fantasy Figure in Classic and Contemporary Film"; Maureen King, for "Contemporary Women Writers and the 'New Evil': The Vampires of Anne Rice and Suzy McKee Charnas"

66. THE INTERNATIONAL FANTASY AWARD
(INTERNATIONAL)

The International Fantasy Awards were created by four British SF personalities—Leslie Flood, John Beynon Harris, G. Ken Chapman, and Frank A. Cooper—at the 1951 British Science Fiction Convention. The awards were selected by an international panel (including the four above named), and honored works of fantastic literature and nonfiction books of interest to the field. Among the sometime judges were: Judith Merril, Anthony Boucher, P. Schuyler Miller, Groff Conklin, Basil Davenport, E. J. "Ted" Carnell, and others. After 1952 the awards were presented at a special dinner party. The Nonfiction category was dropped in 1954, and the Fiction awards were ultimately discontinued in 1958. The IFA was the first major award created specifically to honor fantastic literature, and of all the accolades mentioned in this book, has maintained the most consistent historical reputation for excellence and critical discernment.

INTERNATIONAL FANTASY AWARDS

1949/50 (1951)
Fiction—*Earth Abides*, by George R. Stewart
Nonfiction—*The Conquest of Space*, by Willy Ley and Chesley Bonestell

1951 (1952)
Fiction—*Fancies and Goodnights*, by John Collier
2nd—*The Day of the Triffids*, by John Wyndham
3rd—*The Illustrated Man*, by Ray Bradbury

Nonfiction—*The Exploration of Space*, by Arthur C. Clarke
2nd—*Dragons in Amber*, by Willy Ley
3rd—*Rockets, Jets, Guided Missiles and Spaceships*, by Jack Coggins and Fletcher Pratt

1952 (1953)
Fiction—*City*, by Clifford D. Simak
2nd—*Takeoff*, by Cyril M. Kornbluth
3rd—*Player Piano*, by Kurt Vonnegut, Jr.

Nonfiction—*Lands Beyond*, by Willy Ley and L. Sprague de Camp

1953 (1954)
Fiction—*More Than Human*, by Theodore Sturgeon
2nd—*The Demolished Man*, by Alfred Bester

1954 (1955)
Fiction—*A Mirror for Observers*, by Edgar Pangborn
2nd—*Mission of Gravity*, by Hal Clement

1955 (1956)
No awards

1956 (1957)
Fiction—*The Lord of the Rings Trilogy*, by J. R. R. Tolkien
Awards discontinued.

67. THE INVISIBLE LITTLE MAN AWARD
(UNITED STATES)

The Invisible Little Man Award is given for service to the SF field, and consists of a base with two footprints set into it. Tradition says that the winner must hold the base with one hand and mime the other holding the invisible man. The award was created and is given by The Elves', Gnomes', and Little Men's Science Fiction, Chowder and Marching Society of Berkeley, California. Only a partial list of winners is known.

INVISIBLE LITTLE MAN AWARDS

19??—Catherine L. Moore

1951—George Pal
1960—Ray Bradbury
1961—Cele Goldsmith
1962—Hal Clement
1963—Andre Norton
1964—Frederik Pohl
1965—L. Sprague de Camp
1966—Cordwainer Smith
1967—Charles Schneeman
1968—J. Francis McComas
1985—Algis Budrys

68. THE J. LLOYD EATON MEMORIAL AWARD
(UNITED STATES)

The Eaton Award honors the late San Francisco physician and science fiction fan, Dr. J. Lloyd Eaton, whose major SF collection forms the basis of the largest publicly-accessible library of fantastic literature, at the Rivera Library, University of California, Riverside. The Eaton Award is presented annually to the author of the best nonfiction work in fantastic literature published two years prior to the year the award is given. Occasional special lifetime awards were presented beginning in 1988. The award was mentioned by Robert Reginald and George Edgar Slusser in their initial 1978 proposal to UCR outlining the annual J. Lloyd Eaton Conference on Science Fiction and Fantasy Literature, and was included as part of the program for the first conference in 1979. The prize is chosen by a panel of judges consisting of Dr. George Slusser, Curator of the J. Lloyd Eaton Collection and other members of each Eaton Conference. The actual prize consists of a bronze plaque mounted on wood, presented at the Eaton Conference.

J. LLOYD EATON MEMORIAL AWARDS

1976/77 (1979)—*The Creation of Tomorrow: Fifty Years of Magazine Science Fiction*, by Paul A. Carter
1978 (1980)—*Future Tense: The Cinema of Science Fiction*, by John Brosnan
1979 (1981)—*The Known and the Unknown: The Iconography of Science Fiction*, by Gary K. Wolfe
1980 (1982)—*Robert A. Heinlein: America As Science Fiction*, by H. Bruce Franklin
1981 (1983)—*Alien Encounters*, by Mark Rose
1982 (1984)—*The Logic of Fantasy*, by John Huntington
1983 (1985)—*The Entropy Exhibition*, by Colin Greenland
1984 (1986)—*Fantasy and Mimesis*, by Kathryn Hume
1985 (1987)—(tie) *Some Kind of Paradise*, by Thomas D. Clareson; *Scientific Romance in Britain, 1890-1950*, by Brian Stableford
1986 (1988)—*Trillion Year Spree*, by Brian W. Aldiss; **Lifetime Achievement**—Reginald Bretnor
1987 (1989)—*Origins of Futuristic Fiction*, by Paul K. Alkon

1988 (1990)—*Jules Verne Rediscovered*, by Arthur B. Evans
1989 (1991)—*Science Fiction, Fantasy & Horror 1988*, by Charles N. Brown, William G. Contento, and Hal W. Hall
1991 (1992)—*The Last Frontier: Imagining Other Worlds, From the Copernican Revolution to Modern Science Fiction*, by Karl S. Guthke; **Lifetime Achievement**—James E. Gunn

69. THE JACK GAUGHAN MEMORIAL AWARD
(UNITED STATES)

The Gaughan Award is presented annually at the Boskone convention to the most promising new artist in the SF field; the artist is selected by a jury of three persons serving overlapping three-year terms. The jury is chosen by the president of the New England Science Fiction Association (NESFA), subject to ratification by the membership of NESFA. The award honors the memory of well-known SF artist Jack Gaughan (1930-1985).

JACK GAUGHAN MEMORIAL AWARD

1986—Stephen Hickman
1987—Val Lakey Lindahn
1988—Bob Eggleton
1989—Dell Harris
1990—Richard Hescox
1991—Keith Parkinson
1992—Jody Lee

70. JAMES TIPTREE JR. MEMORIAL AWARD
(UNITED STATES)

This award, originally proposed by Karen Joy Fowler and Pat Murphy at the 1991 WisCon, recognizes "gender-bending" science fiction or fantasy from the previous year, and honors the memory of writer James Tiptree, Jr. (1915-1987). Funds to support the award are raised through donations, sales of cookbooks, and bake sales.

THE JAMES TIPTREE JR. MEMORIAL AWARDS

1991 (1992)

1st—*White Queen*, by Gwyneth Jones
2nd—*A Woman of the Iron People*, by Eleanor Arnason

71. JAPAN FANTASY NOVEL AWARD
(JAPAN)

This prize is chosen by a five-member jury, and sponsored by a large Japanese newspaper and a real estate company. The prize consists of five million yen; the winning novel is made into a television movie (similar to the Turner Tomorrow Award). Only one award year is known.

THE JAPAN FANTASY NOVEL AWARDS

1988 (1989)—*Tales of the Inner Palace*, by Kenichi Sakami

72. JERÓNIMO MONTIERO CONTEST
(BRAZIL)

The Jerónimo Montiero Contest is a science fiction contest promoted by the Brazilian edition of *Isaac Asimov's Science Fiction Magazine* (*IAM*). The award is named for Brazilian SF pioneer Montiero, who edited twenty issues of the Brazilian edition of *The Magazine of Fantasy & Science Fiction* in the 1970s. Winners are announced in April.

THE JERÓNIMO MONTIERO CONTEST WINNERS

1989 (1990)
1st—"Como a Neve de Maio" ("As the Snow of May"), by Roberto Schima
2nd—"Lost," by Cid Fernandez
3rd—"Patrulha para o Desconhecido" ("Patrol to the Unknown"), by Roberto de Sousa Causo

73. THE JERRY OLTION REALLY GOOD STORY AWARD
(UNITED STATES)

The Jerry Oltion Really Good Story Award is presented to anyone writing a story which science fiction writer Jerry Oltion considers to be good. It may be awarded up to four times a year. Winners receive a stylized acrylic spaceship on a mahogany base, hand-built by Oltion.

THE JERRY OLTION REALLY GOOD STORY AWARD

1992—"Clarence to Land," by Adam-Troy Castro; "Hard Landing," by Algis Budrys

74. THE JOHN W. CAMPBELL JR. MEMORIAL AWARD & THE THEODORE STURGEON MEMORIAL AWARD
(UNITED STATES)

The John W. Campbell, Jr. Memorial Award honors the best science fiction novel of the preceding year, and is given in memory of the well-known science fiction writer and editor, one of the founding fathers of modern SF. The award is chosen by an international panel of SF professionals, and presented annually by administrator James E. Gunn at the University of Kansas, Lawrence, KS. The trophy, which was designed by Eldon Tefft, consists of a large iron ring perched on a tall wooden base with a name plate. This award should not be confused with the John W. Campbell, Jr. (Hugo) Award for best new author of the year.

In 1987 a companion award, The Theodore Sturgeon Award, was created to honor the best science fiction short story under 17,500 words published during the previous calendar year in English.

JOHN W. CAMPBELL, JR. MEMORIAL AWARDS

1972 (1973)—*Beyond Apollo*, by Barry N. Malzberg
1973 (1974)—(tie) *Rendezvous with Rama*, by Arthur C. Clarke; *Malevil*, by Robert Merle; **Special Award**—*The Cosmic Connection*, by Carl Sagan
1974 (1975)—*Flow My Tears, the Policeman Said*, by Philip K. Dick
1975 (1976)—No award; **Special Award**—*The Year of the Quiet Sun* (1970), by Wilson Tucker
1976 (1977)—*The Alteration*, by Kingsley Amis
1977 (1978)—*Gateway*, by Frederik Pohl
1978 (1979)—*Gloriana*, by Michael Moorcock
1979 (1980)—*On Wings of Song*, by Thomas M. Disch
1980 (1981)—*Timescape*, by Gregory Benford

1981 (1982)—*Riddley Walker*, by Russell Hoban
1982 (1983)—*Helliconia: Spring*, by Brian W. Aldiss

1983 (1984)

Winner—*The Citadel of the Autarch*, by Gene Wolfe
2nd—*The Birth of the People's Republic of Antarctica*, by John Calvin Batchelor
3rd—*Tik-Tok*, by John Sladek

1984 (1985)—*The Years of the City*, by Frederik Pohl
1985 (1986)—*The Postman*, by David Brin

1986 (1987)

Winner—*A Door into Ocean*, by Jean Slonczewski
2nd—*This is the Way the World Ends*, by James Morrow
3rd—*Speaker for the Dead*, by Orson Scott Card

1987 (1988)

Winner—*Lincoln's Dreams*, by Connie Willis
2nd—*The Sea and Summer*, by George Turner
3rd—*The Unconquered Country*, by Geoff Ryman

1988 (1989)

Winner—*Islands in the Net*, by Bruce Sterling
2nd—*The Gold Coast*, by Kim Stanley Robinson
3rd—*Dragonsdawn*, by Anne McCaffrey

1989 (1990)

Winner—*The Child Garden*, by Geoff Ryman
2nd—*Farewell Horizontal*, by K. W. Jeter
3rd—*Good News from Outer Space*, by John Kessel

1990 (1991)

Winner—*Pacific Edge*, by Kim Stanley Robinson
2nd—*Queen of Angels*, by Greg Bear
3rd—*Only Begotten Daughter*, by James Morrow

1991 (1992)

Winner—*Buddy Holly is Alive and Well on Ganymede*, by Bradley Denton
2nd—*The Difference Engine*, by William Gibson & Bruce Sterling
3rd—(3-way tie) *The Silicon Man*, by Charles Platt; *A Woman of the Iron People*, by Eleanor Arnason; *Stations of the Tide*, by Michael Swanwick

THE THEODORE STURGEON MEMORIAL AWARDS

1986 (1987)

Winner—"Surviving," by Judith Moffett
2nd—"Elephant," by Susan Palwick
3rd—"The Grave Angels," by Richard Kearns

1987 (1988)

Winner—"Rachel In Love," by Pat Murphy
2nd—"Buffalo Gals, Won't You Come Out Tonight?," by Ursula K. Le Guin
3rd—""The Evening and the Morning and the Night," by Octavia E. Butler

1988 (1989)

Winner—"Schrödinger's Kitten," by George Alec Effinger
2nd—"Do Ya, Do Ya, Wanna Dance," by Howard Waldrop
3rd—"Stairs," by Neal Barrett Jr.

1989 (1990)
Winner—"The Edge of the World," by Michael Swanwick
2nd—"Silver Lady and the Fortyish Man," by Megan Lindholm
3rd—"Dori Bangs," by Bruce Sterling

1990 (1991)
Winner—"Bears Discover Fire," by Terry Bisson
2nd—*Episodes of the Argo*, by R. A. Lafferty
3rd—"My Advice to the Civilized," by John Barnes

1991 (1992)
Winner—"Buffalo," by John Kessel
2nd—"Ma Qui," by Alan Brennert
3rd—"The Happy Man," by Jonathan Lethem

75. THE JULES VERNE AWARD
(UNITED STATES)

Nothing is known of the background of this award.

JULES VERNE AWARDS

1982 (1983)
Life Achievement in SF—A. E. van Vogt
Life Achievement in Comics—Al Williamson

1983 (1984)
Life Achievement in SF—Andre Norton
Life Achievement in Comics—Julius Schwartz
Awards discontinued?

76. THE JUPITER AWARD
(UNITED STATES)

The Jupiter Awards were given by the Instructors of Science Fiction in Higher Education, a scholarly organization founded and presided over by Marshall B. Tymn. The society dissolved in 1979. The physical award consisted of a certificate framed in plastic.

THE JUPITER AWARDS

1973 (1974)
Novel—*Rendezvous With Rama*, by Arthur C. Clarke
Novella—"The Feast of St. Dionysus," by Robert Silverberg
Novelette—"The Deathbird," by Harlan Ellison
Short Story—"A Supplicant in Space," by Robert Sheckley

1974 (1975)
Novel—*The Dispossessed*, by Ursula K. Le Guin
Novella—"Riding the Torch," by Norman Spinrad
Novelette—"The Seventeen Virgins," by Jack Vance
Short Story—"The Day Before the Revolution," by Ursula K. Le Guin

1975 (1976)
No awards

1976 (1977)
Novel—*Where Late the Sweet Birds Sang*, by Kate Wilhelm
Novella—"Houston, Houston, Do You Read?" by James Tiptree, Jr.
Novelette—"The Diary of the Rose," by Ursula K. Le Guin
Short Story—"I See You," by Damon Knight

1977 (1978)
Novel—*A Heritage of Stars*, by Clifford D. Simak
Novella—"In the Hall of the Martian Kings," by John Varley
Novelette—"Time Storm," by Gordon R. Dickson
Short Story—"Jeffty Is Five," by Harlan Ellison

Awards discontinued.

77. THE KAREL AWARD
[THE WORLD SCIENCE FICTION AWARD]
(INTERNATIONAL)

The World Science Fiction Award, known as the Karel Award, is presented annually by the World Science Fiction Society (WSFS) for excellence in the translation of science fiction, fantasy, and horror literature. The award was created by Frederik Pohl during his term as President of WSFS. The name honors the memory of Czech SF author, Karel Capek (1890-1938); it should not be confused with the Karel Capek Award (Czechoslovakia). The physical trophy consists of a hand-blown glass figurine designed by Steve Sherer (United States), depicting a robot reading a book while sitting on a globe.

Two additional (occasional) awards initiated by Brian W. Aldiss include: The President's Award, a lucite plaque which honors independence of thought in science fiction; and The Harry Harrison Award, also a plaque, which honors individuals who have improved the international image of science fiction. Other awards occasionally honor the guest who has travelled furthest to the annual World SF convention, or to note dedicated service to the organization.

THE KAREL AWARDS

1981 (1982)
Karel—Norio Ito (Japan), Krsto Mazuranic (Yugoslavia), Roberta Rambelli (Italy), Annemarie van Eioyck (Holland), Peter Kuczka (Hungary)

1982 (1983)
President's Award—Josef Nesvadba (Czechoslovakia)
Harrison Award—Sam J. Lundwall (Sweden), Bruce Gillespie (Australia), Krsto Mazuranic (Yugoslavia)
Dedicated Service Award—Gerald Bishop (United Kingdom); Elizabeth Anne Hull (United States)
Long Distance Award—Wang Fengzhen (China)

1983 (1984)
Karel—Vasily Zakharchencko (USSR), George Balanos (Greece), Maxim Jakubowski (UK/France), Marcial Souto (Uruguay)
Special Award—Annemarie van Eioyck (Holland)
Harrison Award—Ion Hobana (Romania), John Bush (United Kingdom)
President's Award—Takumi Shibano (Japan), Donald A. Wollheim (United States)

1984 (1985)
Karel—Georges Barlov (France), Walter Brimm (West Germany), Donna Dprita (Romania), Gianpaolo Cossato (Italy), Sandro Sandrelli (Italy), Tetsu Yano (Japan), Frantisek Novotny (Czechoslovakia), Theodor Rotreki (Czechoslovakia)

1985 (1986)
Karel—Francesco Porrua (Spain), Roland Adlerberth (Sweden), Lev Djdanov (USSR), Marek Marsol (Poland), Joe Randolph (United States)
Dedicated Service Award—Leslie Flood (United Kingdom), Peter Szabo (Hungary)
President's Award—Everett F. Bleiler (United States), Pierre Versins (France/Switzerland)
Harrison Award—Roulof Goudrian (Belgium), Denise Terrel (France)

1986 (1987)
Karel—Annarita Guarnieri (Italy), Wiktor Bukato (Poland)
Harrison Award—Carlo Pagetti (Italy), Wolfgang Jeschke (West Germany)
President's Award—Patrick Parrinder (United Kingdom), Arkady and Boris Strugatsky (USSR)
Special President's Award—Thomas Olander (Finland), Elisabeth Gille (France), Peter Kuczka (Hungary), Adam Hollanck (Poland), Charles N. Brown (United States), Pierre Barbet (France), Jacques Goimard (France), Lino Aldani (Italy), Neil Barron (United States), Marshall B. Tymn (United States)

1987 (1988)
President's Award—Thomas Olander (Finland), Eremei Parnov (USSR), Brian W. Aldiss (United Kingdom)
Harrison Award—Edward L. Ferman (United States), Patrice Duvic (France)

1988 (1989)
Karel—Erik Simon (East Germany), Hélène Collon (France), Tauno Petolo (Finland), William Wheeler (United States)
President's Award—Neil Barron (United States); Roger de Garis (United States)
Harrison Award—Vladimir Gopman (USSR)
Long Distance Award—Yang Xiao (China), Boris Zavgorodny (USSR)

1989 (1990)
Karel—Guy Abadia (France), Sam J. Lundwall (Sweden), Dan Fukami (Japan)
Special Award—Staff of *Orphia*, an English-language magazine of Slavic authors (Bulgaria)

1990 (1991)
Karel—Guo Jianzhong (China), Takumi Shibano (Japan)
President's Award—Wang Fengzhen (China)
Harrison Award—Arthur C. Clarke (Sri Lanka)
Special Award—*Ikarie* magazine, Jaroslav Olsa Jr., ed., (Czechoslovakia); *SF World* magazine, Yang Xiao, ed. (China)

---

78. THE KAREL CAPEK AWARD
(CZECHOSLOVAKIA)

The Karel Capek Award (Cena Karla Capka), presented annually to the writer of the best short SF story of the year written in Czech, was established in 1982. Originally intended to honor authors who had not yet published a book, in 1988 it was opened to all writers. The primary award is called the Mlok (or "Newt"), after the monsters in Capek's well-known novel, *War with the Newts* (*Valka s Mloky*). The prize is chosen by a jury of writers, editors, and fans, and is presented at the annual Parcon. Although other categories have been established in recent years, the "Mlok" is reserved only for the short story category.

THE KAREL CAPEK AWARDS

1981 (1982)
Mlok—"Kdyz Jsou Hoste v Dome" ("When the Guests are at Home"), by Ladislav Kubic
Short Story by Juvenile—"Nova Atlantida" ("New Atlantis"), by Petr Jedlinsky

1982 (1983)
Mlok—"Syntamor Zasahuje" ("Syntamor in Action"), by Ivan Kminek
Short Story by a Juvenile—"Vyroci" ("Anniversary"), by Jana Rosipalova
Special Award (Professional)—Vojtech Kantor, for editing Mlada Fronta publishers

1983 (1984)
Mlok—"Druhy Vstup do Teze Reky" ("The Second Entry into the Same River") or "Kam s ni?" ("What to Do with Her?"), by Ivan Kminek
Short Story—"Nanos" ("Deposit"), by Petr Burian
New Author—Dagmara Outla
Special Award (Professional)—Ivo Zelezny, for editing Svoboda publishers

1984 (1985)
Mlok—"Legenda o Madone z Vrakoviste" ("The Legend of Madonna from the Wrecking Place"), by Frantisek Novotny
Short Story—"Jsem Hodny, Tichy Chlapec" ("I Am a Good, Silent Boy"), by Frantisek Novotny
New Author—Natasa Krejci
Juvenile Author—Natasa Krejci
Antiwar Story—"Raketyr" ("The Rocketeer"), by Vladimir Veverka
Special Award (Professional)—Theodor Rotreki, for his illustrations

1985 (1986)
Mlok—"Jeji Velicenstvo" ("Her Majesty"), by Josef Pecinovsky
Short Story—"Pan René Nosi Saty" ("Mr. René Is Wearing Clothes"), Frantisek Novotny
Antiwar Story—"Jsme Tady Doma" ("We are Here at Home"), by Jan Hlavicka
Juvenile Writer—Pavel Kocis
Short Story by Student—"Hrali Jsme Fausta" ("We Played Faustus"), by Zdenek Tichy
Special Award (Professional)—Josef Nesvadba, for his writing

1986 (1987)
Mlok—"Nos to Zavazi" ("Carry the Weight!"), by Josef Pecinovsky
Juvenile Writer—Vilma Kadleckova
Short Story—"Uzonrnej Prisar" (Untranslatable), by Barbara Jezkova
Special Award (Professional)—Ondrej Neff, for his writing and translating

1987 (1988)
Mlok—"U nas v Agonii" ("With Us in Agony"), by Eva Hauserova
Short Story—"Sodovka" ("Soda Water"), by Jan Hlavicka
Juvenile Writer—Longin Albert Wdowiak
Short Story by Student—"Kruta je Noc" ("Sharp Is the Night"), by Ivan Adamovic
Special Award (Professional)—Kaja Saudek, for his comics

1988 (1989)
Mlok—"Hlavou Proti Vzduchu" ("By Head Against the Air"), by Jan Hlavicka
Short Story—"Uchem" ("Through the Ear"), by Zdenek Pav

79. THE KEN McINTYRE AWARD
(UNITED KINGDOM)

The Ken McIntyre Award is given for the best artwork appearing in a fanzine during the preceding year in England. It is chosen by a panel of judges. Only three award years are known.

THE KEN MCINTYRE AWARDS

1987 (1988)—SMS, for the cover of the *Follycon Progress Report #2*
1989 (1990)—Jim Porter

1990 (1991)—Colin Johnston

80. THE KING KONG AWARD
(NETHERLANDS)

The King Kong Award, which honors the best Dutch SF short story of the year, is chosen by a panel of professionals in the field, and is open to any Dutch writer who submits a story. The prize consists of 1,000 Dutch Guilden (approximately $500 US), the funds being donated by fans and pros.

THE KING KONG AWARDS

1987—Jan J. B. Kuipers
1990—"The Winter Garden," by Paul Harland

81. KURD LASSWITZ AWARD
[THE GERMAN SCIENCE FICTION AND FANTASY ACHIEVEMENT AWARD]
(GERMANY)

The Kurd Lasswitz Awards (the German equivalent of the American Nebulas) honor the memory of German science fiction author and philosopher, Kurd Lasswitz (1848-1910). The awards are chosen annually by a jury of SF professionals for best science fiction published published in Germany during the previous year.

THE KURD LASSWITZ AWARDS

1980 (1981)
Novel—*Die Enkel der Raketenbauer*, by Georg Zauner
Novella—"Die Sensitiven Jahre" ("The Sensitive Year"), by Thomas Ziegler
Short Story—"Auf dem Grossen Strom," by Ronald M. Hahn
Translator—Horst Pukallus
Artist—Thomas Franke
Special Award—Hans Joachim Alpers, Werner Fuchs, Ronald M. Hahn, and Wolfgang Jeschke, for *Lexicon der Science Fiction Literatur (The Lexicon of Science Fiction Literature)*

1981 (1982)
Novel—*Der Letzte tag der Schoepfung*, by Wolfgang Jeschke
Novella—"Dokumente Über den Zustand des Landes vor der Verheerung," by Wolfgang Jeschke
Short Story—"Ein Paar Kurze Durch die Zensur Geschmuggelte Szenen aus den Akten der Abenteuer und Freiheit GMBH," by Ronald M. Hahn
Translator—Horst Pukallus
Artist—Thomas Franke
Special Award—Wolfgang Jeschke, for publishing SF magazines

1982 (1983)
Novel—*Im Jahre 95 Nach Hiroshima (The 95th Year After Hiroshima)*, by Richard Hey
Novella—"Osiris Land," by Wolfgang Jeschke
Short Story—"Die Planktofischer" ("The Plankton Fisher"), by Andreas Brandhorst
Translator—Michael Kubiak
Artist—Ulf Herholz
Special Award—Hans Joachim Alpers, Werner Fuchs, and Ronald M. Hahn, for *Reclams Science Fiction Führer*

1983 (1984)
Novel—*Das Sakriversum (The Sacriverse)*, by Thomas R. P. Mielke
Novella—"Die Stimmen der Nacht" ("Voices of the Night"), by Thomas Ziegler
Short Story—"Atem der Sonne" ("Breath of the Sun"), by Herbert W. Franke
Translator—Horst Pukallus
Artist—Helmut Wenske
Special Award—Heinrich Wimmer, for publishing of SF
Foreign Novel—*Helliconia: Spring*, by Brian W. Aldiss (United Kingdom)

1984 (1985)
Novel—*Die Kälte des Weltraums*, by Herbert W. Franke
Novella—"Nekyomanteion," by Wolfgang Jeschke
Short Story—"Nur Einen Sommer Gönnt Ihr Gewaltigen," by Carl Amery
Translator—Horst Pukallus
Artist—Helmut Wenske
Special Award—Joachim Körber and Covian Publishers, for *Bibliographical Dictionary of Utopian and Fantastic Literature*
Foreign Novel—*Valis*, by Philip K. Dick (United States)

1985 (1986)
Novel—*End Zeit (End Time)*, by Herbert W. Franke
Novella—"Traumjäger" ("Dreamtime"), by Hans Joachim Alpers and Ronald M. Hahn
Short Story—"Polarlicht" ("Polar Light"), by Reinmar Cunis
Translator—Lore Strassl
Artist—Helmut Wenske
Special Award—Dr. Deiter Hasselblatt, for promoting science fiction radio plays
Foreign Novel—*The Minds of Billy Milligan*, by Daniel Keyes (United States)

1986 (1987)
Novel—*Die Wallfahrer (The Pilgrim)*, by Carl Amery
Novella—"Umkreisungen" ("Orbits"), by Karl Michael Armer
Short Story—"Play Future," by Rainer Erler
Translator—Lore Strassl
Artist—Klaus Holitzka
Film/TV Play—"News-Bericht Über die Reise in Eine Strahlende Zukunft" ("News Report on a Voyage into a Beaming Future"), by Rainer Erler
Radio Play—"Totenfloss" ("Raft of the Dead"), by Harald Mueller
Special Award—Science Fiction Media
Foreign Novel—*Elleander Morning*, by Jerry Yulsman (United States)

1987 (1988)
Novel—*Die Wolke (The Cloud)*, by Gudrun Pausewang
Short Fiction—"Die Endlosung der Arbeitslosenfrage" ("Final Solution to the Problem of Unemployment"), by Karl Michael Armer
Translator—Lore Strassl
Artist—Klaus Holitzka
Film/TV Play—*Der Himmel Über Berlin (The Sky Above Berlin)*
Radio Play—*Pas Penthouse-Protokoll*, by Carl Amery
Special Award—Wolfgang Jeschke, for "Das Science Fiction Jahre" ("The Science Fiction Year")
Foreign Novel—*The Glamour*, by Christopher Priest (United Kingdom)

1988 (1989)
Novel—*New York Ist Himmlisch (New York is Heaven)*, by Norbert Stöbe
Novelette—"Malessen Mite Biotechnik" ("Problems with Biotechnic"), by Karl Michael Armer
Short Story—"Der Käse" ("A Piece of Cheese"), by Rainer Erler
Translator—Walter Brumm
Artist—Helmut Wenske
Film—*Münchhausen*

Radio Play—*Jona im Feuerofen (Jonah in the Furnace)*, by Wolfgang Jeschke
Foreign Novel—*Speaker for the Dead*, by Orson Scott Card (United States)
Special Award—*Science Fiction Media* (news magazine)

1989 (1990)

Novel—*Midas*, by Wolfgang Jeschke
Novelette—"Siebzhen Satza" ("Seventeen Sentences"), by Werner Zillig
Short Story—"Wanderlust," by Gisbert Haefs
Translator—Irene Holicki
Artist—Dieter Rottermund
Film/TV Play—No Award
Radio Play—*Project Ichthantropus Gescheitert (Project Ichthantropus Wrecked)*, by Dieter Hasselblatt
Special Award—Walter Froneberg, Mayor of Wetzlar, for supporting the city's science fiction library
Foreign Novel—*Life During Wartime*, by Lucius Shepard (United States)

82. L. RON HUBBARD'S WRITERS OF THE FUTURE AWARD/ ILLUSTRATORS OF THE FUTURE AWARD
(UNITED STATES)

The L. Ron Hubbard Writers of the Future Awards were created to encourage new writers by giving cash prizes for stories submitted to a panel of judges. There are four contests annually, the best stories from each quarter being published in a paperback anthology, and each quarterly winner of the $1,000 (plus plaque and trophy) first prize eligible to win the annual Gold Award of an additional $4,000, plaque, and trophy. The awards were established in 1985 to honor the memory of SF writer and Dianetics founder, L. Ron Hubbard (1911-1986), and are administered by Author Services Inc., in the persons of Fred Harris and SF writers Algis Budrys and Dave Wolverton.

Awarded simultaneously with this prize is the L. Ron Hubbard Illustrators of the Future Award, created in 1990 to honor SF artists, the first presentation having been made at the American Booksellers Association (ABA) Convention in Las Vegas. The three illustrators chosen quarterly each receive $500, plaque, and trophy, and all are eligible for the Illustrators Gold Award of $4,000.

THE WRITERS OF THE FUTURE AWARDS
THE ILLUSTRATORS OF THE FUTURE AWARDS

1984 (1985)

First Quarter
1st—"Arcadus Arcane," by Dennis J. Pimple
2nd—"The Ebbing," by Leonard Carpenter
3rd—"A Step Into Darkness," by Nina Kiriki Hoffman

Second Quarter
1st—"Tiger Hunt," by Jor Jennings
2nd—"A Way Out," by Mary Frances Zambreno
3rd—"Anthony's Wives," by Randy Crump

Third Quarter
1st—"Shanidar," by David Zindell
2nd—"The Two Tzaddicks," by Ira Herman
3rd—"Tyson's Turn," by Michael D. Miller

Fourth Quarter—unknown

No Gold Awarded.

1985 (1986)

First Quarter
1st—"The Book of Time," by Camilla Decarnin
2nd—"A Sum of Moments," by Laura E. Campbell
3rd—"Dream in a Bottle," by Jerry T. Meredith & Dennis E. Smirl

Second Quarter
1st—"Mudpuppies," by Robert Touzalin (pseud. of Robert Reed)
2nd—"Redmond," by Kenneth Schulze
3rd—"The Cinderella Caper," by Sansoucy Kathenor (Walker)

Third Quarter
1st—"In the Smoke," by Howard Hendrix
2nd—"All You Can Eat!," by Don Baumgart
3rd—"They That Go Down to the Sea in Ships," by Marina Fitch

Fourth Quarter
1st—"The Old Organ Trail," by Bridget McKenna
2nd—"The Helldivers," by Parris ja Young
3rd—"Click," by Ray Aldridge

Gold—"Mudpuppies," by Robert Touzalin

1986 (1987)

First Quarter
1st—"Circumstance," by Eric M. Heideman
2nd—"The Very Last Party at #13 Mallory Way," by Lucy E. Carroll
3rd—"In the Sick Bay," by R. V. Branham

Second Quarter
1st—"Jacob's Ladder," by M. Shayne Bell
2nd—"The Language of the Sea," by Carolyn Ives Gilman
3rd—"Old Mickey Flip Had a Marvelous Ship," by Lori Ann White

Third Quarter
1st—"Living in the Jungle," by Martha Soukup
2nd—"No Pets," by T(awn) J. Stokes
3rd—"Monsters," by Jean Reitz

Fourth Quarter
1st—"On My Way to Paradise," by Dave Wolverton
2nd—"Long Knives," by J(eff) R. Dunn as G. R. O'DOINN
3rd—"A Little of What You Fancy," by Mary Catherine McDaniel

Gold—"On My Way to Paradise," by Dave Wolverton

1987 (1988)

First Quarter
1st—"Buffalo Dreams," by Jane Mailander
2nd—"What Do I See In You?," by Mary A. Turzillo (i.e., Mary Brizzi)
3rd—"A Winter's Night," by Pat MacEwen

Second Quarter
1st—"The Mirror," by Nancy Farmer
2nd—"The Zombie Corps: Nine-Lives Charlie," by Rayson Lorrey (i.e., R. Rayson Deike)
3rd—"The Cause," by Mark D. Haw

Third Quarter
1st—"Heroic Measures," by Paul E. Clinco as PAUL EDWARDS
2nd—"Black Sun and Dark Companion," by R. Garcia y Robertson (i.e., Rod Garcia)

3rd—"The Gas Man," by Richard "Rick" Urdiales

Fourth Quarter
1st—"River of Stone," by Michael Green
2nd—"The Troublesome Kordae Alliance and How It Was Settled," by Flonet Biltgen
3rd—"Growlers," by Larry England

Gold—"The Mirror," by Nancy Farmer

1988 (1989)

First Quarter
1st—"The Nomalers," by Jamil E. Nasir
2nd—"A Walk By Moonlight," by Mark Anthony
3rd—"Dear Mom," by Stephen C. Fisher

Second Quarter
1st—"The Disambiguation of Captain Shroud," by Gary W. Shockley
2nd—"Blue Shift," by Stephen M. Baxter
3rd—"Prosthetic Lady," by Paula May

Third Quarter
1st—"Rachel's Wedding," by Virginia Baker
2nd—"Under Ice," by Calvin W. Johnson
3rd—"StarBird," by J. Steven York

Fourth Quarter
1st—"The Wallet and Maudie," by Alex Wexelblat & Dan'l Danehy-Oakes
2nd—"Despite and Still," by J. Marc Matz
3rd—"Daddy's Girls," by Kathy D. Wentworth

Gold—"The Disambiguation of Captain Shroud," by Gary Shockley
Special Golden Age Award—Edd Cartier for art
Special Golden Age Award—Jack Williamson for writing

1989 (1990)

First Quarter
1st—"The Children of Creche," by James Gardner
2nd—"The Magician," by Michael T. Landweber
3rd—"Dancing With Dinosaurs," by Charles D. Eckert
Illustrator Winners—Allison Hershey, Timothy Standish, & Jeff Fennel

Second Quarter
1st—"Water," by John W. Randal
2nd—"Flutterbyes," by Jo Etta Ledgerwood
3rd—"A Foreign Exchange," by Matthew Willis
Illustrator Winners—Beryl Bush, Ruth Thompson, & Derek J. Hegsted

Third Quarter
1st—"A Branch in the Wind," by Bruce Holland Rogers
2nd—"Riches Like Dust," by Scot Noel
3rd—"Under Glass," by David Carr
Illustrator Winners—Daniel S. Oman, Kelly Faltermeyer, & Timothy Winkler

Fourth Quarter
1st—"The Vintager," by James Gleason Bishop
2nd—"Kansas City Kitty," by Michael L. Scanlon
3rd—"Winter's Garden," by Sharon Wahl
Illustrator Winners—Kevin Dzuban, Kevin Hopkins, & Peggy Ranson

Writers Gold—"The Children of Creche," by James Gardner

Illustrators Gold—Derek Hegsted

1990 (1991)

First Quarter
1st—"Georgi," by James C. Glass
2nd—"17 Short Essays on the Relationship Between Art and Science," by Michael C. Berch
3rd—"Hopes and Dreams," by Mark Andrew Garland
Illustrator Winners:
"17 Short Essays on the Relationship Between Art and Science," by Christopher C. Beau
"Georgi," by Thomas Denmark
"Hopes and Dreams," by Jim Reece

Second Quarter
1st—"The Trashman of Auschwitz," by Barry H. Reynolds
2nd—"Yarena's Daughter," by Terri Trimble
3rd—"The Cab Driver From Hell in the Land of the Pioux Hawques," by Allen J. M. Smith
Illustrator Winners:
"Yarena's Daughter," by Charles Dougherty
"The Trashman of Auschwitz," by Harold J. Fox
"The Cab Driver From Hell in the Land of the Pioux Hawques," by Micheal Grossman

Third Quarter
1st—"Sensations of the Wind," by Valerie J. Freireich
2nd—"A Plea For Mercy," by Ojvind Bernander
3rd—"Balanced Ecology," by William Esrac as WILLIAM CARSE
Illustrator Winners:
"A Plea For Mercy & Pandora's Box 2055," by Rob Sanford
"Balanced Ecology & An Exultation of Tears," by Ferenc Temil Temesvari
"Sensations of the Mind & Raid on the Gold Horn," by Lawrence Allen Williams

Fourth Quarter
1st—"The Relay," by Michelle L. Levigne
2nd—"A Plumber's Tale," by Merritt Severson
3rd—"Crow's Curse," by Michael H. Payne
Illustrator Winners:
"Relay," by Rob Alexander
"Crow's Curse," by Peter H. Francis
"A Plumber's Tale," by Sergey V. Poyarkov

Writers Gold—"Georgi," by James C. Glass
Illustrators Gold—Sergey Poyarkov

1991 (1992)

First Quarter
1st—"Anne of a Thousand Faces," by Michael Paul Meltzer
2nd—"Invisible Man," by Larry Ferrill
3rd—"A Cold Fragrant Air," by Connie Maria Plieger
Illustrator Winners:
"A Cold Fragrant Air," by John Caponigro
"Anne of a Thousand Years," by Ira Crowe
"Invisible Man," by Bob E. Hobbs

Second Quarter
1st—"The Last Indian War," by Brian Burt
2nd—"Bringing Sissy Home," by Astrid Julian
3rd—"Subterranean Pests," by James S. Dorr
Illustrator Winners:
"The Last Indian War," by Evan T. Thomas
"Subterranean Pests," by Allen Koszowski
"Bringing Sissy Home," by Jane Walker

Reginald's Science Fiction & Fantasy Awards, Third Edition

Third Quarter
1st—"Surrogate," by M. C. Sumner
2nd—"Pale Marionettes," by (Robert) Mark Budz
3rd—"Winter Night, With Kittens," by Sam Wilson
Illustrator Winners:
"Winter Night, With Kittens," by Shaun C. Y. Tan
"Pale Marionettes," by Matthew Stork
"Surrogate," by Darren J. Albertson

Fourth Quarter
1st—"Scary Monsters," by Stephen Woodworth
2nd—"The Augmented Man," by Wendy Rathbone
3rd—"Timepieces," by Mike E. Swope
Illustrator Winners:
"Timepieces," by Omar Rayyan
"Scary Monsters," by Yevgeny Rzhanov
"The Augmented Man," by Thomas Whittaker

Writers Gold—"The Last Indian War," by Brian Burt
Illustrators Gold—"The Last Indian War," by Evan T. Thomas

1992 (1993)

First Quarter
1st—"M," by Lisa Maxwell
2nd—"Fire," by Elizabeth Wein
3rd—"Ghosts of the Fall," by Sean Williams
Illustrator Winners:
"Ghosts of the Fall," by Denis Martynec
"Fire," by Juriy Galitsin
"M," by Gary Davis

Second Quarter
1st—"Adjusting the Moon," by Kara Wynn Long
2nd—"The Dictates," by Vaughn Heppner
3rd—"Lady's Portrait, Executed in Archaic Colors," by Charles Michael Saplak
Illustrator Winners:
"Lady's Portrait, Executed in Archaic Colors," by Brian Lee Durfee
"Adjusting the Moon," by Sebastijan Camagajevec
"The Dictates," by Jody C. McMurrian

83. THE LAMBDA LITERARY AWARD
(UNITED STATES)

The Lambda Literary Awards are given to works by gay/lesbian authors or works which present alternative sexual and personal relationships in a positive fashion. Only the science fiction and fantasy components of these awards are listed here.

THE LAMBDA LITERARY AWARDS

1989 (1990)
Lesbian Science Fiction/Fantasy—*What Did Miss Darrington See? An Anthology of Feminist Supernatural Fiction*, edited by Jessica Amanda Salmonson
Gay Science Fiction/Fantasy—*Somewhere in the Night*, by Jeffrey N. McMahan

1990 (1991)
Lesbian Science Fiction/Fantasy—*Gossamer Axe*, by Gael Baudion
Gay Science Fiction/Fantasy—(tie) *Magic's Price*, by Mercedes Lackey; *Secret Matters*, by Toby Johnson

84. THE LAZAR KOMARCIC AWARD
[THE YUGOSLAVIAN SCIENCE FICTION AND FANTASY ACHIEVEMENT AWARD]
(YUGOSLAVIA)

The Yugoslavian Science Fiction and Fantasy Achievement Awards, better known as the Lazar Komarcic Awards, are the equivalent of the American Hugo Awards, and are chosen by the membership of the Yugoslavian Science Fiction Society to honor the best SF of the previous year published in Yugoslavia.

THE LAZAR KOMARCIC AWARDS

1981 (1982)
Novel—*Prepoznavanje (Recognition)*, by Miha Remec
Short Story—(tie) "Prsten" ("The Ring"), by Goran Hudec; "Hajka" ("Posse"), by Radovan Devlic
Film—*Visitors From the Arkana Galaxy*, by Dusan Vukotic
Lifetime Achievement—Zvonimir Furtinger

1984 (1985)
Long Fiction—"Protir Irvinga" ("Against Irving"), by Boban Knezvic
Short Fiction—"Nemacka 1942" ("Germany 1942"), by Andrija Lavrek
Novel—*Regata Plerus (The Plerus Sailing)*, by Nikola Panic
Translator—Alexander B. Nedelkovich
Artist—Zeljko Panek
Foreign Novel—*Beyond the Blue Event Horizon*, by Frederik Pohl (United States)

1985 (1986)
Long Fiction—*Noc Koja Nece Doci (The Night That Will Not Come)*, by Boban Knezevic
Short Fiction—"Most" ("The Bridge"), by Slobodan Petrovski
Novel—(tie) *1999*, by Borislav Panic; *Mnogo Vike Nizasto*, by Predrag Raos
Translator—Alexander B. Nedelkovich
Foreign Short Story—"Flowers for Algernon," by Daniel Keyes (United States)
Foreign Novel—*Lord of Light*, by Roger Zelazny (United States)

1986 (1987)
Novel—No award
Novella—"Varnica" ("A Spark"), by Radmilo Andelkovic
Short Story—No award
Translator—Zoran Jaksic
Artist—Bob Zivkovic
Foreign Short Story—"Sailing to Byzantium," by Robert Silverberg (United States)
Foreign Novel—*The Forever War*, by Joe Haldeman (United States)

1987 (1988)
Novel—*The Universe Stealers*, by David G. Strorm (Zoran Jaksic)
Artist—Igor Kordej
Short Story—"The Shit Stealer," by Dragan R. Filipovic
Novella—"Sokolar" ("The Falconer"), by Vladimir Lazovic
Translator—Alexander B. Nedelkovich
Foreign Short Story—"Thor Meets Captain America," by David Brin (United States) [award not given due to a glitch in the voting procedure]
Foreign Novel—*Dying Inside*, by Robert Silverberg (United States)

1988 (1989)
Novel—(tie) *Atlantis*, by Borislav Panic; *Golden Book*, by Dragan R. Filipovic
Novella—"Can't Be Done in the Evening," by Zoran Neskovic
Short Story—"Day Fourteenth," by Boban Knezevic
Translator—Zoran Jaksic
Artist—Bob Zivkovic

Foreign Short Story—"Pardoner's Tale," by Robert Silverberg (United States)
Foreign Novel—*Flow My Tears, the Policeman Said*, by Philip K. Dick (United States)

1989/1990 (1991)

Novel—*Null Effort*, by Predrag Raos
Long Story—"I Am Running into the Night," by Dragan R. Filipovic
Short Story—"About the Advancement of Agriculture, Generally," by Slobodan Ivkov
Artist—Dobrilo Nikolic, Ratomir Dimitrijevic, and Seka Kresovic-Buneta, for the cover of *Encyclopedia of Science Fiction*
Foreign Novel—*The Book of Skulls*, by Robert Silverberg (United States)
Foreign Short Story—"Gilgamesh in the Outback," by Robert Silverberg (United States)

> NOTE: Robert Silverberg, while grateful for the honor implicit in this (and previous) "Lazar Komarcic Awards," has protested the unauthorized and unrecompensed pirating of his work for these Yugoslavian editions.—*Locus*

85. THE *LOCUS* AWARD
(UNITED STATES)

The Locus Awards were created by Charles N. Brown, publisher and editor of *Locus, the Newspaper of the Science Fiction Field*, and are voted upon annually by the readers of that publication. No physical award was presented originally, although in 1986 David Brin was given a golden inflatable plastic sunflower. The physical shape of the award has varied considerably from year to year. This award consistently attracts one of the largest voting audiences of any award in the genre.

THE *LOCUS* AWARDS

1970 (1971)

Novel—*Ringworld*, by Larry Niven
Short Fiction—"The Region Between," by Harlan Ellison
Anthology/Collection—*Science Fiction Hall of Fame, Vol. 1*, Robert Silverberg, ed.
Magazine—*The Magazine of Fantasy & Science Fiction*, Edward L. Ferman, ed.
Fanzine—*Locus*, Charles and Dena Brown, eds.
Single Issue of Fanzine—*Locus* #70, Charles and Dena Brown, eds.
Paperback Cover Illustrator—Leo and Diane Dillon
Fan Writer—Harry Warner, Jr.
Fan Artist—(tie) Alicia Austin; William Rotsler
Fan Critic—Ted Pauls

1971 (1972)

Novel—*The Lathe of Heaven*, by Ursula K. Le Guin
Short Fiction—"The Queen of Air and Darkness," by Poul Anderson
Original Anthology/Collection—*Universe 1*, Terry Carr, ed.
Reprint Anthology/Collection—*World's Best Science Fiction: 1971*, Donald A. Wollheim and Terry Carr, eds.
Publisher—Ballantine Books, Betty Ballantine, ed.
Magazine—*The Magazine of Fantasy & Science Fiction*, Edward L. Ferman, ed.
Paperback Artist—Gene Szafran
Fanzine—*Locus*, Charles and Dena Brown, eds.
Fan Writer—Charles N. Brown
Fan Artist—William Rotsler
Convention—Noreascon

1972 (1973)

Novel—*The Gods Themselves*, by Isaac Asimov
Novella—"The Gold at the Starbow's End," by Frederik Pohl
Short Fiction—"Basilisk," by Harlan Ellison
Reprint Anthology/Collection—*The Best Science Fiction of the Year: 1972*, Terry Carr, ed.

Original Anthology/Collection—*Again, Dangerous Visions*, Harlan Ellison, ed.
Magazine—*The Magazine of Fantasy & Science Fiction*, Edward L. Ferman, ed.
Publisher—Ballantine Books, Betty Ballantine and Judy-Lynn del Rey, eds.
Professional Artist—Frank Kelly Freas
Fanzine—*Locus*, Charles and Dena Brown, eds.
Fan Artist—Tim Kirk
Fan Critic—Richard E. Geis

1973 (1974)

Novel—*Rendezvous with Rama*, by Arthur C. Clarke
Novella—"The Death of Doctor Island," by Gene Wolfe
Short Fiction—"The Deathbird," by Harlan Ellison
Original Anthology/Collection—*Astounding*, Harry Harrison, ed.
Reprint Anthology/Collection—*The Best Science of the Year: 1973*, Terry Carr, ed.
Magazine—*The Magazine of Fantasy & Science Fiction*, Edward L. Ferman, ed.
Publisher—Ballantine Books, Betty Ballantine and Judy-Lynn del Rey, eds.
Professional Artist—Frank Kelly Freas
Fanzine—*Locus*, Charles and Dena Brown, eds.
Fan Artist—Tim Kirk
Fan Critic—Richard E. Geis

1974 (1975)

Novel—*The Dispossessed*, by Ursula K. Le Guin
Novella—"Born with the Dead," by Robert Silverberg
Novelette—"Adrift, Just Off the Islets of Langerhans...," by Harlan Ellison
Short Story—"The Day Before the Revolution," by Ursula K. Le Guin
Magazine—*The Magazine of Fantasy & Science Fiction*, Edward L. Ferman, ed.
Publisher—Ballantine Books, Judy-Lynn del Rey, ed.
Original Anthology/Collection—*Universe 4*, Terry Carr, ed.
Reprint Anthology/Collection—*Before the Golden Age*, Isaac Asimov, ed.
Professional Artist—Frank Kelly Freas
All-Time Best Novel—*Dune*, by Frank Herbert
Fanzine—*Outworlds*, Bill Bowers, ed.
Fan Artist—Tim Kirk
Fan Critic—P. Schuyler Miller

1975 (1976)

Novel—*The Forever War*, by Joe Haldeman
Novella—"The Storms of Windhaven," by George R. R. Martin and Lisa Tuttle
Novelette—"The New Atlantis," by Ursula K. Le Guin
Short Story—"Croatoan," by Harlan Ellison
Anthology—*Epoch*, Roger Elwood and Robert Silverberg, eds.
Collection—*The Wind's Twelve Quarters*, by Ursula K. Le Guin
Associational Item—*Alternate Worlds*, by James E. Gunn
Magazine—*The Magazine of Fantasy & Science Fiction*, Edward L. Ferman, ed.
Hardcover Publisher—Science Fiction Book Club
Paperback Publisher—Ballantine Books, Judy-Lynn del Rey, ed.
Professional Artist—Rick Sternbach
Fan Critic—Richard E. Geis
Fanzine—*Locus*, Charles and Dena Brown, eds.

1976 (1977)

Novel—*Where Late the Sweet Birds Sang*, by Kate Wilhelm
Novella—"The Samurai and the Willows," by Michael Bishop
Novelette—"The Bicentennial Man," by Isaac Asimov
Short Story—"Tricentennial," by Joe Haldeman
Collection—*A Song for Lya*, by George R. R. Martin
Reprint Anthology—*The Best Science Fiction of the Year #5*, Terry Carr, ed.
Original Anthology—*Stellar #2*, Judy-Lynn del Rey, ed.
Publisher—Ballantine Books, Judy-Lynn del Rey, ed.

Magazine—*The Magazine of Fantasy & Science Fiction*, Edward L. Ferman, ed.
Professional Artist—Rick Sternbach
Fanzine—*Locus*, Charles and Dena Brown, eds.
Fan Critic—Spider Robinson
Best All-time Author—Robert A. Heinlein
Special Award—John Varley
Special Award—Peter Weston, for *Andromeda*

1977 (1978)

SF Novel—*Gateway*, by Frederik Pohl
Novella—"Stardance," by Spider and Jeanne Robinson
Short Fiction—"Jeffty Is Five," by Harlan Ellison
Fantasy Novel—*The Silmarillion*, by J. R. R. Tolkien
Publisher—Ballantine/Del Rey Books, Judy-Lynn del Rey, ed.
Magazine—*The Magazine of Fantasy & Science Fiction*, Edward L. Ferman, ed.

1978 (1979)

Novel—*Dreamsnake*, by Vonda N. McIntyre
Novella—"The Persistence of Vision," by John Varley
Novelette—"The Barbie Murders," by John Varley
Short Story—"Count the Clock That Tells Time," by Harlan Ellison

1979 (1980)

SF Novel—*Titan*, by John Varley
Fantasy Novel—*Harpist in the Wind* by Patricia McKillip
Novella—"Enemy Mine," by Barry B. Longyear
Novelette—"Sandkings," by George R. R. Martin
Short Story—"The Way of Cross and Dragon," by George R. R. Martin
Anthology—*Universe 9*, Terry Carr, ed.
Collection—*Convergent Series*, by Larry Niven
Art Book—*Barlowe's Guide to the Extraterrestrials*, by Wayne Barlowe and Ian Summers
Magazine—*The Magazine of Fantasy & Science Fiction*, Edward L. Ferman, ed.
Publisher—Ballantine/Del Rey Books, Judy-Lynn and Lester del Rey, eds.
Professional Artist—Michael Whelan
Nonfiction—*The Science Fiction Encyclopedia*, Peter Nicholls and John Clute, eds.

1980 (1981)

SF Novel—*The Snow Queen*, by Joan D. Vinge
Fantasy Novel—*Lord Valentine's Castle*, by Robert Silverberg
First Novel—*Dragon's Egg*, by Dr. Robert L. Forward
Novella—"Nightflyers," by George R. R. Martin
Novelette—"The Brave Little Toaster," by Thomas M. Disch
Short Story—"Grotto of the Dancing Deer," by Clifford D. Simak
Anthology—*The Magazine of Fantasy & Science Fiction: A 30-Year Retrospective*, Edward L. Ferman, ed.
Collection—*The Barbie Murders*, by John Varley
Nonfiction—*In Joy Still Felt*, by Isaac Asimov
Professional Artist—Michael Whelan
Magazine—*The Magazine of Fantasy & Science Fiction*, Edward L. Ferman, ed.
Publisher—Ballantine/Del Rey Books, Judy-Lynn and Lester del Rey, eds.

1981 (1982)

SF Novel—*The Many Colored Land*, by Julian May
Fantasy Novel—*The Claw of the Conciliator*, by Gene Wolfe
First Novel—*Starship and Haiku*, by S. P. Somtow (Somtow Sucharitkul)
Novella—"Blue Champagne," by John Varley
Novelette—"Guardians," by George R. R. Martin
Short Story—"The Pusher," by John Varley
Anthology—*Shadows of Sanctuary*, Robert Asprin, ed.
Collection—*Sandkings*, by George R. R. Martin

Nonfiction—*Danse Macabre*, by Stephen King
Professional Artist—Michael Whelan
Magazine—*The Magazine of Fantasy & Science Fiction*, Edward L. Ferman, ed.
Publisher—Pocket/Timescape Books, David G. Hartwell, ed.

1982 (1983)

SF Novel—*Foundation's Edge*, by Isaac Asimov
Fantasy Novel—*The Sword of the Lictor*, by Gene Wolfe
First Novel—*Courtship Rite*, by Donald Kingsbury
Novella—"Souls," by Joanna Russ
Novelette—"Djinn, No Chaser," by Harlan Ellison
Short Story—"Sur," by Ursula K. Le Guin
Anthology—*The Best Science Fiction of the Year #11*, Terry Carr, ed.
Collection—*The Compass Rose*, by Ursula K. Le Guin
Nonfiction—*The Engines of the Night*, by Barry N. Malzberg
Professional Artist—Michael Whelan
Magazine—*Locus*, Charles N. Brown, ed.
Publisher—Pocket/Timescape Books, David Hartwell, ed.

1983 (1984)

SF Novel—*Startide Rising*, by David Brin
Fantasy Novel—*The Mists of Avalon*, by Marion Zimmer Bradley
First Novel—*Tea with the Black Dragon*, by R. A. MacAvoy
Novella—"Her Habiline Husband," by Michael Bishop
Novelette—"The Monkey Treatment," by George R. R. Martin
Short Story—"Beyond the Dead Reef," by James Tiptree, Jr.
Nonfiction—*Dream Makers, Volume 2*, Charles Platt, ed.
Collection—*Unicorn Variations*, by Roger Zelazny
Anthology—*The Best Science Fiction of the Year #12*, Terry Carr, ed.
Professional Artist—Michael Whelan
Magazine—*Locus*, Charles N. Brown, ed.
Publisher—Ballantine/Del Rey Books, Judy-Lynn and Lester del Rey, eds.

1984 (1985)

SF Novel—*The Integral Trees*, by Larry Niven
Fantasy Novel—*Job: A Comedy of Justice*, by Robert A. Heinlein
First Novel—*The Wild Shore*, by Kim Stanley Robinson
Novella—"Press ENTER ▮," by John Varley
Novelette—"Bloodchild," by Octavia E. Butler
Short Story—"Salvador," by Lucius Shepard
Nonfiction—*Sleepless Nights in the Procrustean Bed: Essays*, by Harlan Ellison, edited by Marty Clark
Collection—*The Ghost Light*, by Fritz Leiber
Anthology—*Light Years and Dark*, Michael Bishop, ed.
Professional Artist—Michael Whelan
Magazine—*Locus*, Charles N. Brown, ed.
Publisher—Ballantine/Del Rey Books, Judy-Lynn and Lester del Rey, eds.

1985 (1986)

SF Novel—*The Postman*, by David Brin
Fantasy Novel—*Trumps of Doom*, by Roger Zelazny
First Novel—*Contact*, by Carl Sagan
Novella—"The Only Neat Thing to Do," by James Tiptree, Jr.
Novelette—"Paladin of the Lost Ark," by Harlan Ellison
Short Story—"With Virgil Oddum at the East Pole," by Harlan Ellison
Nonfiction—*Beachmarks: Galaxy Bookshelf*, by Algis Budrys
Collection—*Skeleton Crew*, by Stephen King
Anthology—*Medea: Harlan's World*, Harlan Ellison, ed.
Professional Artist—Michael Whelan
Magazine—*Locus*, Charles N. Brown, ed.

Reginald's Science Fiction & Fantasy Awards, Third Edition

Publisher—Ballantine/Del Rey Books, Lester del Rey, ed.

1986 (1987)

SF Novel—*Speaker for the Dead*, by Orson Scott Card
Fantasy Novel—*Soldier of the Mist*, by Gene Wolfe
First Novel—*The Hercules Text*, by Jack McDevitt
Novella—"R and R," by Lucius Shepard
Novelette—"Thor Meets Captain America," by David Brin
Short Story—"Robot Dreams," by Isaac Asimov
Nonfiction—*Trillion Year Spree*, by Brian W. Aldiss
Collection—*Blue Champagne*, by John Varley
Anthology—*The Year's Best Science Fiction, Third Annual Collection*, Gardner Dozois, ed.
Professional Artist—Michael Whelan
Magazine—*The Magazine of Fantasy & Science Fiction*, Edward L. Ferman, ed.
Publisher—Ballantine/Del Rey Books, Lester del Rey, ed.

1987 (1988)

SF Novel—*The Uplift War*, by David Brin
Fantasy Novel—*Seventh Son*, by Orson Scott Card
First Novel—*War for the Oaks*, by Emma Bull
Novella—"The Secret Sharer," by Robert Silverberg
Novelette—"Rachel in Love," by Pat Murphy
Short Story—"Angel," by Pat Cadigan
Nonfiction—*Watchmen*, by Alan Moore and Dave Gibbons
Collection—*The Jaguar Hunter*, by Lucius Shepard
Anthology—*The Year's Best Science Fiction, Fourth Annual Collection*, Gardner Dozois, ed.
Professional Artist—Michael Whelan
Magazine—*The Magazine of Fantasy & Science Fiction*, Edward L. Ferman, ed.
Publisher—Tor Books
All-Time Author—Robert A. Heinlein
1980's Author—David Brin

1988 (1989)

SF Novel—*Cyteen*, by C. J. Cherryh
Fantasy Novel—*Red Prophet*, by Orson Scott Card
Horror Novel—*Those Who Hunt the Night*, by Barbara Hambly
First Novel—*Desolation Road*, by Ian McDonald
Novella—"The Scalehunter's Beautiful Daughter," by Lucius Shepard
Novelette—"The Function of Dream Sleep," by Harlan Ellison
Short Story—"Eidolons," by Harlan Ellison
Nonfiction—*First Maitz*, by Don Maitz
Anthology—*Full Spectrum*, Lou Aronica and Shawna McCarthy, eds.
Collection—*Angry Candy*, by Harlan Ellison
Editor—Gardner Dozois
Artist—Michael Whelan
Publisher—Tor/St. Martin's Books
Magazine—*Isaac Asimov's Science Fiction Magazine*, Gardner Dozois, ed.

1989 (1990)

SF Novel—*Hyperion*, by Dan Simmons
Fantasy Novel—*Prentice Alvin*, by Orson Scott Card
Horror Novel—*Carrion Comfort*, by Dan Simmons
First Novel—*Orbital Decay*, by Allen Steele
Novella—"The Father of Stones," by Lucius Shepard
Novelette—"Dogwalker," by Orson Scott Card
Short Story—"Lost Boys," by Orson Scott Card
Nonfiction—*Grumbles From the Grave*, by Robert A. Heinlein, edited by Virginia Heinlein [posthumous]
Anthology—*The Year's Best SF, Sixth Annual Collection*, Gardner Dozois, ed.

Collection—*Patterns*, by Pat Cadigan
Magazine—*Isaac Asimov's Science Fiction Magazine*, Gardner Dozois, ed.
Editor—Gardner Dozois
Artist—Michael Whelan
Publisher—Tor/St. Martin's Books

1990 (1991)

SF Novel—*The Fall of Hyperion*, by Dan Simmons
Fantasy Novel—*Tehanu: The Last Book of Earthsea*, by Ursula K. Le Guin
Horror/Dark Fantasy Novel—*The Witching Hour*, by Anne Rice
First Novel—*In the Country of the Blind*, by Michael F. Flynn
Novella—*A Short, Sharp Shock*, by Kim Stanley Robinson
Novelette—*Entropy's Bed at Midnight*, by Dan Simmons
Short Story—"Bears Discover Fire," by Terry Bisson
Nonfiction—*SFWA Handbook: The Professional Writer's Guide to Writing Professionally*, Kristine Kathryn Rusch and Dean Wesley Smith, eds.
Anthology—*The Year's Best SF, Seventh Annual Collection*, Gardner Dozois, ed.
Collection—*Maps in a Mirror: The Short Fiction of Orson Scott Card*, by Orson Scott Card
Magazine—*Isaac Asimov's Science Fiction Magazine*, Gardner Dozois, ed.
Editor—Gardner Dozois
Artist—Michael Whelan
Publisher—Tor/St. Martin's Press Books

1991 (1992)

SF Novel—*Barrayar*, by Lois McMaster Bujold
Fantasy Novel—*Beauty*, by Sheri S. Tepper
Horror/Dark Fantasy Novel—*Summer of Night*, by Dan Simmons
First Novel—*The Cipher*, by Kathe Koja
Novella—"The Gallery of His Dreams," by Kristine Kathryn Rusch
Novelette—"All Dracula's Children," by Dan Simmons
Short Story—"Buffalo," by John Kessel
Nonfiction—*Science Fiction: The Early Years*, by Everett F. Bleiler
Anthology—*Full Spectrum 3*, Lou Aronica, Amy Stout, Betsy Mitchell, eds.
Collection—*Night of the Cooters: More Neat Stories*, by Howard Waldrop
Magazine—*Isaac Asimov's Science Fiction Magazine*, Gardner Dozois, ed.
Editor—Gardner Dozois
Artist—Michael Whelan
Publisher—Tor/St. Martin's Press Books

86. THE LUDVIK SOUCEK AWARD
[THE CZECHOSLOVAKIAN SCIENCE FICTION AND FANTASY ACHIEVEMENT AWARD]
(CZECHOSLOVAKIA)

The Ludvik Soucek Awards (the Czech equivalent of the Hugo Awards) honor the memory of Czech SF writer Ludvik Soucek (1926-1978), and are presented for the best science fiction novel published in Czechoslovakia in the previous year. Awards are made annually at the Czechoslovakian National Science Fiction Convention (Parcon). The Golem Award is voted upon by readers of *Ikarie*, the only semi-prozine in Czechoslovakia, the *Locus* of that country.

THE LUDVIK SOUCEK AWARDS

1983 (1984)

Novel—*Zelezo Pcichazi z Hvezd* (*Iron Comes From the Stars*), by Vojtech Kantor
Anthology—*Experiment Clovek* (*Experiment Man*), Ivo Zelezny, ed.

1985 (1986)
Fanzine—*Ikarie*, Jaroslav Olsa, Jr., ed.
Short Story—Ondrej Neff
Collection—*Vejce Naruby*
Life Achievement—Josef Nesvadba
Anthology—Mlade Leta Publishers, ed.
Golem Award—*Vejce Naruby*, by Ondrej Neff
Special Award—Ondrej Neff, for popularizing SF with *Tri Eseje o Ceske Sci-fi* (*Three Essays on Czech SF*)

87. THE MANNESMANN-TALLY AWARD
(FRANCE)

The Mannesmann-Tally Award is sponsored by Mannesmann-Tally, a French computer printer manufacturer, to honor the best book of the year about computers. The prize consists of a monetary award of 100,000 French francs (about $16,000 US).

THE MANNESMANN-TALLY AWARDS

1985 (1986)—*Oracle*, by Kevin O'Donnell (United States)
1986 (1987)—*Netwar*, by Thierry Barton (FRA)
Awards discontinued?

88. THE MAS ALLA AWARD
[THE ARGENTINIAN SCIENCE FICTION AND FANTASY ACHIEVEMENT AWARD]
(ARGENTINA)

The Más Alla Awards are chosen annually by members of the Argentine Science Fiction and Fantasy Circle (the Argentine professional writers' organization), as a rough equivalent of the American Hugo and Nebula Awards combined, and are presented at the annual national science fiction convention in Argentina.

THE MAS ALLA AWARDS

1983 (1984)
Novel—*Kalpa Imperial I: The House of Power*, by Angelica Gorodischer
Short Fiction—Mario Levrero
Fanzine—*Sinergia*

1984 (1985)
Novel—*Un Paseo por Camarjali* (*A Walk by Camarjali*), by Eduardo Abel
Short Fiction—Mario Levrero
Fanzine—*Sinergia*

1985 (1986)
Novel—*Un Paseo con Gerónimo* (*A Walk with Gerónimo*), by Daniel Barberi
Short Fiction—Eduardo Carletti
Fanzine—*Minotauro*
Prozine—*Sinergia*

89. THE MILFORD AWARD
(UNITED STATES)

The Milford Award is presented annually at the J. Lloyd Eaton Conference on Science Fiction and Fantasy Literature for lifetime contributions to the publishing and editing of science fiction, fantasy, and horror literature. Originally established (and presented) in 1980 by Robert Reginald, publisher of *Science Fiction & Fantasy Book Review*, it was transferred with the demise of that publication to the Eaton Conference, where it has remained ever since. The award is chosen by a jury chaired by Conference co-founder Reginald, with the participation of Daryl F. Mallett. The first award consisted of a hand-lettered scroll mounted under glass; subsequent prizes have taken the form of a bronze engraved plaque mounted on a wood base.

THE MILFORD AWARDS

1980—Donald A. Wollheim
1981—Robert Silverberg
1982—Judy-Lynn del Rey; Lester del Rey
1983—Terry Carr
1984—Edward L. Ferman
1985—Thaddeus E. Dikty
1986—Harlan Ellison
1987—H. L. Gold
1988—Lloyd Arthur Eshbach
1989—Martin Harry Greenberg
1990—David G. Hartwell
1991—Judith Merril
1992—Betty Ballantine; Ian Ballantine

90. THE MINNESOTA FANTASY AWARD
(UNITED STATES)

The Minnesota Fantasy Award, presented annually for lifetime achievement by a Minnesota SF writer, is sponsored by Jwindz Publishing and *The Minnesota Fantasy Review*, and chosen by a jury.

THE MINNESOTA FANTASY AWARDS

1989—Gordon R. Dickson
1990—unknown
1991—Charles V. DeVet

91. THE MYTHOPOEIC SOCIETY FANTASY AWARD
(INTERNATIONAL)

The MSF Awards are presented annually by the Mythopoeic Society to honor the best English-language fantasy novel and the best book of scholarship on mythopoeic literature published during the preceding year. The physical award consists of a trophy depicting a white lion lying on a rectangular pedestal. Beginning in 1992 the Fantasy Fiction category was split into two new categories, Adult Literature and Children's Literature, and the nonfiction award into Inklings Studies and Myth and Fantasy Studies.

Reginald's Science Fiction & Fantasy Awards, Third Edition

THE MYTHOPOEIC SOCIETY FANTASY AWARDS

1982 (1983)
Fantasy—*The Firelings*, by Carol Kendall
Scholarship—*Companion to Narnia*, by Paul F. Ford

1983 (1984)
Fantasy—*When Voiha Wakes*, by Joy Chant
Scholarship—*The Road to Middle Earth*, by Thomas A. Shippey

1984 (1985)
unknown

1985 (1986)
Fantasy—*Bridge of Birds*, by Barry Hughert
Scholarship—*Charles Williams: Poet of Theology*, by Glen Cavaliero

1986 (1987)
unknown

1987 (1988)
Fantasy—*Seventh Son*, by Orson Scott Card
Scholarship—*C. S. Lewis*, by Joe R. Christopher

1988 (1989)
Fantasy—*Unicorn Mountain*, by Michael Bishop

1989 (1990)
Fantasy—*The Stress of Her Regard*, by Tim Powers
Scholarship—*The Annotated Hobbit*, by J. R. R. Tolkien; Douglas A. Anderson, ed.

1990 (1991)
Fantasy—*Thomas the Rhymer*, by Ellen Kushner
Scholarship—*Jack: C. S. Lewis and His Times*, by George Sayer

1991 (1992)
Adult Literature—*A Woman of the Iron People*, by Eleanor Arnason
Children's Literature—*Haroun and the Sea of Stories*, by Salman Rushdie
Scholarship for Inklings Studies—*Word and Story in C. S. Lewis*, by Peter J. Schakel & Charles A. Huttar, eds.
Scholarship for Myth & Fantasy Studies—*The Victorian Fantasists: Essays on Culture, Society, and Belief in the Mythopoeic Fiction of the Victorian Age*, Kath Filmer, ed.

92. THE N3F AMATEUR SHORT STORY CONTEST
(UNITED STATES)

The N3F Amateur Short Story Contest is sponsored by the SF club N3F. Prizes of $25, $15, and $10 respectively are given to the three best short stories of the previous year.

THE N3F AMATEUR SHORT STORY CONTEST WINNERS

1990 (1991)
1st—"The Flowers Still Smell the Same," by Warren Rochelle
2nd—"Autie Insurance," by Scott Southworth
3rd—"Coffin Nails," by Brian Hall

1991 (1992)
1st—"Port City Excursion," by Andrew W. Mackie
2nd—"Pelmatozoa," by Jeffrey Kasten
3rd—"The Surgeon's Hands," by Helen E. Davis
Hon. Mention—"The Moon Song Goddess and Her Ultimate Lonely Hearts Club Band," by B. J. Thrower

93. THE NEBULA AWARD
(UNITED STATES)

The Nebula Awards are presented by the Science Fiction Writers of America (SFWA) at its annual banquet. Stories are nominated by active members of SFWA throughout the year. Members may not nominate the same work more than once, writers may not nominate their own works, and editors may not nominate works they have edited. At the end of the year, a ballot with the nominated titles (the top five vote-getters in each category) is distributed to active members; the awards jury may add a sixth item to each category if they choose. The returned ballots are tabulated according to the Australian vote system by an outside agency.

Judith Blish (J. A. Lawrence) created the physical award from a drawing done by Kate Wilhelm. It consists of a rectangular block of transparent lucite with a quartz crystal or silver glitter spiral nebula enclosed within. No two trophies are identical. A special Grand Master Award for lifetime achievement may also be given by the officers of the SFWA in no more than six years out of every decade. Lisa Tuttle is the only writer thus far to refuse a Nebula (1982).

THE NEBULA AWARDS

1965 (1966)
Novel—*Dune*, by Frank Herbert
Novella—(tie) "He Who Shapes," by Roger Zelazny; "The Saliva Tree," by Brian W. Aldiss
Novelette—"The Doors of His Face, the Lamps of His Mouth," by Roger Zelazny
Short Story—"'Repent, Harlequin,' said the Ticktockman," by Harlan Ellison

1966 (1967)
Novel—(tie) *Babel-17*, by Samuel R. Delany; *Flowers for Algernon*, by Daniel Keyes
Novella—"The Last Castle," by Jack Vance
Novelette—"Call Him Lord," by Gordon R. Dickson
Short Story—"The Secret Place," by Richard McKenna [posthumous]

1967 (1968)
Novel—*The Einstein Intersection*, by Samuel R. Delany
Novella—"Behold the Man," by Michael Moorcock
Novelette—"Gonna Roll Them Bones," by Fritz Leiber
Short Story—"Aye, and Gomorrah," by Samuel R. Delany

1968 (1969)
Novel—*Rite of Passage*, by Alexei Panshin
Novella—"Dragon Rider," by Anne McCaffrey
Novelette—"Mother to the World," by Richard Wilson
Short Story—"The Planners," by Kate Wilhelm

1969 (1970)
Novel—*The Left Hand of Darkness*, by Ursula K. Le Guin
Novella—"A Boy and His Dog," by Harlan Ellison
Novelette—"Time Considered As a Helix of Semi-Precious Stones," by Samuel R. Delany
Short Story—"Passengers," by Robert Silverberg

1970 (1971)
Novel—*Ringworld*, by Larry Niven

Reginald's Science Fiction & Fantasy Awards, Third Edition

Novella—"Ill Met in Lankhmar," by Fritz Leiber
Novelette—"Slow Sculpture," by Theodore Sturgeon
Short Story—No award

1971 (1972)
Novel—*A Time of Change*, by Robert Silverberg
Novella—"The Missing Man," by Katherine MacLean
Novelette—"The Queen of Air and Darkness," by Poul Anderson
Short Story—"Good News from the Vatican," by Robert Silverberg

1972 (1973)
Novel—*The Gods Themselves*, by Isaac Asimov
Novella—"A Meeting with Medusa," by Arthur C. Clarke
Novelette—"Goat Song," by Poul Anderson
Short Story—"When It Changed," by Joanna Russ

1973 (1974)
Novel—*Rendezvous with Rama*, by Arthur C. Clarke
Novella—"The Death of Dr. Island," by Gene Wolfe
Novelette—"Of Mist, and Grass, and Sand," by Vonda N. McIntyre
Short Story—"Love Is the Plan, the Plan Is Death," by James Tiptree, Jr.
Dramatic Presentation—*Soylent Green*, screenplay by Stanley Greenberg

1974 (1975)
Novel—*The Dispossessed*, by Ursula K. Le Guin
Novella—"Born with the Dead," by Robert Silverberg
Novelette—"The Stars Are Gods," by Gregory Benford
Short Story—"The Day Before the Revolution," by Ursula K. Le Guin
Dramatic Presentation—*Sleeper*, screenplay by Woody Allen
Grand Master—Robert A. Heinlein

1975 (1976)
Novel—*The Forever War*, by Joe Haldeman
Novella—"Home Is the Hangman," by Roger Zelazny
Novelette—"San Diego Lightfoot Sue," by Tom Reamy
Short Story—"Catch That Zeppelin," by Fritz Leiber
Dramatic Presentation—*Young Frankenstein*, by Mel Brooks and Gene Wilder
Grand Master—Jack Williamson
Special Plaque—George Pal, for his work in films

1976 (1977)
Novel—*Man Plus*, by Frederik Pohl
Novella—"Houston, Houston, Do You Read?," by James Tiptree, Jr.
Novelette—"The Bicentennial Man," by Isaac Asimov
Short Story—"A Crowd of Shadows," by Charles L. Grant
Dramatic Presentation—No award
Grand Master—Clifford D. Simak

1977 (1978)
Novel—*Gateway*, by Frederik Pohl
Novella—"Stardance," by Spider and Jeanne Robinson
Novelette—"The Screwfly Solution," by Racoona Sheldon (James Tiptree, Jr.)
Short Story—"Jeffty Is Five," by Harlan Ellison
Special Plaque—George Lucas, for *Star Wars*

1978 (1979)
Novel—*Dreamsnake*, by Vonda N. McIntyre
Novella—"The Persistence of Vision," by John Varley
Novelette—"A Glow of Candles, a Unicorn's Eye," by Charles L. Grant
Short Story—"Stone," by Edward Bryant

Grand Master—L. Sprague de Camp

1979 (1980)
Novel—*The Fountains of Paradise*, by Arthur C. Clarke
Novella—"Enemy Mine," by Barry B. Longyear
Novelette—"Sandkings," by George R. R. Martin
Short Story—"giANTS," by Edward Bryant

1980 (1981)
Novel—*Timescape*, by Gregory Benford
Novella—"Unicorn Tapestry," by Suzy McKee Charnas
Novelette—"The Ugly Chickens," by Howard Waldrop
Short Story—"Grotto of the Dancing Deer," by Clifford D. Simak
Grand Master—Fritz Leiber

1981 (1982)
Novel—*The Claw of the Conciliator*, by Gene Wolfe
Novella—"The Saturn Game," by Poul Anderson
Novelette—"The Quickening," by Michael Bishop
Short Story—"The Bone Flute," by Lisa Tuttle [refused]

1982 (1983)
Novel—*No Enemy But Time*, by Michael Bishop
Novella—"Another Orphan," by John Kessel
Novelette—"Fire Watch," by Connie Willis
Short Story—"A Letter From the Clearys," by Connie Willis

1983 (1984)
Novel—*Startide Rising*, by David Brin
Novella—"Hardfought," by Greg Bear
Novelette—"Blood Music," by Greg Bear
Short Story—"The Peacemaker," by Gardner Dozois
Grand Master—Andre Norton

1984 (1985)
Novel—*Neuromancer*, by William Gibson
Novella—"Press Enter ■," by John Varley
Novelette—"Bloodchild," by Octavia E. Butler
Short Story—"Morning Child," by Gardner Dozois
Special Award—Ian and Betty Ballantine, for contributions to science fiction publishing

1985 (1986)
Novel—*Ender's Game*, by Orson Scott Card
Novella—"Sailing to Byzantium," by Robert Silverberg
Novelette—"Portraits of His Children," by George R. R. Martin
Short Story—"Out of All Them Bright Stars," by Nancy Kress
Grand Master—Arthur C. Clarke

1986 (1987)
Novel—*Speaker for the Dead*, by Orson Scott Card
Novella—"R and R," by Lucius Shepard
Novelette—"The Girl Who Fell into the Sky," by Kate Wilhelm
Short Story—"Tangents," by Greg Bear
Grand Master—Isaac Asimov

1987 (1988)
Novel—*The Falling Woman*, by Pat Murphy
Novella—"The Blind Geometer," by Kim Stanley Robinson
Novelette—"Rachel In Love," by Pat Murphy
Short Story—"Forever Yours, Anna," by Kate Wilhelm

Grand Master—Alfred Bester [posthumous]

1988 (1989)
Novel—*Falling Free*, by Lois McMaster Bujold
Novella—"The Last of the Winnebagos," by Connie Willis
Novelette—"Schrödinger's Kitten," by George Alec Effinger
Short Story—"Bible Stories for Adults, #17: The Deluge," by James Morrow
Grand Master—Ray Bradbury

1989 (1990)
Novel—*The Healer's War*, by Elizabeth Ann Scarborough
Novella—"The Mountains of Mourning," by Lois McMaster Bujold
Novelette—"At the Rialto," by Connie Willis
Short Story—"Ripples in the Dirac Sea," by Geoffrey A. Landis

1990 (1991)
Novel—*Tehanu: The Last Book of Earthsea*, by Ursula K. Le Guin
Novella—"The Hemingway Hoax," by Joe Haldeman
Novelette—"Tower of Babylon," by Ted Chiang
Short Story—"Bears Discover Fire," by Terry Bisson
Grand Master—Lester del Rey

1991 (1992)
Novel—*Stations of the Tide*, by Michael Swanwick
Novella—"Beggars in Spain," by Nancy Kress
Novelette—"Guide Dog," by Mike Conner
Short Story—"Ma Qui," by Alan Brennert

---

94. NIHON SCIENCE FICTION TAISHO
[THE JAPANESE SCIENCE FICTION AWARD]
(JAPAN)

The Nihon Science Fiction Taisho, the Japanese equivalent of the Nebula Award, is presented by the Japan Science Fiction Writers Club for the best work of science fiction by a Japanese writer during the preceding year. Nominations are made by members of the club, with final decisions by a panel of judges. The prize was designed by science fiction illustrator, Naoyuki Kato, and consists of a thirteen-inch golden rocket mounted on a wooden base, plus a monetary award of one million Japanese yen. The Taisho is sponsored by Tokuma Shoten, publishers of *SF Adventure*.

THE JAPANESE SCIENCE FICTION AWARDS

1980 (1981)—*Taiyofu Koten* [*Solar Wind*], by Hori Akira
1983 (1984)—*Genshi Kari* [*Pursuit of the Dream Poem*], by Chiaki Kawamata
1984 (1985)—*Minstrel of the Laughing Cosmos*, by Musashi Kanbei
1985 (1986)—*The Capital Vanishes!*, by Sakyo Komatsu
1986 (1987)—*Teito Monogatari* (*Tales of the Imperial City Dekalogy*), by Hiroshi Aramata
1987 (1988)—(tie) *The Resistance of Ichiro Misaki*, by Ryo Hanmura; *Shunro Oshikawa*, by Junya Yokota and Shingo Aizu
1988 (1989)—*The Lion that Ate the Crescent Moon*, by Baku Yumemakura
1989 (1990)—*Ad Bird*, by Makoto Shiina

95. THE NOVA AWARD
(BRAZIL)

The Nova Award is judged by and given by the Brazilian fanzine, *Annuario Brasiliero de Ficçao Científica* (*Brazilian Science Fiction Yearbook*).

THE NOVA AWARDS

1988 (1989)

Novel—*O Planeta do Rio (Riverworld)*, by Philip José Farmer (United States)
Short Story—"Pela Voloruzacao de Vida," by Ivan Carlos Regina
Fanzine—*Somnium*, R. C. Nacimento, ed.
Special Award—L. Ron Hubbard (United States), for special achievement in SF

1989 (1990)

Fan Illustrator—Roberto Schima

1990 (1991)

Novel—*A Espinha Dorsal da Memória (The Backbone of Memory)*, by Braulio Tavares
Short Story—"Mestre de Armas" ("Weapons Master"), by Braulio Tavares
Foreign Novel—*O Jogo Do Exterminador (Ender's Game)*, by Orson Scott Card (United States)
Artist—R. S. Causo, for interior artwork in *IAM*
Reviewer—Orson Scott Card (United States)
Fanzine—*Megalon*, Marcello S. Branco and Renato Rosatti, eds.
Fan Illustrator—Roberto Schima
Fan Short Story—"Projeto Mulah de Tróia," by Osame Kinouche Filho

96. THE PHILIP K. DICK MEMORIAL AWARD
(UNITED STATES)

The Philip K. Dick Memorial Award was created by Thomas M. Disch, David Hartwell, and Charles N. Brown shortly after Dick's death, to honor the Best American Original SF Paperback Book of the year. The prize is awarded annually by the Philadelphia SF Society at Norwescon, and consists of a cash prize of $1,000 for first prize and $500 for second. Both prizes come with a certificate, a gold logo for first, silver for second. A five-person jury comprises each year's panel; each juror names his/her successor for the following year. There is always at least one academic and one editor on the panel, in addition to working SF and fantasy authors. The award is administered by four directors: David Hartwell, Paul O. Williams, Algis Budrys, and Russell Galen. Prize monies are obtained by soliciting contributions from paperback publishers.

THE PHILIP K. DICK MEMORIAL AWARDS

1982 (1983)

1st—*Software*, by Rudy Rucker
2nd—*The Prometheus Man*, by Ray F. Nelson

1983 (1984)

1st—*The Anubis Gates*, by Tim Powers
2nd—*Tea with the Black Dragon*, by R. A. MacAvoy

1984 (1985)

1st—*Neuromancer*, by William Gibson
2nd—*The Wild Shores*, by Kim Stanley Robinson

1985 (1986)

1st—*Dinner at Deviant's Palace*, by Tim Powers

2nd—*Saraband of Lost Time*, by Richard Grant

1986 (1987)
1st—*Homunculus*, by James P. Blaylock
2nd—*The Hercules Text*, by Jack McDevitt

1987 (1988)
1st—*Strange Toys*, by Patricia Geary
2nd—*Memories*, by Mike McQuay

1988 (1989)
1st—*Wetware*, by Rudy Rucker
2nd—*400 Billion Stars*, by Paul J. McCauley

1989 (1990)
1st—*Subterranean Gallery*, by Richard Paul Russo
2nd—*On My Way to Paradise*, by Dave Wolverton

1990 (1991)
1st—*Points of Departure*, by Pat Murphy
2nd—*The Schizogenic Man*, by Raymond Harris

1991 (1992)
1st—*King of Morning, Queen of Day*, by Ian McDonald
2nd—*Bone Dance*, by Emma Bull

97. THE PHOENIX AWARD/THE REBEL AWARD
(UNITED STATES)

The Phoenix Award honors outstanding contributions to science fiction by a professional writer, editor, publisher, artist, cartoonist, or collector living in the Southern United States. The award is presented annually at the Deep South Science Fiction Convention. An associated prize, The Rebel Award, is given for outstanding science fiction fan activity in the Southern United States. Only a partial list of award dates is known.

THE PHOENIX AWARDS

1977 (1978)—Karl Edward Wagner
1982 (1983)—Doug Chaffee; Joe Haldeman
1983 (1984)—David Drake
1984 (1985)—Sharon Webb
1986 (1987)—Orson Scott Card; Hugh B. Cave

THE REBEL AWARDS

1983—Lin Hickman; John Henry
1987—Penny Frierson; Lee Hoffman

98. THE PILGRIM AWARD/THE PIONEER AWARD
(INTERNATIONAL)

The Pilgrim Award was created in 1970 by the Science Fiction Research Association (SFRA) to honor lifetime contributions to science fiction and fantasy scholarship. The award was named for J. O. Bailey's pioneering text, *Pilgrims Through Space and Time*. A five-member committee appointed by the President of SFRA selects both nominees and the winner. The physical award originally consisted of a bronze trophy sculpted by Elden Tefft, one copy of which was housed at the headquarters of SFRA in Lawrence, Kansas; the recipient actually received just a certificate through 1989. Beginning in 1990, a bronze plaque with black inset design was created by Mead, and was also presented retroactively to past winners. Traditionally, the winner gives an acceptance speech at the annual SFRA conference in July. The Pioneer Award was created in 1990 to honor the best single critical work of the year (of any length), and is presented simultaneously with the Pilgrim Award at the annual SFRA conference.

THE PILGRIM AWARDS

1970—J. O. Bailey
1971—Marjorie Hope Nicholson
1972—Julius Kagarlitski (Russia)
1973—Jack Williamson
1974—I. F. Clarke (United Kingdom)
1975—Damon Knight
1976—James E. Gunn
1977—Thomas D. Clareson
1978—Brian W. Aldiss (United Kingdom)
1979—Darko Suvin (Canada)
1980—Peter Nicholls (Canada)
1981—Sam Moskowitz
1982—Neil Barron
1983—H. Bruce Franklin
1984—Everett F. Bleiler
1985—Samuel R. Delany
1986—George E. Slusser
1987—Gary K. Wolfe
1988—Joanna Russ
1989—Ursula K. Le Guin
1990—Marshall B. Tymn
1991—Pierre Versins (France/Switzerland)
1992—Mark R. Hillegas

THE PIONEER AWARDS

1990—Veronica Hollinger, for "The Vampire and the Alien: Variations on the Outsider"
1991—H. Bruce Franklin, for "The Vietnam War as American Science Fiction and Fantasy"
1992—Istvan Csiscery-Ronay Jr., for "The SF of Theory: Baudrillard and Haraway"

99. THE POLISH SCIENCE FICTION AND FANTASY ACHIEVEMENT AWARD
(POLAND)

The Polish Science Fiction and Fantasy Achievement Awards are given annually by the Silesian Science Fiction Club (Slaski Klub Fantastyki—or Slafka), to honor achievements by Polish SF authors and editors. The awards are chosen by a jury consisting of the leaders of Slafka, and presented at the annual Silicon convention held around Easter. The physical award is a statue in the form of a female figure in robes. The Polish Fandom Award, originally called the "SFinks" Award, and later renamed the Janusz A. Zajdel Award in memory of its first recipient, consists of a diploma, and is voted upon by attending members of the Polish National Science Fiction Convention.

POLISH SCIENCE FICTION AND FANTASY ACHIEVEMENT AWARDS

1983 (1984)

Author—Juliusz Machulski
Publisher—Jacek Rodek

Fan—No award

1984 (1985)

Author—Janusz A. Zajdel
Publisher—Jerzy Luczak
Fan—Rafal Surmacz
Polish Fandom Award—Janusz A. Zajdel

1985 (1986)

Author—Marek Baraniecki
Publisher—Wiktor Bukato
Fan—Robert Szmidt
Polish Fandom/Zajdel Award—Marek Baraniecki
Novel—*Arsenal*, by Marek Oramus
Collection—*Glowa Kasandry (The Head of Cassandra)*, by Marek Baraniecki
Short Story—Grzegorz Krukarczyk, for his short stories
Special Award—Maciej Makowski, for a series of articles in *Fantastyka*
Special Award—Andrzej Wojcik, for *Spotkanie w Przestworzach (The Encounter in Space 3)*
Golden Meteor Award—(tie) Z. Lekiewicz, for *The Philosophy of Science Fiction*; B. Gogolewslea and J. Skowronski, for *Nerses VIII Is Attacking* and *A Billion Years for an Hour*

1987 (1988)

Novel—*Imaginary Wars*, by Andrzej Ziemianski
Foreign Novel—*Foundation*, by Isaac Asimov
Publication—*Alfa*
Author—Stanislaw Lem
Publisher—Maroslaw Kowalski
Fan—Krzysztof Papierkowski

100. THE PONG AWARD
(UNITED STATES)

The Pong Awards were only given once, to honor various fan activities. They were chosen by readers of *Pong*, a fanzine edited by Ted White and Dan Steffan.

THE PONG AWARDS

1982 (1983)

Fan Writer—D. West
Fan Artist—Dan Steffan
Fan Editor—Malcolm Edwards
New Fan—Steve Bieler
Single Publication—*Warhoon* #30, Richard Bergeron, ed.
Fugghead of the Year—Seth Breidbart
#1 Fan Face—Dan Steffan

Awards discontinued.

101. PREMIOS COMETA D'ARGENTO
(ITALY)

Nothing is known about the background of these Italian awards.

PREMIOS COMETA D'ARGENTO

1973 (1974)
Fiction—*Dune*, by Frank Herbert (United States)
Film—*1984*, screenplay by William Templeton and Ralph Bettinson (United Kingdom)
Chronicles of Tomorrow—*Soylent Green*, screenplay by Stanley Greenberg (United Kingdom)
Special Award—Rusconi Editore, publishers of *Il Signore degli Anelli* (*The Lord of the Rings*), by J. R. R. Tolkien) (Italy)

1974 (1975)
Novel—*A Time of Changes*, by Robert Silverberg (United States)
Film—*Zardoz*, screenplay by John Boorman (United States)
SF Artist—Karel Thole (Italy)
Fantasy Artist—Karel Thole (Italy)

1975 (1976)
Novel—*The Sheep Look Up*, by John Brunner (United Kingdom)
Film—*Cuore di Cane* (Italy)
Critical Work—*La Storia della Fantascienza*, by Jacques Sadoul (France)

1976 (1977)
Novel—*The Dispossessed*, by Ursula K. Le Guin (United States)

1977 (1978)
Novel—*Stand on Zanzibar*, by John Brunner (United Kingdom)
Editor—Inisero Cremaschi (Italy)

Awards discontinued.

---

102. PREMIOS GILGAMÉS DE NARRATIVA FANTASTICA
(SPAIN)

The Premios Gilgamés de Narrativa Fantástica, the Spanish equivalent of the Locus Award, was created in 1984 by Alejo Cuervo, a well-known Spanish fan and professional, and named by him for bookshop and newszine, *Gilgamés*. The awards, which honor the best science fiction, fantasy, and horror works published during the preceding year, consist of an inscribed diploma. Stories, novels, and individuals are nominated annually by Cuervo and a group of panelists, which have included such professionals as Miguel Barcelo. The finalists are then voted upon by customers of the Gilgamés Bookstore, readers of *Gilgamés*, and the panelists.

PREMIOS GILGAMES DE NARRATIVA FANTASTICA

1983 (1984)
SF Novel—(tie) *Los Desposeidos* (*The Dispossessed*), by Ursula K. Le Guin (United States); *Rascacielos* (*High Rise*), by J. G. Ballard (United Kingdom)
Fantasy Novel—*Un Mago de Terramar* (*A Wizard of Earthsea*), by Ursula K. Le Guin (United States)
Horror Novel—*Sueño del Fevre* (*Fever Dreams*), by George R. R. Martin (United States)
SF Collection—*Visiones Peligrosas* (*Dangerous Visions*), by Harlan Ellison (United States)
Fantasy Collection—No award
Horror Collection—No award
SF Short Story—No Award
Fantasy Short Story—"El Díos Gris Pasa," by Robert E. Howard (United States)
Horror Short Story—No award
Specialized Line—*Minotauro*
Magazine—No award
Fanzine—(tie) *Tránsito*; *Maser*

Special Award—Jadwiga Mauricio, for translating Stanislaw Lem
Special Award—*Minotauro*, for innovative character
Special Award—Ediciones Anaya (Italy) publisher, for reprinting *Ella (She)* by H. Rider Haggard (United States)

1984 (1985)

SF Novel—(tie) *La Transmigración de Timothy Archer (The Transmigration of Timothy Archer)*, by Philip K. Dick (United States); *Cronopaisaje (Timescape)*, by Gregory Benford (United States)
Fantasy Novel—(tie) *Jurgen*, by James Branch Cabell (United States); *El Silmarillión (The Silmarillion)*, by J. R. R. Tolkien (United Kingdom)
Horror Novel—No award
SF Collection—*La Persistencia de la Visión (The Persistence of Vision)*, by John Varley (United States)
Fantasy Collection—No award
Horror Collection—No award
SF Short Story—"Escape," by J. G. Ballard (United Kingdom)
Fantasy Short Story—No award
Horror Short Story—No award
Specialized Line—No award
Magazine—No award
Fanzine—No award
Special Award—Juan Perucho, for *Los Laberintos Bizantinos*
Special Award—Javier Martín Lalanda, for *La Canción de las Espadas*
Special Award—Ediciones Sireula (publisher), for the line Selección de Lecturas Medievales

1985 (1986)

SF Novel—(tie) *Orbita Inestable (The Jagged Orbit)*, by John Brunner (United Kingdom); *El Jinete en la Onda de Shock (The Shockwave Rider)*, by John Brunner (United Kingdom)
Fantasy Novel—*Volkhavaar*, by Tanith Lee (United Kingdom)
Horror Novel—No award
SF Collection—*Las Doce Moradas del Viento (The Wind's Twelve Quarters)*, by Ursula K. Le Guin (United States)
Fantasy Collection—*Espadas y Demonios (Swords and Deviltry)*, by Fritz Leiber (United States)
Horror Collection—No award
SF Short Story—"Quiramir," by Eduardo Abel Gimenez
Fantasy Short Story—(3-way tie) "Acerca de las Ciudades que Creced Descontro-Ladeamente," by Angelica Gorodischer (France); "Aciago Encuentro en Lankhmar" ("Ill Met in Lankhmar"), by Fritz Leiber (United States); "Tal Cómo Está," by Robert Silverberg (United States)
Horror Short Story—"Largo, Largo Camino que Serpentea," by Russell Kirk (United States)
Specialized Line—Alejo Cuervo, fantasy editor
Magazine—No award
Fanzine—No award
Special Award—Salman Rushdie (United Kingdom), for *Los Hijos de la Medianoche* and *Verquenza*
Special Award—Ediciones Ultramar (publisher), for *Latinoamericana Fantástica* by Augusto Uribe
Special Award—Ediciones Orbis (publisher), for the series, Biblioteca de Ciencia Ficción

1986 (1987)

SF Novel—No award
Fantasy Novel—(tie) *Elric of Melnibone*, by Michael Moorcock (United Kingdom); *El Señor de la Noche (Master of Night)*, by Tanith Lee (United Kingdom)
Horror Novel—No award
SF Collection—No award
Fantasy Collection—*Swords Against Death*, by Fritz Leiber (United States)

Horror Collection—(tie) *Canciones que Cantan los Muertos* (*Songs the Dead Men Sing*), by George R. R. Martin (United States); *Libros Sangrientos 1* (*Books of Blood 1*), by Clive Barker (United States)
SF Short Story—No award
Fantasy Short Story—(tie) "Casa de Ladrones" ("House of Thieves"), by Fritz Leiber (United States); "El Bazar de lo Extraño" ("Bazaar of the Bizarre"), by Fritz Leiber (United States)
Horror Short Story—(3-way tie) "En las Colinas en las Ciudades" ("Into the Hills, the Cities"), by Clive Barker (UK/USA); "The Midnight Meat Train," by Clive Barker (UK/USA); "Entre los Muertos" ("Down Among the Dead Men"), by Gardner Dozois and Jack Dann (United States)
Specialized Line—Alejo Cuervo
Magazine—No award
Fanzine—*Tránsito*
Special Award—*Cuasar* (fanzine), for quality
Special Award—Ediciones Glauco (publisher), for the line l'Arca
Special Award—Albert Sole (Italy), for translating *Night's Master* by Tanith Lee (United Kingdom)

1987 (1988)

SF Novel—*Muerto por Dentro* (*Dying Inside*), by Robert Silverberg (United States)
Fantasy Novel—(tie) *La Saga de Cugel* (*Cugel's Saga*), by Jack Vance (United States); *La Costa mas Lejana* (*The Farthest Shore*), by Ursula K. Le Guin (United States)
Horror Novel—No award
SF Collection—No award
Fantasy Collection—*Espadas entre la Niebla* (*Sword in the Mist*), by Fritz Leiber (United States)
Horror Collection—(tie) *La Tía de Seaton*, by Walter de la Mare (United States); *Libros Sangrientos 3* (*Books of Blood 3*), by Clive Barker (UK/USA)
SF Short Story—No award
Fantasy Short Story—"Tiempos Dificiles en Lankhmar," by Fritz Leiber (United States)
Horror Short Story—"La Condición Inhumana" ("The Inhuman Condition"), by Clive Barker (UK/USA)
Specialized Line—(tie) Alejo Cuervo for fantasy editing; Alejo Cuervo for SF editing
Magazine—No award
Fanzine—(tie) *Cuasar*; *Tránsito*
Special Award—Francisco Porrua, for lifetime achievement in science fiction
Special Award—Ediciones Orbis (Italy) publisher, for translating *Science in Science Fiction* by Peter Nicholls (United Kingdom)
Special Award—Ediciones Pleniluni (publisher), for the line Pleniluni Ciencia Ficción
Special Award—*El Péndulo* (fanzine) for quality

1988 (1989)

SF Novel—(3-way tie) *Now Wait for Last Year*, by Philip K. Dick (United States); *Tuf Voyaging*, by George R. R. Martin (United States); *The Demon Princes, Vol. 1*, by Jack Vance (United States)
Fantasy Novel—(tie) *The Anubis Gates*, by Tim Powers (United States); *Mr. Weston's Good Wine*, by T. F. Powys (United Kingdom)
Horror Novel—(tie) *Hawksmoor*, by Peter Ackroyd (United States); *The Ice Maiden*, by Marc Behn (United States)
SF Collection/Anthology—*Blue Champagne*, by John Varley (United States)
Fantasy Collection/Anthology—*En el País del Tiempo* (*Beyond the Fields We Know*), by Lord Dunsany (United Kingdom), edited by Lin Carter (United States)
Horror Collection/Anthology—No award
SF Short Story—"Press ENTER ■," by John Varley (United States)
Fantasy Short Story—No award
Horror Short Story—No award
Specialized Programs—(tie) "Nova Ciencia Ficción," Miquel Barcelo, ed.; "Gran Fantasy," Alevo Cuervo, ed.

Fanzine—(tie) *Cuasar*, Luis M. Pestarini and Monica Nicastro, eds.; *Tránsito*, Miguel Mas and Juan Manuel Ortiz, eds.
Special Award—José María Latorre, for *El Cine Fantástico*
Special Award—Valemar Editores (Italy) publisher, for their bilingual edition of *Fungi From Yuggoth*, by H. P. Lovecraft (United States)
Special Award—Ediciones Alcor (Italy) publisher, for their edition of *Puttering Around in a Small Land*, by Philip K. Dick (United States)

1989 (1990)

SF Novel—*The Shadow of the Torturer*, by Gene Wolfe (United States)
Fantasy Novel—(tie) *Mythago Wood*, by Robert Holdstock (United Kingdom); *The Colour of Magic*, by Terry Pratchett (United Kingdom)
Horror Novel—*Conjure Wife*, by Fritz Leiber (United States)
SF Short Story—No award
Fantasy Short Story—(tie) "The Lord of Quarmall," by Fritz Leiber (United States); "Old Ghosties," by Richard Matheson (United States)
Horror Short Story—(5 winners) "The Hospice," by Robert Aickman (United States); "The Ancient Mind at Work," by Suzy McKee Charnas (United States); "The Unicorn Tapestry," by Suzy McKee Charnas (United States); "Night-Side," by Joyce Carol Oates (United States); "Quiet Voices in Passenham," by T. H. White (United Kingdom)
SF Collection/Anthology—*Beyond the Wub: Collected Works, Vol. 1*, by Philip K. Dick (United States)
Fantasy Collection/Anthology—*Swords Against Magic*, by Fritz Leiber (United States)
Horror Collection/Anthology—*Dark Descent*, David Hartwell, ed. (United States)
Fanzine—*Cuasar*, Luis M. Pestarini and Monica Nicastro, eds.
Series—*Gran Fantasy*
Special Award (Fanzine)—*Destino*, Alvaro Cunqueiro Library
Special Award (Fanzine)—*Olaneta*, Tale of Wonder Library, Cristine Macia, ed.

103. PREMIOS ITALIANO DI FANTASCIENZA
(ITALY)

Nothing is known about the background of these Italian awards.

PREMIOS ITALIANO DI FANTASCIENZA

1971 (1972)

Novel—*Autocrisi*, by Pierfrancesco Prosperi
Short Fiction—"Dove Muore l'Astragalo," by Livio Horrakh
Dramatic Presentation—*La Ragazza di Latta*, Marcello Aliprandi, Writer
Artist—Karel Thole
Specialized Prozine—*Galassia*
Nonspecialized Prozine—*Fenarete*
Fanzine—*Notizario CCSF*
Reference Work—"Il Senso del Futuro," by Carlo Pagetti
Comic—*Valentina*, by Guido Crepax

1972 (1973)-1973 (1974)

No awards

1974 (1975)

Novel—*La Donna Immortale*, by Gustavo Gasparini
Artist—Karel Thole
Specialized Professional Publication—Cosmo Serie Argento
Fanzine—*Notizario CCSF*
Special Award—Bob Shaw (United Kingdom)

1975 (1976)
Novel—*Giungla Domestica*, by Gilda Musa
Short Fiction—"L'Accessorio Indispensabile," by Stefano Sudria
TV Show—*Spazio 1999 (Space 1999)*, RAI-TV, co-producers
Professional Publication—Cosmo Serie Argento
Fanzine—*Bollettino del CCSF*
Artist—Karel Thole
Comic Artist—Roberto Bonadimani

1976 (1977)
Novel—*Oltre il Cristallo*, by Besana and Caroglio
Short Fiction—"Servocasa," by Virginio Marafante
Dramatic Presentation—*Spazio 1999 (Space 1999)*, RAI-TV, co-producers
Artist—Karel Thole
Prozine—*Robot*
Book Series—Cosmo Serie Oro, Editrice Nord, publisher
Fanzine—*The Time Machine*, C. P. F. di Padova, ed.
Scholar—Riccardo Valla
Comic Artist—Roberto Bonadimani
Critical Work—"Quando Arrivano i Marziani," by Remo Guerrini

1977 (1978)
Novel—*Reazione a Catena*, by Luigi Menghini
Short Fiction—"Gil ex Bambini," by Gilda Musa
Professional Publication—Cosmo Serie Argento
Fanzine—*The Time Machine*, C. P. F. di Padova, ed.
Artist—Franco Storchi
Critical Book—*Ieri il Futuro*, by Gianni Montanari
Critical Article—"Fantascienza Story," by Franco Scaglia
Comic—*Eram Nel Sogno*, by Roberto Bonadimani
Prozine—*Urania*

1978 (1979)
Novel—*Amazon*, by Gianluigi Zuddas
Short Fiction—"Sindrome Lunare," by Vittorio Curtoni
Artist—Karel Thole
Prozine—*Robot*
Fanzine—*The Time Machine*, C. P. F. di Padova, ed.
Comic—*Rosa di Stelle*, by Roberto Bonadimani
Critical Work—"Introduzione al Libro," by Inisero Cremaschi
Dramatic Presentation—*Scontri Stellari (Star Crash)*

1979 (1980)
Novel—*L'Insidia kei Kryan*, by Virginio Marafante
Short Fiction—"Dove Sono le Nevi," by Adalberto Cersosimo
Artist—Franco Storchi
Prozine—*SF Anticipazione*
Fanzine—*SF...ERE*
Comic—*Metamorfosi*, by Roberto Bonadimani
Critical Work—*Lovecraft*, by De Turris and Fusco
Dramatic Presentation—(tie) *Racconti di Fantascienza*, Alessandro Blasetti, writer; *Allegro Non Troppo*, Bruno Bozzetto, writer

1980 (1981)
Special Award—A. E. van Vogt, for the body of his work (CAN/USA)
Special Award—Forrest J Ackerman, for lifetime achievement in science fiction (United States)

1990 (1991)
Novel—*Gli Universi di Moras*, by Vittorio Catani

Short Fiction (Professional)—"Rulli di Tamburi," by Miriam Poloniato
Short Fiction (Fan)—"Valzer," by Donato Altomare
Book Length Essay—*Lo Schermo Insanguinato*, by A. Colombo and F. Tentori
Critical Article—"L'Ateneo Esoterico di Howard e Lovecraft," by Mariella Bernacchi
Artist—Alessandro Bani
Editor—Piergiorgio Nicolazzini
Translator—Annarita Guarnieri
Published Line—Cosmo Argento, by Editrice Nord
Magazine—*Dimensione Cosmica*
Fanzine—*Yorick*

1991 (1992)

Novel—*La Proposto*, by Nino Filastò
Short Fiction (Professional)—"La Baracca degli Angeli Neri," by Dario Tonani
Short Fiction (Fan)—"Go to Label Zero," by Domenico Gallo
Book Length Essay—*La Scienza della Fantascienza*, by Renato Giovannoli
Critical Article (Professional)—"Il Caso Tolkien," by Gianfranco de Turris
Critical Article (Fan)—"Il Futuro della Fantascienza," by Gianfranco de Turris
Artist—Alessandro Bani
Editor—Piergiorgio Nicolazzini
Translator—Annarita Guarnieri
Published Line—Cosmo Argento, by Editrice Nord
Magazine—*L'Eternauta*
Fanzine—*Yorick*

104. THE *PRISONERS OF GRAVITY* REALITY 1 COMMENDATION AWARDS
(CANADA)

Prisoners of Gravity, a weekly SF/comics discussion/interview television series produced in Ontario, Canada, sponsors this viewer award, also known as the R1ckie Award.

THE *PRISONERS OF GRAVITY* REALITY 1 AWARDS

1991 (1992)

SF Novel—*Barrayar*, by Lois McMaster Bujold
Fantasy Novel—*Good Omens*, by Terry Pratchett and Neil Gaiman
Horror Novel—(3-way tie) *The Witching Hour*, by Anne Rice; *Dark Matter*, by Garfield Reeves-Stevens; *Blood Price*, by Tanya Huff
Short Fiction—"Daughter Earth," by James Morrow
Favorite *PoG* Guest—Neil Gaiman
Graphic Novel—unknown
Comic Book Series—unknown

105. PRIX APOLLO
(FRANCE)

The Prix Apollo is given annually to honor for the best science fiction novel (original or translated) published in French during the preceding year. The award is voted upon by a rotating panel of three judges. The awards were suspended in 1991.

PRIX APOLLO

1971 (1972)—*Isle of the Dead*, by Roger Zelazny (United States)
1972 (1973)—*Stand on Zanzibar*, by John Brunner (United Kingdom)
1973 (1974)—*The Iron Dream*, by Norman Spinrad (USA/France)

1974 (1975)—*The Embedding*, by Ian Watson (United Kingdom)
1975 (1976)—*Nightwings*, by Robert Silverberg (United States)
1976 (1977)—*Cette Chère Humanité*, by Philippe Curval (France)
1977 (1978)—*Hellstrom's Hive*, by Frank Herbert (United States)
1978 (1979)—*Gateway*, by Frederik Pohl (United States)
1980 (1981)—*Juniper Time*, by Kate Wilhelm (United States)
1981 (1982)—*The Idiot King*, by Scott Baker (France)
1982 (1983)—*L'Orbe et la Roue*, by Michel Jeury (France)
1983 (1984)—*Les Semeurs d'Abîme*, by Serge Brussolo (France)
1984 (1985)—*The Citadel of the Autarch*, by Gene Wolfe (United States)
1985 (1986)—*Blood Music*, by Greg Bear (United States)
1986 (1987)—*The Anubis Gates*, by Tim Powers (United States)
1987 (1988)—*La Compagnie des Glaces* (*The Ice Corporation*), by G. J. Arnaud (France)
1989 (1990)—*Argentine*, by Joël Houssin (France)

Awards discontinued.

106. PRIX BORÉAL
(CANADA)

The Prix Boréal is presented annually at the Boréal Science Fiction Convention at Québec, Canada, to honor achievement in French language science fiction.

PRIX BORÉAL

1986 (1987)
Novel—*L'Épuisement du Soleil* (*The End of the Sun*), by Esther Rochon
Short Story—"Compost," by Agnes Guitard
Artist—Sue Krinard
Author—Yves Menard (Garth Spencer)

1988 (1989)
Novel—*Les Gélules Utopiques*, by Guy Bouchard
Short Story—"Geisha Blues," by Michel Martin and Guy Sirois
Critical Work—"L'Horreur Anglosaxonne...," by Luc Pomerleau
Artist—Sylvain Bellemare

107. PRIX COSMOS 2000
(FRANCE)

The Prix Cosmos 2000 is sponsored by the Parisian science fiction bookstore, Cosmos 2000, and its owner Annick Beguin, and voted upon by the store customers in an annual poll. The award honors the best science fiction novel of the year published throughout the world, and is similar in scope and origin to the Saturn Award given by Forbidden Planet bookstore.

PRIX COSMOS 2000

1981 (1982)—*Shadrach in the Furnace*, by Robert Silverberg (United States)
1982 (1983)—*L'Orbe et la Roue*, by Michel Jeury (France)
1983 (1984)—*Radix*, by A. A. Attanasio (United States)
1984 (1985)—*The Robots of Dawn*, by Isaac Asimov (United States)
1985 (1986)—*Heretics of Dune*, by Frank Herbert (United States)
1986 (1987)—*Phénix*, by Bernard Simonay (France)
1987 (1988)—*La Voix des Morts* (*Speaker for the Dead*), by Orson Scott Card (United States)
1988 (1989)—*Mission Earth Dekalogy*, by L. Ron Hubbard (United States)

108. PRIX JULES VERNE
(SWEDEN)

Nothing is known about the background of this Swedish award.

PRIX JULES VERNE

1975—Roland Adlerberth, Rolf Ahlgren, Eugen Semitjov, and Lars-Olov Strandberg, for services to Swedish science fiction
1976—*The Left Hand of Darkness*, by Ursula K. Le Guin (United States)
1977—*Non-Stop*, by Brian W. Aldiss (United Kingdom)
1978—*Spring of Light*, by Vladimir Gakov (USSR)
1979—*Roadside Picnic*, by Arkady and Boris Strugatsky (USSR)
1980—*Make Room! Make Room!*, by Harry Harrison (USA/Ireland)
Awards discontinued.

109. PRIX JULIA VERLANGER
(FRANCE)

Related to the Prix Cosmos 2000, the Prix Julia Verlanger is given for best SF novel published in France in the previous year, and chosen in the same way as the Cosmos 2000. The physical award consists of a 5,000-Franc prize.

THE JULIA VERLANGER AWARDS

1985 (1986)—*Le Jeu du Monde*, by Michel Jeury (France); **Life Achievement Award**—Stefan Wul (France)
1986 (1987)—*Phénix*, by Bernard Simonay (France)
1987 (1988)—*Le Portrait du Mal*, by Graham Masterton (United States)

110. PRIX ROSNY-AÎNÉ
(FRANCE)

The Rosny-Aîné was created in 1980 by the organizers of the Rambouillet French National Science Fiction Convention to honor French fantasy writer J.-H. Rosny, *Aîné* (1856-1940), and received its current name in 1983 (previously being known as the "Prix de la Convention"). The award recognizes original French-language works of SF or fantasy published during the preceding year. The award is administered by a committee of science fiction professionals, including Pascal J. Thomas, Roland Wagner, Francis Valéry, Pierre Barbet, and Francis Saint-Martin. The winner is determined by an Australian-ballot vote of the members of the convention. There is usually no physical award as such, although some conventions have honored the winners by giving them original pieces of science fiction artwork.

PRIX ROSNY-AÎNÉ

1980
Novel—*Le Territoire Humain*, by Michel Jeury
Novelette—"La Créode," by Joëlle Wintrebert

1981
Novel—*Les Yeux Géants*, by Michel Jeury
Novelette—(tie) "Chronique de la Vallée," by Jacques Boireau; "Subway," by Serge Brussolo

1982
Novel—*Le Silence de la Cité*, by Elisabeth Vonarburg (Canada)

Novelette—"La Nuit des Albiens," by Christine Renard

1983
Novel—*Damiers Imaginaires*, by Emmanuel Jouanne
Novelette—"Faire-Part," by Roland C. Wagner

1984
Novel—*Le Champ du Rêveur*, by Jean-Pierre Hubert
Novelette—"Le Clavier Incendié," by Lionel Evrard

1985
Novel—*Ici-Bas*, by Emmanuel Jouanne
Novelette—"Pleine Peau," by Jean-Pierre Hubert

1986
Novel—*Ombromanies*, by Jean-Pierre Hubert
Novelette—"Le Chemin de la Rencontre," by Sylvie Laine

1987
Novel—*La Ville au Fond de L'Oeil*, by Francis Berthelot
Novelette—"Mémoire Vive, Mémoire Morte," by Gérard Klein

1988
Novel—(tie) *Le Serpent d'Angoisse*, by Roland C. Wagner; *Les Olympiades Truquées*, by Joëlle Wintrebert
Novelette—"Roulette Mousse," by Jean-Pierre Hubert

1989
Novel—*Poupée aux Yeux Morts (Dead-eyed Doll)*, by Roland C. Wagner
Novelette—"Bumpie (TM)," by Francis Valéry
Awards discontinued?

111. PRIX ROTARY
(FRANCE)

The Prix Rotary is given for the best science fiction short story published during the previous year in France.

PRIX ROTARY

1985 (1986)—"Voyage au Pays des Bords du Gouffre," by Alain Nadaud

112. THE PROMETHEUS AWARDS
(UNITED STATES)

The Prometheus Award was created in 1978 to promote "pro-freedom" fiction which dramatizes such themes as the evolution of an ideal free society and the persistent human drive toward self-liberation, self-realization, and personal growth. L. Neil Smith was prominent in establishing the prize. The first award was $2,500 in gold. The current award is a half-ounce gold coin imprinted with the image of economist F. A. Hayak. The awards were suspended between 1980-1981. In 1982 Michael Grossberg created the Libertarian Futurist Society (LFS), which reinstated the awards and now maintains them. Any member of LFS is eligible to nominate books for the Prometheus Award, but only the Advisory members may vote on nominations.

The Prometheus Hall of Fame Award was created by the LFS in 1982 as a retrospective counterpart to the Prometheus. The award is open to any work of fiction over five years old; titles are nominated and chosen by the entire membership of LFS. The awards were given to two works annually from 1983-1987, and to one work beginning in 1988. The physical prize consists of a silver coin stamped with the image of economist Adam Smith plus a certificate (to authors living at the time they receive the award), or just a certificate to the heirs of deceased writers.

THE PROMETHEUS AWARDS

1978 (1979)—*Wheels within Wheels*, by F. Paul Wilson
1979 (1980)—No award
1980 (1981)—No award
1981 (1982)—*The Probability Broach*, by L. Neil Smith
1982 (1983)—*Voyage from Yesteryear*, by James P. Hogan
1983 (1984)—*The Rainbow Cadenza*, by J. Neil Schulman
1984 (1985)—No award
1985 (1986)—*The Cybernetic Samurai*, by Victor Milán
1986 (1987)—*Marooned in Realtime*, by Vernor Vinge
1987 (1988)—*The Jehovah Contract*, by Victor Koman
1988 (1989)—*Moon of Ice*, by Brad Linaweaver
1989 (1990)—*Solomon's Knife*, by Victor Koman
1990 (1991)—*In the Country of the Blind*, by Michael Flynn

THE PROMETHEUS HALL OF FAME AWARDS

1983—*The Moon is a Harsh Mistress*, by Robert A. Heinlein; *Atlas Shrugged*, by Ayn Rand
1984—*Fahrenheit 451*, by Ray Bradbury; *Nineteen Eighty-Four*, by George Orwell
1985—*Trader to the Stars*, by Poul Anderson; *The Great Explosion*, by Eric Frank Russell
1986—*The Syndic*, by C. M. Kornbluth; The *Illuminatus Trilogy*, by Robert Shea and Robert Anton Wilson
1987—*Stranger in a Strange Land*, by Robert A. Heinlein; *Anthem*, by Ayn Rand
1988—*The Stars My Destination*, by Alfred Bester
1989—*Alongside Night*, by J. Neil Schulman
1990—*Healer*, by F. Paul Wilson
1991—*An Enemy of the People*, by F. Paul Wilson

113. THE PYRAMID BOOKS/*F&SF*/KENT PRODUCTIONS SCIENCE FICTION NOVEL CONTEST
(UNITED STATES)

Pyramid Books, *The Magazine of Fantasy & Science Fiction*, and Kent Productions sponsored this one-time $5,000 contest for best original science fiction novel of the year.

THE PYRAMID BOOKS/*F&SF*/KENT PRODUCTIONS SCIENCE FICTION NOVEL CONTEST WINNER

1968—*Sos the Rope*, by Piers Anthony

114. THE READERCON SMALL PRESS SCIENCE FICTION AWARD
(UNITED STATES)

The Small Press Science Fiction Awards are presented annually at Noreascon by the Small Press Writers and Artists Organization (SPWAO), and chosen by the members of that group, subject to ratification by a panel of judges. Past judges have included: Algis Budrys, Robert Colby, David Hartwell, Mark V. Ziesing, Terri Windling, and Arthur Hlavaty.

The Readercon Small Press Awards

1979 (1980)

Magazine (Small Circ.)—*Space and Time*, Gordon Linzer, ed.
Magazine (Large Circ.)—*Whispers*, Stuart David Schiff, ed.
SF Writer—Jon Inouye
Fantasy Writer—Charles R. Saunders
Horror Writer—Galad Elflandsson
Nonfiction Writer—Charles R. Saunders
SF Artist—Steve Fabian
Fantasy Artist—Tim Hammell
Horror Artist—Allen Koszowski
Cover Artist—Gene Day
Overall Artistic Achievement—Gene Day
Dale Donaldson Memorial Award—C. C. Clingan

1983 (1984)

Magazine (Small Circ.)—*Space and Time*, Gordon Linzer, ed.
Magazine (Large Circ.)—*Owlflight*, Millea Kenin, ed.
SF Writer—Margaret Lindholm
Fantasy Writer—Janet Fox
Horror Writer—Janet Fox
SF Artist—Brad Foster
Fantasy Artist—Steve Fabian
Horror Artist—Allen Koszowski
Cover Artist—Brad Foster
Overall Artistic Achievement—(tie) Allen Koszowski; Brad Foster
Dale Donaldson Memorial Award—Janet Fox
Poet—Steve Eng

1986 (1987)

Editor—Peggy Nadramia
Magazine—*Grue*, Peggy Nadramia, ed.
Writer—Colleen Drippe
Poet—D. M. Vosk
Artist—Allen Koszowski
Comic Writer/Artist—Larry Dickinson
Nonfiction Writer—Joe Lansdale
Dale Donaldson Memorial Award—W. Paul Ganley; David B. Silva

1987 (1988)

Editor—Peggy Nadramia
Fiction Writer—Janet Fox
Nonfiction Writer—Jeanette M. Hooper
Poet—Bruce D. Boston
Artist—Allen Koszowski
Comics—Marge Simon
Dale Donaldson Memorial Award—David B. Silva

1988 (1989)

Magazine Design—*Midnight Grafitti*, Jessie Horsting, ed.
Novel—*Fool on the Hill*, by Matt Ruff
Collection—*Co-Orbital Moons*, by Robert Frazier
Anthology—*Night Visions #6*
Short Work—"The Drowned Man's Reef," by Charles de Lint
Nonfiction—*Strokes: Essays and Reviews, 1966-1986*, by John Clute
Jacket Illustrator—Don Maitz, for *First Maitz*
Interior Illustrator—Michael W. Kaluta, for *Metropolis*
Value in Bookcraft—Chris Drumm, for Drumm Booklets Series
Reissued Item—*VALIS*, by Philip K. Dick

Reginald's Science Fiction & Fantasy Awards, Third Edition

Fiction/Poetry Magazine—*Interzone*, David Pringle, ed.
Reviewer/Criticism Magazine—(tie) *Mystery Scene*; *New York Review of Science Fiction*, David Hartwell, ed.

1989 (1990)
Novel—No award
Short Work—"A Dozen Tough Jobs," by Howard Waldrop
Collection—*Richard Matheson: Collected Stories*, by Richard Matheson
Anthology—*What Did Miss Darrington See?: An Anthology of Feminist Supernatural Fiction*, Jessica Amanda Salmonson, ed.
Nonfiction—*The Dark-Haired Girl*, by Philip K. Dick
Reference/Bibliography—No award
Reprint—Mark Ziesing, for *The Anubis Gates* by Tim Powers
Jacket Illustration—J. K. Potter, for *The Anubis Gates* by Tim Powers
Interior Illustration—Mark Ferrari and Tom Sullivan, for *S. Peterson's Field Guide to Creatures of the Dreamlands*
Value in Bookcraft—Scream/Press, for *Richard Matheson: Collected Stories*, by Richard Matheson
Magazine (Fiction)—*Interzone*, David Pringle, ed.
Magazine (Criticism)—*Science Fiction Eye*, Stephen P. Brown and Daniel J. Steffan, eds.
Magazine (Design)—*Science Fiction Eye*, Stephen P. Brown and Daniel J. Steffan, eds.

1990 (1991)
Novel—*Red Spider, White Web*, by Misha
Short Work—"Entropy's Bed at Midnight," by Dan Simmons
Collection—*The Brains of Rats*, by Michael Blumlein
Anthology—*When the Black Lotus Blooms*, Elizabeth Saunders, ed.
Nonfiction—*Across the Wounded Galaxies*, by Larry McCaffery
Reference/Bibliography—No award
Reprint—Re/Search, for *The Atrocity Exhibition*, by J. G. Ballard
Jacket Illustration—H. R. Giger, for *H. R. Giger's Biomechanics*, by H. R. Giger
Interior Illustration—H. R. Giger, for *H. R. Giger's Biomechanics*, by H. R. Giger
Value in Bookcraft—Mark Ziesing (Ursus/Ziesing), for *Slow Dancing Through Time*, by Gardner Dozois
Magazine (Fiction)—*Journal Wired*, Mark Ziesing & Andy Watson, eds.
Magazine (Criticism)—*New York Review of Science Fiction*, David Hartwell, ed.
Magazine (Design)—*Journal Wired*, Mark Ziesing & Andy Watson, eds.

115. THE REUBEN AWARD
(UNITED STATES)

The Reuben Award, named in honor of the late Rube Goldberg, is given by the National Cartoonists Society (NCS), the winner being selected by secret ballot of the membership.

THE REUBEN AWARD

1946—Milton Caniff, for *Steve Canyon*
1947—Al Capp, for *Li'l Abner*
1948—Chic Young, for *Blondie*
1949—Alex Raymond, for *Rip Kirby*
1950—Roy Crane, for *Buzz Sawyer*
1951—Walt Kelly, for *Pogo*
1952—Hank Ketcham, for *Dennis the Menace*
1953—Mort Walker, for *Beetle Bailey*
1954—Willard Mullin, for *Sports* cartoons
1955—Charles Schulz, for *Peanuts*
1956—Herblock, for Editorial cartoons
1957—Hal Foster, for *Prince Valiant*

1958—Frank King, for *Gasoline Alley*
1959—Chester Gould, for *Dick Tracy*
1960—Ronald Searle, for Illustrations
1961—Bill Mauldin, for Editorial cartoons
1962—Dik Browne, for *Hi & Lois*
1963—Fred Lasswell, for *Barney Google and Snuffy Smith*
1964—Charles Schulz, for *Peanuts*
1965—Leonard Starr, for *On Stage*
1966—Otto Soglow, for *The Little King*
1967—Rube Goldberg, for *Humor in Sculpture*
1968—(tie) John Hart, for *B.C.* and *Wizard of Id*; Pat Oliphant, for Editorial cartoons
1969—Walter Berndt, for *Smitty*
1970—Alfred Andriola, for *Kerry Drake*
1971—Milton Caniff, for *Steve Canyon*
1972—Pat Oliphant, for Editorial cartoons
1973—Dik Browne, for *Hagar the Horrible*
1974—Dick Moores, for *Gasoline Alley*
1975—Bob Dunn, for *They'll Do It Every Time*
1976—Ernie Bushmiller, for *Nancy*
1977—Chester Gould, for *Dick Tracy*

116. THE RHYSLING AWARD
(UNITED STATES)

The Rhyslings were created by the Science Fiction Poetry Association (SFPA) in 1978. Suzette Haden Elgin, founder of SFPA, was instrumental in establishing the award. The award is presented in two categories: long poem (fifty lines or over), and shorter lengths (anything less). The award is voted upon by the membership of SFPA. Each member may nominate one poem annually in each category.

THE RHYSLING AWARDS

1977 (1978)
Long Poem—"The Computer Iterates the Greater Trump," by Gene Wolfe
Short Poem—(3-way tie) "The Starman," by Duane Ackerson; "Corruption of Metals," by Sonya Dorman; "Asleep in the Arms of Mother Night," by Andrew Joron

1978 (1979)
Long Poem—"For the Lady of a Physician," by Michael Bishop
Short Poem—(tie) "Fatalities," by Duane Ackerson; "Story Books and Treasure Maps," by Steve Eng

1979 (1980)
Long Poem—"The Sonic Waterfall of Primes," by Andrew Joron
Short Poem—(tie) "Encased in the Amber of Eternity," by Robert Frazier; "The Migration of Darkness," by Peter Payack

1980 (1981)
Long Poem—"On Science Fiction," by Thomas M. Disch
Short Poem—"Meeting Place," by Ken Duffin

1981 (1982)
Long Poem—"The Well of Baln," by Ursula K. Le Guin
Short Poem—"On the Speed of Sight," by Raymond DiZazzo

1982 (1983)
Long Poem—"Your Time and You," by Adam Cornford
Short Poem—"In Computers," by Alan P. Lightman

1983 (1984)
Long Poem—"Saul's Death," by Joe W. Haldeman
Short Poem—"Two Sonnets," by Helen Ehrlich

1984 (1985)
Long Poem—"A Letter from Caroline Herschel," by Siv Cederling
Short Poem—"For Spacers Snarled in the Hair of Comets," by Bruce D. Boston

1985 (1986)
Long Poem—"Shipwrecked on Destiny Five," by Andrew Joron
Short Poem—"The Neighbor's Wife," by Susan Palwick

1986 (1987)
Long Poem—"Daedalus," by W. Gregory Stewart
Short Poem—(tie) "A Dream of Heredity," by John Calvin Rezmerski; "Before the Big Bang," by Jonathan V. Post

1987 (1988)
Long Poem—"White Trains," by Lucius Shepard
Short Poem—(tie) "Rocky Road to Hoe," by Suzette Haden Elgin; "The Nightmare Collector," by Bruce D. Boston

1988 (1989)
Long Poem—(tie) "In the Darkened Hours," by Bruce D. Boston; "Winter Solstice, Camelot Station," by Walter Jon Williams
Short Poem—"Salinity," by Robert Frazier

1989 (1990)
Long Poem—"Dear Spaceman," by Patrick McKinnon
Short Poem—"Epitaph for Dreams," by G. Sutton Breiding

1990 (1991)
Long Poem—"Eighteen Years Old, October Eleventh," by Joe Haldeman
Short Poem—"The Aging Cryonicist in the Arms of His Mistress Contemplates the Survival of the Species While the Phoenix is Consumed by Fire," by David Memmott

---

117. THE ROBBIE AWARD
[THE AUSTRALIAN SCIENCE FICTION MEDIA AWARD]
(AUSTRALIA)

The Robbies are given for best SF in the media in Australia, and are presented at the annual Australian National SF Media Convention.

THE ROBBIE AWARDS

1988 (1989)

Fanzine—*Spock*, Pam Rendell, ed.
Fan Writer—Edwina Harvey
Fan Media Artist—Gail Adams

---

118. THE RUSS MANNING AWARD
(UNITED STATES)

The Russ Manning Award is given to the most promising new artist of the year, and is presented jointly by the West Coast Comics Club and the San Diego Comic-Con. The Manning honors the memory of Russ Manning, a comic artist best known for his work on *Tarzan* and *Magnus, Robot Fighter*.

THE RUSS MANNING AWARDS

1982—Dave Stevens
1983—Jan Duursema
1984—Steve Rude
1985—Scott McCloud
1986—Art Adams
1987—Eric Shanower
1988—Kevin Maguire
1989—Richard Piers Rayner
1990—Daniel Brereton
1991—Darick Gross
1992—Mike Okomoto

119. THE SATURN AWARD
[THE SCIENCE FICTION, FANTASY, AND HORROR FILM AWARD]
(UNITED STATES)

The Science Fiction, Fantasy and Horror Film Awards are given by the Academy of Science Fiction, Fantasy, and Horror Films for recognition of outstanding achievement and merit in fantastic films released during the preceding year; categories are similar to those of the Oscar Awards. A Golden Scroll Award is awarded monthly, but the main award is called the Saturn Award. The awards were established in 1972 by Dr. Donald A. Reed, founder of the Academy. This accolade should not be confused with the literary Saturn Award given by Forbidden Planet.

THE SATURN AWARDS

1972 (1973)
SF Film—*Slaughterhouse-Five*, screenplay by Stephen Geller (Universal)
Fantasy Film—No award.
Horror Film—*Blacula*, screenplay by Joan Torres and Raymond Koenig (AIP)
Special Award—The Count Dracula Society, for recognition of its pioneering efforts since 1962 in presenting awards of merit and recognition in science fiction, fantasy, and horror genres.

1973/74 (1975)
SF Film—*Soylent Green*, screenplay by Stanley Greenberg (MGM)
Fantasy Film—*The Golden Voyage of Sinbad*, screenplay by Brian Clemens (Columbia)
Horror Film—*The Exorcist*, screenplay by William Peter Blatty (Warner Bros.)
Makeup—Dick Smith, for *The Exorcist*
Music—Bernard Herrmann, for *It's Alive*
Special Effects—Marcel Veroutère, for *The Exorcist*
Stop Motion Animation—Ray Harryhausen, for *The Golden Voyage of Sinbad*
Special Award—George Pal
Special Award—Charlton Heston
Special Award—Gloria Swanson
Special Award—Fay Wray
Special Award—Don Fanzo
Special Award—C. Dean Andersson

1975 (1976)
SF Film—*Rollerball*, screenplay by William Harrison (United Artists)
Fantasy Film—*Doc Savage*, screenplay by George Pal and Joe Morheim (Warner Bros.)

Reginald's Science Fiction & Fantasy Awards, Third Edition

Horror Film—*Young Frankenstein*, screenplay by Mel Brooks and Gene Wilder (20th Century-Fox)
Actor—(tie) James Caan, for *Rollerball*; Don Johnson, for *A Boy and His Dog*
Actress—Katherine Ross, for *The Stepford Wives*
Supporting Actor—Marty Feldman, for *Young Frankenstein*
Supporting Actress—Ida Lupino, for *The Devil's Rain*
Cinematography—Douglas Slocombe, for *Rollerball*
Director—Mel Brooks, for *Young Frankenstein*
Executive Achievement—Brandon L. Chase, for *The Giant Spider Invasion*
Film Critic—(tie) Forrest J Ackerman; Dale Winogura
Makeup—William Tuttle, for *Young Frankenstein*
Set Decoration—Robert de Vestel and Dale Hennesey, for *Young Frankenstein*
Music—Miklos Rozsa
Art Decoration—Philip Harrison, for *Old Dracula*
Advertisement/Publicity/Public Relations—Clark Ramsey, for *Jaws*
Special Effects—Doug Knapp, Bill Taylor, John Carpenter, and Dan O'Bannon, for *Dark Star*
Stop Motion Animation—Jim Danforth
Writing—(tie) Harlan Ellison, for *A Boy and His Dog*; Ib J. Melchior
Life Career Award—Fritz Lang
Special Award—*Jaws*, for outstanding film of 1975

1976 (1977)

SF Film—*Logan's Run*, screenplay by William F. Nolan and George Clayton Johnson (MGM)
Fantasy Film—*The Holes* (Burbank International Pictures)
Horror Film—*Burnt Offerings*, screenplay by Dan Curtis and William F. Nolan (United Artists)
Actor—(tie) David Bowie, for *The Man Who Fell to Earth*; Gregory Peck, for *The Omen*
Actress—Blythe Danner, for *Futureworld*
Supporting Actor—Jay Robinson, for *Train Ride to Hollywood*
Supporting Actress—Bette Davis, for *Burnt Offerings*
Animation—Charles M. Jones
Cinematography—Ernest Laszlo, for *Logan's Run*
Costumes—Bill Thomas, for *Logan's Run*
Director—Dan Curtis, for *Burnt Offerings*
Executive Achievement—Gene Roddenberry
Film Critic—Arthur Knight
Makeup—William Tuttle, for *Logan's Run*
Music—David Raksin
Set Decoration—Robert de Vestel, for *Logan's Run*
Art Decoration—Dale Hennesey, for *Logan's Run*
Advertisement/Publicity/Public Relations—Don Morgan, for *Logan's Run*
Special Effects—L. B. Abbott
Writing—Jimmy Sangster
Life Career Award—Samuel Z. Arkoff, President American International Pictures
Special Award—*King Kong*, for outstanding film of 1976

1977 (1978)

SF Film—*Star Wars*, screenplay by George Lucas (20th Century-Fox)
Fantasy Film—*Oh, God!* (Warner Bros.)
Horror Film—*The Little Girl Who Lives Down the Lane*, screenplay by Laird Koenig (American International Pictures)
Actor—George Burns, for *Oh, God!*
Actress—Jodie Foster, for *The Little Girl Who Lives Down the Lane*
Supporting Actor—Alec Guiness, for *Star Wars*
Supporting Actress—Susan Tyrell, for *Bad*
Cinematography—Gilbert Taylor, for *Star Wars*
Costumes—John Mollo, for *Star Wars*
Editing—Paul Hirsch, Marcia Lucas, and Richard Chew, for *Star Wars*

Director—(tie) George Lucas, for *Star Wars*; Steven Spielberg, for *Close Encounters of the Third Kind*
Executive Achievement—Richard Albain
Film Critic—Kevin Thomas
Literature—Devendra P. Varma
Makeup—Rick Baker and Stuart Freeborn, for *Star Wars*
Music—John Williams, for *Star Wars* and *Close Encounters of the Third Kind*
Art Decoration—John Barry, Norman Reynolds, and Leslie Dilley, for *Star Wars*
Set Decoration—Roger Christian, for *Star Wars*
Advertisement/Publicity/Public Relations—Charles Lippincott, for *Star Wars*
Recording—Caedmon Records
Sound—Ben Burtt, Don MacDougall, and Sam Shaw, for *Star Wars*
Special Effects—John Dykstra and John Stears, for *Star Wars*
Stop Motion Animation—Ray Harryhausen, for *Sinbad and the Eye of the Tiger*
Television Performance—Jonathan Harris, in *Lost in Space* and *Space Academy*
Writing—George Lucas, for *Star Wars*
Hall of Fame Inductee—George Pal
Hall of Fame Inductee—*War of the Worlds*
Life Career Award—Carl Laemmle, Jr.
Outstanding Service Award—Louis Federici, for his services to the Academy
Special Award—Dr. Donald A. Reed, for founding the Academy of Science Fiction, Fantasy and Horror Films

1978 (1979)

SF Film—*Superman*, screenplay by Mario Puzo, David Newman, Leslie Newman, and Robert Benton (Warner Bros.)
Fantasy Film—*Heaven Can Wait*, screenplay by Elaine May and Warren Beatty (Paramount Pictures)
Horror Film—*The Wicker Man*, screenplay by Anthony Shaffer (International Pictures)
Actor—Warren Beatty, for *Heaven Can Wait*
Actress—Margot Kidder, for *Superman*
Supporting Actor—Burgess Meredith, for *Magic*
Supporting Actress—Dyan Cannon, for *Heaven Can Wait*
Animated Film—*Watership Down*, screenplay by Richard Adams
Cinematography—Russell Boyd, for *Picnic at Hanging Rock*
Costumes—Theoni V. Aldredge, for *The Eyes of Laura Mars*
Editing—Mark Goldblatt and Joe Dante, for *Piranha*
Director—Philip Kaufman, for *Invasion of the Body Snatchers*
Executive Achievement—Gene Booth
Film Critic—Eric Hoffman
Literature—A. E. van Vogt, for his truly immeasurable contributions to the art and science of science fiction writing
Makeup—William Tuttle and Rick Baker, for *The Fury*
Music—John Williams, for *Superman*
Production Design—John Barry, for *Superman*
Advertisement/Publicity/Public Relations—Julian F. Myers, for his work at American International Pictures
Sound—Art Rochester, Mark Berger, and Andrew Wiskes, for *Invasion of the Body Snatchers*
Special Effects—Colin Chilvers, for *Superman*
Television Performance—Eric Greene, for *Space Academy*
Writing—(tie) Elaine May and Warren Beatty, for *Heaven Can Wait*; Anthony Shaffer, for *The Wicker Man*
Life Career Award—Christopher Lee
Special Award—Arnold Shapiro, executive producer of the Annual Science Fiction Film Awards
Special Award—Scott Sternberg, producer of the Annual Science Fiction Film Awards
Special Award—Gilles Kohler, for his performance in *La Merveilleuse Visite*
Special Award—Margaret Hamilton, for her classic role as the Wicked Witch of the West in *The Wizard of Oz*

Reginald's Science Fiction & Fantasy Awards, Third Edition

Special Award—Gloria Swanson, for *Sunset Boulevard* and *Killer Bees*
Special Award—Robert H. Solo, producer of *Invasion of the Body Snatchers*
Special Award—Gayna Shireen, crowned Miss Science Fiction
Special Award—Lawrence D. Foldes, for the Academy Intern Program
Special Award—Helen Gahagan Douglas, for *She*
Special Award—*Battlestar Galactica*, for best television program
Outstanding Service Award—Frank R. Saletri, for his services to the Academy
Outstanding Service Award—Seid H. Mahdavi, for his services to the Academy
TV Actor—Dirk Benedict, for *Battlestar Galactica*
TV Actress—Laurette Spang, for *Battlestar Galactica*
TV Show (Past Achievement)—*Star Trek*
TV Performer (Past Achievement)—William Shatner, for *Star Trek*
Special Literature—Ray Bradbury

1979 (1980)

SF Film—*Alien*, screenplay by Dan O'Bannon and Ronald Shusett (20th Century Fox)
Fantasy Film—*The Muppet Movie* (Associated Film Distribution)
Horror Film—*Dracula* (Universal)
Foreign Film—*Patrick*, screenplay by Everett De Roche (Australia)
Low Budget Film—*Clonus Horror*, screenplay by Robert Fiveson
Actor—George Hamilton, for *Love at First Bite*
Actress—Mary Steenburgen, for *Time After Time*
Supporting Actor—Arte Johnson, for *Love at First Bite*
Supporting Actress—Veronica Cartwright, for *Alien*
Director—Ridley Scott, for *Alien*
Writing—Nicholas Meyer, for *Time After Time*
Music—Miklos Rosza, for *Time After Time*
Makeup—William Tuttle, for *Love at First Bite*
Special Effects—Douglas Trumbull, John Dykstra, and Richard Yuricich, for *Star Trek: The Motion Picture*
Costume—Jean-Pierre Dorleac, for *Buck Rogers in the 25th Century*
Life Career Award—William Shatner
Life Career Award—Gene Roddenberry
George Pal Memorial Award—John Badham
Most Popular International Performer—Roger Moore
Hall of Fame Inductee—*The Empire Strikes Back*, screenplay by George Lucas, Leigh Brackett, and Lawrence Kasdan
Hall of Fame Inductee—*The Rocky Horror Picture Show*, screenplay by Jim Sharman and Richard O'Brien
Special Award (Career)—Kirk Douglas
Special Award (Career)—Donald Pleasance
Special Award (Career)—John Saxon
Special Award—Robert V. Michelucci
Special Award—William G. Wilson, Jr.
Special Award—Richard S. Zdinak
Special Award—Marcy Lafferty, for *Time After Time*
Special Award—Persis Khambatta, for *Star Trek: The Motion Picture*
World SF Film Favorite—Christopher Lee
Outstanding Service Award—Tim Wohlgemuth, for his services to the Academy
Outstanding Service Award—Michael Prichard, for his services to the Academy
SF TV Film—*The Lathe of Heaven*
Fantasy TV Film—*The Girl, the Gold Watch and Everything*, screenplay by George Zateslo
Horror TV Film—*'Salem's Lot*, screenplay by Paul Monash
TV Actor—Gil Gerard, for *Buck Rogers in the 25th Century*
TV Actress—Erin Gray, for *Buck Rogers in the 25th Century*
TV Series—*Buck Rogers in the 25th Century*
TV Performer (Past Achievement)—David Soul, for *'Salem's Lot*
Special TV Award—Rod Serling, for *The Twilight Zone*
Special TV Award—Peter Sellers

1980 (1981)

SF Film—*The Empire Strikes Back*, screenplay by George Lucas, Leigh Brackett, and Lawrence Kasdan
Fantasy Film—*Somewhere In Time*, screenplay by Richard Matheson
Horror Film—*The Shining*, screenplay by Stanley Kubrick and Diane Johnson
Low Budget Film—*Scared to Death*
International Film—*Scanners*, screenplay by David Cronenberg (United Kingdom)
Actor—Mark Hamill, for *The Empire Strikes Back*
Actress—Angie Dickinson, for *Dressed to Kill*
Supporting Actor—Scatman Crothers, in *The Shining*
Supporting Actress—Eve Brent Ashe, for *Fade to Black*
Director—Irvin Kershner, for *The Empire Strikes Back*
Writing—William Peter Blatty, for *Twinkle, Twinkle, Killer Kane*
Special Effects—Brian Johnson and Richard Edlund, for *The Empire Strikes Back*
Music—John Barry, for *Somewhere in Time*
Makeup—Dick Smith, for *Altered States* and *Scanners*
Costumes—Jean-Pierre Dorleac, for *Somewhere in Time*
Life Career Award—John Agar
Special Award—*Harlequin*, screenplay by Everett De Roche, for outstanding film of 1980
Special Award—Robert Culp
Special Award—Lou Ferrigno
Special Award—Rouben Mamoulian
Outstanding Service Award—Natalie Harris, for her services to the Academy
New Star—Sam J. Jones
Exceptional Achievement—Charles Couch

1981 (1982)

SF Film—*Superman II*, screenplay by Mario Puzo, Leslie Newman, and David Newman
Fantasy Film—*Raiders of the Lost Ark*, screenplay by Lawrence Kasdan
Horror Film—*An American Werewolf in London*, screenplay by John Landis
Actor—Harrison Ford, for *Raiders of the Lost Ark*
Actress—Karen Allen, for *Raiders of the Lost Ark*
Supporting Actor—Burgess Meredith, for *Clash of the Titans*
Supporting Actress—Frances Sternhagen, for *Outland*
Director—Steven Spielberg, for *Raiders of the Lost Ark*
Writing—Lawrence Kasdan, for *Raiders of the Lost Ark*
Music—John Williams, for *Raiders of the Lost Ark*
Special Effects—Richard Edlund, for *Raiders of the Lost Ark*
International Film—*Quest for Fire*, screenplay by Anthony Burgess
Special Award—*Quest for Fire*, screenplay by Anthony Burgess
President's Award—*Time Bandits*, screenplay by Terry Gilliam and Michael Palin
Life Career Award—Ray Harryhausen
Makeup—Rick Baker, for *An American Werewolf in London*
George Pal Memorial Award—Michael Gruskoff
Special Award—Gary Sakharoff, for services to the Academy
Special Award—Hans Salter, for music

1982 (1983)

SF Film—*E.T., the Extraterrestrial*, screenplay by Steven Spielberg and Melissa Mathison
Fantasy Film—*The Dark Crystal*, screenplay by Jim Henson and David Odell
Horror Film—*Poltergeist*, screenplay by Steven Spielberg, Mark Grais, and Michael Victor
Low Budget Film—*Eating Raoul*, screenplay by Paul Bartel and Richard Blackburn
International Film—*The Road Warrior*
Animated Film—*The Secret of NIMH*, screenplay by Robert C. O'Brien
Actor—William Shatner, for *Star Trek II*
Actress—Sandahl Bergman, for *Conan the Barbarian*
Supporting Actor—Richard Lynch, for *The Sword and the Sorcerer*
Supporting Actress—Zelda Rubinstein, for *Poltergeist*
Director—Nicholas Meyer, for *Star Trek II*
Music—John Williams, for *E.T., the Extraterrestrial*

Reginald's Science Fiction & Fantasy Awards, Third Edition

Special Effects—Carlo Rambaldi and Dennis Muren, for *E.T., the Extraterrestrial*
Costumes—Elois Jenssen and Rosanna Norton, for *Tron*
Makeup—Dorothy Pearl, for *Poltergeist*
Screenplay—Melissa Mathison, for *E.T., the Extraterrestrial*
Poster Art—John Alvin, for *E.T., the Extraterrestrial*
Life Career Award—Martin B. Cohen
Posthumous Award—Buster Crabbe
Outstanding Service Award—Dr. Robert Karns, for his service to the Academy
Outstanding Service Award—Louis Ramsey, for his service to the Academy
President's Award—Elsa Lanchester

1984 (1985)

SF Film—*The Terminator*, screenplay by James Cameron and Gale Anne Hurd
Fantasy Film—*Ghostbusters*, screenplay by Dan Ackroyd and Harold Ramis
Horror Film—*Gremlins*, screenplay by Chris Columbus
Actor—Jeff Bridges, for *Starman*
Actress—Daryl Hannah, for *Splash!*
Supporting Actor—Tracey Walter, for *Repo Man*
Supporting Actress—Polly Holiday, for *Gremlins*
Director—Joe Dante, for *Gremlins*
Special Effects—Chris Walas, for *Gremlins*
Juvenile Actor—Noah Hathaway, for *The Neverending Story*
Writing—James Cameron and Gale Anne Hurd, for *The Terminator*
Music—Jerry Goldsmith, for *Gremlins*
Costumes—Bob Ringwood, for *Dune*
Makeup—Stan Winston, for *The Terminator*
President's Award—Jack Arnold
George Pal Memorial Award—Douglas Trumbull

1985 (1986)

SF Film—*Aliens*
Fantasy Film—*The Boy Who Could Fly*
Horror Film—*The Fly*

1987 (1988)

SF Film—*Robocop*
Fantasy Film—*The Princess Bride*, screenplay by William Goldman
Horror Film—*The Lost Boys*
Actor—Jack Nicholson, for *The Witches of Eastwick*
Actress—Jessica Tandy, for *Batteries Not Included*
Supporting Actor—Richard Dawson, for *The Running Man*
Supporting Actress—Anne Ramsey, for *Throw Momma From the Train*
Juvenile Actor—Kirk Cameron, for *Like Father, Like Son*
Director—Paul Verhoeven, for *Robocop*
Writing—Michael Miner and Ed Neumier, for *Robocop*
Makeup—Rob Bottin and Stephan Dupuis, for *Robocop*
Special Effects—Peter Kuran, Phil Tippit, Rob Bottin, and Rocco Gioffre, for *Robocop*
Costumes—Phyllis Dalton, for *The Princess Bride*
Music—Alan Silvestri, for *Predator*
George Pal Memorial Award—Larry Cohen, for contributions to genre filmmaking
President's Award—Mike Jittlov and Richard Kaye, for *The Wizard of Speed and Time*
Life Career Award—Roger Corman
Outstanding Service Award—Frank Gueringer, for his services to the Academy

1988 (1989)

SF Film—*Alien Nation*
Fantasy Film—*Who Framed Roger Rabbit?*, screenplay by Jeffrey Price and Peter S. Seaman
Horror Film—*Beetlejuice*
TV Series—*Star Trek: The Next Generation*

Actor—Tom Hanks, for *BIG*
Actress—Catherine Hicks, for *Childsplay*
Supporting Actor—Robert Loggia, for *BIG*
Supporting Actress—Sylvia Sydney, for *Beetlejuice*
Juvenile Actor—Fred Savage, for *Vice Versa*
TV Actor—Patrick Stewart, for *Star Trek: The Next Generation*
TV Actress—Linda Hamilton, for *Beauty and the Beast*
Director—Robert Zemeckis, for *Who Framed Roger Rabbit?*
Writing—Gary Ross and Anne Spielberg, for *BIG*
Music—Christopher Young, for *Hellbound: Hellraiser II*
Costumes—Barbara Lane, for *Willow*
Makeup—Ve Neill, Steve Laporte, and Robert Short, for *Beetlejuice*
Special Effects—George Gibbs, Industrial Light and Magic, Ken Ralston, and Richard Williams, for *Who Framed Roger Rabbit?*
George Pal Memorial Award—David Cronenberg
President's Award—Carrie Fisher
Outstanding Service Award—Frank and Bobbie Bresee, for their services to the Academy
Life Career Award—Ray Walston

1989/90 (1991)

SF Film—*Total Recall*
Fantasy Film—*Ghost*
Horror Film—*Arachnophobia*
George Pal Memorial Award—Gene Roddenberry
Special Award—Ray Harryhausen
Outstanding Service Award—Frank & Delores Costa
Life Career Award—Arnold Schwarznegger
President's Award—Robert Shayne

1991 (1992)

SF Film—*Terminator 2: Judgment Day*
Fantasy Film—*Edward Scissorhands*
Horror Film—*Silence of the Lambs*
Actor—Anthony Hopkins, for *Silence of the Lambs*
Actress—Linda Hamilton, for *Terminator 2: Judgment Day*
Life Career Award—Arnold Schwarznegger
George Pal Memorial Award—Gene Roddenberry
Special Lifetime Achievement Award—Ray Harryhausen

120. THE SATURN AWARD (II)
(UNITED STATES)

The Saturn Award was sponsored by the Forbidden Planet Bookstore in New York City, as voted upon by store customers. The physical award consisted of "a plastic bowler's hat on a pedestal." Only one award presentation is known. This award should not be confused with the Saturn Awards for SF films.

THE SATURN AWARDS

1982 (1983)

SF Novel—*2010: Odyssey Two*, by Arthur C. Clarke
Fantasy Novel—*The One Tree*, by Stephen R. Donaldson
Short Story—"Myths of the Near Future," by J. G. Ballard
Anthology—*Storm Season*, Robert Asprin, ed.
New Writer—Donald Kingsbury
Magazine—*The Magazine of Fantasy & Science Fiction*, Edward L. Ferman, ed.
Book Cover Artist—Michael Whelan, for *2010: Odyssey Two*, by Arthur C. Clarke

Awards discontinued.

121. THE SCIENCE FICTION & FANTASY WORKSHOP AWARD
(UNITED STATES)

THE SCIENCE FICTION & FANTASY WORKSHOP AWARDS

1986 (1987)
Best Short Story Editor—Edward L. Ferman
Best Book Editor—Susan Allison

122. THE SCIENCE FICTION BOOK CLUB AWARD
(UNITED STATES)

The Science Fiction Book Club Award is given and voted upon by members of the Science Fiction Book Club, honoring the best SF book of the previous year. The prize consists of a trophy representing several upright glass books.

THE SCIENCE FICTION BOOK CLUB AWARDS

1986 (1987)—*Killashandra*, by Anne McCaffrey
1987 (1988)—*The Mirror of Her Dreams*, by Stephen R. Donaldson

1988 (1989)
Winner—*A Man Rides Through*, by Stephen R. Donaldson
2nd—*Prelude to Foundation*, by Isaac Asimov
3rd—*Darkmage*, by Barbara Hambly

1989 (1990)
Winner—*Dragonsdawn*, by Anne McCaffrey
2nd—*The Dragonbone Chair*, by Tad Williams
3rd—*Hatrack River*, by Orson Scott Card

1990 (1991)
Winner—*Renegades of Pern*, by Anne McCaffrey
2nd—*Stranger in a Strange Land*, by Robert A. Heinlein
3rd—*The Rowan*, by Anne McCaffrey

123. *THE SCIENCE FICTION CHRONICLE* AWARD
(UNITED STATES)

The *Science Fiction Chronicle* Awards are sponsored by the magazine *Science Fiction Chronicle* and its editor, Andrew Porter, and, like the *Locus* Awards, are voted upon by readers of the magazine.

THE SCIENCE FICTION CHRONICLE AWARDS

1981 (1982)
Novel—*The Claw of the Conciliator*, by Gene Wolfe
Novella—"In the Western Tradition," by Phyllis Eisenstein
Novelette—"Mummer Kiss," by Michael Swanwick
Short Story—"The Pusher," by John Varley
Editor—Edward L. Ferman
Artist—Michael Whelan
Dramatic Presentation—*Raiders of the Lost Ark*, screenplay by Lawrence Kasdan
Fanzine—*Science Fiction Chronicle*, Andrew Porter, ed.

Fan Writer—Richard E. Geis
Fan Artist (Fanzines)—Alexis Gilliland
Fan Artist (Conventions)—Victoria Poyser
Convention—Denvention 2

1982 (1983)

Novel—*The Sword of the Lictor*, by Gene Wolfe
Novella—"Souls," by Joanna Russ
Novelette—"Fire Watch," by Connie Willis
Short Story—"Petra," by Greg Bear
Editor—Edward L. Ferman
Artist—Michael Whelan
Dramatic Presentation—*Blade Runner*, screenplay by Hampton Fancher and David Peoples
Fanzine—*File 770*, Mike Glyer, ed.
Fan Artist (Fanzines)—Alexis Gilliland
Fan Artist (Conventions)—No award
Semiprozine—*Science Fiction Chronicle*, Andrew Porter, ed.
Convention—World Fantasy Convention 1982

1983 (1984)

Novel—*The Anubis Gates*, by Tim Powers
Novella—"Her Habiline Husband," by Michael Bishop
Novelette—"Black Air," by Kim Stanley Robinson
Short Story—"The Peacemaker," by Gardner Dozois
Editor (Magazines)—Edward L. Ferman
Editor (Books)—David Hartwell
Artist—Michael Whelan
Fanzine—*File 770*, Mike Glyer, ed.
Fan Writer—Richard E. Geis
Fan Artist—Alexis Gilliland
Semiprozine—*Science Fiction Chronicle*, Andrew I. Porter, ed.
Cover (Books)—Ace Books, Gene Mydlowski, art ed.
Cover (Magazines)—*Analog*, Ralph Rubino, art ed.
Most Attractive Female Writer—Tanith Lee
Most Attractive Male Writer—(tie) Harlan Ellison; Thomas Monteleone
Most Attractive Female Artist—Dawn Wilson
Most Attractive Male Artist—Don Maitz
Most Attractive Female Editor—Susan Allison
Most Attractive Male Editor—David Hartwell
Most Attractive Female Fan—Tess Kissinger
Most Attractive Male Fan—Jean Gonzalez
Best Buns (Either Gender)—Douglas E. Winter

1984 (1985)

Novel—*Neuromancer*, by William Gibson
Novella—"Press ENTER ■," by John Varley
Novelette—"Bloodchild," by Octavia E. Butler
Short Story—"Salvador," by Lucius Shepard
Editor (Magazines)—Edward L. Ferman
Editor (Books)—Terry Carr
Artist—Michael Whelan
Dramatic Presentation—*2010: Odyssey Two*, screenplay by Peter Hyams
Fanzine—*File 770*, Mike Glyer, ed.
Fan Writer—Richard E. Geis
Fan Artist—Brad Foster
Semiprozine—*Science Fiction Chronicle*, Andrew Porter, ed.

1985 (1986)

Novel—*Ender's Game*, by Orson Scott Card
Novella—"The Only Neat Thing to Do," by James Tiptree, Jr.

Reginald's Science Fiction & Fantasy Awards, Third Edition

Novelette—"Paper Dragons," by James P. Blaylock
Short Story—"Portraits of His Children," by George R. R. Martin
Editor (Magazines)—Shawna McCarthy
Editor (Books)—Judy-Lynn del Rey
Artist—Michael Whelan
Dramatic Presentation—*Back to the Future*, screenplay by Robert Zemeckis and Bob Gale
Fanzine—*File 770*, Mike Glyer, ed.
Fan Writer—Richard E. Geis
Fan Artist—Brad Foster
Semiprozine—*Science Fiction Chronicle*, Andrew Porter, ed.

1986 (1987)

Novel—*Speaker for the Dead*, by Orson Scott Card
Novella—"R and R," by Lucius Shepard
Novelette—"Aymara," by Lucius Shepard
Short Story—"Pretty Boy Crossover," by Pat Cadigan
Editor (Magazines)—Gardner Dozois
Editor (Books)—David Hartwell
Artist—Michael Whelan
Dramatic Presentation—*Aliens*, James Cameron, Writer and director
Fanzine—*Ansible*, Dave Langford, ed.
Fan Writer—Dave Langford
Fan Artist—Brad Foster
Semiprozine—*Science Fiction Chronicle*, Andrew Porter, ed.

1987 (1988)

Novel—*The Urth of the New Sun*, by Gene Wolfe
Novella—"The Secret Sharer," by Robert Silverberg
Novelette—"The Evening and the Morning and the Night," by Octavia E. Butler
Short Story—"The Circular Library of Stones," by Carol Emshwiller
Editor (Magazines)—Gardner Dozois
Editor (Books)—David Hartwell
Artist—Michael Whelan
Dramatic Presentation—*The Princess Bride*, screenplay by William Goldman
Fanzine—*Izzard*, Patrick and Teresa Nielsen Hayden, eds.
Fan Writer—Teresa Nielsen Hayden
Fan Artist—Arthur "ATom" Thompson
Semiprozine—*Science Fiction Chronicle*, Andrew Porter, ed.

1988 (1989)

Novel—*Cyteen*, by C. J. Cherryh
Novella—"Last of the Winnebagos," by Connie Willis
Novelette—"Schrödinger's Kitten," by George Alec Effinger
Short Story—"Kirinyaga," by Mike Resnick
Dramatic Presentation—*Who Framed Roger Rabbit?*, screenplay by Jeffrey Price and Peter S. Seaman
Artist—Don Maitz
Editor (Magazines)—Edward L. Ferman
Editor (Books)—David Hartwell
Semiprozine—*Science Fiction Chronicle*, Andrew Porter, ed.
Fanzine—*Fosfax*, Timothy Lane, ed.
Fan Writer—Mike Glyer
Fan Artist—Brad Foster

1989 (1990)

Novel—*A Fire in the Sun*, by George Alec Effinger
Novella—"The Mountains of Mourning," by Lois McMaster Bujold
Novelette—"For I Have Touched the Sky," by Mike Resnick
Short Story—"Dori Bangs," by Bruce Sterling
Dramatic Presentation—*Field of Dreams*

Artist—Tom Canty
Editor (Magazines)—Gardner Dozois
Editor (Books)—Beth Meacham
Semiprozine—*Science Fiction Chronicle*, Andrew Porter, ed.
Fanzine—*Lan's Lantern*, George Laskowski, ed.
Fan Writer—Dave Langford
Fan Artist—Teddy Harvia

1990 (1991)

Novel—*The Fall of Hyperion*, by Dan Simmons
Novella—"Bully!" by Mike Resnick
Novelette—"The Manamouki," by Mike Resnick
Short Story—"Bears Discover Fire," by Terry Bisson
Dramatic Presentation—*Total Recall*
Artist—Michael Whelan
Editor (Magazines)—Edward Ferman
Editor (Books)—Ellen Datlow
Semiprozine—*Science Fiction Chronicle*, Andrew Porter, ed.
Fanzine—*Lan's Lantern*, George Laskowski, ed.
Fan Writer—Dave Langford
Fan Artist—Teddy Harvia

1991 (1992)

Novel—*Stations of the Tide*, by Michael Swanwick
Novella—"Beggars in Spain," by Nancy Kress
Novelette—"Gate of Faces," by Ray Aldridge
Short Story—"Vinland the Dream," by Kim Stanley Robinson
Dramatic Presentation—*Terminator 2*
Artist—Michael Whelan
Editor (Magazines)—Gardner Dozois
Editor (Books)—Ellen Datlow
Semiprozine—*Science Fiction Chronicle*, Andrew Porter, ed.
Fanzine—*Ansible*, Dave Langford, ed.
Fan Writer—Dave Langford
Fan Artist—Teddy Harvia

124. THE SCIENCE FICTION CLUB DEUTSCHLAND AWARD (GERMANY)

This German equivalent to the American Hugo Award is given by the SF Club Deutschland (SFCD), the largest SF fan club in Germany.

THE SCIENCE FICTION CLUB DEUTSCHLAND AWARDS

1988 (1989)

Novel—*Kiezkoller*, by Fritz Schmoll
Short Fiction—"Der Kase" ("A Piece of Cheese"), by Rainer Erler

1990 (1991)

Novel—*Den Uberlebenden* (*To the Survivors*), by Maria J. Pfannholz
Short Fiction—"Kaperle Ist Wieder DA" ("Hanswurst Is Back Again"), by Gert Prokop

Reginald's Science Fiction & Fantasy Awards, Third Edition

125. THE SCIENCE FICTION GAMES OF THE YEAR AWARD
(UNITED STATES)

First awarded in 1988, these awards are voted upon by jury selection and presented at Davis Magazines awards reception in New York.

THE SCIENCE FICTION GAMES OF THE YEAR AWARDS

1987 (1988)—*Aliens* (Activision); *Cathedral* (Mattel board game); *Defender of the Crown* (Cinemaware computer game); *Dungeonquest* (Games Workshop board game); *Maniac Mansion* (Lucasfilms Games computer game); *Solarquest* (Western Publishing board game); *Shogun* (Milton Bradley board game); *Traveller: 2300* (Games Designer Workshop role-playing game)

---

126. THE SCIENCE FICTION WRITERS OF EARTH SHORT STORY CONTEST
(UNITED STATES)

First place is $100, second is $50, third is $25.

THE SCIENCE FICTION WRITERS OF EARTH AWARDS

1984 (1985)
- **1st**—"Emotion Sickness," by Mark Rhodes
- **2nd**—"The Taking of L-11 and the Last Lady," by Jean Bruce
- **3rd**—"Mind Link," by J. D. Brumbaugh

1985 (1986)
- **1st**—"Song of Wyness," by Catherine Carley
- **2nd**—"Cheating the Devil," by Michaelene Pendleton
- **3rd**—"Merchants of Magick," by L. Dean James

1986 (1987)
- **1st**—"The Wound That Would Not Be Healed," by Eric Carl Wolf
- **2nd**—"The Euphemism," by Stephen V. Ramey
- **3rd**—"Story Drum," by William Gagliani

1987 (1988)
- **1st**—"The Bureau of Reflections," by Ron A. Nyren
- **2nd**—"Live In Concert," by Mary Rosenblum
- **3rd**—"A Simple Matter of Justice," by David F. Hamilton

1988 (1989)
- **1st**—"If Thine Eye Be Single," by E. Rose Sabin
- **2nd**—"Brother Billy's Good News," by K. D. Wentworth
- **3rd**—"Candles on the Pond," by Sue Ellen Sloca

1989 (1990)
- **1st**—"Fusion Effects," by Mary Bachran
- **2nd**—"What Green Altar," by Richard Embs
- **3rd**—"Winds of Quetzalcoatl," by Gary Kim Hayes

1990 (1991)
- **1st**—"Happy Ever After," by Marjorie Richter
- **2nd**—"The Implications of a Grand Unified Theory," by Stephen V. Ramey
- **3rd**—"The Weeders," by Corinne A. Dwyer

Special "Author of the '80s" Contest
1st—"The Misfit," by E. Rose Sabin
2nd—"Due Process," by K. D. Wentworth
3rd—"Love Fix," by Conda V. Douglas

1991 (1992)
1st—"Dust to Dust," by Kent Johnson
2nd—"The Woman in Red," by Rhonda Eikamp
3rd—"The Clinic," by Susana Alicia Sanchez

127. THE SEIUN TAISHO
(JAPAN)

The Seiun Taisho (Seiun Award), the Japanese equivalent of the American Hugo Award, is voted upon by attending members of the annual Japanese National Science Fiction Convention. The physical prize differs from year to year. In 1982 (1983), the award was a golden rocket mounted on a wooden base with a plaque attached to it, plus a certificate. In 1988 (1989) a saki set (4 cups and a carafe) were given with the winners' names inscribed on them. The Takumi Shibano Award is the equivalent of the American Big Heart Award, and is given to a Japanese professional or fan whose contributions to Japanese science fiction have previously gone unrewarded.

THE SEIUN TAISHO

1980 (1981)
Foreign Novel—*Inherit the Stars*, by James P. Hogan (Ireland/USA)
Foreign Novelette—"Relic of Empire," by Larry Niven (United States)

1981 (1982)
Foreign Novel—*The Genesis Machine*, by James P. Hogan (Ireland/USA)
Foreign Novelette—"The Brave Little Toaster," by Thomas M. Disch (United States)

1982 (1983)
Foreign Novel—*Dragon's Egg*, by Robert L. Forward (United States)
Foreign Novelette—"Nightflyers," by George R. R. Martin (United States)
Novel—*Sayonara Jupiter* (*Goodbye Jupiter*), by Sakyo Komatsu
Novelette—"Kotabazukai shi" ("The Word Handler"), by Chohei Kambayashi
Dramatic Presentation—*Blade Runner*, screenplay by Hampton Fancher and David Peoples
Comics—Moto Hagio
Artist—Yoshitaka Amano

1983 (1984)
Foreign Novel—*Garments of Caean*, by Barrington Bayley (United Kingdom)
Foreign Novelette—"The Unicorn Variations," by Roger Zelazny (United States)
Novel—*Teki wa Kaizoku—Kaizoku Ban* (*The Enemy Are Pirates—Pirate Edition*), by Chohei Kambayashi
Novelette—"Super Phoenix," by Chohei Kambayashi
Dramatic Presentation—*The Dark Crystal*
Comics—*Domo* (*Go Ahead*), by Katsuhiro Ootomo
Artist—Yoshitaka Amano
Fanzine—*Horaizuma* Keio University SF Club, eds.
Shibano Award—Takayuki Tatsumi and Tetsu Yano

1984 (1985)
Foreign Novel—*The Zen Gun*, by Barrington Bayley (United Kingdom)
Foreign Novelette—No award
Novel—*Sento Yosei Yukikaze* (*The Icewind Train*), by Chohei Kambayashi
Novelette—No award

Dramatic Presentation—*Kaze no Tani no Nashika* (*Apprentices in the Valley of Wind*)
Comics—*X+Y*, by Moto Hagio
Artist—Yoshitaka Amano
Fanzine—*Palantir*, Yoshito Kobayashi, ed.
Nonfiction—*Koseiki no Sekai (Jewel World)*, by Dr. Fujio Ishihara

1985 (1986)

Foreign Novel—*The Elric Saga*, by Michael Moorcock (United Kingdom)
Foreign Novelette—No award
Novel—*Dirty Pair no Dai Gyakuten* (*The Dirty Pair's Upset*), by Haruka Takachiho
Novelette—"Lemon Pie Oyashiki Yokocho 0 Banchi" ("Address: 0 Lemon Pie Alley"), by Masahiro Noda
Dramatic Presentation—*Back to the Future*
Comics—*Appleseed*, by Masamune Shiro
Artist—Yoshitaka Amano
Fanzine—*Perceptron*, Nagoya University SF Research Group, eds.
Nonfiction—*Science Fiction Hero Sagas*, by Kensho Ikeda

1986 (1987)

Foreign Novel—*Neuromancer*, by William Gibson (Canada)
Foreign Novelette—"Press ENTER ■," by John Varley (United States)
Novel—*Prism*, by Chohei Kambayashi
Novelette—"Martian Railroad 19," by Kosyu Tani
Dramatic Presentation—*Brazil*
Comics—*Urusai Yatura (Be Quiet, Brats)*, by Rumiko Takahashi
Nonfiction—"Dr. Ishihara's Science Fiction Laboratory," by Dr. Fujio Ishihara
Shibano Award—Ken Yamaoka

1987 (1988)

Foreign Novel—*Norstrilia*, by Cordwainer Smith (United States)
Foreign Novelette—"The Only Neat Thing To Do," by James Tiptree, Jr. (United States)
Novel—*Tales of the Galactic Hero* Dekalogy, by Yoshiki Tanaka
Novelette—"Concert on the Mountain," by Norio Nakai
Dramatic Presentation—*Wings of Oneamis*
Artist—Jun Suemi
Comics—*Super-Man R*
Nonfiction—*Wizardry Diary*, by Tetsu Yano
Fanzine—*Talking Heads*

1988 (1989)

Foreign Novel—*Footfall*, by Larry Niven (United States)
Foreign Novelette—"Eye For Eye," by Orson Scott Card (United States)
Novel—*Babylonia Wave*, by Akira Hori
Short Fiction—"Eye of the Jellyfish," by Jin Kusagami
Media—*Tororo Next Door*, Hayao Miyazaki, director
Comics—*Forest of the Mermaid*, by Rumiko Takahashi
Artist—Hiroyuki Kato; Keisuke Goto
Nonfiction—*Writing Space Opera*, by Masahiro Noda
Special Award—Osamu Tezuka

1989 (1990)

Foreign Novel—*Collision Course/Collision with Chronos*, by Barrington J. Bayley (United Kingdom)
Foreign Short Story—"Think Blue, Count Two," by Cordwainer Smith (United States)
Foreign Nonfiction—*Future Magic*, by Robert L. Forward (United States)
Novel—*The Lion That Ate the Crescent Moon*, by Baku Yumemakura
Short Fiction—"Aqua Planet," by Mariko Ohara
Media—*Gunbuster*
Artist—Katsumi Michihara
Comics—*So What?*, by Megumi Wakatsuki

Fanzine—*Paradox*
Shibano Award—Shizuo Matsumiya; Shinji Maki

1990 (1991)
Foreign Novel—*The Uplift War*, by David Brin (United States)
Foreign Short Story—"Schrödinger's Kitten," by George Alec Effinger (United States)
Novel—*Hybrid Child*, by Mariko Ohara
Short Fiction—"Jodan no Tsuki o Kurau Inoshishi," by Baku Yumemakura
Media—*Ginga-Ulchu Odyssey* (*Galactic Odyssey*), written and narrated by Gregory Benford (United States)
Artist—Eiji Yokoyama
Comics—*Galactic Supermarket*, by Eiji Yokoyama
Nonfiction—*SF Handbook*
Fanzine—*Starbase Kobe Books*
Shibano Award—Yasuo Kawai; Norihiro Misaki; Koichi Ohashi

128. THE SHASTA PUBLISHERS/POCKET BOOKS CONTEST
(UNITED STATES)

Shasta Publishers and Pocket Books sponsored this one-time contest for best original science fiction novel of the year, which was won by Philip José Farmer for the book that eventually became the Riverworld series. In one of the major scandals of SF speciality publishing, Farmer was never paid for his novel, and Shasta shut down a few years later, finally going out of business in 1957.

THE SHASTA PUBLISHERS/POCKET BOOKS SCIENCE FICTION NOVEL CONTEST

1952—*I Owe for the Flesh*, by Philip José Farmer

129. THE SKYLARK AWARD
(UNITED STATES)

The Skylark Award, also called The Edward E. "Doc" Smith Memorial Award, honors the Lensman series by Smith (1890-1965), and is voted upon by the New England Science Fiction Association (NESFA) to recognize significant contributions to the science fiction. The physical award consists of a trophy of a magnifying glass mounted on a wooden base.

THE SKYLARK AWARDS

1966—Frederik Pohl
1967—Isaac Asimov
1968—John W. Campbell, Jr.
1969—Hal Clement
1970—Judy-Lynn Benjamin del Rey
1971—No award
1972—Lester del Rey
1973—Larry Niven
1974—Ben Bova
1975—Gordon R. Dickson
1976—Anne McCaffrey
1977—Jack Gaughan
1978—Spider Robinson
1979—David Gerrold
1980—Jack L. Chalker
1981—Frank Kelly Freas
1982—Poul Anderson

1983—Andre Norton
1984—Robert Silverberg
1985—Jack Williamson
1986—Wilson "Bob" Tucker
1987—Vincent DiFate
1988—C. J. Cherryh
1989—Gene Wolfe
1990—Jane Yolen
1991—David Cherry
1992—Orson Scott Card

130. THE SOCCON AWARD
(USSR/RUSSIA)

The Soccon Awards were given at SocCon, the first International Congress of SF for Eastern Bloc countries (Romania, Russia, Bulgaria, East Germany, Czechoslovakia, and Poland), being voted upon by a convention committee.

THE SOCCON AWARDS

1988 (1989)

Fan—Andrei E. Chertkov and Sergey Berezhnoy, for creating the fanzine *Oversun-Inform*, and contributing to the development of fandom in the Soviet Union
Fanzine—*ABS-Panorama*, Vadim Kazakov, ed.
Special Award—Leonid Kurtis, Chief Organizer of SocCon

131. THE SOUTHPAW AWARD
(UNITED STATES)

The Southpaw Award is given each year at DeepSouthCon. The awards may have been discontinued.

THE SOUTHPAW AWARDS

1982 (1983)

Writer—Stephen Carlburg
Artist—Dave Ryan
Humorist—Warren Baddig
Achievement in APA Administration—Lon Atkins
Best APA—SFPA

Awards discontinued?

132. SVENSKA SF PRISET
[THE SWEDISH SCIENCE FICTION AND FANTASY ACHIEVEMENT AWARD]
(SWEDEN)

The Swedish Science Fiction and Fantasy Achievement Awards are voted upon by members of the Scandinavian Science Fiction Association (SSFA) and members of the Swedish National Science Fiction Convention.

THE SVENSKA SF PRISET AWARDS

1985 (1986)
Novel—*Kyss Mej Dodligt* (*Kiss Me Deadly*), by Carl Johan DeGeer
Short Story—Bertil Martensson
Foreign Novel—*Inverted World*, by Christopher Priest (United Kingdom)

133. THE TURNER TOMORROW AWARD
(UNITED STATES)

This one-time prize of $500,000 for best environmental SF novel was offered by Ted Turner through his Turner Broadcasting Co. Also included in the package is guaranteed hardcover publication of the book by Bantam Books, and a motion picture adaptation of the story. Judges were: William Styron, Ray Bradbury, Peter Matthiessen, Wallace Stegner, Carlos Fuentes, Nadine Gordimer, Rodney Hall, and Ian and Betty Ballantine.

THE TURNER TOMORROW AWARDS

1991
Grand Prize—*Ishmael*, by Daniel Quinn
Honorable Mention—*The Bully Pulpit*, by Andrew Goldblatt; *Natural Enemies*, by Sara Cameron; *Necessary Risks*, by Janet Keller

134. THE TWILIGHT DIMENSION AWARD
(UNITED STATES)

The Twilight Dimension Awards were given by *Rod Serling's The Twilight Zone Magazine* for best horror book and film of the year, having been selected by readers of that magazine. With the cessation of this publication, resumption of the awards seems unlikely.

THE TWILIGHT DIMENSION AWARDS

1984 (1985)
Film—*Indiana Jones and the Temple of Doom*
Novel—*The Talisman*, by Stephen King and Peter Straub
Short Story—"Coming Soon to a Theatre Near You," by David J. Schow
Awards discontinued.

135. THE WETZLAR FANTASTIK PREIS
(GERMANY)

The Wetzlar Fantastik Preis is presented by the city of Wetzlar, Germany, to honor the best SF novel of the previous year.

THE WETZLAR FANTASTIK PREIS

1990 (1991)—*Erzahler der Nacht* (*Storyteller of the Night*), by Rafik Schami

Reginald's Science Fiction & Fantasy Awards, Third Edition

136. THE WILL EISNER COMIC INDUSTRY AWARD
(UNITED STATES)

The Will Eisner Awards are the comic book industry's equivalent of the Hugo Award. They are named for famed illustrator Will Eisner, and are given at the annual San Diego Comic-Con. The finalists for the awards are nominated and voted upon by a blue-ribbon committee of professionals in the field.

THE WILL EISNER COMIC INDUSTRY AWARDS

1987 (1988)

Single Issue—*Gumby Summer Fun Special*
Artist—Steve Rude, for *Nexus*
Writer—Alan Moore, for *Watchmen*
Writer/Artist Team—Alan Moore and Dave Gibbons, for *Watchmen*
Art Team—Steve Rude, Willie Blyberg, and Ken Steacy, for *Space Ghost Special*
Graphic Album—*Watchmen*, written by Alan Moore, illustrated by Dave Gibbons
Continuing Series—*Concrete*, written and illustrated by Paul Chadwick
B&W Series—*Concrete*, written and illustrated by Paul Chadwick
Finite Series—Watchmen, written by Alan Moore, illustrated by Dave Gibbons
New Series—*Concrete*, written and illustrated by Paul Chadwick
Hall of Fame Inductees—Milton Caniff

1988 (1989)

Single Issue—*Kings in Disguise* #1
Artist—Brian Bolland, for *The Killing Joke*
Writer—Alan Moore, for *The Killing Joke*
Writer/Artist Team—Paul Chadwick, for *Concrete*
Art Team—Alan Davis and Paul Neary, for *Excalibur*
Graphic Album—The Killing Joke, written by Alan Moore, illustrated by Brian Bolland
Continuing Series—*Concrete*, written and illustrated by Paul Chadwick
B&W Series—*Concrete*, written and illustrated by Paul Chadwick
Finite Series—*Silver Surfer*
New Series—*Kings in Disguise*
Hall of Fame Inductees—Harvey Kurtzman

1990 (1991)

Single Issue or Story—*Concrete Celebrates Earth Day*, by Paul Chadwick, Charles Vess, and Moebius
B&W Series—*Xenozoic Tales*, by Mark Schultz
Continuing Series—*Sandman*, written by Neil Gaiman, illustrated by various artists
Finite Series—*Give Me Liberty*, written by Frank Miller, illustrated by Dave Gibbons
Graphic Album (New)—*Elektra Lives Again*, by Frank Miller & Lynn Varley
Graphic Album (Reprint)—*Sandman: The Doll's House*, by Neil Gaiman, Mike Dringenberg, and Malcolm Jones III
Writer—Neil Gaiman
Artist—Steve Rude
Inker—Al Williamson
Writer/Artist Team—Frank Miller and Geof Darrow
Hall of Fame Inductees—Robert Crumb and Alex Toth

1991 (1992)

Single Issue or Story—"Season of Mists," written by Neil Gaiman, illustrated by various artists, in *Sandman* #22-28.
Continuing Series—*Sandman*, written by Neil Gaiman, illustrated by various artists
Finite Series—*Concrete: Fragile Creatures*, written and illustrated by Paul Chadwick
Anthology—*Dark Horse Presents*, edited by Randy Stradley
Graphic Album (New Material)—*To the Heart of the Storm*, written and illustrated by Will Eisner

Graphic Album (Reprint)—*Maus II: And Here My Troubles Began*, written and illustrated by Art Spiegelman
Comic Strip Collection—*The Revenge of the Baby-sat*, written and illustrated by Bill Watterson
Humor Publication—*Groo the Wanderer*, written and illustrated by Sergio Aragonés, with Mark Evanier
Writer—Neil Gaiman, for *Sandman*; *Books of Magic*; and *Miracleman*
Artist—Simon Bisley, for *Batman/Judge Dredd: Judgment on Gotham*
Colorist—Steve Oliff, for *Legends of the Dark Knight* and *Akira*
Writer/Artist Team—Peter David and Dale Keown, for *The Incredible Hulk*
Editor—Karen Berger, for *Sandman*; *Shade, the Changing Man*; *Kid Eternity*; and *Books of Magic*
Cover Artist—Brian Bolland, for *Animal Man*
Comics-Related Book—*From Aargh! to Zap!: Harvey Kurtzman's Visual History of the Comics*, by Harvey Kurtzman
Comics-Related Periodical—*Comics Buyers Guide*, Don and Maggie Thompson, eds.
Comics-Related Product—Sandman statue, by Randy Bowen
Hall of Fame Inductees—Jerry Siegel; Joe Shuster; Wally Wood

137. THE WORLD FANTASY AWARD
[THE HOWARD AWARD]
(UNITED STATES)

The World Fantasy Award (also called the Howard Award) consists of a misshapen metal bust of horror writer Howard Phillips Lovecraft designed by artist Gahan Wilson. Attending and supporting members of the World Fantasy Convention are eligible to nominate potential winners, the final decisions being made by a panel of judges. Only living persons are eligible. Presentations are made at annually at the World Fantasy Convention. In 1984 Donald Wandrei rejected a lifetime achievement award, stating that the statuette represented "a caricature of H. P. Lovecraft."

THE WORLD FANTASY AWARDS

1973/74 (1975)
Novel—*The Forgotten Beasts of Eld*, by Patricia A. McKillip
Short Fiction—"Pages From a Young Girl's Diary," by Robert Aickman
Single Author Collection/Anthology—*Worse Things Waiting*, by Manly Wade Wellman
Artist—Lee Brown Coye
Lifetime Achievement—Robert Bloch
Special Award (Professional)—Ian and Betty Ballantine, for publishing excellence
Special Award (Nonprofessional)—Stuart David Schiff, for *Whispers*

1975 (1976)
Novel—*Bid Time Return*, by Richard Matheson
Short Fiction—"Belsen Express," by Fritz Leiber
Single Author Collection/Anthology—*The Enquiries of Dr. Esterhazy*, by Avram Davidson
Artist—Frank Frazetta
Lifetime Achievement—Fritz Leiber
Special Award (Professional)—Donald M. Grant, for publishing excellence
Special Award (Nonprofessional)—Carcosa Publishers

1976 (1977)
Novel—*Doctor Rat*, by William Kotzwinkle
Short Fiction—"There's a Long, Long Trail A-Winding," by Russell Kirk
Single Author Collection/Anthology—*Frights*, edited by Kirby McCauley
Artist—Roger Dean
Lifetime Achievement—Ray Bradbury
Special Award (Professional)—Alternate World Recordings

Special Award (Nonprofessional)—Stuart David Schiff, for *Whispers*

1977 (1978)
Novel—*Our Lady of Darkness*, by Fritz Leiber
Short Fiction—"The Chimney," by Ramsey Campbell
Single Author Collection/Anthology—*Murgunstruum and Others*, by Hugh B. Cave
Artist—Lee Brown Coye
Lifetime Achievement—Frank Belknap Long
Special Award (Professional)—Everett F. Bleiler
Special Award (Nonprofessional)—Robert Weinberg

1978 (1979)
Novel—*Gloriana*, by Michael Moorcock
Short Fiction—"Naples," by Avram Davidson
Single Author Collection/Anthology—*Shadows*, by Charles L. Grant
Artist—Alicia Austin; Dale Enzenbacher
Lifetime Achievement—Jorge Luis Borges
Special Award (Professional)—Edward L. Ferman, for *The Magazine of Fantasy & Science Fiction*
Special Award (Nonprofessional)—Donald H. Tuck
Special Award—Kirby McCauley, for starting the World Fantasy Convention

1979 (1980)
Novel—*Watchtower*, by Elizabeth A. Lynn
Short Fiction—(tie) "The Woman Who Loved the Moon," by Elizabeth A. Lynn; "Mackintosh Willy," by Ramsey Campbell
Single Author Collection/Anthology—*Amazons!*, by Jessica Amanda Salmonson
Artist—Don Maitz
Lifetime Achievement—Manly Wade Wellman
Special Award (Professional)—Donald M. Grant, for publishing excellence
Special Award (Nonprofessional)—Paul C. Allen

1980 (1981)
Novel—*The Shadow of the Torturer*, by Gene Wolfe
Short Fiction—"The Ugly Chickens," by Howard Waldrop
Single Author Collection/Anthology—*Dark Forces*, edited by Kirby McCauley
Artist—Michael Whelan
Lifetime Achievement—C. L. Moore
Special Award (Professional)—Donald A. Wollheim
Special Award (Nonprofessional)—Pat Cadigan and Arnold Fenner
Special Award—Gahan Wilson

1981 (1982)
Novel—*Little, Big*, by John Crowley
Novella—"The Fire When It Comes," by Parke Godwin
Short Story—(tie) "The Dark Country," by Dennis Etchison; "Do the Dead Sing?" by Stephen King
Anthology/Collection—*Elsewhere*, Terri Windling and Mark Allan Arnold, eds.
Artist—Michael Whelan
Lifetime Achievement—Italo Calvino
Special Award (Professional)—Edward L. Ferman, for editing *The Magazine of Fantasy & Science Fiction*
Special Award (Nonprofessional)—Paul Allen and Robert Collins, for *Fantasy Newsletter*
Special Award—Roy G. Krenkel
Special Award—Joseph Payne Brennan

1982 (1983)
Novel—*Nifft the Lean*, by Michael Shea
Novella—(tie) "Beyond All Measure," by Karl Edward Wagner; "Confess the Seasons," by Charles L. Grant

Short Story—"The Gorgon," by Tanith Lee
Anthology/Collection—*Nightmare Seasons*, by Charles L. Grant
Artist—Michael Whelan
Lifetime Achievement—Roald Dahl
Special Award (Professional)—Donald M. Grant, for publishing excellence
Special Award (Nonprofessional)—Stuart David Schiff, for *Whispers*
Special Award—Arkham House Publishers

1983 (1984)

Novel—*The Dragon Waiting*, by John M. Ford
Novella—"Black Air," by Kim Stanley Robinson
Short Story—"Elle est Trois (La Mort)," by Tanith Lee
Anthology/Collection—*High Spirits*, by Robinson Davies
Artist—Steve Gervais
Lifetime Achievement—L. Sprague de Camp, E. Hoffmann Price, Donald Wandrei [refused], Richard Matheson, Jack Vance
Special Award (Professional)—Ian and Betty Ballantine, Joy Chant, George Sharp, and David Larking, for *The High Kings*
Special Award (Nonprofessional)—Stephen Jones and David Sutton, for *Fantasy Tales*
Special Award—Donald M. Grant

1984 (1985)

Novel—(tie) *Mythago Wood*, by Robert Holdstock; *Bridge of Birds*, by Barry Hughart
Novella—"The Unconquered Country," by Geoff Ryman
Short Story—(tie) "Still Life With Scorpion," by Scott Baker; "The Bones Wizard," by Alan Ryan
Anthology/Collection—*Books of Blood, Vols. 1-3*, by Clive Barker
Artist—Edward Gorey
Lifetime Achievement—Theodore Sturgeon
Special Award (Professional)—Chris van Allsburg, for *The Mysteries of Harris Burdick*
Special Award (Nonprofessional)—Stuart David Schiff, for *Whispers*
Special Award—Evangeline Walton

1985 (1986)

Novel—*Song of Kali*, by Dan Simmons
Novella—"Nadelman's God," by T. E. D. Klein
Short Story—"Paper Dragons," by James P. Blaylock
Anthology/Collection—*Imaginary Lands*, by Robin McKinley
Artist—Jeff Jones; Thomas Canty
Lifetime Achievement—Avram Davidson
Special Award (Professional)—Pat LoBrutto
Special Award (Nonprofessional)—Douglas E. Winter
Special Award—Donald A. Wollheim

1986 (1987)

Novel—*Perfume*, by Patrick Suskind
Novella—"Hatrack River," by Orson Scott Card
Short Story—"Red Light," by David J. Schow
Anthology/Collection—*Tales of the Quintana Roo*, by James Tiptree, Jr.
Artist—Robert Gould
Lifetime Achievement—Jack Finney
Special Award (Professional)—Jane Yolen
Special Award (Nonprofessional)—Jeff Conner; W. Paul Ganley
Special Award—Andre Norton

1987 (1988)

Novel—*Replay*, by Ken Grimwood
Novella—"Buffalo Gals, Won't You Come Out Tonight," by Ursula K. Le Guin
Short Story—"Friend's Best Man," by Jonathan Carroll
Anthology/Collection—*The Jaguar Hunter*, by Lucius Shepard

Reginald's Science Fiction & Fantasy Awards, Third Edition

Artist—J. K. Potter
Lifetime Achievement—Everett F. Bleiler
Special Award (Professional)—David G. Hartwell
Special Award (Nonprofessional)—David B. Silva, for *The Horror Show*; Robert and Nancy Garcia, for *American Fantasy*

1988 (1989)

Novel—*Koko*, by Peter Straub
Novella—"The Skin Trade," by George R. R. Martin
Short Story—"Winter Solstice, Camelot Station," by John M. Ford
Collection—(tie) *Storeys from the Old Hotel*, by Gene Wolfe; *Angry Candy*, by Harlan Ellison
Anthology—*The Year's Best Fantasy: First Annual Collection*, Ellen Datlow and Terri Windling, eds.
Artist—Edward Gorey
Lifetime Achievement—Evangeline Walton
Special Award (Professional)—Terri Windling; Robert Weinberg
Special Award (Nonprofessional)—Kristine Kathryn Rusch and Dean Wesley Smith, for *Pulphouse*

1989 (1990)

Novel—*Lyonesse: Madouc*, by Jack Vance
Novella—"Great Work of Time," by John Crowley
Short Fiction—"The Illusionist," by Steven Millhauser
Collection—*Richard Matheson: Collected Stories*, by Richard Matheson
Anthology—*The Year's Best Fantasy: Second Annual Collection*, Ellen Datlow and Terri Windling, eds.
Artist—Thomas Canty
Lifetime Achievement—R. A. Lafferty
Special Award (Professional)—Mark V. Ziesing, for Mark V. Ziesing Publications
Special Award (Nonprofessional)—Peggy Nadramia, for *Grue Magazine*

1990 (1991)

Novel—(tie) *Only Begotten Daughter*, by James Morrow; *Thomas the Rhymer*, by Ellen Kushner
Novella—"Bones," by Pat Murphy
Short Fiction—"A Midsummer Night's Dream," by Neil Gaiman and Charles Vess
Collection—*The Start of the End of it All and Other Stories*, by Carol Emshwiller
Anthology—*Best New Horror*, Stephen Jones and Ramsey Campbell, eds.
Artist—Dave McKean
Lifetime Achievement—Ray Russell
Special Award (Professional)—Arnie Fenner
Special Award (Nonprofessional)—Richard Chizmar, for *Cemetery Dance*

1991 (1992)

Novel—*Boy's Life*, by Robert McCammon
Novella—"The Ragthorn," by Robert Holdstock and Gerry Kilworth
Short Fiction—"The Somewhere Doors," by Fred Chappell
Collection—*The Ends of the Earth*, by Lucius Shepard
Anthology—*The Year's Best Fantasy & Horror: Fourth Annual Collection*, Ellen Datlow and Terri Windling, eds.
Artist—Tim Hildebrandt
Lifetime Achievement—Edd Cartier
Special Award (Professional)—George Scithers and Darrell Schweitzer, for *Weird Tales*
Special Award (Nonprofessional)—W. Paul Ganley, for *Weirdbook*

138. THE WRITERS OF THE PAST AWARD
(UNITED STATES)

The Writers of the Past Award trophy was designed by Curtis J. Wood. Nominees write their names on paper bags and place them on tables. Voters place money in the bags and the person with the most money in his/her bag is the winner. Proceeds benefit the Emergency Medical Fund of The Science Fiction Writers of America (SFWA). Only one award date is known.

THE WRITERS OF THE PAST AWARDS

1987 (1988)—*Venus on the Half-Shell*, by Kilgore Trout (Philip José Farmer)

139. THE ZAUBER ZEIT AWARD
(GERMANY)

Nothing is known about the background of this German award.

THE ZAUBER ZEIT AWARDS

1986 (1987)
SF Novel—*Life, The Universe and Everything*, by Douglas Adams (United Kingdom)
Fantasy Novel—*The Book of Lost Tales*, by J. R. R. Tolkien (United Kingdom)

1990 (1991)
SF Novel—*Tommyknockers*, by Stephen King (United States)
Fantasy Novel—*Little Myth Marker*, by Robert Asprin (United States)

PART TWO
NON-GENRE
AWARDS

140. THE ACADEMY OF FAMILY FILMS AND FAMILY TELEVISION AWARD
(UNITED STATES)

1987—Best TV—*Star Trek: The Next Generation*

141. THE A.D.E.-M.L.A. DISTINGUISHED TEACHING AWARD
(UNITED STATES)

Given by the Modern Language Association.

19??—Richard "Dick" Allen

142. THE AEROSPACE COMMUNICATIONS AWARD
(UNITED STATES)

Given by the American Institute of Aeronautics and Astronautics for contributions in areas such as satellite/ground, space/space communications; this award was established in 1967.

1974—Arthur C. Clarke (Sri Lanka)

143. THE AMERICAN AND NATIONAL BOOK AWARDS
(UNITED STATES)

The American Book Awards, originally The National Book Awards, are presented annually by the Association of American Publishers to honor American books of the "highest literary merit," reprints and translations being ineligible. The prize for first place in each category is $10,000. The awards for SF and fantasy were discontinued after 1980 because the committee felt there were already too many awards in these fields.

1970 (1971)
Children's Literature—*The Marvelous Misadventures of Sebastian*, by Lloyd Alexander

1971 (1972)
Children's Literature—*The Slightly Irregular Fire Engine, or, The Hithering Thithering Djinn*, by Donald Barthelme

1972 (1973)
Fiction—*Chimera*, by John Barth
Children's Literature—*The Farthest Shore*, by Ursula K. Le Guin

1973 (1974)
Children's Literature—*The Court of the Stone Children*, by Eleanor Cameron

1979 (1980)
Children's Paperback Novel—*A Swiftly Tilting Planet*, by Madeleine L'Engle
Hardcover Science Fiction Novel—*Jem*, by Frederik Pohl
Paperback Science Fiction Novel—*The Book of the Dun Cow*, by Walter Wangerin, Jr.

1982 (1983)
Original Paperback—*The Red Magician*, by Lisa Goldstein

144. THE AMERICAN MYSTERY AWARD
(UNITED STATES)

Sponsored by the magazine *Mystery Scene*.

1987—**Best Short Story**—"Soft Monkey," by Harlan Ellison

145. THE AMERICAN STUDIES BOOK PRIZE
(USA/JAPAN)

Sponsored by the United States/Japan Friendship Commission.

1988 (1989)—*Cyberpunk America*, by Takayuki Tatsumi (Japan)

146. THE ANTONIUS PRIZE OF DANISH SOCIETY FOR MENTAL HYGIENE
(DENMARK)

1951—*Cafe Paradize* (film), by Johannes Allen.

147. THE ARTS AND LETTERS AWARD
(UNITED STATES)

Given by the National Institute of Arts and Letters to help writers continue their creative work. The award consists of a $5,000 prize.

1951—Vladimir Nabokov (USSR/France/USA)
1954—Ray Bradbury
1957—Leslie Fiedler
1958—H. L. Gold
1970—Kurt Vonnegut, Jr.

148. THE ATHENAEUM LITERARY AWARD
(UNITED STATES)

Given by the Athenaeum of Philadelphia for writers living within thirty miles of Philadelphia City Hall. Established in 1949, the award consists of a bronze medal, and is voted upon by a committee.

1958—*An Elephant for Aristotle*, by L. Sprague de Camp

149. THE AWA WRITING AWARDS
(UNITED STATES)

Presented by the Aviation/Space Writers Association for outstanding achievements in writing and reporting about aviation and space. The prize is $100 and a scroll and is awarded annually in a number of categories.

1961—**Books (Nonfiction)**—Martin Caidin
1964—**Books (Nonfiction)**—Robert J. Serling
1965—**General Magazines**—Arthur C. Clarke (Sri Lanka)

1965—**Books (Nonfiction)**—Martin Caidin; Robert J. Serling
1967—**Books (Fiction)**—Robert J. Serling
1968—**General Magazines**—Ray Bradbury
1968—**Books (Fiction)**—Martin Caidin
1970—**Books (Nonfiction)**—Robert J. Serling
1975—**Books (Nonfiction)**—Robert J. Serling

150. THE AWARD OF MERIT MEDAL
(UNITED STATES)

Given by the American Academy of Arts and Letters, this $3,000 prize is intended to encourage and support writers. There is no public nomination or application process.

1954—Ray Bradbury
1959—Aldous Huxley
1966—John Barth
1969—Vladimir Nabokov (USSR/USA)
1970—Kurt Vonnegut Jr.
1975—William S. Burroughs

151. THE BENSON MEDAL
(UNITED KINGDOM)

Given by the Royal Society of Literature in the UK for distinguished work of the year. Established in 1917, it consists of a silver medal.

1966—*The Middle Earth Saga* [i.e. *The Lord of the Rings*], by J. R. R. Tolkien

152. THE BESS HOKIN PRIZE
(UNITED STATES)

Presented by *Poetry* Magazine, this prize is $100 for the best poetry in the previous two volumes of the magazine.

1974—Margaret Atwood

153. THE *BOSTON GLOBE* HORN BOOK AWARD
(UNITED STATES)

Given by the *Boston Globe* for a juvenile book published in the United States during the preceding year.

1969—**Best Fiction**—*The Wizard of Earthsea*, by Ursula K. Le Guin
1977—**Best Fiction**—*Child of the Owl*, by Lawrence Yep

154. THE BRITISH CRITICS AWARD
(UNITED STATES)

1967—*In the Heat of the Night*, by John Ball

155. THE BROWN UNIVERSITY/ACADEMY OF AMERICAN POETS PRIZE
(UNITED STATES)

19??—Richard "Dick" Allen

156. THE BUENOS AIRES CITY HALL LITERARY PRIZE
(ARGENTINA)

Given by the Buenos Aires City Hall for a book published the previous year.

1934—*Vigilia*, by Enrique Anderson Imbert

157. THE CALDECOTT MEDAL
(UNITED KINGDOM)

Given by the American Library Association's Children's Services Division to the artist or author of the most distinguished children's book of the previous year. The medal bears the likeness of 19th-century British illustrator Randolph Caldecott.

1976—*Why Mosquitoes Buzz in People's Ears*, by Leo & Diane Dillon
1977—*Ashanti to Zulu: African Traditions*, by Leo & Diane Dillon

158. THE CALIFORNIA WRITERS AWARD
(UNITED STATES)

1967—*In the Heat of the Night*, by John Ball

159. THE CARNEGIE MEDAL
(UNITED KINGDOM)

Given by the Library Association of the United Kingdom for outstanding children's novels in the UK in the previous year. Chosen by a committee.

1956—*The Last Battle*, by C. S. Lewis
1972—*Watership Down*, by Richard Adams

160. CATHOLIC LIBRARY ASSOCIATION REGINA MEDAL
(UNITED STATES)

1992—Jane Yolen

161. THE CHILDREN'S BOOK AWARD
(INTERNATIONAL)

Given by the International Reading Association for the first or second children's book by an author, with prize money of $1,000.

1976—*Dragonwings*, by Lawrence Yep

162. THE CLEVELAND CRITICS AWARD
(UNITED STATES)

1967—*In the Heat of the Night*, by John Ball

163. THE DAROFF MEMORIAL FICTION AWARD
(unknown)

For Best Jewish novel of the Year.

1954—*In the Morning Light*, by Charles Angoff

164. THE DUODECIMAL SOCIETY AWARD
(UNITED STATES)

19??—F. Emerson Andrews

165. THE EDGAR (ALLAN POE) AWARD
[THE AMERICAN MYSTERY WRITERS AWARD]
(UNITED STATES)

The Edgar Awards, also known as The American Mystery Writers Awards, are chosen annually by active members of the Mystery Writers Association of America (MWA). The physical award consists of a statuette of "Edgar" Allen Poe, to honor that famous American writer.

1946—**Best Criticism**—Anthony Boucher
1948—**Best First Mystery Novel**—*The Fabulous Clipjoint*, by Frederic Brown
1950—**Best Criticism**—Anthony Boucher
1953—**Best Criticism**—Anthony Boucher
1960—**Best Half-hour Television Suspense Show]**—Bill S. Ballinger
1961—**Best First Mystery Novel**—*The Man in the Cage*, by John Holbrook "Jack" Vance
1971—**Special Award**—*Space for Hire*, by William F. Nolan
1972—*Night Fall*, by Joan Aiken
1974—**Best Short Story**—"The Whimper of Whipped Dogs," by Harlan Ellison
1987—**Best Short Story**—"Soft Monkey," by Harlan Ellison

166. THE EMMY AWARD
(UNITED STATES)

Given by the National Academy of Television Arts and Sciences. Established in 1948.

1966—**Supporting Actress in Comedy**—Alice Pearce, for *Bewitched*
1967—**Children's Program**—*Jack and the Beanstalk*
1968—**Supporting Actress in Comedy**—Marion Lorne, for *Bewitched*; **Makeup Design**—John Chambers, for "Survival" segment of *Primal Man*
1969—**Best Actress in Comedy**—Hope Lange, for *The Ghost and Mrs. Muir*
1970—**Best Actress in Comedy**—Hope Lange, for *The Ghost and Mrs. Muir*
1977—**Best Actress in Drama**—Lindsay Wagner, for *The Bionic Woman*

Reginald's Science Fiction & Fantasy Awards, Third Edition

1979
Best Actress in Drama—Mariette Hartley, for *The Incredible Hulk*
Outstanding Costume Design for a Series—Jean-Pierre Dorleac, for "Furlon" episode of *Battlestar Galactica*

1981
Outstanding Individual Achievement in a Creative Technical Craft—Rick Sternbach, for *Cosmos*

1986
Outstanding Achievement in Makeup—Red Wilson, for "The Horn of Plenty" episode of *Airwolf*
Outstanding Achievement in Special Visual Effects—Michael McAllister, for *Ewoks: The Battle for Endor*

1988
Outstanding Art Direction for a Series—John Mansbridge, Art Director, and Chuck Korian, Set Decorator, for *Beauty and the Beast*
Outstanding Achievement in Makeup—Werner Keppler, Michael Westmore, and Gerald Quist, for "Conspiracy" episode of *Star Trek: The Next Generation*
Outstanding Cinematography for a Series—Roy H. Wagner, for *Beauty and the Beast*
Outstanding Costume Design for a Series—William Ware Theiss, for "The Big Goodbye" episode of *Star Trek: The Next Generation*
Outstanding Sound Editing—*Star Trek: The Next Generation*

1989
Outstanding Achievement in Hairstyling—Virginia Kearns, Hairstylist, for "Double Identity" episode of *Quantum Leap*
Outstanding Achievement in Music and Lyrics—Lee Holdridge, Composer and Melanie Holdridge, Lyricist, for "A Distant Shore" episode of *Beauty and the Beast*
Outstanding Cinematography for a Series—Roy H. Wagner, Director of Photography, for pilot episode of *Quantum Leap*
Outstanding Costume Design for a Series—Judy Evans, Costume Designer, for "The Outsiders" episode of *Beauty and the Beast*
Outstanding Sound Editing—*Star Trek: The Next Generation*
Outstanding Sound Mixing—*Star Trek: The Next Generation*

1990
Outstanding Art Direction for a Series—Richard D. James, Production Designer and James J. Mees, Set Decorator, for "Sins of the Father" episode of *Star Trek: The Next Generation*
Outstanding Achievement in Makeup—Rick Stratton, Makeup Effects Supervisor; Michelle Burke, Head Makeup Artist; Richard Snell, Katalin Elek, Ken Diaz, Makeup Artists, for "Chains of Love" episode of *Alien Nation*
Outstanding Cinematography for a Series—Michael Watkins, for "Pool Hall Blues" episode of *Quantum Leap*
Outstanding Sound Editing—*Star Trek: The Next Generation*

1991
Outstanding Sound Editing—*Star Trek: The Next Generation*
Outstanding Sound Mixing—*Star Trek: The Next Generation*
Best Producer in Dramatic Series—Alan Brennert, for *L.A. Law*

1992
Outstanding Individual Achievement in Special Visual Effects (Juried)—*Star Trek: The Next Generation*
Outstanding Individual Achievement in Special Visual Effects (Juried)—*Star Trek: The Next Generation*
Outstanding Music Composition for a Series—*Star Trek: The Next Generation*
Outstanding Costume Design for a Series—*Star Trek: The Next Generation*

Outstanding Makeup for a Series—*Star Trek: The Next Generation*

167. THE EMPIRE STATE AWARD FOR EXCELLENCE IN LITERATURE
(UNITED STATES)

1992—Madeleine L'Engle

168. THE EUNICE TIETJENS MEMORIAL AWARD
(UNITED STATES)

Given by the editors of *Poetry* magazines for the best poem in the magazine from the previous two years, with prize money of $200.

1973—Judith Moffett

169. THE FREEDOM FOUNDATION AT VALLEY FORGE HONOR MEDAL
(UNITED STATES)

1973—Holmes Alexander

170. THE GOLDEN GLOBE AWARD
(UNITED STATES)

1967—*In the Heat of the Night*, by John Ball

171. GOVERNOR GENERAL'S LITERARY AWARD
(CANADA)

This $5,000 prize is given annually to up to six authors, three each who have written in either English or French. An eighteen-member committee selects one work in fiction, non-fiction, and poetry/drama in each language.

1967—*The Circle Game*, by Margaret Atwood

172. THE HALL OF FAME COLONNADE INDUCTEES
(UNITED STATES)

Honors "Great Americans" who have been deceased at least twenty-five years by inducting them into the Hall of Fame Colonnade Museum at Bronx Community College. The award commemorates achievements of Americans of historical significance in the arts, sciences, humanities, government, business, or labor. Established in 1900, the award was presented every five years until 1970, after which time it is given every three years.

1910—Edgar Allan Poe
1920—Mark Twain (Samuel Langhorne Clemens)

Reginald's Science Fiction & Fantasy Awards, Third Edition

173. HANS CHRISTIAN ANDERSEN INTERNATIONAL MEDAL
(INTERNATIONAL)

The Hans Christian Andersen is given every two years to a living author and artist for contributions in children's literature. It is administered by the International Board on Books for Young People. It is voted upon by a jury selected by the board's executive committee.

1968—Jiri Trnka (Czechoslovakia)

174. HAROLD D. VURSELL MEMORIAL AWARD
(UNITED STATES)

Consists of $5,000 for "recent writing in book form that merits recognition for the quality of its prose style."

1990 (1991)—Ursula K. Le Guin

175. THE HEINEMANN AWARD
(UNITED KINGDOM)

Given by the Royal Society of Literature in the United Kingdom for best work of poetry, biography, or history, with a cash prize of £200.

1951—*Gormenghast*, by Mervyn Peake

176. THE IMAGE AWARD
(UNITED STATES)

The Image Awards are sponsored and presented by the National Association for the Advancement of Colored People (NAACP) for outstanding service by Black public figures.

1989

Best Actor—Michael Dorn, for his role as Lt. Worf on "The Emissary" episode of *Star Trek: The Next Generation*

177. THE INTERNATIONAL FORUM FOR NEUROLOGICAL ORGANIZATION AWARD
(INTERNATIONAL)

1970—Robert Ardrey (United States)

178. THE JACK I. & LILLIAN L. POSES/ BRANDEIS UNIVERSITY CREATIVE ARTS AWARD
(UNITED STATES)

The Jack I. and Lillian L. Poses Brandeis University Creative Arts Award is given annually to recognize talent in literature, and consists of $1,000 plus a medal or citation. A jury chosen by the Brandeis University Commission Office decides the winner.

1964—**Medal**—Vladmir Nabokov (USSR/USA)
1966—**Citation**—John Barth

179. THE JAMES J. STREBIG AWARD
(UNITED STATES)

The James B. Strebig Award is sponsored by Teledyne Continental Motors Co. and is presented for outstanding aviation writing in any medium. The prize is $500.

1958—Martin Caidin
1961—Martin Caidin
1964—Robert J. Serling

180. JAMES TAIT BLACK MEMORIAL PRIZE
(UNITED KINGDOM)

The James Tait Black Memorial Prize is given by the University of Edinburgh to honor novels published during the previous year by British authors. The prize consists of £1,000.

1940—*After Many a Summer Dies the Swan*, by Aldous Huxley

181. THE JERUSALEM PRIZE
(ISRAEL)

Awarded biennially by the City of Jerusalem, Israel, to the writer whose work best expresses the ideals of freedom for individuals in society, winners being chosen by a panel of Israeli scholars. The prize consists of $3,000 and a citation.

1971—Jorge Luis Borges (Argentina)

182. JOHN LLEWELYN RHYS MEMORIAL PRIZE
(UNITED KINGDOM)

The John Llewelyn Rhys Memorial Prize is given annually for a book by an author under thirty years of age who is a citizen of the United Kingdom and Commonwealth. The prize is £300.

1968—*The Magic Toyshop*, by Angela Carter.

183. THE JOHN MASEFIELD AWARD
(UNITED STATES)

Given by the Poetry Society of America for best narrative verse.

1979—"Dragon Raid," by G. N. Gabbard

184. THE KNIGHTHOOD OF MARK TWAIN
(UNITED STATES)

19??—Poul Anderson
19??—William C. Anderson, for *The Headstrong Housebeat*

185. THE LENIN PEACE PRIZE
(USSR/RUSSIA)

1966—Miguel Angel Asturias

186. THE LEVINSON PRIZE
(UNITED STATES)

Given by *Poetry* Magazine, this prize carries a $300 honorarium to recognize the best poetry published in the previous two volumes of the magazine.

1976—Judith Moffett

187. THE MACMILLAN COCK ROBIN AWARD
(UNITED STATES)

Honors the best mystery novel published by Macmillan in the previous year.

1959—*Perish by the Sword*, by Poul Anderson

188. *MANCHESTER GUARDIAN* FICTION PRIZE
(UNITED KINGDOM)

1969—*The Whispering Mountain*, by Joan Aiken
1972—*Watership Down*, by Richard Adams
1991—*Shapeshifter*, by Pauline Melville

189. THE MARY LYONS AWARD
(UNITED STATES)

1989—Judith Tarr

190. THE MEDICIS PRIZE
(FRANCE)

Established in 1958, the Medicis Prize is awarded annually for *avant-garde* prose, either in novel or collection form. It is given to relatively unknown French authors. An award for foreign authors was added in 1970.

1976—*The Golden Notebook*, by Doris Lessing (United Kingdom)

191. THE MELVILLE CANE AWARD
(UNITED STATES)

The $500 Melville Cane Award is annually honors the best book of poems by an American (odd-numbered years), or the best book about poetry or poets (even-numbered years). Chosen by jury.

1971—*Yeats*, by Harold Bloom

192. THE MORTON DAUWEN ZABEL AWARD
(UNITED STATES)

This $2,500 prize is given annually to an American poet, writer, or critic of literature for "progressive, original, and experimental tendencies rather than academic and conservative tendencies." Chosen by jury.

1972—Donald Barthelme
1973—Marjorie Hope Nicholson

193. NASA HEADQUARTERS EXCEPTIONAL PERFORMANCE AWARD
(UNITED STATES)

1990—Gary L. Bennett, for his work as manager of the Advanced Space Power Systems in NASA's Propulsion, Power, and Energy Division

194. THE NCR BOOK AWARD FOR NONFICTION
(UNITED KINGDOM)

1990—*The Godwins and the Shelleys*, by William St. Clair; *C. S. Lewis*, by A. N. Wilson

195. THE NEW YORK CRITICS AWARD
(UNITED STATES)

1967—*In the Heat of the Night*, by John Ball

196. THE NEWBERY MEDAL
(UNITED STATES)

Given by the American Library Association to the author of a book published during the preceding year which has made a distinguished contribution to American children's literature.

1963—*A Wrinkle In Time*, by Madeleine L'Engle
1969—*The High King*, by Lloyd Alexander
1972—*Mrs. Frisby and the Rats of NIMH*, by Robert C. O'Brien
1990—*Afternoon of the Elves*, by Janet Taylor Lisle

197. THE NOBEL PRIZE
(INTERNATIONAL)

1967—Literature—Miguel Angel Asturias

198. THE OKLAHOMA PROFESSIONAL WRITERS HALL OF FAME
(UNITED STATES)

Writers from Oklahoma are eligible to be inducted into this hall of fame.

1991—C. J. Cherryh; Dwight V. Swain

199. THE OSCAR AWARD
(UNITED STATES)

The Oscar Award is given by the Academy of Arts and Sciences for contributions to honor achievements in the medium of film.

1932
Actor—Fredric March, for *Dr. Jekyll and Mr. Hyde* (Paramount)

1939
Original Music Score—Herbert Sothart, for *The Wizard of Oz*

1940
Original Music Score—Leigh Harline, Paul J. Smith, and Ned Washington, for *Pinocchio*

1941
Music Score for a Musical Picture—Frank Churchill and Oliver Wallace, for *Dumbo*, Score of a Musical Picture
Music Score for a Dramatic or Comedy Picture—Bernard Hermann, for *All That Money Can Buy*, Score of a Dramatic or Comedy Picture
Irving Thalberg Memorial Award—Walt Disney

1943
Color Cinematography—*The Phantom of the Opera*
Color Art Direction—*The Phantom of the Opera*

1945
Black and White Cinematography—*The Picture of Dorian Gray*

1949
Special Effects—*Mighty Joe Young*

1950
Special Effects—*Destination Moon* (Eagle-Lion)

1951
Special Effects—*When Worlds Collide* (Paramount)

1953
Special Effects—*The War of the Worlds* (Paramount)

1954
Special Effects—*20,000 Leagues Under the Sea* (Walt Disney Studios)
Art Direction—John Meehan, for *20,000 Leagues Under the Sea* (Walt Disney Studios)
Set Decoration—Emile Kuri, for *20,000 Leagues Under the Sea* (Walt Disney Studios)

1960
Special Effects—*The Time Machine* (Galaxy Films/MGM)

1962
Costume Design (Black & White)—Norma Koch, for *What Ever Happened to Baby Jane?*
Costume Design (Color)—Mary Wills, for *The Wonderful World of the Brothers Grimm*

1964
Sound Effects—Norman Westfall, for *Goldfinger* (Eon Productions/United Artists)
Makeup Achievement—William Tuttle, for *The Seven Faces of Dr. Lao* (MGM)
Best Actress—Julie Andrews, for *Mary Poppins*
Special Visual Effects—Peter Ellenshaw, Hamilton Luske, and Eustace Lycett, for *Mary Poppins*

1965
Special Visual Effects—John Stears, for *Thunderball* (United Artists)

1966
Art Direction—Jack Martin Smith and Dale Kennessy, for *Fantastic Voyage* (20th Century Fox)
Set Decoration—Walter M. Scott and Stuart A. Reiss, for *Fantastic Voyage* (20th Century Fox)
Special Visual Effects—Art Cruickshank, for *Fantastic Voyage* (20th Century Fox)

1967
Irving Thalberg Memorial Award—Alfred Hitchcock
Special Visual Effects—Lyle B. Abbott, for *Doctor Doolittle*
Writing (Screenplay Based on Material from Another Medium)—*In the Heat of the Night*, screenplay by Stirling Silliphant, based on the novel by John Ball
Best Story of the Year—*In the Heat of the Night*, screenplay by Stirling Silliphant, based on the novel by John Ball

1968
Makeup Design—John Chambers, for *Planet of the Apes* (20th Century Fox)
Actress—Ruth Gordon, for *Rosemary's Baby*
Special Visual Effects—Stanley Kubrick, for *2001: A Space Odyssey* (Polaris Productions/MGM)

1969
Special Visual Effects—Robbie Robertson, for *Marooned* (Columbia)

1973
Visual Effects—Alan Maley, Eustace Lycett, and Danny Lee, for *Bedknobs and Broomsticks*

1973
Sound—Robert Knudson and Chris Newman, for *The Exorcist*
Writing (Screenplay Based on Material from Another Medium)—William Peter Blatty, for *The Exorcist*

1975
Sound—*Jaws*
Editing—*Jaws*
Original Music Score—*Jaws*

1976
Special Achievement (Visual Effects)—Carlo Rambaldi, Glen Robinson and Frank Van Der Veer, for *King Kong* (De Laurentiis/Paramount)
Special Achievement (Visual Effects)—Lyle B. Abbott, Glen Robinson and Matthew Yuricich, for *Logan's Run* (Saul David/MGM)
Original Music Score for a Motion Picture (Not a Musical)—Jerry Goldsmith, for *The Omen*

1977
Original Music Score for a Motion Picture (Not a Musical)—John Williams, for *Star Wars* (20th Century Fox)
Sound—Don MacDouglass, Ray West, Bob Minkler and Derek Ball, for *Star Wars* (20th Century Fox)
Special Achievement (Sound Effects Creation)—Benjamin Burtt Jr., for the alien, creature, and robot voices featured in *Star Wars* (20th Century Fox)
Special Achievement (Sound Effects Editing)—Frank E. Warner, for *Close Encounters of the Third Kind* (Columbia)
Cinematography—Wilmos Zsigmond, for *Close Encounters of the Third Kind* (Columbia)

Visual Effects Special Achievement Award—Roy Arbogast, Douglas Trumbull, Matthew Yuricich, Gregory Jein and Richard Yuricich, for *Close Encounters of the Third Kind* (Columbia)
Costume Design—John Mollo, for *Star Wars* (20th Century Fox)
Film Editing—Paul Hirsch, Marcia Lucas and Richard Chew, for *Star Wars* (20th Century Fox)
Art Direction—John Barry, Norman Reynolds, Leslie Dilley, for *Star Wars* (20th Century Fox)
Set Decoration—Roger Christian, for *Star Wars* (20th Century Fox)
Visual Effects—John Stears, John Dykstra, Richard Edlund, Grant McCune and Robert Blalack, for *Star Wars* (20th Century Fox)

1978
Special Achievement (Visual Effects)—Les Bowie, Colin Chilvers, Denys Coop, Roy Field, Derek Meddings, and Zoran Perisic, for *Superman*

1979
Visual Effects—H. R. Giger, Carlo Rambaldi, Brian Johnson, Nick Allder, and Denys Ayling, for *Alien*

1980
Sound—Bill Varney, Steve Maslow, Gregg Landaker, and Peter Sutton, for *The Empire Strikes Back*
Special Achievement (Visual Effects)—Brian Johnson, Richard Edlund, Dennis Muren, and Bruce Nicholson, for *The Empire Strikes Back*

1981
Sound—Bill Varney, Steve Maslow, Gregg Landaker, and Roy Charman, for *Raiders of the Lost Ark*
Special Achievement (Sound Effects Editing)—Ben Burtt and Richard L. Anderson, for *Raiders of the Lost Ark*
Makeup—*An American Werewolf in London*
Art Direction—Norman Reynolds and Leslie Dilley, for *Raiders of the Lost Ark*
Set Decoration—Michael Ford, for *Raiders of the Lost Ark*
Visual Effects—Richard Edlund, Kit West, Bruce Nicholson, and Joe Johnston, for *Raiders of the Lost Ark*

1982
Original Music Score—John Williams, for *E.T., the Extraterrestrial*
Sound—Robert Knudson, Robert Glass, Jonathan Bates, and Simon Kaye, for *E.T., the Extraterrestrial*
Sound Effects Editing—Charles L. Campbell and Ben Burtt, for *E.T., the Extraterrestrial*
Visual Effects—Carlo Rambaldi, Dennis Muren, and Kenneth F. Smith, for *E.T., the Extraterrestrial*

1983
Special Achievement (Visual Effects)—Richard Edlund, Dennis Muren, Ken Ralston, and Phil Tippett, for *Return of the Jedi*

1984
Visual Effects—Dennis Muren, Michael McAllister, Lorne Peterson, and George Gibbs, for *Indiana Jones and the Temple of Doom*

1985
Sound Effects Editing—Charles L. Campbell and Robert Rutledge, for *Back to the Future*
Best Supporting Actor—Don Ameche, for *Cocoon*
Visual Effects—Ken Ralston, Ralph McQuarrie, Scott Farrar, and David Berry, for *Cocoon*

1986
Sound Effects Editing—Don Sharpe, for *Aliens*
Irving Thalberg Memorial Award—Steven Spielberg
Makeup—Chris Walas and Stephan Dupuis, for *The Fly*
Visual Effects—Robert Skotak, Stan Winston, John Richardson, and Suzanne Benson, for *Aliens*

1987
Special Achievement (Special Effects Editing)—Stephen Flick and John Pospisil, for *Robocop*
Makeup—Rick Baker, for *Harry and the Hendersons*
Visual Effects—William George, Kenneth Smith, Dennis Muren, and Harley Jessup, for *Innerspace*

1988
Original Music Score—Alan Merken, for *The Little Mermaid*
Sound Effects Editing—Charles L. Campbell and Louis L. Edemann, for *Who Framed Roger Rabbit?*
Special Achievement (Animation Direction)—Richard Williams, for *Who Framed Roger Rabbit?*
Makeup—Ve Neill, Steve La Porte, and Robert Short, for *Beetlejuice*
Visual Effects—Ken Ralston, Richard Williams, Edward Jones, and George Gibbs, for *Who Framed Roger Rabbit?*

1989
Sound Effects Editing—Ben Burtt and Richard Hymns, for *Indiana Jones and the Last Crusade*
Art Direction—Anton Furst, for *Batman*
Set Decoration—Peter Young, for *Batman*
Visual Effects—John Bruno, Dennis Muren, Hoyt Yeatman, and Dennis Skotak, for *The Abyss*

1990
Special Achievement (Visual Effects)—Eric Brevig, Rob Bottin, Tim McGovern, and Alex Funke, for *Total Recall*
Best Actress—Kathy Bates, for *Misery*
Best Supporting Actress—Whoopi Goldberg, for *Ghost*
Art Direction—Richard Sylbert, for *Dick Tracy*
Set Decoration—Rick Simpson, for *Dick Tracy*
Writing (Original Screenplay)—Bruce Joel Rubin, for *Ghost*

200. THE PATSY AWARD
(UNITED STATES)

Given by the American Humane Society as the animal equivalent of the Oscar.

1970—Scruffy the dog, for *The Ghost and Mrs. Muir*
1970—Algae the seal, for *The Ghost and Mrs. Muir*

1971—Margie the elephant, for *The Wonderful World of Disney*
1976—17 the cat, for *Dr. Shrinker*
1976—Neal the lion, for *The Bionic Woman*

201. THE PEABODY AWARD
(UNITED STATES)

1987—*Star Trek: The Next Generation*

202. THE *PLAYBOY* WRITING AWARD
(UNITED STATES)

Given by *Playboy* Magazine for the best fiction or nonfiction work contributed to *Playboy* during the preceding year, as chosen by the editors. The award consists of a cash prize of $1,000.

1956—**Fiction Short Story**—"The Right Kind of Pride," by H. L. Gold
1958—**Fiction Short Story**—"The Distributor," by Richard Matheson
1960—**Nonfiction/Article**—"Chaplin," by Charles Beaumont
1965—**Fiction Short Story**—"The Visitor," by Roald Dahl (United Kingdom)
1966—**Fiction Short Story**—"Despair," by Vladimir Nabokov (USSR/USA)
1969—**Fiction Short Story**—"Ada," by Vladimir Nabokov (USSR/USA)
1972—**Nonfiction Essay**—"In the Community of Girls and the Commerce of Culture," by H. L. Gold
1976—**Fiction Short Story**—"Slapstick, or, Lonesome No More," by Kurt Vonnegut
1980—**New Fiction Writer**—"Frozen Journey," by Philip K. Dick

203. THE PRESIDENTIAL MEDAL OF FREEDOM
(UNITED STATES)

Given for outstanding contributions to national interest or security of the United States, the advancement of world peace, or endeavors in the field of culture or other public or private endeavors beneficial to the U.S., it is the highest civilian honor awarded by the U.S. government. The award consists of a gold medallion, and is presented by the President of the United States. Established in 1963 by John F. Kennedy.

1964—Walt Disney

204. THE PRIX DU MEILLEUR ROMAN ETRANGER
(FRANCE)

1952—*El Señor Presidente*, by Miguel Angel Asturias

205. THE PRIX SYLLA MONSEGUR
(FRANCE)

1931—*Leyendas de Guatemala*, by Miguel Angel Asturias

206. THE PULITZER PRIZE
(UNITED STATES)

Created through the will of Joseph Pulitzer, founder of the *St. Louis Post Dispatch*, it is administered by Columbia University. The prize is $1,000 in each category of fiction, nonfiction, history, biography, journalism, drama, music, and public service.

1975—Fiction—*The Killer Angels*, by Michael Shaara

207. THE ROBERT S. BALL MEMORIAL AWARD
(UNITED STATES)

The Robert S. Ball Memorial Award is sponsored by Chrysler Corp. and is presented for outstanding writing about space in any medium. The prize is $500.

1965—Arthur C. Clarke (Sri Lanka)
1968—Ray Bradbury

208. THE SIDNEY HOWARD MEMORIAL AWARD
(unknown)

Named in honor Sidney Howard, a playwright, this award is given for best play of the year by The Playwright's Company.

1940—*Thunder Rock*, by Robert Ardrey

209. THE SOMERSET MAUGHAM AWARD
(UNITED KINGDOM)

1955—*Lucky Jim*, by Kingsley Amis
1969—*Heroes and Villains*, by Angela Carter.

210. THE SOUTHWEST BOOK AWARD
(UNITED STATES)

Given for literary excellence and contributions to the cultural heritage of the Southwest.

1990—*Cyber Way*, by Alan Dean Foster

211. THE SPUR AWARD
(UNITED STATES)

Given by the Western Writers of America (WWA) for best western fiction and nonfiction of the previous year.

1966—*Walk the World's Rim*, by Betty Baker
1967—*The Wolf Is My Brother*, by Chad Oliver

212. THE THERESA HELBURN MEMORIAL AWARD
(United Kingdom)

Named in honor Theresa Helburn, this award is given for best play of the year by the Theatre Guild.

1961—*Shadow of Heroes*, by Richard Ardrey

213. THE TOP HANDS AWARD
(UNITED STATES)

Given by the Colorado Authors League to honor works by Colorado Authors.

1989
Adult Short Story—"While She Was Out," by Edward Bryant
Juvenile Short Story—"Good Kids," by Edward Bryant
Original Adult Fiction Paperback—*Deep Quarry*, by John E. Stith

214. U.S. AIR FORCE ACADEMY SPECIAL ACHIEVEMENT AWARD
(UNITED STATES)

This award consists of a white falcon on a black base.

1989—Ray Bradbury, David Brin, Octavia E. Butler, Joe Haldeman, Susan Shwartz

215. U.S. INDUSTRIAL FILM AND VIDEO FESTIVAL AWARD
(UNITED STATES)

This certificate honors creative excellence in video, television, and film.

1992—*Prisoners of Gravity* (Canada)

216. THE U.S.S.R. WRITERS' UNION AWARD
(USSR/RUSSIA)

Given by the Soviet Writer's Union for best works published in the Soviet Union the previous year.

1960 (1961)—**Best Short Story**—Aleksandr Abramov

217. THE UNION LEAGUE ARTS AND CIVIC FOUNDATION POETRY PRIZE
(UNITED STATES)

19??—Richard "Dick" Allen

218. UNIVERSITY OF CHICAGO PROFESSIONAL ACHIEVEMENT AWARD
(UNITED STATES)

Given for outstanding achievement in any profession by an alumni of the school.

1972—Robert Ardrey

219. THE UNIVERSITY OF MICHIGAN/ AVERY HOPWOOD DRAMA AWARD
(UNITED STATES)

1955—George Bamber

220. THE UNIVERSITY OF OKLAHOMA/DWIGHT V. SWAIN AWARD
(UNITED STATES)

The University of Oklahoma established The Dwight V. Swain Award in 1975 for Outstanding Seniors in its professional writing program to honor the late Oklahoman science fiction writer Dwight V(reeland) Swain (1915-1992). No winners qualify for listing here.

221. UNIVERSITY OF TEXAS/CARL HERTZOG AWARD
(UNITED STATES)

Given for excellence in book design during the previous year.

1990 (1991)—Cheap Street Publishers, for *Blood and Gingerbread*, by John Sladek

222. THE ViRA AWARD
(UNITED STATES)

Given by the Videocassette Industry, and presented by *Video Review*, to honor videocassettes released the previous year.

1989—**Best Vintage TV**—"Demon with a Glass Hand," *The Outer Limits*, by Harlan Ellison

223. THE W. H. SMITH ILLUSTRATION AWARD
(UNITED KINGDOM)

British publisher W. H. Smith & Co. sponsors this annual award for book illustration.

1986 (1987)

1st—Ralph Steadman, for *I, Leonardo*
2nd—Justin Todd, for *Alice in Wonderland* and *Through the Looking Glass*, by Lewis Carroll

224. WALDO AWARD
(UNITED STATES)

Given by Waldenbooks to honor "various persons involved in the publishing industry."

1989 (1990)—[Bestselling Author of the Year]—*Plains of Passage*, by Jean M. Auel

225. THE WESTERN HERITAGE AWARD
(UNITED STATES)

Given by the National Cowboy Hall of Fame annually for works depicting the Old West. The trophy is the Wrangler Trophy, a replica of the painting *Night Herder* by Charles Russell. Voted upon by the trustees of the Hall of Fame.

19??—*Killer-of-Death*, by Betty Baker
1963—"The Prairie Schooner Got Them There," by George R. Stewart

226. THE WHITBREAD AWARD
(UNITED KINGDOM)

The Whitbread Award of £1,000 is sponsored by Whitbread & Co. Brewery, and is administered by the Bookseller's Association of Great Britain and Northern Ireland. It is awarded to authors who have lived in the U.K. for at least five years and covers fiction, biography, first books, and children's literature.

1974—**Children's Book**—*How Tom Beat Captain Najork and His Hired Sportsmen*, by Russell Hoban and Quentin Blake

227. WILLIAM ALLEN WHITE CHILDREN'S BOOK AWARD
(UNITED STATES)

Given by the William Allen White Library at Kansas State Teacher's College. Voted upon by children.

1974—*Mrs. Frisby and the Rats of NIMH*, by Robert C. O'Brien; *The Headless Cupid*, by Zilpha K. Snyder

228. THE WRITERS GUILD AWARD
(UNITED STATES)

Given by the Writers Guild of America, West for the best teleplays or radio plays of the year. The Valentine Davies Award is presented annually for contributions to the motion picture community that bring dignity and honor to writers everywhere. The Laurel Award honors lifetime television writing achievement.

1965—**Best Anthology Script**—"Demon with a Glass Hand" episode of *The Outer Limits*, by Harlan Ellison
1967—**Best Dramatic/Episodic Script**—"The City on the Edge of Forever" episode of *Star Trek*, by Harlan Ellison
1972—**Best Adapted Anthology**—*The Night Stalker*, an *ABC Movie of the Week*, by Richard Matheson
1973—**Best Dramatic/Episodic Script**—"Phoenix Without Ashes," the original pilot episode (as written, not shown) of *The Starlost*, by Harlan Ellison

1974—Valentine Davies Award—Ray Bradbury
1976—Laurel Award—Rod Serling
1987—Best Dramatic/Episodic Script—(tie) "Paladin of the Lost Hour" episode of *The Twilight Zone*, by Harlan Ellison; "The Last Defender of Camelot" episode of *The Twilight Zone*, by George R. R. Martin; "Her Pilgrim Soul" episode of *The Twilight Zone*, by Alan Brennert; "The Doll" episode of *Amazing Stories*, by Richard Matheson

APPENDIX I

OFFICERS OF THE SCIENCE FICTION AND FANTASY WRITERS OF AMERICA, INC.
(UNITED STATES)

The Science Fiction and Fantasy Writers of America, Inc. (SFWA) organization was started in 1965 by Damon Knight, "to inform its membership of writers on matters of professional interest, to promote their general welfare, and to help them deal effectively with publishers, editors and anthologists."—*SFWA Bulletin.* Terms run from one summer to the next.

1965-1966
President—Damon Knight
Vice President—Harlan Ellison
Secretary/Treasurer—Lloyd Biggle

1966-1967
President—Damon Knight
Vice President—James Blish
Secretary/Treasurer—Lloyd Biggle

1967-1968
President—Robert Silverberg
Vice President—James Blish
Secretary/Treasurer—Roger Zelazny

1968-1969
President—Alan E. Nourse
Vice President—Harry Harrison
Secretary/Treasurer—Anne McCaffrey

1969-1970
President—Gordon R. Dickson
Vice President—Ron Goulart
Secretary/Treasurer—Anne McCaffrey

1970-1971
President—Gordon R. Dickson
Vice President—Tom Purdom
Secretary—Chelsea Quinn Yarbro
Treasurer—Joe W. Haldeman

1971-1972

President—James E. Gunn
Vice President—Tom Purdom
Secretary—Chelsea Quinn Yarbro
Treasurer—Joe W. Haldeman

1972-1973

President—Poul Anderson
Vice President—Norman Spinrad
Secretary—Robert Coulson
Treasurer—Joe W. Haldeman

1973-1974

President—Jerry Pournelle
Vice President—Norman Spinrad
Secretary—Robert Coulson
Treasurer—andrew j. offutt

1974-1975

President—Frederik Pohl
Vice President—F. M. Busby
Secretary—Theodore Cogswell
Treasurer—andrew j. offutt

1975-1976

President—Frederik Pohl
Vice President—F. M. Busby
Secretary—Thomas Monteleone
Treasurer—andrew j. offutt

1976-1977

President—andrew j. offutt
Vice President—Mildred Downey Broxon
Secretary—Thomas Monteleone
Treasurer—Joan Hunter Holly

1977-1978

President—andrew j. offutt
Vice President—Mildred Downey Broxon
Secretary—Thomas Monteleone
Treasurer—Joan Hunter Holly

1978-1979

President—Jack Williamson
Vice President—Marion Zimmer Bradley
Secretary—David Bischoff
Treasurer—Joan Hunter Holly

1979-1980

President—Jack Williamson
Vice President—Robert E. Vardeman
Secretary—David Bischoff
Treasurer—Jack L. Chalker

1980-1981

President—Norman Spinrad
Vice President—David Bischoff
Secretary—Somtow Sucharitkul (S. P. Somtow)
Treasurer—Jack L. Chalker

1981-1982

President—Norman Spinrad
Vice President—Marta Randall
Secretary—Somtow Sucharitkul (S. P. Somtow)
Treasurer—Jack L. Chalker

1982-1983

President—Marta Randall
Vice President—Charles Sheffield
Secretary—David Brin
Treasurer—John F. Carr

1983-1984

President—Marta Randall
Vice President—Charles Sheffield
Secretary—David Brin
Treasurer—John F. Carr

1984-1985

President—Charles Sheffield
Vice President—Roland Green
Secretary—C. J. Cherryh
Treasurer—John F. Carr

1985-1986

President—Charles Sheffield
Vice President—Roland Green
Secretary—C. J. Cherryh
Treasurer—John F. Carr

1986-1987

President—Jane Yolen
Vice President—John F. Carr
Secretary—Lee Killough
Treasurer—Harry Turtledove

1987-1988

President—Jane Yolen
Vice President—Greg Bear
Secretary—Lee Killough
Treasurer—D. Alexander Smith

1988-1989

President—Greg Bear
Vice President—Michael Cassutt
Secretary—Frank Catalano
Treasurer—D. Alexander Smith

1989-1990

President—Greg Bear
Vice President—Dean R. Lambe
Secretary—Martha Soukoup
Treasurer—D. Alexander Smith

1990-1991

President—Ben Bova
Vice President—Dean R. Lambe
Secretary—Martha Soukoup
Treasurer—Bruce Bethke

1991-1992

President—Ben Bova
Vice President—Sheila Finch
Secretary—C. J. Cherryh
Treasurer—Bruce Bethke

1992-1993

President—Joe Haldeman
Vice President—Sheila Finch
Secretary—C. J. Cherryh
Treasurer—Michael Capobianco

APPENDIX II

OFFICERS OF THE SCIENCE FICTION RESEARCH ASSOCIATION
(UNITED STATES)

The Science Fiction Research Association (SFRA) was founded in 1970 by Dr. Thomas D. Clareson "to improve classroom teaching, encourage and assist scholarship, and evaluate and publicize new books, new teaching methods and materials and allied media performances"—(SFRA bylaws). The membership consists of individuals who are interested in furthering the study and scholarship of science fiction, fantasy, and horror (speculative fiction), including professors, teachers, students, and writers.

1970-1971 - 1976-1977
President—Thomas D. Clareson

1977-1978
President—Arthur O. Lewis, Jr.
Vice President—Darko Suvin
Secretary—L. W. Currey
Treasurer—Marshall B. Tymn

1978-1979
President—Arthur O. Lewis, Jr.

1979-1980
President—Joe DeBolt
Vice President—Marshall B. Tymn
Secretary—Robert Galbreath
Treasurer—Elizabeth Cummins Cogell

1980-1981
President—Joe DeBolt
Secretary—Robert Galbreath
Treasurer—Elizabeth Cummins Cogell

1981-1982
President—James E. Gunn
Vice President—Mary Kenny Badami
Secretary—Robert Galbreath
Treasurer—Elizabeth Cummins Cogell

1982-1983
President—James E. Gunn
Secretary—William H. Hardesty III
Treasurer—Elizabeth Cummins Cogell

1983-1984

President—Patricia S. Warrick
Vice President—Elizabeth Cummins Cogell
Secretary—William H. Hardesty III
Treasurer—Donald M. Hassler

1984-1985

President—Patricia S. Warrick
Vice President—Elizabeth Cummins Cogell
Secretary—William H. Hardesty III
Treasurer—Donald M. Hassler

1985-1986

President—Donald M. Hassler
Vice President—Stephen M. Goldman
Secretary—William H. Hardesty III
Treasurer—Charlotte Donsky

1986-1987

President—Donald M. Hassler
Vice President—Stephen M. Goldman
Secretary—William H. Hardesty III
Treasurer—Charlotte Donsky

1987-1988

President—William H. Hardesty III
Vice President—Martin H. Greenberg
Secretary—Elizabeth Anne Hull
Treasurer—Charlotte Donsky

1988-1989

President—William H. Hardesty III
Vice President—Martin H. Greenberg
Secretary—Elizabeth Anne Hull
Treasurer—Charlotte Donsky

1989-1990

President—Elizabeth Anne Hull
Vice President—Neil Barron
Secretary—David G. Mead
Treasurer—Thomas J. Remington

1990-1991

President—Elizabeth Anne Hull
Vice President—Neil Barron
Secretary—David G. Mead
Treasurer—Thomas J. Remington

1991-1992

President—Peter Lowentrout
Vice President—Muriel Rogow Becker
Secretary—David G. Mead
Treasurer—Edra Bogle

1992-1993

President—Peter Lowentrout
Vice President—Muriel Rogow Becker
Secretary—David G. Mead
Treasurer—Edra Bogle

1993-1994

President—David Mead
Vice President—Muriel Rogow Becker
Secretary—Joan Gordon
Treasurer—Robert J. Ewald

Newsletter Editors

1971-1974—Fred Lerner
1974-1978—Beverly Friend
1978-1981—Roald Tweet
1981-1984—Elizabeth Anne Hull
1984-1988—Richard W. Miller
1988-1990—Robert A. Collins
1990-1992—Betsy Harfst
1992-DATE—Daryl F. Mallett

APPENDIX III

OFFICERS OF THE HORROR WRITERS OF AMERICA
(UNITED STATES)

The Horror Writers of America (HWA) was founded in 1987 by Richard McCammon for professionals and those with associated interests.

1987-1988

President—Dean R. Koontz
Vice President—Paul Dale Anderson
Secretary—J. N. Williamson
Treasurer—Joe Lansdale

1988-1989

President—Charles L. Grant
Vice President—Tom Monteleone
Secretary—Besty Engstrom
Treasurer—Maxine O'Callaghan

1989-1990

President—Chelsea Quinn Yarbro
Vice President—Joe Lansdale
Secretary—Lisa Cantrell
Treasurer—Joseph L. Citro
Executive Secretary—Theresa P. Gladden
Pres. of Trustees—Charles L. Grant

1990-1991

President—Craig Shaw Gardner
Vice President—Chet Williamson
Secretary—Chris Curry
Treasurer—Matthew J. Costello
Executive Secretary—Leanne Johnson
Pres. of Trustees—Charles L. Grant

1991-1992

President—Craig Shaw Gardner
Vice President—Rick Hautala
Secretary—Chris Curry
Treasurer—Matthew J. Costello
Executive Secretary—Leanne Johnson
Pres. of Trustees—Charles L. Grant

1992-1993

President—Dennis Etchison
Vice President—Charles de Lint
Secretary—Claudia O'Keefe
Treasurer—Christopher Golden
Pres. of Trustees—Chelsea Quinn Yarbro

APPENDIX IV

THE WORLD SCIENCE FICTION CONVENTIONS

[GoH = Guest of Honor; FGoH = Fan Guest of Honor; AGoH = Artist Guest of Honor]

1. 1939—Nycon [I], New York, NY; GoH—Frank R. Paul
2. 1940—Chicon [I], Chicago, IL; GoH—Edward E. "Doc" Smith
3. 1941—Denvention [I], Denver, CO; GoH—Robert A. Heinlein
   [Conventions suspended due to World War II]
4. 1946—Pacificon [I], Los Angeles, CA; GoHs—A. E. van Vogt and E. Mayne Hull
5. 1947—Philcon [I], Philadelphia, PA; GoH—John W. Campbell, Jr.
6. 1948—Torcon [I], Toronto, Canada; GoH—Robert Bloch
7. 1949—Cinvention, Cinncinnati, OH; GoH—Lloyd Arthur Eshbach
8. 1950—Norwescon, Portland, OR; GoH—Anthony Boucher
9. 1951—Nolacon [I], New Orleans, LA; GoH—Fritz Leiber
10. 1952—Chicon II, Chicago, IL; GoH—Hugo Gernsback
11. 1953—Philcon II, Philadelphia, PA; GoH—Willy Ley
12. 1954—SFCon, San Francisco, CA; GoH—John W. Campbell, Jr.
13. 1955—Clevention, Cleveland, OH; GoH—Isaac Asimov
14. 1956—Nycon II, New York, NY; GoH—Arthur C. Clarke
15. 1957—Loncon [I], London, England; GoH—John W. Campbell, Jr.
16. 1958—Solacon, Los Angeles, CA; GoH—Richard Matheson
17. 1959—Detention, Detroit, MI; GoH—Poul Anderson
18. 1960—Pittcon, Pittsburgh, PA; GoH—James Blish
19. 1961—Seacon, Seattle, WA; GoH—Robert A. Heinlein
20. 1962—Chicon III, Chicago, IL; GoH—Theodore Sturgeon
21. 1963—Discon [I], Washington, DC; GoH—Murray Leinster
22. 1964—Pacificon II, Oakland, CA; GoHs—Edmond Hamilton and Leigh Brackett; FGoH—Forrest J Ackerman
23. 1965—Loncon II, London, England; GoH—Brian W. Aldiss
24. 1966—Tricon, Cleveland, OH; GoH—L. Sprague de Camp
25. 1967—Nycon III, New York, NY; GoH—Lester del Rey; FGoH—Wilson Tucker
26. 1968—Baycon, Oakland, CA; GoH—Philip José Farmer [substituting for Anthony Boucher, who died before the convention]; FGoH—Walter J. Daugherty; TM—Robert Silverberg
27. 1969—St. Louiscon, St. Louis, MO; GoH—Jack Gaughan; FGoH—Eddie Jones
28. 1970—Heicon '70, Heidelberg, Germany; GoHs—Robert Silverberg, E. C. Tubb and Herbert W. Franke; FGoH—Elliot K. Shorter
29. 1971—Noreascon [I], Boston, MA; GoH—Clifford D. Simak; FGoH—Harry Warner
30. 1972—LA Con [I], Los Angeles, CA; GoH—Frederik Pohl; FGoHs—Robert and Juanita Coulson
31. 1973—Torcon II, Toronto, Canada; GoH—Robert Bloch; FGoH—William Rotsler
32. 1974—Discon II, Washington, DC; GoH—Roger Zelazny; FGoH—J. K. Klein
33. 1975—Aussicon [I], Sydney, Australia; GoHs—Ursula K. Le Guin and Donald H. Tuck
34. 1976—Midamericon, Kansas City, MO; GoH—Robert A. Heinlein; FGoH—George Barr
35. 1977—Suncon, Orlando, FL; GoH—Jack Williamson; FGoH—Robert Madle
36. 1978—Iguanacon, Phoenix, AZ; GoH—Harlan Ellison; FGoH—Bill Bowers

37.	1979—	Seacon '79, Brighton, England; GoHs—Fritz Leiber and Brian W. Aldiss; FGoH—Harry Bell
38.	1980—	Noreascon II, Boston, MO; GoHs—Kate Wilhelm and Damon Knight; FGoH—Bruce Pelz
39.	1981—	Denvention II, Denver, CO; GoHs—Clifford D. Simak and C. L. Moore; FGoH—Rusty Hevelin
40.	1982—	Chicon IV, Chicago, IL; GoH—A. Bertram Chandler; AGoH—Frank Kelly Freas; FGoH—Lee Hoffman
41.	1983—	Constellation, Baltimore, MD; GoH—John Brunner; FGoH—David Kyle
42.	1984—	LA Con II, Los Angeles, CA; GoH—Gordon R. Dickson; FGoH—Dick Eney
43.	1985—	Aussiecon II, Melbourne, Australia; GoH—Gene Wolfe; FGoH—Ted White
44.	1986—	Confederation, Atlanta, GA; GoH—Ray Bradbury; FGoH—Terry Carr
45.	1987—	Conspiracy, Brighton, England; GoHs—Doris Lessing; Alfred Bester; FGoHs—Joyce and Ken Slater; Dave Langford; AGoH—Jim Burns
46.	1988—	Nolacon II, New Orleans, LA; GoH—Donald A. Wollheim; FGoH—Roger Sims
47.	1989—	Noreascon III, Boston, MO; GoHs—Andre Norton, and Ian and Betty Ballantine; FGoH—The Stranger Club
48.	1990—	Confiction, The Hague, Netherlands; GoHs—Joe Haldeman; Wolfgang Jeschke; Harry Harrison; FGoH—Andrew Porter
49.	1991—	Chicon V, Chicago, IL; GoHs—Hal Clement; Martin H. Greenberg; AGoH—Richard Powers; FGoHs—Jon and Joni Stopa
50.	1992—	Magicon, Orlando, FL; GoH—Jack Vance; AGoH—Vincent DiFate; FGoH—Walter A. Willis; TM—Spider Robinson
51.	1993—	ConFrancisco, San Francisco, CA; GoH—Larry Niven, Tom Digby; AGoH—Alicia Austin; FGoH—jan howard finder; DGoH—Mark Twain
52.	1994—	Conadian, Winnipeg, Manitoba, Canada; GoH—Anne McCaffrey; AGoH—George Barr; FGoH—Robert Runté

APPENDIX V

THE WORLD FANTASY CONVENTIONS

[GoH = Guest of Honor; FGoH = Fan Guest of Honor; AGoH = Artist Guest of Honor; TM = Toastmaster]

1. 1975—Providence, Rhode Island; GoH—Robert Bloch
2. 1976—New York, New York; GoHs—C. L. Moore and Michael Moorcock
3. 1977—Los Angeles, California; GoH—Richard Matheson
4. 1978—Fort Worth, Texas; GoH—Fritz Leiber; AGoH—Alicia Austin
5. 1979—Providence, Rhode Island; GoHs—Stephen King and Frank Belknap Long; AGoH—Michael Whelan
6. 1980—Baltimore, Maryland; GoH—Jack Vance; AGoH—Boris Vallejo
7. 1981—Oakland, California; GoH—Peter Beagle; AGoH—Brian Froud; FGoH—Alan Garner
8. 1982—New Haven, Connecticut; GoH—Peter Straub; AGoH—Don Maitz; FGoH—Joseph Payne Brennan
9. 1983—Chicago, Illinois; GoHs—Gene Wolfe and Manly Wade Wellman; AGoH—Rowena Morrill
10. 1984—Ottawa, Canada; GoHs—Jane Yolen and Tanith Lee; AGoH—Jeffrey Jones
11. 1985—Tucson, Arizona; GoHs—Evangeline Walton and Stephen R. Donaldson; AGoH—Victoria Poyser; FGoH—Michael Hague
12. 1986—Providence, Rhode Island; GoHs—Ramsey Campbell and Charles L. Grant; AGoH—J. K. Potter
13. 1987—Nashville, Tennessee; GoH—Piers Anthony; AGoH—Frank Kelly Freas
14. 1988—London, England; GoH—James Herbert
15. 1989—Seattle, Washington; GoHs—Ursula K. Le Guin, S. P. Somtow and Robert McCammon
16. 1990—Chicago, Illinois; GoHs—F. Paul Wilson and L. Sprague de Camp; AGoH—David Mattingly; Editor GoH—Susan Allison
17. 1991—Tucson, Arizona; GoHs—Harlan and Susan Ellison, and Stephen R. Donaldson; AGoH—Arlin Robins
18. 1992—Pine Mountain, Georgia; GoHs—Michael Bishop, John Farris, Martin H. Greenberg, and Anne McCaffrey

APPENDIX VI

THE WORLD HORROR CONVENTIONS

[GoH=Guest of Honor; FGoH=Fan Guest of Honor; AGoH=Artist Guest of Honor; TM=Toastmaster]

1. **1991**—Nashville, TN
2. **1992**—Nashville, TN; GoH—Richard Matheson; MGoH—Richard Christian Matheson; AGoH—Harry O. Morris; TM—Brian Lumley
3. **1993**—Stamford, CT; GoHs—Peter Straub, Les Daniels, Stanley Wiater; AGoH—J. K. Potter

AUTHOR INDEX

[GoH = Guest of Honor; FGoH = Fan Guest of Honor; AGoH = Artist Guest of Honor; TM = Toastmaster]

ABADIA, Guy. Karel, 1989 (1990).
ABEL, Eduardo. Más Alla [Novel], 1984 (1985).
ABBOTT, Bud. Count Dracula Society [Special], 1968 (1969).
ABBOTT, Lyle B. Oscar [Special Visual Effects], 1967; [Special Achievement (Visual Effects)], 1976. Saturn [Special Effects], 1976 (1977).
ABRAMOV, Aleksandr. USSR Writers' Union [Short Story], 1960 (1961).
ACKERMAN, Forrest J
  Atlanta Fantasy Faire, 1982.
  Clampett, 1984.
  Count Dracula Society [Literature], 1962 (1963), 1965 (1966); [Fauria], 1967 (1968); [Cunningham], 1974 (1975).
  E. E. Evans/Paul Frehafer, 1946 (1972).
  Frank R. Paul, 19??
  Grimmy, 1990.
  Hugo [Number One Fan Personality], 1952 (1953).
  Inkpot, 1974.
  Premios Italiano di Fantascienza [Special], 1980 (1981).
  Saturn [Film Critic], 1975 (1976).
  FGoH World SF Convention, 1964.
ACKERSON, Duane. Rhysling [Short Poem], 1977 (1978); 1978 (1979).
ACKROYD, Dan. Saturn [Fantasy Film], 1984 (1985).
ACKROYD, Peter. Gilgamés [Horror Novel], 1988 (1989).
ADAMOVIC, Ivan. Karel Capek [Short Story by Student], 1987 (1988).
ADAMS, Art. Manning, 1986.
ADAMS, Douglas. Ditmar [International Fiction], 1979 (1980); [Pat Terry], 1979 (1980). BSFA [Media Presentation], 1979 (1980), 1980 (1981). Inkpot, 1983. Zauber Zeit [SF Novel], 1986 (1987).
ADAMS, Gail. Robbie [Fan Media Artist], 1988 (1989).
ADAMS, Neal. Inkpot, 1976.
ADAMS, Richard. Carnegie Medal, 1972. Manchester Guardian, 1972. Saturn [Animated Film], 1978 (1979).
ADDAMS, Charles. Hugo [Nonfiction], 1991 (1992).
ADLERBERTH, Roland. Karel, 1985 (1986). Prix Jules Verne, 1975.
AGAR, John. Saturn [Life Career], 1980 (1981).
AHLGREN, Rolf. Prix Jules Verne, 1975.
AICKMAN, Robert. British Fantasy [Short Story], 1980 (1981). Gilgamés [Horror Short Story], 1989 (1990). World Fantasy [Short Fiction], 1973/1974 (1975).
AIKEN, Joan. Edgar, 1972. Manchester Guardian, 1969.
AIZU, Shingo. Nihon SF Taisho, 1987 (1988).
AKIRA, Hori. Nihon SF Taisho, 1980 (1981).
ALBAIN, Richard. Saturn [Executive Achievement], 1977 (1978).
ALBERTSON, Darren J. L. Ron Hubbard's Illustrators of the Future [3rd Quarter], 1991 (1992).
ALCALA, Alfredo. Inkpot, 1977.
ALDANI, Lino. Karel [Special President's], 1986 (1987).
ALDISS, Brian W.
  BSFA [Novel], 1971 (1972), 1982 (1983), 1985 (1986); [Special], 1969 (1970), 1973 (1974).
  Ditmar [Contemporary Author], 1968 (1969).

Hugo [Short Fiction], 1961 (1962); [Nonfiction], 1986 (1987); [Special Plaque], 1957 (1958).
IAFA [Distinguished Scholarship], 1985 (1986).
J. Lloyd Eaton, 1986 (1988).
John W. Campbell, Jr. Memorial, 1982 (1983).
Karel [President's], 1987 (1988).
Kurd Lasswitz [Foreign Novel], 1983 (1984).
Locus [Nonfiction], 1986 (1987).
Nebula [Novella], 1965 (1966).
Pilgrim, 1978.
Prix Jules Verne, 1977.
GoH World SF Convention, 1965, 1979.
ALDREDGE, Theoni V. Saturn [Costumes], 1978 (1979).
ALDRIDGE, Ray. L. Ron Hubbard's Writers of the Future [4th Quarter, 3rd Place], 1985 (1986).
ALDRIN, Edwin "Buzz." Hugo [Special], 1968 (1969).
ALEKSIEVA, Tekla. Graviton [Illustrator], 1989 (1990).
ALEXANDER, Holmes. Freedom Foundation at Valley Forge Honor Medal, 1973.
ALEXANDER, Lloyd. American Book [Children's Literature], 1970 (1971). Newbery Medal, 1969.
ALEXANDER, Rob. L. Ron Hubbard's Illustrators of the Future [4th Quarter], 1990 (1991).
ALF, Richard. Inkpot, 1989.
ALFONSO, Barry. Inkpot, 1975.
ALIPRANDI, Marcello. Premios Italiano di Fantascienza [Dramatic Presentation], 1971 (1972).
ALKON, Paul K. J. Lloyd Eaton Memorial, 1987 (1988).
ALLDER, Nick. Oscar [Visual Effects], 1979.
ALLEN, Johannes. Antonius Prize, 1951.
ALLEN, Karen. Saturn [Actress], 1981 (1982).
ALLEN, Paul C. Balrog [Outstanding Amateur Achievement], 1978 (1979), 1979 (1980), 1980 (1981); [Amateur Publication], 1979 (1980), 1980 (1981). World Fantasy [Special (Nonprofessional)], 1979 (1980), 1981 (1982).
ALLEN, Richard "Dick." A.D.E.-M.L.A. Distinguished Teaching, 19??. Brown University/Academy of American Poets Prize, 19??. Union League Arts and Civic Foundation Poetry Prize, 19??.
ALLEN, Roger MacBride. Davis Readers (Analog) [Short Story], 1986 (1987).
ALLEN, Susan. Balrog [Amateur Publication], 1980 (1981); [Outstanding Amateur Achievement], 1980 (1981).
ALLEN, Woody. Hugo [Dramatic Presentation], 1973 (1974). Nebula [Dramatic Presentation], 1974 (1975).
ALLISON, Susan. SF Chronicle [Most Attractive Female Editor], 1983 (1984). Science Fiction & Fantasy Workshop [Book Editor], 1986 (1987). Editor GoH World Fantasy Convention, 1990.
ALPERS, Hans Joachim. Kurd Lasswitz [Special], 1980 (1981); [Special], 1982 (1983); [Novella], 1985 (1986).
ALTOMARE, Donato. Premios Italiano di Fantascienza [Short Fiction (Fan)], 1990 (1991).
ALTON, Andrea I. Andre Norton Fantasy/SF Short Story [2nd], 1990 (1991).
ALVIN, John. Saturn [Poster Art], 1982 (1983).
ALYN, Kirk. Inkpot, 1974.
ALZMANN, Maeheah. Inkpot, 1983.
AMANO, Yoshitaka. Seiun Taisho [Artist], 1982 (1983), 1983 (1984), 1984 (1985), 1985 (1986).
AMECHE, Don. Oscar [Best Supporting Actor], 1985.
AMERY, Carl. Kurd Lasswitz [Short Story], 1984 (1985); [Novel], 1986 (1987); [Radio Play], 1987 (1988).
AMIS, Kingsley. John W. Campbell, Jr. Memorial, 1976 (1977). Somerset Maugham, 1955.
ANDELKOVIC, Radmilo. Lazar Komarcic [Novella], 1986 (1987).

ANDERSON, Brad. Inkpot, 1975.
ANDERSON, Brent. Inkpot, 1985.
ANDERSON, C. Dean. Saturn [Special], 1973/74 (1975).
ANDERSON, Craig. Inkpot, 1979.
ANDERSON, Douglas A. Mythopoeic [Scholarship], 1989 (1990).
ANDERSON, Murphy. Inkpot, 1984.
ANDERSON, Paul Dale. HWA Vice President, 1987-1988.
ANDERSON, Poul.
   British Fantasy [August Derleth], 1974 (1975).
   Forry, 1968.
   Gray Mouser, 1984.
   Hugo [Novella], 1971 (1972), 1981 (1982); [Novelette], 1968 (1969), 1972 (1973), 1978 (1979); [Short Story], 1960 (1961); [Short Fiction], 1963 (1964); [Gandalf Grand Master], 1977 (1978).
   Inkpot, 1986.
   Knight of Mark Twain, 19??
   Locus [Short Fiction], 1971 (1972).
   Macmillan Cock Robin, 1959.
   Nebula [Novelette], 1971 (1972), 1972 (1973); [Novella], 1981 (1982).
   Prometheus Hall of Fame, 1985.
   Skylark, 1982.
   SFWA President, 1972-1973.
   GoH World SF Convention, 1959.
ANDERSON, Richard L. Oscar [Special Achievement (Sound Effects Editing)], 1981.
ANDERSON, William C. Knight of Mark Twain, 19??.
ANDERSON IMBERT, Enrique. Buenos Aires City Hall Literary Prize, 1934.
ANDERSSON, Erik. Alvar Appletofft Memorial, 1979 (1980).
ANDREASSON, Malte. Alvar Appletofft Memorial, 1987 (1988).
ANDREASSON, Martin. Alvar Appletofft Memorial, 1987 (1988).
ANDREVON, Jean-Pierre. Grand Prix de la SF Française [Juvenile], 1980 (1981).
ANDREWS, F. Emerson. Duodecimal Society Award, 19??.
ANDREWS, Graham. Aisling Gheal [1st], 1979 (1980).
ANDREWS, Julie. Oscar [Best Actress], 1964.
ANDRIOLA, Alfred. Reuben, 1970.
ANGOFF, Charles. Daroff Memorial Fiction, 1954.
ANKER, Roger. Bram Stoker [Collection], 1988 (1989).
ANSARA, Edward. Count Dracula Society [Summers], 1977 (1978).
ANSARA, Michael. Count Dracula Society [Special], 1978 (1979).
ANTHONY, Mark. L. Ron Hubbard's Writers of the Future [1st Quarter, 2nd Place], 1988 (1989).
ANTHONY, Piers. British Fantasy [August Derleth], 1977 (1978). Pyramid Books/*F&SF*/Kent Productions SF Novel, 1968. GoH World Fantasy Convention, 1987.
ANTONELLI, Roberto. Festival Internazionale del Film [Silver Asteroid—Actor], 1970 (1971).
APPLETOFFT, Alvar. Alvar Appletofft Memorial, 1977 (1978).
ARAGONÉS, Sergio. Clampett, 1990. Inkpot, 1976. Will Eisner Comic Industry [Humor Publication], 1991 (1992).
ARAMATA, Hiroshi. Nihon SF Taisho, 1986 (1987).
ARAMBOLA, Ramon. Inkpot, 1984.
ARBOGAST, Roy. Oscar [Visual Effects Special Achievement], 1977.
ARDREY, Robert. International Forum for Neurological Organization, 1970. Sidney Howard Memorial, 1940. Theresa Helburn Memorial, 1961. University of Chicago Professional Achievement, 1972.
ARKOFF, Samuel Z. Saturn [Life Career], 1976 (1977).
ARMER, Karl Michael. Kurd Lasswitz [Novella], 1986 (1987); [Novelette], 1988 (1989); [Short Fiction], 1987 (1988).
ARMSTRONG, Neil. Hugo [Special], 1968 (1969).
ARNASON, Eleanor. James Tiptree Jr. Memorial Award [2nd], 1991 (1992). John W. Campbell Jr. Memorial [3rd], 1991 (1992). Mythopoeic [Adult Literature], 1991 (1992).

ARNAUD, G. J. Grand Prix de la SF Française [Special], 1980 (1981). Prix Apollo, 1987 (1988).
ARNOLD, Jack. Saturn [President's], 1984 (1985).
ARNOLD, Mark Allan. World Fantasy [Anthology/Collection], 1981 (1982).
ARONICA, Lou. Locus [Anthology], 1988 (1989), 1991 (1992).
ASHE, Eve Brent. Saturn [Supporting Actress], 1980 (1981).
ASIMOV, Isaac.
Collectors [Most Collectible over Lifetime], 1991 (1992).
Davis Readers (IASFM) [Short Story], 1986 (1987).
Ditmar [International Fiction], 1972 (1973).
Forry, 1990.
Hugo [Special Plaque], 1962 (1963); [All-Time Series], 1965 (1966); [Novel], 1972 (1973), 1982 (1983); [Novelette], 1976 (1977), 1991 (1992).
Locus [Novel], 1972 (1973), 1982 (1983); [Novelette], 1976 (1977); [Short Story], 1986 (1987); [Reprint Anthology/Collection], 1974 (1975); [Nonfiction], 1980 (1981).
Nebula [Novel], 1972 (1973); [Novelette], 1976 (1977); [Grand Master], 1986 (1987).
Polish SF & Fantasy Achievement [Foreign Novel], 1987 (1988).
Prix Cosmos 2000, 1984 (1985).
Science Fiction Book Club [2nd], 1988 (1989).
Skylark, 1967.
GoH World SF Convention, 1955.
ASPRIN, Robert. Balrog [Collection/Anthology], 1981 (1982), 1982 (1983). Inkpot, 1988. Locus [Anthology], 1981 (1982). Saturn [Anthology], 1982 (1983). Zauber Zeit [Fantasy Novel], 1990 (1991).
ASTURIAS, Miguel Angel. Prix du Meilleur Roman Etranger, 1952. Lenin Peace Prize, 1966. Nobel [Literature], 1967. Prix Sylla Monsegur, 1931.
ATKINS, Lon. Southpaw [Achievement in APA Administration], 1982 (1983).
ATTANASIO, A. A. Prix Cosmos 2000, 1983 (1984).
ATTEBERY, Brian. IAFA [Distinguished Scholarship], 1990 (1991).
ATWATER, Barry. Count Dracula Society [Television], 1972 (1973).
ATWOOD, Margaret. Arthur C. Clarke, 1986 (1987).
AUEL, Jean M. Waldo, 1989 (1990).
AULISIO, Janet. Chesley [Interior Illustration], 1987 (1988). Davis Readers (IASFM) [Interior Artist], 1989 (1990), 1990 (1991).
AUSTIN, Alicia.
Balrog [Professional Publication], 1978 (1979).
Hugo [Fan Artist], 1970 (1971).
Inkpot, 1991.
Locus [Fan Artist], 1970 (1971).
World Fantasy [Artist], 1978 (1979).
AGoH World Fantasy Convention, 1978.
AGoH World SF Convention, 1993.
AUSTIN, Terry. Inkpot, 1980.
AYLING, Denys. Oscar [Visual Effects], 1979.
BABENKO, Viktor. Aëlita [Yefremov], 1989 (1990).
BACHRAN, Mary. SF Writers of Earth [1st], 1989 (1990).
BACON, Jonathan. Balrog [Judges' Choice], 1978 (1979).
BADAMI, Mary Kenny. SFRA Vice President, 1981-1982.
BADDIG, Warren. Southpaw [Humorist], 1982 (1983).
BADHAM, John. Saturn [George Pal Memorial], 1979 (1980).
BAILEY, J. O. Pilgrim, 1970.
BAILS, Jerry. Inkpot, 1981.
BAKER, Betty. Spur, 1966. Western Heritage, 19??.
BAKER, Rick. Oscar [Makeup], 1987. Saturn [Makeup], 1977 (1978), 1978 (1979), 1981 (1982).
BAKER, Scott. Prix Apollo, 1981 (1982). World Fantasy [Short Story], 1984 (1985).
BAKER, Virginia. L. Ron Hubbard's Writers of the Future [3rd Quarter, 1st Place], 1988 (1989).
BALANOS, George. Karel, 1983 (1984).
BALIK, Jaroslav. Festival Internazionale del Film [Special], 1973 (1974).

BALL, Derek. Oscar [Sound], 1977.
BALL, John.
British Critics, 1967.
California Writers, 1967.
Cleveland Critics, 1967.
Edgar, 1966 (1967).
Golden Globe, 1967.
New York Critics, 1967.
Oscar [Writing (Screenplay Based on Material from Another Medium)], 1967; [Best Story of the Year], 1967.
BALLANTINE, Betty.
Balrog [Special], 1979 (1980).
Hugo [Publisher], 1964 (1965).
Locus [Publisher], 1971 (1972), 1972 (1973), 1973 (1974).
Milford, 1992.
Nebula [Special], 1984 (1985).
World Fantasy [Special (Professional)], 1973/1974 (1975), 1983 (1984).
GoH World SF Convention, 1989.
BALLANTINE, Ian.
Balrog [Special], 1979 (1980).
Hugo [Publisher], 1964 (1965).
Milford, 1992.
Nebula [Special], 1984 (1985).
World Fantasy [Special (Professional)], 1973/1974 (1975), 1983 (1984).
GoH World SF Convention, 1989.
BALLARD, J. G. BSFA [Novel], 1979 (1980). Gilgamés [SF Novel], 1983 (1984); [SF Short Story], 1984 (1985). Saturn [Short Story], 1982 (1983).
BALLINGER, Bill S. Edgar [Half-hour Television Suspense Show], 1960.
BAMBER, George. University of Michigan/Avery Hopwood, 1955.
BANGSUND, John. Ditmar [Australian Fanzine], 1968 (1969).
BANI, Alessandro. Premios Italiano di Fantascienza [Artist], 1990 (1991), 1991 (1992).
BARANIECKI, Marek. Fantastyka [Short Fiction], 1983 (1984). Polish SF & Fantasy Achievement [Author], 1985 (1986); [Polish Fandom/Zajdel], 1985 (1986); [Collection], 1985 (1986).
BARBEE, Chuck. Festival Internazional del Film [Golden Seal], 1973 (1974).
BARBERI, Daniel. Más Alla [Novel], 1985 (1986).
BARBERI, Jacques. Grand Prix de la SF Française [Short Fiction], 1986 (1987).
BARBET, Pierre. Karel [Special President's], 1986 (1987).
BARCELO, Miguel. Gilgamés [Specialized Program], 1988 (1989).
BARKER, Clive.
British Fantasy [Short Story], 1984 (1985); [Film], 1987 (1988).
Gilgamés [Horror Collection], 1986 (1987), 1987 (1988); [Horror Short Story], 1986 (1987), 1987 (1988).
Inkpot, 1991.
World Fantasy [Anthology/Collection], 1984 (1985).
BARKS, Carl. Inkpot, 1977.
BARLOV, Georges. Karel, 1984 (1985).
BARLOWE, Wayne. Locus [Art Book], 1979 (1980).
BARNES, John. Theodore Sturgeon Memorial [3rd], 1990 (1991).
BARNETT, Charles. Festival Internazional del Film [Special], 1978 (1979).
BARON, Mike. Inkpot, 1988.
BARR, George. Hugo [Fan Writer], 1967 (1968). FGoH World SF Convention, 1976. AGoH World SF Convention, 1994.
BARRETT, Neal Jr. Theodore Sturgeon Memorial [3rd], 1988 (1989).
BARRON, Neil. Karel [Special President's], 1986 (1987); [President's], 1988 (1989). Pilgrim, 1982. SFRA Vice President, 1989-1991.
BARRY, Dan. Inkpot, 1988.
BARRY, John. Oscar [Art Direction], 1977. Saturn [Art Decoration], 1977 (1978); [Production Design], 1978 (1979); [Music], 1980 (1981).
BARRY, Lynda. Inkpot, 1988.

BARTEL, Paul. Saturn [Low Budget Film], 1982 (1983).
BARTH, John. American Book [Fiction], 1972 (1973). Arts and Letters, 1966. Jack I. and Lillian L. Poses Brandeis University Creative Arts [Citation], 1966.
BARTHELME, Donald. American Book [Children's Literature], 1971 (1972). Zabel, 1972.
BARTLETT, Sally Ann. IAFA [Graduate Scholarship], 1987 (1988).
BARTON, Thierry. Mannesmann-Tally, 1986 (1987).
BARWOOD, Lee. Gryphon, 1989 (1990).
BASS, Saul. Festival Internazionale del Film [Silver Seal], 1968 (1969); [Golden Asteroid], 1974 (1975).
BATCHELOR, John Calvin. John W. Campbell Jr. Memorial [2nd], 1983 (1984).
BATES, Jonathan. Oscar [Sound], 1982.
BATES, Kathy. Oscar [Best Actress], 1990.
BAUDINO, Gael. Lambda Literary [Lesbian SF/Fantasy], 1990 (1991).
BAUMGART, Don. L. Ron Hubbard's Writers of the Future [3rd Quarter, 2nd Place], 1985 (1986).
BAXTER, John. Ditmar [Special], 1970 (1971).
BAXTER, Stephen M. L. Ron Hubbard's Writers of the Future [2nd Quarter, 2nd Place], 1988 (1989).
BAYLEY, Barrington. Seiun Taisho [Foreign Novel], 1983 (1984), 1984 (1985), 1989 (1990).
BAZZONNI, Camillo. Festival Internazionale del Film [Golden Seal], 1964 (1965).
BEAGLE, Peter. GoH World Fantasy Convention, 1981.
BEAR, Greg.
  Atlanta Fantasy Faire, 1991.
  Hugo [Novelette], 1983 (1984); [Short Story], 1986 (1987).
  Inkpot, 1984.
  John W. Campbell Jr. Memorial [2nd], 1990 (1991).
  Nebula [Novella], 1983 (1984); [Novelette], 1983 (1984); [Short Story], 1986 (1987).
  Prix Apollo, 1985 (1986).
  SF Chronicle [Short Story], 1982 (1983).
  SFWA President, 1988-1990.
BEATTY, Warren. Saturn [Actor], 1978 (1979); [Writing], 1978 (1979); [Fantasy Film], 1978 (1979).
BEAU, Christopher C. L. Ron Hubbard's Illustrators of the Future [1st Quarter], 1990 (1991).
BEAUMONT, Charles. Bram Stoker [Collection], 1988 (1989). Playboy Writing [Nonfiction/Article], 1960.
BECHTEL, Amy. Davis Readers (Analog) [Short Story], 1988 (1989); [Short Story], 1989 (1990).
BECHTOLD, Alan. Balrog [Outstanding Amateur Achievement], 1982 (1983).
BECK, C. C. Inkpot, 1977.
BECKER, Muriel Rogow. SFRA Vice President, 1991- .
BEHN, Marc. Gilgamés [Horror Novel], 1988 (1989).
BELL, Harry. FGoH World SF Convention, 1979.
BELL, M. Shayne. L. Ron Hubbard's Writers of the Future [2nd Quarter, 1st Place], 1986 (1987).
BELLEMARE, Sylvain. Prix Boréal [Artist], 1988 (1989).
BENEDICT, Dirk. Saturn [TV Actor], 1978 (1979).
BENFORD, Gregory.
  BSFA [Novel], 1980 (1981).
  Ditmar [International Fiction], 1980 (1981).
  Gilgamés [SF Novel], 1984 (1985).
  John W. Campbell, Jr. Memorial, 1980 (1981).
  Nebula [Novelette], 1974 (1975); [Novel], 1980 (1981).
  Seiun Taisho [Media Presentation], 1990 (1991).
BENNETT, Gary L. NASA Headquarters Exceptional Performance, 1990.
BENSON, Suzanne. Oscar [Visual Effects], 1986.
BENTON, Robert. Hugo [Dramatic Presentation], 1978 (1979). Saturn [SF Film], 1978 (1979).

BERCH, Michael C. L. Ron Hubbard's Writers of the Future [1st Quarter, 2nd Place], 1990 (1991).
BERES, Stanislaw. Fantastyka [Nonfiction], 1984 (1985).
BEREZHNOY, Sergey. Fond Fantastiki [Small-Circ. Fanzine], 1990 (1991). SocCon [Fan], 1988 (1989).
BERGER, Karen. Inkpot, 1990. Will Eisner Comic Industry [Editor], 1991 (1992).
BERGER, Mark. Saturn [Sound], 1978 (1979).
BERGERON, Alain. Casper [Short Fiction], 1987 (1988).
BERGERON, Richard. Hugo [Amateur Magazine], 1961 (1962). Pong [Single Publication], 1982 (1983).
BERGMAN, Sandahl. Saturn [Actress], 1982 (1983).
BERMAN, Alex. Collectors [Most Collectible Book], 1988 (1989).
BERNACCHI, Mariella. Premios Italiano di Fantascienza [Critical Article], 1990 (1991).
BERNANDER, Ojvind. L. Ron Hubbard's Writers of the Future [3rd Quarter, 2nd Place], 1990 (1991).
BERNDT, Walter. Reuben, 1969.
BERRY, David. Oscar [Visual Effects], 1985.
BERTHELOT, Francis. Grand Prix de la SF Française [Short Fiction], 1986 (1987); [Novel], 1989 (1990). Prix Rosny-Aîné [Novel], 1987.
BESANA. Premios Italiano di Fantascienza [Novel], 1976 (1977).
BESTER, Alfred.
   Hugo [Novel], 1952 (1953).
   International Fantasy [2nd Fiction], 1953 (1954).
   Nebula [Grand Master], 1987 (1988).
   Prometheus Hall of Fame, 1988.
   GoH World SF Convention, 1987.
BETHKE, Bruce. SFWA Treasurer, 1990-1992.
BETTINSON, David. Premios Cometa d'Argenta [Film], 1973 (1974).
BETZ, Al. Casper [Fan Achievement (Other)], 1990 (1991).
BIELER, Steve. Pong [New Fan], 1982 (1983).
BIGGLE, Lloyd. SFWA Secretary/Treasurer, 1965-1967.
BILENKIN, Dmitri. Aëlita [Yefremov], 1987 (1988).
BILLON, Pierre. Grand Prix de la SF Française [Novel], 1981 (1982).
BILTGEN, Flonet. L. Ron Hubbard's Writers of the Future [4th Quarter, 2nd Place], 1987 (1988).
BINDIG, Bob. Inkpot, 1982.
BINNS, Merv. Ditmar [Australian Fanzine], 1984 (1985).
BISCHOFF, David. SFWA Secretary, 1978-1980; Vice President, 1980-1981.
BISHOFF, Murray. Inkpot, 1980.
BISHOP, Gerald. Karel [Dedicated Service], 1982 (1983).
BISHOP, James Gleason. L. Ron Hubbard's Writers of the Future [4th Quarter, 1st Place], 1989 (1990).
BISHOP, Michael.
   Locus [Novella], 1976 (1977), 1983 (1984); [Anthology], 1984 (1985).
   Mythopoeic [Fantasy], 1988 (1989).
   Nebula [Novelette], 1981 (1982); [Novel], 1982 (1983).
   Rhysling [Long Poem], 1978 (1979).
   SF Chronicle [Novella], 1983 (1984).
   GoH World Fantasy Convention, 1992.
BISLEY, Simon. Will Eisner Comic Industry [Artist], 1991 (1992).
BISSON, Terry.
   Davis Readers (IASFM) [Short Story], 1990 (1991).
   Hugo [Short Story], 1990 (1991).
   Locus [Short Story], 1990 (1991).
   Nebula [Short Story], 1990 (1991).
   SF Chronicle [Short Story], 1990 (1991).
   Theodore Sturgeon Memorial [Winner], 1990 (1991).
BITSCH, Charles. Festival Internazionale del Film [Golden Asteroid], 1968 (1969).
BLACK, Nick. Gollancz/BBC Radio 4 *Bookshelf* First Fantasy Novel, 1990 (1991).
BLACKBURN, Richard. Saturn [Low Budget Film], 1982 (1983).

BLACKFORD, Russell. Ditmar [Atheling], 1986 (1987); [Atheling], 1988 (1989).
BLACKWOOD, Christian. Festival Internazionale del Film [Silver Asteroid—TV Film], 1979 (1980).
BLAKE, Jacob. Ditmar [Fanzine], 1988 (1989).
BLALACK, Robert. Oscar [Visual Effects], 1977.
BLANC, Mel. Inkpot, 1976.
BLASETTI, Alessandro. Premios Italiano di Fantascienza [Dramatic Presentation], 1979 (1980).
BLATTY, William Peter. British Fantasy [Film], 1974 (1975). Oscar [Writing (Screenplay Based on Material from Another Medium)], 1973. Saturn [Horror Film], 1973/74 (1975); [Writing], 1980 (1981).
BLAYLOCK, James P. Philip K. Dick Memorial [1st], 1986 (1987). SF Chronicle [Novelette], 1985 (1986). World Fantasy [Short Story], 1985 (1986).
BLEILER, Everett F. Karel [President's], 1985 (1986). Locus [Nonfiction], 1991 (1992). Pilgrim, 1984. World Fantasy [Special (Professional)], 1977 (1978); [Lifetime Achievement], 1987 (1988).
BLISH, James. Hugo [Novel], 1958 (1959). SFWA Vice President, 1966-1968. GoH World SF Convention, 1960.
BLOCH, Robert.
Atlanta Fantasy Faire, 1984.
Count Dracula Society [Television], 1965 (1966); [Literature], 1968 (1969).
First Fandom, 1985.
Forry, 1974.
Hugo [Short Story], 1958 (1959); [Special], 1983 (1984).
Inkpot, 1975.
World Fantasy [Lifetime Achievement], 1973/1974 (1975).
GoH World Fantasy Convention, 1975; World SF Convention, 1948, 1973.
BLOOM, Harold. Melville Cane, 1971.
BLUMLEIN, Michael. Readercon [Collection], 1990 (1991).
BLUTH, Don. Inkpot, 1983.
BLYBERG, Willie. Will Eisner Comic Industry [Art Team], 1987 (1988).
BOAM, Jeffrey. British Fantasy [Film], 1989 (1990). Hugo [Dramatic Presentation], 1989 (1990).
BODÉ, Vaughn. Hugo [Fan Artist], 1968 (1969). Inkpot, 1975.
BODROSSY, Felix. Festival Internazionale del Film [Special], 1974 (1975).
BOGLE, Edra. SFRA Treasurer, 1991-1993.
BOIREAU, Jacques. Prix Rosny-Aîné [Novelette], 1981.
BOK, Hannes. Hugo [Cover Artist], 1952 (1953).
BOLLAND, Brian. Inkpot, 1982. Will Eisner Comic Industry [Artist], 1988 (1989); [Graphic Album], 1988 (1989); [Cover Artist], 1991 (1992).
BOLOTOVA, Jana. Festival Internazionale del Film [Silver Asteroid—Actress], 1973 (1974).
BOLTON, John. Inkpot, 1988.
BONADIMANI, Roberto. Premios Italiano di Fantascienza [Comic Artist], 1975 (1976), 1976 (1977); [Comic], 1977 (1978), 1978 (1979), 1979 (1980).
BONESTELL, Chesley. Hugo [Special Hugo], 1973 (1974). International Fantasy [Nonfiction], 1949/1950 (1951).
BOORMAN, John. Premios Cometa d'Argento [Film], 1974 (1975).
BOOTH, Gene. Saturn [Executive Achievement], 1978 (1979).
BORGES, Jorge Luis. Balrog [Special], 1980 (1981). Jerusalem Prize, 1971. World Fantasy [Lifetime Achievement], 1978 (1979).
BOSTON, Bruce D. Boomerang [Poem], 1988 (1989). Davis Readers (IASFM) [Poem], 1989 (1990). Readercon [Poet], 1987 (1988). Rhysling [Short Poem], 1984 (1985), 1987 (1988); [Long Poem], 1988 (1989).
BOTTIN, Rob. Oscar [Special Achievement (Visual Effects)], 1990. Saturn [Makeup], 1987 (1988); [Special Effects], 1987 (1988).
BOUCHARD, Guy. Prix Boréal [Novel], 1988 (1989).
BOUCHER, Anthony. Edgar Allen Poe [Criticism], 1946, 1950, 1953. Hugo [Professional Magazine], 1957 (1958); [Professional Magazine], 1958 (1959). GoH World SF Convention, 1950.

BOVA, Ben.
Balrog [Professional Publication], 1979 (1980), 1981 (1982); [Outstanding Professional Achievement], 1982 (1983).
Hugo [Editor], 1972 (1973); [Professional Editor], 1973 (1974), 1974 (1975), 1975 (1976), 1976 (1977), 1978 (1979).
Inkpot, 1985.
Skylark, 1974.
SFWA President, 1990-1992.
BOWEN, Randy. Will Eisner Comic Industry [Comics-Related Product], 1991 (1992).
BOWERS, Bill. Locus [Fanzine], 1974 (1975). FGoH World SF Convention, 1978.
BOWIE, David. Saturn [Actor], 1976 (1977).
BOWIE, Les. Oscar [Special Achievement (Visual Effects)], 1978.
BOYD, Russell. Saturn [Cinematography], 1978 (1979).
BOYETTE, Pat. Inkpot, 1980.
BOZZETTO, Bruno. Festival Internazionale del Film [Golden Seal], 1979 (1980). Premios Italiano di Fantascienza [Dramatic Presentation], 1979 (1980).
BRACKETT, Leigh.
Balrog [SF Film Hall of Fame], 1980 (1981).
British Fantasy [Film], 1980 (1981).
Forry, 1978.
Hugo [Dramatic Presentation], 1980 (1981).
Saturn [Hall of Fame], 1979 (1980); [SF Film], 1980 (1981).
GoH World SF Convention, 1964.
BRADBURY, Ray.
Arts and Letters, 1954.
AWA Writing [General Magazines], 1968.
Balrog [Poet], 1978 (1979).
Bram Stoker [Life Achievement], 1988 (1989).
Clampett, 1987.
Count Dracula Society [Literature], 1964 (1965), 1970 (1971).
Forry, 1966.
Hugo [Gandalf Grand Master], 1979 (1980).
Inkpot, 1974.
International Fantasy [3rd Fiction], 1951 (1952).
Invisible Little Man, 1960.
Nebula [Grand Master], 1988 (1989).
Prometheus Hall of Fame, 1984.
Robert S. Ball Memorial, 1968.
Saturn [Special Literature], 1978 (1979).
U. S. Air Force Academy Special Achievement, 1989.
Valentine Davies, 1974.
World Fantasy [Lifetime Achievement], 1976 (1977).
GoH World SF Convention, 1986.
BRADLEY, Marion Zimmer. Forry, 1976. Gray Mouser, 1981. Inkpot, 1986. Locus [Fantasy Novel], 1983 (1984). SFWA Vice President, 1978-1979.
BRANCO, Marcello S. Nova [Fanzine], 1990 (1991).
BRANDHORST, Andreas. Kurd Lasswitz [Short Story], 1982 (1983).
BRANHAM, R. V. L. Ron Hubbard's Writers of the Future [1st Quarter, 3rd Place], 1986 (1987).
BREIDBART, Seth. Pong [Fugghead of the Year], 1982 (1983).
BREIDING, G. Sutton. Rhysling [Short Poem], 1989 (1990).
BRENNAN, Joseph Payne. World Fantasy [Special], 1981 (1982). FGoH World Fantasy Convention, 1982.
BRENNERT, Alan. Emmy, 1991. Nebula [Short Story], 1991 (1992). Theodore Sturgeon Memorial [2nd], 1991 (1992). Writers Guild of America TV/Radio [Dramatic/Episodic Script], 1986.
BRERETON, Daniel. Manning, 1990.
BRESEE, Bobbie. Saturn [Outstanding Service], 1988 (1989).
BRESEE, Frank. Saturn [Outstanding Service], 1988 (1989).

BRETNOR, Reginald. J. Lloyd Eaton Memorial [Special Lifetime Achievement], 1986 (1988).
BREVIG, Eric. Oscar [Special Achievement (Visual Effects)], 1990.
BRIDGES, Jeff. Saturn [Actor], 1984 (1985).
BRIMM, Walter. Karel, 1984 (1985).
BRIN, David.
  Balrog [Novel], 1984 (1985).
  Collectors [Most Collectible Book], 1988 (1989).
  Hugo [Novel], 1983 (1984), 1987 (1988); [Short Story], 1984 (1985).
  Inkpot, 1985.
  John W. Campbell, Jr. Memorial, 1985 (1986).
  Lazar Komarcic [Foreign Short Story], 1987 (1988).
  Locus [SF Novel], 1983 (1984), 1985 (1986), 1987 (1988); [Novelette], 1986 (1987); [1980s Author], 1987 (1988).
  Nebula [Novel], 1983 (1984).
  Seiun Taisho [Foreign Novel], 1990 (1991).
  U.S. Air Force Academy Special Achievement, 1989.
  SFWA Secretary, 1983-1984.
BRIZZI, Mary A. T.—SEE: TURZILLO, Mary A.
BRODERICK, Damien. Ditmar [Australian Novel], 1980 (1981); [Australian Long Fiction], 1988 (1989).
BROOKS, Mel. Hugo [Dramatic Presentation], 1974 (1975). Nebula [Dramatic Presentation], 1975 (1976). Saturn [Director], 1975 (1976); [Horror Film], 1975 (1976).
BROSNAN, John. J. Lloyd Eaton Memorial, 1978 (1980).
BROSSARD, Jacques. Casper [French Long Form], 1989 (1990).
BROWN, Charles N.
  Hugo [Amateur Magazine], 1970 (1971), 1971 (1972); [Fanzine], 1975 (1976), 1977 (1978), 1979 (1980), 1980 (1981), 1981 (1982), 1982 (1983); [Semiprozine], 1983 (1984), 1984 (1985), 1985 (1986), 1986 (1987), 1987 (1988), 1988 (1989), 1989 (1990), 1990 (1991), 1991 (1992).
  J. Lloyd Eaton Memorial, 1989 (1991).
  Karel [Special President's], 1986 (1987).
  Locus [Fanzine], 1970 (1971), 1971 (1972), 1972 (1973), 1973 (1974), 1975 (1976), 1976 (1977); [Single Issue of Fanzine], 1970 (1971); [Fan Writer], 1971 (1972); [Magazine], 1982 (1983), 1983 (1984), 1984 (1985), 1985 (1986).
BROWN, Dena. Hugo [Amateur Magazine], 1970 (1971), 1971 (1972); [Fanzine], 1975 (1976), 1977 (1978). Locus [Fanzine], 1970 (1971), 1971 (1972), 1972 (1973), 1973 (1974), 1975 (1976), 1976 (1977); [Single Issue of Fanzine], 1970 (1971).
BROWN, Frederic. Edgar Allen Poe [First Novel], 1948.
BROWN, Hi. Count Dracula Society [Special], 1974 (1975).
BROWN, Molly. BSFA [Short Fiction], 1991 (1992).
BROWN, Pat. Doc Weir, 1991.
BROWN, Stephen P. Readercon [Criticism Magazine], 1989 (1990); [Magazine Design], 1989 (1990).
BROWNE, Dik. Reuben, 1962, 1973.
BROXON, Mildred Downey. SFWA Vice President, 1976-1978.
BRUCE, Jean. SF Writers of Earth [2nd], 1984 (1985).
BRUMBAUGH, J. D. SF Writers of Earth [3rd], 1984 (1985).
BRUMM, Walter. Kurd Lasswitz [Translator], 1988 (1989).
BRUNNER, Frank. British Fantasy [Comics], 1978 (1979). Inkpot, 1976.
BRUNNER, John.
  BSFA [Novel], 1969 (1970), 1970 (1971).
  Gilgamés [SF Novel], 1985 (1986).
  Hugo [Novel], 1968 (1969).
  Premios Cometa d'Argento [Novel], 1975 (1976), 1977 (1978).
  Prix Apollo, 1972 (1973).
  GoH World SF Convention, 1983.
BRUNO, John. Oscar [Visual Effects], 1989.

BRUSSOLO, Serge. Grand Prix de la SF Française [Novelette], 1978 (1979); [Novel], 1980 (1981), 1986 (1987). Prix Apollo, 1983 (1984). Prix Rosny-Aîné [Novelette], 1981.
BRYANT, Edward. Nebula [Short Story], 1978 (1979), 1979 (1980). Top Hands [Adult Short Story], 1989; [Juvenile Short Story], 1989.
BRYNYCH, Zbynek. Festival Internazional del Film [Special], 1967 (1968).
BUDRYS, Algis. Invisible Little Man, 1985. Locus [Nonfiction], 1985 (1986).
BUDZ, Mark. L. Ron Hubbard's Writers of the Future [3rd Quarter, 2nd Place], 1991 (1992).
BUDZ, Robert Mark—SEE: BUDZ, Mark.
BUGAJSKI, Leszek. Fantastyka [Nonfiction], 1983 (1984).
BUGROV, Vitaly. Aëlita [Yefremov], 1987 (1988).
BUJOLD, Lois McMaster.
Davis Readers (Analog) [Novella/Novelette], 1989 (1990), 1990 (1991).
Hugo [Novel], 1990 (1991), 1991 (1992); [Novella], 1989 (1990).
Locus [SF Novel], 1991 (1992).
Nebula [Novel], 1988 (1989); [Novella], 1989 (1990).
Prisoners of Gravity Reality 1 [SF Novel], 1991 (1992).
SF Chronicle [Novella], 1989 (1990).
BUKATO, Wiktor. Fantastyka [Special], 1986/1987 (1988). Karel, 1986 (1987). Polish SF & Fantasy Achievement [Publisher], 1985 (1986).
BULGAKOV, Mikhail. Premios Cometa d'Argento [Film], 1975 (1976).
BULL, Emma. *Chronic Rift* Roundtable [Short Story], 1991 (1992). Locus [First Novel], 1987 (1988). Philip K. Dick [2nd], 1991 (1992).
BULYCHEV, Kir. Alkor [Novel], 1989 (1990).
BURDEN, Bob. Inkpot, 1990.
BURGESS, Anthony. Hugo [Dramatic Presentation], 1971 (1972). Saturn [International Film], 1981 (1982); [Special], 1981 (1982).
BURIAN, Pĕtr. Karel Capek [Short Story], 1983 (1984).
BURKE, John. Festival Internazional del Film [Golden Asteroid], 1967 (1968).
BURKE, Michelle. Emmy [Outstanding Achievement in Makeup], 1990.
BURNHAM, Crispin. Balrog [Amateur Publication], 1981 (1982), 1984 (1985).
BURNS, George. Saturn [Actor], 1977 (1978).
BURNS, Jim. BSFA [Artist], 1979 (1980), 1984 (1985), 1985 (1986), 1987 (1988), 1989 (1990). Hugo [Professional Artist], 1986 (1987). AGoH World SF Convention, 1987.
BURNS, Peter. Ditmar [Australian Fanzine], 1986 (1987).
BURNS-CHENELLE, Carina. Inkpot, 1992.
BURROUGHS, Edgar Rice. Gernsback [Novel], 1926 (1983). Inkpot, 1975.
BURROUGHS, William S. Arts and Letters, 1975.
BURT, Brian. L. Ron Hubbard's Writers of the Future [Gold], 1991 (1992); [2nd Quarter, 1st Place], 1991 (1992).
BURTT, Ben(jamin Jr.). Oscar [Special Achievement (Sound Effects Creation)], 1977; [Sound Effects Editing], 1982, 1989; [Special Achievement (Sound Effects Editing)], 1981. Saturn [Sound], 1977 (1978).
BUSBY, F. M. Hugo [Amateur Magazine], 1959 (1960). SFWA Vice President, 1974-1976.
BUSCEMA, John. Inkpot, 1978.
BUSH, Beryl. L. Ron Hubbard's Illustrators of the Future [2nd Quarter], 1989 (1990).
BUSH, John. Karel [Harrison], 1983 (1984).
BUSHMILLER, Ernie. Reuben, 1976.
BUTLER, Dawn. Inkpot, 1975.
BUTLER, Octavia.
Hugo [Short Story], 1983 (1984); [Novelette], 1984 (1985).
Locus [Novelette], 1984 (1985).
Nebula [Novelette], 1984 (1985).
SF Chronicle [Novelette], 1984 (1985), 1987 (1988).
Theodore Sturgeon Memorial [3rd], 1987 (1988).
U.S. Air Force Academy Special Achievement, 1989.
BUTNER, Richard. Inkpot, 1975.
BYRNE, John. Inkpot, 1980.

CABELL, James Branch. Gilgamés [Fantasy Novel], 1984 (1985).
CADGER, Rick. Fear Fiction [Newcomer], 1990 (1991).
CADIGAN, Pat.
Arthur C. Clarke [Winner], 1991 (1992).
Balrog [Short Fiction], 1978 (1979); [Amateur Publication], 1978 (1979), 1982 (1983).
Locus [Short Story], 1987 (1988); [Collection], 1989 (1990).
SF Chronicle [Short Story], 1986 (1987).
World Fantasy [Special (Nonprofessional)], 1980 (1981).
CAIDIN, Martin. AWA Writing [Books (Nonfiction)], 1961, 1965; [Books (Fiction)], 1968. James J. Strebig, 1958, 1961.
CALVINO, Italo. Ditmar [International Fiction], 1969 (1970). World Fantasy [Lifetime Achievement], 1981 (1982).
CAMAGAJEVEC, Sebastijan. L. Ron Hubbard's Illustrators of the Future [2nd Quarter], 1992 (1993).
CAMERON, Eleanor. American Book [Children's Literature], 1973 (1974).
CAMERON, James.
British Fantasy [Film], 1986 (1987).
BSFA [Media Presentation], 1986 (1987).
Hugo [Dramatic Presentation], 1979 (1980), 1986 (1987).
Saturn [Writing], 1984 (1985); [SF Film], 1984 (1985).
SF Chronicle [Dramatic Presentation], 1986 (1987).
CAMERON, Kirk. Saturn [Juvenile Actor], 1987 (1988).
CAMERON, Sara. Turner Tomorrow [Hon. Mention], 1991.
CAMPBELL, Charles L. Oscar [Sound Effects Editing], 1982, 1985, 1988.
CAMPBELL, John W., Jr.
Hugo [Professional Magazine], 1952 (1953), 1954 (1955), 1955 (1956), 1960 (1961), 1961 (1962), 1963 (1964), 1964 (1965); [American Professional Magazine], 1956 (1957).
Skylark, 1968.
GoH World SF Convention, 1947, 1954, 1957.
CAMPBELL, Laura. L. Ron Hubbard's Writers of the Future [1st Quarter; 2nd Place], 1985 (1986).
CAMPBELL, Ramsey.
British Fantasy [August Derleth], 1980 (1981), 1987 (1988), 1988 (1989), 1990 (1991); [Short Story], 1977 (1978); [Anthology/Collection], 1990 (1991).
World Fantasy [Short Fiction], 1977 (1978), 1979 (1980); [Anthology], 1990 (1991).
GoH World Fantasy Convention, 1986.
CANAL, Richard. Grand Prix de la SF Française [Short Fiction], 1987 (1988).
CANIFF, Milton. Inkpot, 1974. Reuben, 1946, 1971. Will Eisner Comic Industry [Hall of Fame Inductee], 1987 (1988).
CANN, James. Saturn [Actor], 1975 (1976).
CANNON, Dyan. Saturn [Supporting Actress], 1978 (1979).
CANTOR, Robbie. E. E. Evans/Paul Frehafer, 1989.
CANTRELL, Lisa. Bram Stoker [First Novel], 1987 (1988). HWA Secretary, 1989-1990.
CANTY, Thomas. SF Chronicle [Artist], 1989 (1990). World Fantasy [Artist], 1985 (1986), 1989 (1990).
CAPOBIANCO, Michael. SFWA Treasurer, 1992- .
CAPONIGRO, John. L. Ron Hubbard's Illustrators of the Future [1st Quarter], 1991 (1992).
CAPP, Al. Inkpot, 1978. Reuben, 1947.
CAPRA, Frank. Inkpot, 1974.
CARD, Orson Scott.
Davis Readers (IASFM) [Novelette], 1988 (1989).
Ditmar [International Fiction], 1988 (1989).
Kurd Lasswitz [Foreign Novel], 1988 (1989).
Hugo [Novel], 1985 (1986), 1986 (1987); [Novella], 1987 (1988); [Nonfiction], 1990 (1991); [Campbell], 1977 (1978).
IAM [Novelette], 1990 (1991).
John W. Campbell Jr. Memorial [3rd], 1986 (1987).

Locus [SF Novel], 1986 (1987); [Fantasy Novel], 1987 (1988), 1988 (1989), 1989 (1990); [Novelette], 1989 (1990); [Short Story], 1989 (1990); [Collection], 1990 (1991).
Mythopoeic [Fantasy], 1987 (1988).
Nebula [Novel], 1985 (1986), 1986 (1987).
Nova [Foreign Novel], 1990 (1991); [Reviewer], 1990 (1991).
Phoenix, 1986 (1987).
Prix Cosmos 2000, 1987 (1988).
SF Chronicle [Novel], 1985 (1986), 1986 (1987).
Seiun Taisho [Foreign Novelette], 1988 (1989).
Skylark, 1992.
World Fantasy [Novella], 1986 (1987).

CAREY, Peter. Ditmar [Australian Novel], 1985 (1986).
CARLBURG, Stephen. Southpaw [Writer], 1982 (1983).
CARLETTI, Eduardo. Más Alla [Short Fiction], 1985 (1986).
CARLEY, Catherine. SF Writers of Earth [1st], 1985 (1986).
CARNELL, Edward J. Hugo [British Professional Magazine], 1956 (1957).
CARO. Grand Prix de la SF Française [Special], 1981 (1982).
CAROGLIO. Premios Italiano di Fantascienza [Novel], 1976 (1977).
CARPENTER, John. Saturn [Special Effects], 1975 (1976).
CARPENTER, Leonard. L. Ron Hubbard's Writers of the Future [1st Quarter; 2nd Place], 1984 (1985).
CARR, David. L. Ron Hubbard's Writers of the Future [3rd Quarter, 3rd Place], 1989 (1990).
CARR, John F. SFWA Treasurer, 1982-1986; Vice President, 1986-1987.
CARR, Terry.
Hugo [Amateur Magazine], 1958 (1959); [Fan Writer], 1972 (1973); [Professional Editor], 1984 (1985), 1986 (1987).
Locus [Original Anthology/Collection], 1971 (1972), 1974 (1975); [Reprint Anthology/Collection], 1971 (1972), 1972 (1973), 1973 (1974), 1976 (1977); [Anthology], 1979 (1980), 1982 (1983), 1983 (1984).
Milford, 1983.
SF Chronicle [Book Editor], 1984 (1985).
FGoH World SF Convention, 1986.
CARRADINE, John. Count Dracula Society [Cinema], 1968 (1969).
CARRAZÉ, Alain. Grand Prix de la SF Française [Nonfiction], 1989 (1990).
CARRERE, Emmanuel. Grand Prix de la SF Française [Special], 1985 (1986).
CARROLL, Jonathan. Arthur C. Clarke [2nd], 1989 (1990). British Fantasy [August Derleth], 1991 (1992). World Fantasy [Short Story], 1987 (1988).
CARROLL, Lucy E. L. Ron Hubbard's Writers of the Future [1st Quarter, 2nd Place], 1986 (1987).
CARSE, William. L. Ron Hubbard's Writers of the Future [3rd Quarter, 3rd Place], 1990 (1991).
CARSON, Dave. British Fantasy [Artist], 1980 (1981), 1981 (1982), 1982 (1983), 1988 (1989), 1989 (1990).
CARTER, Angela. John Llewelyn Rhys Memorial Prize, 1968. Somerset Maugham, 1969.
CARTER, Lin. Gilgamés [Fantasy Collection/Anthology], 1988 (1989).
CARTER, Margaret L. Count Dracula Society [Walpole Medal], 1975 (1976).
CARTER, Paul A. J. Lloyd Eaton Memorial, 1976/1977 (1979).
CARTIER, Edd. First Fandom, 1990. L. Ron Hubbard's Writers of the Future [Special Golden Age], 1988 (1989). World Fantasy [Lifetime Achievement], 1991 (1992).
CARTWRIGHT, Veronica. Saturn [Supporting Actress], 1979 (1980).
CASSUTT, Michael. SFWA Vice President, 1988-1989.
CASTLE, William. Count Dracula Society [Cinema], 1974 (1975).
CASTLEBERRY, May. Collectors [Most Collectible Book], 1989 (1990).
CATALANO, Frank. SFWA Secretary, 1988-1989.
CATANI, Vittorio. Premios Italiano di Fantascienza [Novel], 1990 (1991).
CAUSO, Roberto de Sousa. Jeronimo Montiero [3rd], 1990 (1991). Nova [Artist], 1990 (1991).

CAVALIERO, Glen. Mythopoeic [Scholarship], 1985 (1986).
CAVE, Hugh B. Bram Stoker [Life Achievement], 1990 (1991). Phoenix, 1986 (1987). World Fantasy [Single Author Collection/Anthology], 1977 (1978).
CAZADESSUS, Camille. Hugo [Amateur Magazine], 1965 (1966).
CEDERLING, Siv. Rhysling [Long Poem], 1984 (1985).
CEROSIMO, Adalberto. Premios Italiano di Fantascienza [Short Fiction], 1979 (1980).
CHADBORN, Mark. Fear Fiction [Newcomer], 1989 (1990).
CHADWICK, Paul. *Will Eisner Comic Industry* [Continuing Series], 1987 (1988), 1988 (1989); [B&W Series], 1987 (1988), 1988 (1989); [New Series], 1987 (1988); [Writer/Artist Team], 1988 (1989); [Single Issue or Story], 1990 (1991); [Finite Series], 1991 (1992).
CHAFFEE, Doug. Phoenix, 1982 (1983).
CHALKER, Jack L. Hamilton/Brackett Memorial, 1980. Skylark, 1980. SFWA Treasurer, 1980-1982.
CHAMBERS, John. Emmy [Makeup Design], 1968. Oscar [Makeup Design], 1968.
CHAMPETIER, Joël. Casper [French Short Form], 1988 (1989).
CHAN, Ernie. Inkpot, 1980.
CHANDLER, A. Bertram. Ditmar [Australian Fiction], 1968 (1969), 1970 (1971), 1974 (1975), 1975 (1976). GoH World SF Convention, 1982.
CHANEY, Lon Jr. Count Dracula Society [Cinema], 1965 (1966).
CHANT, Joy. Mythopoeic [Fantasy], 1983 (1984). World Fantasy [Special (Professional)], 1983 (1984).
CHAPMAN, Bob. Inkpot, 1992.
CHAPPELL, Fred. World Fantasy [Short Story], 1991 (1992).
CHARMAN, Roy. Oscar [Sound], 1981.
CHARNAS, Suzy McKee. Gilgamés [Horror Short Story], 1989 (1990). Hugo [Short Story], 1989 (1990). Nebula [Novella], 1980 (1981).
CHASE, Brandon L. Saturn [Executive Achievement], 1975 (1976).
CHAYKIN, Howard. Inkpot, 1977.
CHERRY, David A.
  Chesley [Cover Illustration (Hardback)], 1986 (1987); [Cover Illustration (Paperback)], 1991 (1992); [Unpublished Color], 1986 (1987), 1991 (1992); [Special], 1988 (1989), 1989 (1990).
  Skylark, 1991.
CHERRYH, C. J.
  Balrog [Short Fiction], 1981 (1982).
  Hugo [Campbell], 1976 (1977); [Short Story], 1978 (1979); [Novel], 1981 (1982), 1988 (1989).
  Locus [SF Novel], 1988 (1989).
  Oklahoma Professional Writers Hall of Fame Inductee, 1991.
  SF Chronicle [Novel], 1988 (1989).
  Skylark, 1988.
  SFWA Secretary, 1984-1986, 1991- .
CHERTKOV, Andrei E. SocCon [Fan], 1988 (1989).
CHETWYND-HAYES, Ronald. Bram Stoker [Life Achievement], 1988 (1989). British Fantasy [Special], 1988 (1989).
CHEW, Richard. Oscar [Film Editing], 1977. Saturn [Editing], 1977 (1978).
CHIANG, Ted. Dell Readers (Analog) [Novelette], 1991 (1992). Hugo [John W. Campbell], 1991 (1992). Nebula [Novelette], 1990 (1991).
CHILVERS, Colin. Oscar [Special Achievement (Visual Effects)], 1978. Saturn [Special Effects], 1978 (1979).
CHIZMAR, Richard. World Fantasy [Special (Nonprofessional)], 1990 (1991).
CHRISTENSEN, James C. Chesley [3-D Art], 1990 (1991).
CHRISTIAN, Roger. Oscar [Set Decoration], 1977. Saturn [Set Decoration], 1977 (1978).
CHRISTOPHER, Joe R. Mythopoeic [Scholarship], 1987 (1988).
CHURCHILL, Frank. Oscar [Music Score of a Musical Picture], 1941.
CITRO, Joseph L. HWA Treasurer, 1989-1990.
CLAESSON, Maths. Alvar Appleotfft Memorial, 1983 (1984).
CLAMPETT, Bob. Count Dracula Society [Summers], 1972 (1973). Inkpot, 1974.
CLAREMONT, Chris. Inkpot, 1980.

CLARESON, Thomas D. J. Lloyd Eaton Memorial, 1985 (1987). Pilgrim, 1977. SFRA President, 1970-1977.
CLARK, Marty. Locus [Nonfiction], 1984 (1985).
CLARKE, Arthur C.
Aerospace Communications, 1974.
Alkor [Translated Novel], 1989 (1990).
AWA Writing [General Magazines], 1965.
Balrog [SF Film], 1979 (1980).
BSFA [Novel], 1973 (1974).
Forry, 1982.
Hugo [Short Story], 1955 (1956); [Dramatic Presentation], 1968 (1969), 1984 (1985); [Novel], 1973 (1974), 1979 (1980).
International Fantasy [Nonfiction], 1951 (1952).
John W. Campbell, Jr. Memorial, 1973 (1974).
Jupiter [Novel], 1973 (1974).
Karel [Harrison], 1990 (1991).
Locus [Novel], 1973 (1974).
Nebula [Novella], 1972 (1973); [Novel], 1973 (1974), 1979 (1980); [Grand Master], 1985 (1986).
Robert S. Ball Memorial, 1965.
Saturn [SF Novel], 1982 (1983).
SF Chronicle [Dramatic Presentation], 1984 (1985).
GoH World SF Convention, 1956.
CLARKE, I. F. Pilgrim, 1974.
CLAYPOOL, Gavin. E. E. Evans/Paul Frehafer, 1984.
CLEMENS, Brian. Saturn [Fantasy Film], 1973/74 (1975).
CLEMENS, Samuel Langhorne—SEE: TWAIN, Mark.
CLEMENT, Hal. Forry, 1992. International Fantasy [2nd Fiction], 1954 (1955). Invisible Little Man, 1962. Skylark, 1969. GoH World SF Convention, 1991.
CLIFTON, Mark. Hugo [Novel], 1954 (1955).
CLINGAN, C. C. Readercon [Dale Donaldson Memorial], 1979 (1980).
CLUTE, John. Hugo [Nonfiction], 1979 (1980). Locus [Nonfiction], 1979 (1980). Readercon [Nonfiction], 1988 (1989).
COBLENTZ, Stanton A. First Fandom, 1981.
COCHRAN, Russ. Inkpot, 1982.
COCKRUM, David. Inkpot, 1982.
COCOMAN, Tracy. Collectors [Most Collectible Book], 1991 (1992).
COGELL, Elizabeth Cummins. SFRA Treasurer, 1979-1983; Vice President, 1983-1985.
COGGINS, Jack. International Fantasy [3rd Nonfiction], 1951 (1952).
COGSWELL, Theodore. SFWA Secretary, 1974-1975.
COHEN, Herman. Count Dracula Society [Cinema], 1963 (1964).
COHEN, Larry. Saturn [George Pal Memorial], 1987 (1988).
COHEN, Martin B. Saturn [Life Career], 1982 (1983).
COLAN, Gene. Inkpot, 1978.
COLE, L. B. Inkpot, 1981.
COLEBORN, Peter. British Fantasy [Special], 1989 (1990).
COLLIER, John. International Fantasy [Fiction], 1951 (1952).
COLLINGS, Michael J. IAFA [Graduate Scholarship], 1988 (1989).
COLLINS, Max Allen. Inkpot, 1982.
COLLINS, Michael. Hugo [Special], 1968 (1969).
COLLINS, Nancy. Bram Stoker [First Novel], 1989 (1990).
COLLINS, Robert. Balrog [Outstanding Amateur Achievement], 1981 (1982); [Amateur Publication], 1983 (1984). World Fantasy [Special (Nonprofessional)], 1981 (1982). SFRA Newsletter Editor, 1988-1989.
COLLON, Hélène. Karel, 1988 (1989).
COLOMBO, A. Premios Italiano di Fantascienza [Book Length Essay], 1990 (1991).
COLUMBUS, Chris. Saturn [Horror Film], 1984 (1985).
COMIC BOOK LEGAL DEFENSE FUND. Clampett, 1991.
CONEY, Michael G. BSFA [Novel], 1976 (1977).
CONNER, Jeff. World Fantasy [Special (Nonprofessional)], 1986 (1987).

CONNER, Mike. Nebula [Novelette], 1991 (1992).
CONTENTO, William G. J. Lloyd Eaton Memorial, 1989 (1991).
COOK, Rick. Davis Readers (Analog) [Science Fact Article], 1986 (1987).
COOP, Denys. Oscar [Special Achievement (Visual Effects)], 1978.
COOPER, Merian C. Count Dracula Society [Special], 1970 (1971).
COPPOLA, Francis Ford. Inkpot, 1992.
CORDESSE, Gerard. Grand Prix de la SF Française [Special], 1983 (1984).
CORMAN, Roger. Count Dracula Society [Cinema], 1970 (1971). Saturn [Life Career], 1987 (1988).
CORNFORD, Adam. Rhysling [Long Poem], 1982 (1983).
CORRELL, Rich. Count Dracula Society [Fauria], 1971 (1972).
COSSATO, Gianpaolo. Karel, 1984 (1985).
COSTA, Delores. Saturn [Outstanding Service], 1989/90 (1991).
COSTA, Frank. Saturn [Outstanding Service], 1989/90 (1991).
COSTELLO, Matthew J. HWA Treasurer, 1990-1992.
COUCH, Charles. Saturn [Exceptional Achievement], 1980 (1981).
COULSON, Juanita. Hugo [Amateur Magazine], 1964 (1965). FGoH World SF Convention, 1972.
COULSON, Robert. Hugo [Amateur Magazine], 1964 (1965). SFWA Secretary, 1972-1974. FGoH World SF Convention, 1972.
COVILLE, Bruce. Golden Duck [Children's SF Book], 1991 (1992).
COWPER, Richard. Balrog [Short Fiction], 1980 (1981).
COWPERTHWAITE, David. British Fantasy [Small Press Magazine], 1990 (1991).
COYE, Lee Brown. World Fantasy [Artist], 1973/1974 (1975), 1977 (1978).
CRABBE, Buster. Saturn [Posthumous], 1982 (1983).
CRAIG, Chase. Inkpot, 1982.
CRANE, Roy. Reuben, 1950.
CRAVEN, Wes. British Fantasy [Film], 1984 (1985).
CRAWFORD, William L. Big Heart, 1985. Count Dracula Society [Summers], 1971 (1972). First Fandom, 1982.
CRAYNE, Chuck. E. E. Evans/Paul Frehafer, 1968.
CREELMAN, James A. Balrog [Fantasy Film Hall of Fame], 1981 (1982).
CREMASCHI, Inisero. Premios Cometa d'Argento [Editor], 1977 (1978); [Critical Work], 1978 (1979).
CREMER, Robert. Count Dracula Society [Literature], 1976 (1977).
CREPAX, Guido. Premios Italiano di Fantascienza [Comic], 1971 (1972).
CRONENBERG, David. British Fantasy [Film], 1983 (1984). Saturn [International Film], 1980 (1981); [George Pal Memorial], 1988 (1989).
CROTHERS, Scatman. Saturn [Supporting Actor], 1980 (1981).
CROWE, Ira. L. Ron Hubbard's Illustrators of the Future [1st Quarter], 1991 (1992).
CROWLEY, John. World Fantasy [Novel], 1981 (1982); [Novella], 1989 (1990).
CRUICKSHANK, Art. Oscar [Special Visual Effects], 1966.
CRUMB, Robert. Inkpot, 1989. Will Eisner Comic Industry [Hall of Fame Inductee], 1990 (1991).
CRUMP, Randy. L. Ron Hubbard's Writers of the Future [2nd Quarter; 3rd Place], 1984 (1985).
CRUSE, Howard. Inkpot, 1989.
CSISCERY-RONAY, Istvan Jr. Pioneer, 1992.
CUERVO, Alejo. Gilgamés [Specialized Line], 1985 (1986), 1986 (1987), 1987 (1988); [Specialized Program], 1988 (1989); [Special], 1989 (1990).
CULP, Robert. Saturn [Special], 1980 (1981).
CUMMINGS, Jack. Inkpot, 1985.
CUNIS, Reinmar. Kurd Lasswitz [Short Story], 1985 (1986).
CUNNINGHAM, Frank. Count Dracula Society [Fauria], 1968 (1969); [Summers], 1969 (1970).
CURREY, L. W. SFRA Secretary 1977-1978.
CURRY, Chris. HWA Secretary, 1990-1992.
CURTIS, Dan. Count Dracula Society [Television], 1969 (1970), 1973 (1974). Saturn [Director], 1976 (1977); [Horror Film], 1976 (1977).
CURTONI, Vittorio. Premios Italiano di Fantascienza [Short Fiction], 1978 (1979).

CURVAL, Phillipe. Grand Prix de la SF Française [Novel], 1974 (1975). Prix Apollo, 1976 (1977).
CUSHING, Peter. Count Dracula Society [Special], 1969 (1970).
CWIKIEL, Agnieszka. Fantastyka [Nonfiction], 1985 (1986).
DAHL, Roald. Playboy Writing [Fiction Short Story], 1965. World Fantasy [Lifetime Achievement], 1982 (1983).
DALTON, Phyllis. Saturn [Costumes], 1987 (1988).
DANEHY-OAKES, Dan'l. L. Ron Hubbard's Writers of the Future [4th Quarter, 1st Place], 1988 (1989).
DANFORTH, Jim. Saturn [Stop Motion Animation], 1975 (1976).
DANIELS, Les. GoH World Horror Convention, 1993.
DANN, Jack. Gilgamés [Horror Short Story], 1986 (1987).
DANNER, Blythe. Saturn [Actress], 1976 (1977).
DANTE, Joe. Saturn [Editing], 1978 (1979); [Director], 1984 (1985).
DARROW, Geof. Will Eisner Comic Industry [Writer/Artist Team], 1990 (1991).
DATLOW, Ellen. SF Chronicle [Book Editor], 1990 (1991). World Fantasy [Anthology], 1988 (1989), 1989 (1990), 1991 (1992).
DAUGHERTY, Walter J. Big Heart, 1968. Count Dracula Society [Fauria], 1967 (1968); [Special], 1968 (1969). FGoH World SF Convention, 1968.
DAVENPORT, Emily. Boomerang [Short Story], 1988 (1989).
DAVID, Peter. Will Eisner Comic Industry [Writer/Artist Team], 1991 (1992).
DAVIDSON, Avram.
  Hugo [Short Story], 1957 (1958); [Professional Magazine], 1962 (1963).
  World Fantasy [Single Author Collection/Anthology], 1975 (1976); [Short Fiction], 1978 (1979); [Lifetime Achievement], 1985 (1986).
DAVIES, Robinson. World Fantasy [Anthology/Collection], 1983 (1984).
DAVIS, Alan. Will Eisner Comic Industry [Art Team], 1988 (1989).
DAVIS, Bette. Saturn [Supporting Actress], 1976 (1977).
DAVIS, Gary. L. Ron Hubbard's Illustrators of the Future [1st Quarter], 1992 (1993).
DAVIS, Helen. N3F [3rd], 1991 (1992).
DAVIS, Jack. Inkpot, 1985.
DAWSON, Richard. Saturn [Supporting Actor], 1987 (1988).
DAY, Gene. Readercon [Cover Artist], 1979 (1980); [Overall Artistic Achievement], 1979 (1980).
DE CAMP, L. Sprague.
  Athenaeum Literary, 1958.
  Davis Readers (Analog) [Science Fact Article], 1989 (1990).
  First Fandom, 1989.
  Forry, 1977.
  Hugo [Gandalf Grand Master], 1975 (1976).
  International Fantasy [Nonfiction], 1952 (1953).
  Invisible Little Man, 1965.
  Nebula [Grand Master], 1978 (1979).
  World Fantasy [Lifetime Achievement], 1983 (1984).
  GoH World Fantasy Convention, 1990; World SF Convention, 1966.
DE GARIS, Roger. Karel [President's], 1988 (1989).
DE LA MARE, Walter. Gilgamés [Horror Collection], 1987 (1988).
DE LINT, Charles. Casper [Novel], 1987 (1988). IAFA [Crawford], 1984 (1985). Readercon [Short Work], 1988 (1989). HWA Vice President, 1992- .
DE ROCHE, Everette. Festival Fantastique d'Avoriaz, 1979. Saturn [Foreign Film], 1979 (1980); [Special] 1980 (1981).
DE TURRIS, Gianfranco. Premios Italiano di Fantascienza [Critical Work], 1979 (1980); [Critical Article (Professional)], 1991 (1992); [Critical Article (Fan)], 1991 (1992).
DE VESTEL, Robert. Saturn [Set Decoration], 1975 (1976), 1976 (1977).
DEAN, Roger. World Fantasy [Artist], 1976 (1977).
DeBOLT, Joe. SFRA President, 1979-1981.
DeCARLO, Dan. Inkpot, 1991.
DECARNIN, Camilla. L. Ron Hubbard's Writers of the Future [1st Quarter; 1st Place], 1985 (1986).
DeFALCO, Tom. Inkpot, 1990.

DEGEER, Carl Johan. Svenska SF Priset [Novel], 1985 (1986).
DEL REY, Judy-Lynn.
Hugo [Professional Editor], 1985 (1986) [refused].
Locus [Publisher], 1972 (1973), 1973 (1974), 1974 (1975), 1976 (1977), 1977 (1978), 1979 (1980), 1980 (1981), 1983 (1984), 1984 (1985); [Paperback Publisher], 1975 (1976); [Original Anthology], 1976 (1977).
Milford, 1982.
SF Chronicle [Book Editor], 1985 (1986).
Skylark, 1970.
DEL REY, Lester.
Balrog [Special], 1984 (1985).
Galaxy SF Novel, 1955.
Locus [Publisher], 1979 (1980), 1980 (1981), 1983 (1984), 1984 (1985), 1985 (1986), 1986 (1987).
Milford, 1982.
Nebula [Grand Master], 1990 (1991).
Skylark, 1972.
GoH World SF Convention, 1967.
DELANY, Samuel R.
Hugo [Short Story], 1969 (1970); [Nonfiction], 1988 (1989).
Nebula [Novel], 1966 (1967), 1967 (1968); [Short Story], 1967 (1968); [Novelette], 1969 (1970).
Pilgrim, 1985.
DELMAS, H. Grand Prix de la SF Française [Special], 1982 (1983).
DEMPSEY, Jeff. British Fantasy [Small Press Magazine], 1990 (1991).
DEMUTH, Michel. Grand Prix de la SF Française [Novel], 1976 (1977).
DENMARK, Thomas. L. Ron Hubbard's Illustrators of the Future [1st Quarter], 1990 (1991).
DENT, Lester. Inkpot, 1977.
DENTON, Bradley. John W. Campbell, Jr. Memorial [Winner], 1991 (1992).
DERLETH, August. Count Dracula Society [Literature], 1966 (1967).
DERMEZE, Yves. Grand Prix de la SF Française [Special], 1976 (1977).
DEROCHE, Everett. Saturn [Foreign Film], 1979 (1980); [Special], 1980 (1981).
DESMOND, Fae Gates. Inkpot, 1984.
DEVET, Charles. Minnesota Fantasy, 1991.
DEVLIC, Radovan. Lazar Komarcic [Short Story], 1981 (1982).
DI PADOVA, C. P. F. Premios Italiano di Fantascienza [Fanzine], 1976 (1977), 1977 (1978), 1978 (1979).
DIAZ, Ken. Emmy [Outstanding Achievement in Makeup], 1990.
DICK, Philip K.
Alkor [Translated Short Story], 1989 (1990).
Daedalus [SF Novel], 1986 (1987).
Gilgamés [SF Novel], 1984 (1985), 1988 (1989); [SF Collection/Anthology], 1989 (1990).
Hugo [Novel], 1962 (1963); [Dramatic Presentation], 1982 (1983).
John W. Campbell, Jr. Memorial, 1974 (1975).
Kurd Lasswitz [Foreign Novel], 1984 (1985).
Lazar Komarcic [Foreign Novel], 1988 (1989).
Playboy Writing [New Fiction Writer], 1980.
Readercon [Reissued Item], 1988 (1989); [Nonfiction], 1989 (1990).
SF Chronicle [Dramatic Presentation], 1982 (1983).
Seiun Taisho [Dramatic Presentation], 1982 (1983).
DICKINSON, Angie. Saturn [Actress], 1980 (1981).
DICKINSON, Larry. Readercon [Comic Writer/Artist], 1986 (1987).
DICKSON, Gordon R.
British Fantasy [August Derleth], 1976 (1977).
Hugo [Short Fiction], 1964 (1965); [Novella], 1980 (1981); [Novelette], 1980 (1981).
Jupiter [Novelette], 1977 (1978).
Minnesota Fantasy, 1989.
Nebula [Novelette], 1966 (1967).

Skylark, 1975.
SFWA President, 1969-1971.
GoH World SF Convention, 1984.
DiFATE, Vincent. Davis Readers (Analog) [Cover Artist], 1987 (1988), 1988 (1989), 1990 (1991). Hugo [Professional Artist], 1978 (1979). Skylark, 1987. AGoH World SF Convention, 1992.
DIGBY, Tom. E. E. Evans/Paul Frehafer, 1975. GoH World SF Convention, 1993.
DIKTY, T. E. Milford, 1985.
DILLON, Diane. Caldecott Medal, 1976, 1977. Hugo [Professional Artist], 1970 (1971). Locus [Paperback Cover Illustrator], 1970 (1971).
DILLON, Leo. Caldecott Medal, 1976, 1977. Hugo [Professional Artist], 1970 (1971). Locus [Paperback Cover Illustrator], 1970 (1971).
DILLEY, Leslie. Oscar [Art Direction], 1977, 1981. Saturn [Art Decoration], 1977 (1978).
DISCH, Thomas M.
BSFA [Short Fiction], 1980 (1981).
Ditmar [International Fiction], 1968 (1969).
John W. Campbell, Jr. Memorial, 1979 (1980).
Locus [Novelette], 1980 (1981).
Rhysling [Long Poem], 1980 (1981).
Seiun Taisho [Foreign Novelette], 1981 (1982).
DISNEY, Walt. Oscar [Thalberg], 1941.
DiZAZZO, Raymond. Rhysling [Short Poem], 1981 (1982).
DJDANOV, Lev. Karel, 1985 (1986).
DMITRIJEVIC, Ratomir. Lazar Komarcic [Artist], 1989/1990 (1991).
DOBYNSKI, Charles. Grand Prix de la SF Française [Short Fiction], 1984 (1985).
DOIG-COLLS, Robin. Inkpot, 1992.
DOLLENS, Morris Scott. Count Dracula Society [Special], 1969 (1970).
DONALDSON, Stephen R.
Balrog [Novel], 1980 (1981), 1982 (1983); [Collection/Anthology], 1984 (1985).
British Fantasy [August Derleth], 1978 (1979).
Hugo [Campbell], 1978 (1979).
Saturn [Fantasy Novel], 1982 (1983).
SF Book Club [Winner], 1987 (1988), 1988 (1989).
GoH World Fantasy Convention, 1985, 1991.
DONNER, Richard. Count Dracula Society [Special], 1979 (1980).
DONSKY, Charlotte. SFRA Treasurer, 1985-1989.
DOREA, Gumercindo Rocha. Homage Trophy, 1991.
DORF, Shel. Inkpot, 1975.
DORLEAC, Jean-Pierre. Emmy [Outstanding Costume Design for a Series], 1979. Saturn [Costumes], 1979 (1980), 1980 (1981).
DORMAN, Sonya. Rhysling [Short Poem], 1977 (1978).
DORN, Michael. Image [Best Actor], 19??, (19??).
DORR, James S. L. Ron Hubbard's Writers of the Future [2nd Quarter, 3rd Place], 1991 (1992).
DORSEY, Candas Jane. Casper [English Short Form], 1988 (1989).
DOUAY, Dominique. Grand Prix de la SF Française [Novelette], 1974 (1975); [Special], 1987 (1988).
DOUGHERTY, Charles. L. Ron Hubbard's Illustrators of the Future [2nd Quarter], 1990 (1991).
DOUGLAS, Conda V. SF Writers of Earth [Author of the '80s—3rd], 1990 (1991).
DOUGLAS, Helen Gahagen. Count Dracula Society [Special], 1973 (1974). Saturn [Special], 1978 (1979).
DOUGLAS, Kirk. Saturn [Special (Career)], 1979 (1980).
DOVNIKOVIC, Boris. Festival Internazional del Film [Golden Seal], 1970 (1971).
DOWLING, Terry. Ditmar [Australian Fiction], 1982 (1983); [Atheling], 1982 (1983); [Australian Short Fiction], 1984 (1985), 1985 (1986), 1986 (1987), 1987 (1988); [Australian Long Fiction], 1987 (1988); [Australian Long Fiction/Anthology], 1990 (1991).
DOZOIS, Gardner.

Daedalus [Zeus], 1986 (1987).
Gilgamés [Horror Short Story], 1986 (1987).
Hugo [Professional Editor], 1987 (1988), 1988 (1989), 1989 (1990), 1990 (1991), 1991 (1992).
Locus [Anthology], 1986 (1987), 1987 (1988), 1989 (1990), 1990 (1991); [Professional Editor], 1988 (1989), 1989 (1990), 1990 (1991), 1991 (1992).
Nebula [Short Story], 1983 (1984), 1984 (1985).
SF Chronicle [Short Story], 1983 (1984); [Magazine Editor], 1986 (1987), 1987 (1988), 1989 (1990).
DPRITA, Donna. Karel, 1984 (1985).
DRAGIC, Nedelijiko. Festival Internazional del Film [Special], 1972 (1973).
DRAKE, David. Phoenix, 1983 (1984).
DRAKE, Stan. Inkpot, 1984.
DREW, Les. Festival Internazional del Film [Silver Seal], 1966 (1967).
DRINGENBERG, Mike. Will Eisner Comic Industry [Graphic Album (Reprint)], 1990 (1991).
DRIPPE, Colleen. Readercon [Writer], 1986 (1987).
DRUKARCZYK, Grzegorz. Fantastyka [New Author], 1985 (1986).
DRUMM, Chris. Readercon [Value in Bookcraft], 1988 (1989).
DUFFIN, Ken. Rhysling [Short Poem], 1980 (1981).
DUFFY, Hugo. Aisling Gheal [3rd], 1979 (1980).
DUNCAN, Dave. Casper [English Long Form], 1989 (1990).
DUNIN, Vadim. Fantastyka [Special], 1986/1987 (1988).
DUNN, Bob. Reuben, 1975.
DUNSANY, Lord. Gilgamés [Fantasy Collection/Anthology], 1988 (1989).
DUNYACH, Jean-Claude. Grand Prix de la SF Française [Short Fiction], 1982 (1983).
DUPUIS, Stephan. Oscar [Makeup], 1986. Saturn [Makeup], 1987 (1988).
DURFEE, Brian Lee. L. Ron Hubbard's Illustrators of the Future [2nd Quarter], 1992 (1993).
DUURSEMA, Jan. Manning, 1983.
DUVIC, Patrice. Karel [Harrison], 1987 (1988).
DWYER, Corinne A. SF Writers of Earth [3rd], 1990 (1991).
DYKSTRA, John. Oscar [Visual Effects], 1977. Saturn [Special Effects], 1977 (1978), 1979 (1980).
DZUBAN, Kevin. L. Ron Hubbard's Illustrators of the Future [4th Quarter], 1989 (1990).
EAMES, Charles. Festival Internazional del Film [Special], 1978 (1979).
EAMES, Ray. Festival Internazional del Film [Special], 1978 (1979).
EASTMAN, Kevin. Inkpot, 1989.
ECKERT, Charles D. L. Ron Hubbard's Writers of the Future [1st Quarter, 3rd Place], 1989 (1990).
ECKLAR, Julia. Hugo [Campbell], 1990 (1991).
EDEMANN, Louis L. Oscar [Sound Effects Editing], 1988.
EDLUND, Richard. Oscar [Visual Effects], 1977, 1981; [Special Achievement (Visual Effects)], 1980, 1983. Saturn [Special Effects], 1980 (1981), 1981 (1982).
EDMONDS, Leigh. Ditmar [Australian Fanzine], 1975 (1976), 1983 (1984); [Australian Fan Writer], 1983 (1984), 1984 (1985), 1985 (1986).
EDWARDS, Les. British Fantasy [Artist], 1990 (1991).
EDWARDS, Malcolm. BSFA [Short Fiction], 1983 (1984). Pong [Fan Editor], 1982 (1983).
EDWARDS, Paul. L. Ron Hubbard's Writers of the Future [3rd Quarter, 1st Place], 1987 (1988).
EFFINGER, George Alec. Hugo [Novelette], 1988 (1989). Nebula [Novelette], 1988 (1989). SF Chronicle [Novelette], 1988 (1989); [Novel], 1989 (1990). Seiun Taisho [Foreign Short Story], 1990 (1991). Theodore Sturgeon Memorial [Winner], 1988 (1989).
EGGLETON, Bob.
Boomerang [Artist], 1990 (1991).
Chesley [Cover Illustration (Magazine)], 1986 (1987), 1988 (1989), 1990 (1991).
Davis Readers (IASFM) [Cover Artist], 1987 (1988).
Dell Readers (IASFM) [Cover Artist], 1991 (1992).

Jack Gaughan Memorial, 1988.
EHRLICH, Helen. Rhysling [Short Poem], 1983 (1984).
EICHNER, Henry. Count Dracula Society [Fauria], 1970 (1971); [Literature], 1971 (1972).
EIKAMP, Rhonda. SF Writers of Earth [2nd], 1991 (1992).
EISENSTEIN, Phyllis. Balrog [Collection/Anthology], 1978 (1979). SF Chronicle [Novella], 1981 (1982).
EISNER, Will. Atlanta Fantasy Faire, 1985. Inkpot, 1975. Will Eisner Comic Industry [Graphic Album (New)], 1991 (1992).
ELDER, Barbara. Count Dracula Society [Fauria], 1974 (1975).
ELEK, Katalin. Emmy [Outstanding Achievement in Makeup], 1990.
ELFLANDSSON, Galad. Readercon [Horror Writer], 1979 (1980).
ELGIN, Suzette Haden. Rhysling [Short Poem], 1987 (1988).
ELIASSON, Holger. Alvar Appletofft Memorial, 1988 (1989).
ELLENSHAW, Peter. Oscar [Special Visual Effects], 1964.
ELLERS, Marjii. E. E. Evans/Paul Frehafer, 1983.
ELLIK, Ron. Hugo [Amateur Magazine], 1958 (1959).
ELLISON, Harlan.
  American Mystery Award, 1988.
  Bram Stoker [Collection], 1987 (1988); [Nonfiction], 1989 (1990).
  British Fantasy [Short Story], 1978 (1979).
  Collectors [Most Collectible over Lifetime], 1989 (1990).
  Edgar Allen Poe, 1974, 1987.
  Festival Internazional del Film [Certificate of Honor], 1969 (1970).
  Forry, 1970.
  Georges Méliès, 1972, 1973.
  Gilgamés [SF Collection], 1983 (1984).
  Hugo [Short Fiction], 1965 (1966); [Short Story], 1967 (1968), 1968 (1969), 1977 (1978); [Dramatic Presentation], 1967 (1968), 1975 (1976); [Special Plaque], 1967 (1968), 1971 (1972); [Novelette], 1974 (1975), 1985 (1986).
  Inkpot, 1987.
  Jupiter [Novelette], 1973 (1974); [Short Story], 1977 (1978).
  Locus [Short Fiction], 1970 (1971), 1972 (1973), 1973 (1974), 1977 (1978); [Original Anthology/Collection], 1972 (1973); [Novelette], 1974 (1975), 1982 (1983), 1985 (1986), 1988 (1989); [Short Story], 1975 (1976), 1978 (1979), 1985 (1986), 1988 (1989); [Nonfiction], 1984 (1985); [Anthology], 1985 (1986); [Collection], 1988 (1989).
  Milford, 1986.
  Nebula [Short Story], 1965 (1966), 1977 (1978); [Novella], 1969 (1970).
  SF Chronicle [Most Attractive Male Writer], 1983 (1984).
  Saturn [Writing], 1975 (1976).
  ViRA [Vintage TV].
  World Fantasy [Collection], 1988 (1989).
  Writers Guild of America TV/Radio [Anthology Script], 1965; [Dramatic/Episodic Script], 1967, 1973, 1986.
  SFWA Vice President, 1965-1966.
  GoH World Fantasy Convention, 1991; World SF Convention, 1978.
ELLISON, Susan. GoH World Fantasy Convention, 1991.
ELWOOD, Roger. Locus [Anthology], 1975 (1976).
EMBS, Richard. SF Writers of Earth [2nd], 1989 (1990).
EMSHWILLER, Carol. SF Chronicle [Short Story], 1987 (1988). World Fantasy [Collection], 1990 (1991).
EMSHWILLER, Ed. Hugo [Cover Artist], 1952 (1953); [Illustrator], 1959 (1960), 1960 (1961), 1961 (1962); [Professional Artist], 1963 (1964).
ENEY, Dick. FGoH World SF Convention, 1984.
ENG, Steve. Readercon [Poet], 1983 (1984). Rhysling [Short Poem], 1978 (1979).
ENGEL, Tobias. Festival Internazional del Film [Silver Asteroid—Actor], 1968 (1969).
ENGHOLM, Ahrvid. Alvar Appletofft Memorial, 1978 (1979).
ENGLAND, Larry. L. Ron Hubbard's Writers of the Future [4th Quarter, 3rd Place], 1987 (1988).

ENGLEHART, Steve. Inkpot, 1979.
ENGSTROM, Betsy. HWA Secretary, 1988-1989.
ENZENBACHER, Dale. Inkpot, 1979. World Fantasy [Artist], 1978 (1979).
ERLANGER, Dominique. Festival Internazional del Film [Silver Asteroid—Actress], 1971 (1972).
ERLER, Rainer. Festival Internazional del Film [Golden Asteroid], 1977 (1978); [Silver Asteroid—TV Film], 1978 (1979). Kurd Lasswitz [Short Story], 1986 (1987), 1988 (1989); [Film/TV Play], 1986 (1987). SFCD [Short Fiction], 1988 (1989).
ESCARPIT, Robert. Grand Prix de la SF Française [Juvenile], 1983 (1984).
ESHBACH, Lloyd Arthur. Collectors [Most Collectible over Lifetime], 1990 (1991). First Fandom, 1988. Milford, 1988. GoH World SF Convention, 1949.
ESRAC, William—SEE: CARSE, William.
ESTRADA, Jackie. Inkpot, 1977.
ETCHISON, Dennis. British Fantasy [Short Story], 1981 (1982), 1986 (1987). World Fantasy [Short Story], 1981 (1982). HWA President, 1992- .
EVANIER, Mark. Inkpot, 1975. Will Eisner Comic Industry [Humor Publication], 1991 (1992).
EVANS, Arthur B. J. Lloyd Eaton Memorial, 1988 (1990).
EVANS, Bruce A. Balrog [SF Film Hall of Fame], 1984 (1985).
EVANS, Judy. Emmy [Outstanding Costume Design for a Series], 1989.
EVRARD, Lionel. Grand Prix de la SF Française [Short Fiction], 1986 (1987). Prix Rosny-Aîné [Novelette], 1984.
EWALD, Robert J. SFRA Treasurer, 1993- .
EWART, Claire. Golden Duck [Children's SF Picture Book], 1991 (1992).
FABIAN, Stephen. British Fantasy [Artist], 1979 (1980). Readercon [SF Artist], 1979 (1980); [Fantasy Artist], 1983 (1984).
FAHNESTALK, Lynne Taylor. Aurora [Artistic Achievement], 1990 (1991).
FALK, Lee. Inkpot, 1989.
FALTERMEYER, Kelly. L. Ron Hubbard's Illustrators of the Future [3rd Quarter], 1989 (1990).
FANCHER, Hampton. British Fantasy [Film], 1982 (1983). British Science Fiction [Film], 1982 (1983). Hugo [Dramatic Presentation], 1982 (1983).
FANG, Chi. China SF Constellation, 1990 (1991).
FANZO, Don. Saturn [Special], 1973/74 (1975).
FARMER, Nancy. L. Ron Hubbard's Writers of the Future [2nd Quarter, 1st Place], 1987 (1988); [Gold], 1987 (1988).
FARMER, Philip José.
Hugo [New Author/Artist], 1952 (1953); [Novella], 1967 (1968); [Novel], 1971 (1972).
Nova [Novel], 1988 (1989).
Shasta SF Novel, 1952?
Writers of the Past (as Kilgore Trout), 1987 (1988).
GoH World SF Convention, 1968.
FARRAR, Scott. Oscar [Visual Effects], 1985.
FARRIS, John. GoH World Fantasy Convention, 1992.
FARWAGI, André. Festival Internazional del Film [Special], 1970 (1971).
FAURIA, Inez. Count Dracula Society [Fauria], 1965 (1966).
FAURIA, Virgil. Count Dracula Society [Fauria], 1965 (1966).
FEDERICI, Louis. Saturn [Outstanding Service], 1977 (1978).
FEIFFER, Jules. Inkpot, 1988.
FEIST, Raymond E. HOMer [Fantasy Novel], 1990 (1991). Inkpot, 1988.
FELDMAN, Marty. Saturn [Supporting Actor], 1975 (1976).
FENGZHEN, Wang. Karel [President's], 1990 (1991).
FENNEL, Jeff. L. Ron Hubbard's Illustrators of the Future [1st Quarter], 1989 (1990).
FENNER, Arnold. Balrog [Amateur Publication], 1978 (1979), 1982 (1983). World Fantasy [Special (Professional)], 1990 (1991); [Special (Nonprofessional)], 1980 (1981).
FERMAN, Edward L.
Balrog [Professional Publication], 1980 (1981), 1982 (1983), 1983 (1984).
Hugo [Professional Magazine], 1968 (1969), 1969 (1970), 1970 (1971), 1971 (1972); [Professional Editor], 1980 (1981), 1981 (1982), 1982 (1983).
Karel [Harrison], 1987 (1988).

Locus [Magazine], 1970 (1971), 1971 (1972), 1972 (1973), 1973 (1974), 1974 (1975), 1975 (1976), 1976 (1977), 1977 (1978), 1979 (1980), 1980 (1981), 1981 (1982), 1986 (1987), 1987 (1988); [Anthology], 1980 (1981).
Milford, 1984.
Saturn [Magazine], 1982 (1983).
Science Fiction & Fantasy Workshop [Short Story Editor], 1986 (1987).
SF Chronicle [Editor], 1981 (1982), 1982 (1983); [Magazine Editor], 1983 (1984), 1984 (1985); 1988 (1989), 1990 (1991).
World Fantasy [Special (Professional)], 1978 (1979), 1981 (1982).
FERNANDEZ, Cid. Jeronimo Montiero [2nd], 1990 (1991).
FERRARI, Mark. Readercon [Interior Illustration], 1989 (1990).
FERRIGNO, Lou. Saturn [Special], 1980 (1981).
FERRILL, Larry. L. Ron Hubbard's Writers of the Future [1st Quarter, 2nd Place], 1991 (1992).
FERTIG, Matt. Chesley [Special], 1986 (1987).
FIEDLER, Leslie. Arts and Letters, 1957.
FIELD, John. Inkpot, 1984.
FIELD, Roy. Oscar [Special Achievement (Visual Effects)], 1978.
FILASTO, Nino. Premios Italiano di Fantascienza [Novel], 1991 (1992).
FILHO, Osame Kinouche. Nova [Fan Short Story], 1990 (1991).
FILIPOVIC, Dragan R. Lazar Komarcic [Short Story], 1987 (1988); [Novel], 1988 (1989); [Long Story], 1989/1990 (1991).
FILMER, Kath. Mythopoeic [Scholarship for Myth & Fantasy Studies], 1991 (1992).
FINCH, Sheila. Crook/Tall, 1985 (1986). SFWA Vice President, 1991- .
FINDER, Jan Howard. FGoH World SF Convention, 1993.
FINLAY, Virgil. Hugo [Interior Illustrator], 1952 (1953).
FINNEY, Jack. World Fantasy [Lifetime Achievement], 1986 (1987).
FISHER, Carrie. Saturn [President's], 1988 (1989).
FISHER, Stephen C. L. Ron Hubbard's Writers of the Future [1st Quarter, 3rd Place], 1988 (1989).
FITCH, Don. E. E. Evans/Paul Frehafer, 1970.
FITCH, Marina. L. Ron Hubbard's Writers of the Future [3rd Quarter, 3rd Place], 1985 (1986).
FITZPATRICK, Jim. Inkpot, 1981.
FIVESON, Robert. Saturn [Low Budget Film], 1979 (1980).
FLEISCHMAN, Paul. Golden Duck [Children's SF Picture Book], 1991 (1992).
FLEMING, Victor. Balrog [Fantasy Film Hall of Fame], 1980 (1981).
FLENNIKEN, Shary. Inkpot, 1980.
FLESSEL, Creig. Inkpot, 1992.
FLICK, Stephen. Oscar [Special Achievement (Special Effects Editing)], 1987.
FLINGA, Rolf. Count Dracula Society [Fauria], 1969 (1970).
FLOOD, Leslie. British Fantasy [Special], 1984 (1985). Karel [Dedicated Service], 1985 (1986).
FLORESCU, Radu. Count Dracula Society [Walpole Medal], 1972 (1973); [Special], 1975 (1976).
FLYNN, Michael F. Crook/Tall, 1990 (1991). Davis Readers (Analog) [Novelette], 1986 (1987); [Science Fact Article], 1988 (1989), 1990 (1991). Locus [First Novel], 1990 (1991). Prometheus, 1990 (1991).
FOGLIO, Phil. Hugo [Fan Artist], 1976 (1977), 1977 (1978).
FOKY, Otto. Festival Internazional del Film [Special], 1976 (1977).
FOLDES, Lawrence D. Saturn [Special], 1978 (1979).
FORAY, June. Clampett, 1988. Inkpot, 1974.
FORD, Carl. British Fantasy [Small Press Magazine], 1987 (1988), 1988 (1989); [Icarus], 1987 (1988).
FORD, Harrison. Saturn [Actor], 1981 (1982).
FORD, John M. World Fantasy [Novel], 1983 (1984); [Short Story], 1988 (1989).
FORD, Michael. Oscar [Set Decoration], 1981.
FORD, Paul F. Mythopoeic [Scholarship], 1982 (1983).
FORDE, Pat. Davis Readers (Analog) [Novelette], 1987 (1988).

FORWARD, Robert L. Locus [First Novel], 1980 (1981). Seiun Taisho [Foreign Novel], 1982 (1983); [Foreign Nonfiction], 1989 (1990).
FOSTER, Alan Dean. Southwest Book, 1990.
FOSTER, Brad.
  Chesley [Unpublished Monochrome], 1988 (1989).
  Hugo [Fan Artist], 1986 (1987), 1987 (1988), 1988 (1989), 1991 (1992).
  Readercon [SF Artist], 1983 (1984); [Cover Artist], 1983 (1984); [Overall Artistic Achievement], 1983 (1984).
  SF Chronicle [Fan Artist], 1984 (1985), 1985 (1986), 1986 (1987), 1988 (1989).
FOSTER, Hal. Inkpot, 1977. Reuben, 1957.
FOSTER, Jodie. Saturn [Actress], 1977 (1978).
FOSTER, Robert "Grimsley". Count Dracula Society [Special], 1976 (1977).
FOWLER, Karen Joy. Hugo [Campbell], 1986 (1987).
FOX, Gil. Inkpot, 1978.
FOX, Harold J. L. Ron Hubbard's Illustrators of the Future [2nd Quarter], 1990 (1991).
FOX, Janet. Readercon [Fantasy Writer], 1983 (1984); [Horror Writer], 1983 (1984); [Dale Donaldson Memorial], 1983 (1984); [Fiction Writer], 1987 (1988).
FOYSTER, John. Ditmar [Australian Fanzine], 1969 (1970), 1978 (1979); [Australian Fiction], 1972 (1973).
FRAHM, Leanne. Ditmar [Australian Fan Writer], 1979 (1980); [Australian Short Fiction], 1980 (1981).
FRANCIS, Peter H. L. Ron Hubbard's Illustrators of the Future [4th Quarter], 1990 (1991).
FRANK, Mike. E. E. Evans/Paul Frehafer, 1986.
FRANKE, Herbert W. Kurd Lasswitz [Short Story], 1983 (1984); [Novel], 1984 (1985), 1985 (1986). GoH World SF Convention, 1970.
FRANKE, Thomas. Kurd Lasswitz [Artist], 1980 (1981), 1981 (1982).
FRANKLIN, H. Bruce. IAFA [Distinguished Scholarship], 1989 (1990). J. Lloyd Eaton Memorial, 1980 (1982). Pilgrim, 1983. Pioneer, 1991.
FRAZETTA, Frank. Balrog [Artist], 1980 (1981). Chesley [Artistic Achievement], 1987 (1988). Hugo [Professional Artist], 1965 (1966). World Fantasy [Artist], 1975 (1976).
FRAZIER, Robert. Davis Readers (IASFM) [Poem], 1990 (1991). Readercon [Collection], 1988 (1989). Rhysling [Short Poem], 1979 (1980), 1988 (1989).
FREAS, Frank Kelly.
  Chesley [Cover Illustration (Magazine)], 1989 (1990).
  Dell Readers (Analog) [Cover Artist], 1991 (1992).
  Forry, 1983.
  Hugo [Illustrator], 1954 (1955), 1955 (1956), 1957 (1958), 1958 (1959); [Professional Artist], 1969 (1970), 1971 (1972), 1972 (1973), 1973 (1974), 1974 (1975), 1975 (1976).
  Inkpot, 1979.
  Locus [Professional Artist], 1972 (1973), 1973 (1974), 1974 (1975).
  Skylark, 1981.
  AGoH World Fantasy Convention, 1987, 1982.
FREAS, Laura Brodian. Chesley [Cover Illustration (Magazine)], 1989 (1990).
FREEBORN, Stuart. Saturn [Makeup], 1977 (1978).
FREEMAN, Gary. Dell Readers (IASFM) [Cover Artist], 1991 (1992).
FREIREICH, Valerie J. L. Ron Hubbard's Writers of the Future [3rd Quarter, 1st Place], 1990 (1991).
FRÉMION, Yves. Aurora [French Short Form], 1991 (1992). Casper [Novel], 1985 (1986). Grand Prix de la SF Française [Novelette], 1977 (1978). Prix Boréal [Author (as Yves Menard)], 1986 (1987).
FRENCH, Tom. Inkpot, 1978.
FRENCH, Virginia. Inkpot, 1979.
FREUND, Karl. Count Dracula Society [Special], 1966 (1967).
FRID, Jonathan. Count Dracula Society [Television], 1968 (1969).
FRIED, Helen. Andre Norton Fantasy/SF Short Story [3rd], 1990 (1991).
FRIED, Sol. Count Dracula Society [Cunningham], 1971 (1972).
FRIEDRICH, Mike. Inkpot, 1980.
FRIEND, Beverly. SFRA Newsletter Editor, 1974-1978.

FRIERSON, Penny. Rebel, 1987.
FRONEBERG, Walter. Kurd Lasswitz [Special], 1989 (1990).
FROUD, Brian. AGoH World Fantasy Convention, 1981.
FUCHS, Werner. Kurd Lasswitz [Special], 1980 (1981), 1982 (1983).
FUKAMI, Dan. Karel, 1989 (1990).
FUNKE, Alex. Oscar [Special Achievement (Visual Effects)], 1990.
FURST, Anton. Oscar [Art Direction], 1989.
FURTINGER, Zvonimir. Lazar Komarcic [Lifetime Achievement], 1981 (1982).
FUSCO. Premios Italiano di Fantascienza [Critical Work], 1979 (1980).
GABBARD, G. N. John Masefield, 1979.
GAGLIANI, William. SF Writers of Earth [3rd], 1986 (1987).
GAIMAN, Neil.
  Inkpot, 1991.
  Prisoners of Gravity Reality 1 [Fantasy Novel], 1991 (1992); [Favorite *PoG* Guest], 1991 (1992).
  Will Eisner Comic Industry [Graphic Album (Reprint)], 1990 (1991); [Continuing Series], 1990 (1991), 1991 (1992); [Single Issue or Story], 1991 (1992); [Writer], 1990 (1991), 1991 (1992).
  World Fantasy [Short Fiction], 1990 (1991).
GAINES, William. Inkpot, 1990.
GAKOV, Vladimir. Prix Jules Verne, 1978.
GALBREATH, Robert. SFRA Secretary, 1979-1982.
GALE, Bob. SF Chronicle [Dramatic Presentation], 1985 (1986).
GALITSIN, Juriy. L. Ron Hubbard's Illustrators of the Future [1st Quarter], 1992 (1993).
GALLAGHER, Diana G. Hugo [Fan Artist], 1988 (1989).
GALLO, Domenico. Premios Italiano di Fantascienza [Short Fiction (Fan)], 1991 (1992).
GANLEY, W. Paul. Readercon [Dale Donaldson Memorial], 1986 (1987). World Fantasy [Special (Nonprofessional)], 1986 (1987), 1991 (1992).
GANSOVSKII, Sever. Aëlita, 1988 (1989).
GARCIA, Nancy. World Fantasy [Special (Nonprofessional)], 1987 (1988).
GARCIA, Robert. World Fantasy [Special (Nonprofessional)], 1987 (1988).
GARCIA, Rod—SEE: GARCIA Y ROBERTSON, R.
GARCIA y ROBERTSON, R. L. Ron Hubbard's Writers of the Future [3rd Quarter, 2nd Place], 1987 (1988).
GARDNER, Craig Shaw. HWA President, 1990-1992.
GARDNER, James Alan. Casper [English Short Form], 1990 (1991). L. Ron Hubbard's Writers of the Future [1st Quarter, 1st Place], 1989 (1990); [Gold], 1989 (1990).
GARDNER, Stan. Balrog [Outstanding Amateur Achievement], 1983 (1984).
GARDNIER, Mas Massimino. Festival Internazional del Film [Special], 1971 (1972).
GARLAND, Mark Andrew. L. Ron Hubbard's Writers of the Future [1st Quarter, 3rd Place], 1990 (1991).
GARNER, ALan. FGoH World Fantasy Convention, 1981.
GARRETT, Randall. Ditmar [Pat Terry], 1981 (1982).
GARTON, Ray. Collectors [Most Collectible Book], 1991 (1992).
GASPARINI, Gustavo. Premios Italiano di Fantascienza [Novel], 1974 (1975).
GAUGHAN, Jack. Hugo [Professional Artist], 1966 (1967), 1967 (1968), 1968 (1969); [Fan Artist], 1966 (1967). Skylark, 1977. GoH World SF Convention, 1969.
GEARY, Patricia. Philip K. Dick Memorial [1st], 1987 (1988).
GEARY, Rick. Inkpot, 1980.
GEECK, Larry. Inkpot, 1987.
GEIS, Richard E.
  Hugo [Amateur Magazine], 1968 (1969), 1969 (1970); [Fan Writer], 1970 (1971), 1974 (1975), 1975 (1976), 1976 (1977), 1977 (1978), 1981 (1982), 1982 (1983); [Fanzine], 1973 (1974), 1974 (1975), 1976 (1977), 1978 (1979).
  Locus [Fan Critic], 1972 (1973), 1973 (1974), 1975 (1976).
  SF Chronicle [Fan Writer], 1981 (1982), 1983 (1984), 1984 (1985), 1985 (1986).
GEISEL, Ted—SEE: Seuss, Dr.
GELLER, Stephen. Saturn [SF Film], 1972 (1973).
GENTLE, Mary. Arthur C. Clarke [2nd], 1990 (1991).
GEORGE, Peter. Hugo [Dramatic Presentation], 1964 (1965).

GEORGE, William. Oscar [Visual Effects], 1987.
GEPHARDT, Jan Sherrell. Chesley [Special], 1991 (1992).
GERARD, Gil. Saturn [TV Actor], 1979 (1980).
GERBER, Steve. Inkpot, 1978.
GERMESHAUSEN, Alvin. Count Dracula Society [Fauria], 1969 (1970).
GERNSBACK, Hugo. Gernsback [Editor], 1926 (1983). Hugo [Special], 1959 (1960). GoH World SF Convention, 1952.
GERROLD, David. Skylark, 1979.
GERVAIS, Steve. World Fantasy [Artist], 1983 (1984).
GIBBONS, Dave.
  Hugo [Other Forms], 1987 (1988).
  Inkpot, 1986.
  Locus [Nonfiction], 1987 (1988).
  Will Eisner Comic Industry [Writer/Artist Team], 1987 (1988); [Graphic Album], 1987 (1988); [Finite Series], 1987 (1988), 1990 (1991).
GIBBS, George. Oscar [Visual Effects], 1984, 1988. Saturn [Special Effects], 1988 (1989).
GIBSON, Walter. Inkpot, 1977.
GIBSON, William.
  Casper [English Long Form], 1988 (1989).
  Chronic Rift Roundtable [Hall of Fame Inductee], 1990 (1991).
  DASA [SF Novel], 1990 (1991).
  Ditmar [International Fiction], 1984 (1985).
  Hugo [Novel], 1984 (1985).
  John W. Campbell Jr. Memorial [2nd], 1991 (1992).
  Nebula [Novel], 1984 (1985).
  Philip K. Dick Memorial [1st], 1984 (1985).
  SF Chronicle [Novel], 1984 (1985).
  Seiun Taisho [Foreign Novel], 1986 (1987).
GIDEON, Raynold. Balrog [SF Film Hall of Fame], 1984 (1985).
GIFFEN, Keith. Inkpot, 1991.
GIGER, H. R. Inkpot, 1979. Oscar [Visual Effects], 1979. Readercon [Jacket Illustration], 1990 (1991); [Interior Illustration], 1990 (1991).
GILBERT, John. British Fantasy [Icarus], 1988 (1989).
GILBERT, Sheila. Chesley [Art Direction], 1989 (1990), 1991 (1992).
GILLE, Elisabeth. Karel [Special President's], 1986 (1987).
GILLESPIE, Bruce. Ditmar [Australian Fanzine], 1971 (1972), 1972 (1973), 1976 (1977), 1979 (1980), 1985 (1986); [Atheling], 1981 (1982); [Australian Editor], 1984 (1985); [Fan Writer], 1988 (1989); [Fan Writer], 1990 (1991); [Atheling], 1990 (1991). Karel [Harrison], 1982 (1983).
GILLIAM, Terry. British Science Fiction [Film], 1981 (1982), 1985 (1986).
GILLILAND, Alexis. Hugo [Fan Artist], 1979 (1980), 1982 (1983), 1983 (1984), 1984 (1985); [Campbell], 1981 (1982). SF Chronicle [Fan Aritst (Fanzines)], 1981 (1982), 1982 (1983); [Fan Artist], 1983 (1984).
GILMAN, Carolyn Ives. L. Ron Hubbard's Writers of the Future [2nd Quarter, 2nd Place], 1986 (1987).
GILMAN, Greer Ilene. IAFA [Crawford], 1991 (1992).
GIMENEZ, Eduardo Abel. Gilgamés [SF Short Story], 1985 (1986).
GIOFFRE, Rocco. Saturn [Special Effects], 1987 (1988).
GIORDANO, Dick. Inkpot, 1981.
GIOVANNOLI, Renato. Premios Italiano di Fantascienza [Book Length Essay], 1991 (1992).
GIRAUD, Jean—SEE: MOEBIUS.
GIRCZYC, Catherine. Casper [Fan Achievement (Fanzine)], 1990 (1991).
GIULIANI, Pierre. Grand Prix de la SF Française [Novelette], 1979 (1980).
GLADDEN, Theresa P. HWA Executive Secretary, 1989-1990.
GLADIR, Heorge. Inkpot, 1991.
GLASS, James C. L. Ron Hubbard's Writers of the Future [1st Quarter, 1st Place], 1990 (1991); [Gold], 1990 (1991).
GLASS, Jim. E. E. Evans/Paul Frehafer, 1978.

GLASS, Robert. Oscar [Sound], 1982.
GLICKSOHN, Michael. Hugo [Fanzine], 1972 (1973).
GLICKSOHN, Susan—SEE: **WOOD, Susan.**
GLUT, Donald F. Count Dracula Society [Summers], 1975 (1976). Inkpot, 1980.
GLYER, Mike. Hugo [Special], 1981 (1982); [Fanzine], 1983 (1984), 1984 (1985), 1988 (1989); [Fan Writer], 1983 (1984), 1985 (1986), 1987 (1988). SF Chronicle [Fanzine], 1982 (1983), 1983 (1984), 1984 (1985), 1985 (1986); [Fan Writer], 1988 (1989).
GODDARD, Jean-Luc. Festival Internazionale del Film [Golden Asteroid], 1964 (1965).
GODWIN, Parke. World Fantasy [Novella], 1981 (1982).
GOGOLEWSLEA, B. Polish SF & Fantasy Achievement [Golden Meteor], 1985 (1986).
GOIMARD, Jacques. Karel [Special President's], 1986 (1987).
GOLD, H. L. Arts and Letters, 1958. Playboy Writing [Fiction Short Story], 1956; [Nonfiction Essay], 1972.
GOLD, Horace L. Forry, 1981. Hugo [Professional Magazine], 1952 (1953). Milford, 1987.
GOLD, Lee. E. E. Evans/Paul Frehafer, 1974.
GOLDBERG, Rube. Reuben, 1967.
GOLDBERG, Whoopi. Oscar [Best Supporting Actress], 1990.
GOLDBLATT, Andrew. Turner Tomorrow [Hon. Mention], 1991.
GOLDBLATT, Mark. Saturn [Editing], 1978 (1979).
GOLDEN, Christopher. HWA Treasurer, 1992- .
GOLDMAN, Stephen M. SFRA Vice President, 1985-1987.
GOLDMAN, William. Hugo [Dramatic Presentation], 1987 (1988). Saturn [Fantasy Film], 1987 (1988). SF Chronicle [Dramatic Presentation], 1987 (1988).
GOLDSMITH, Cele. Hugo [Special Plaque], 1961 (1962). Invisible Little Man, 1961.
GOLDSMITH, Jerry. Oscar [Original Score for a Motion Picture (Not a Musical)], 1976. Saturn [Music], 1984 (1985).
GOLDSTEIN, Lisa. American Book [Original Paperback], 1982 (1983). Arthur C. Clarke [3rd], 1989 (1990).
GONZALEZ, Jean. SF Chronicle [Most Attractive Male Fan], 1983 (1984).
GOODWIN, Archie. Clampett, 1992. Inkpot, 1982.
GOPMAN, Vladimir. Karel [Harrison], 1988 (1989).
GORDON, Joan. SFRA Secretary, 1993- .
GOREY, Edward. World Fantasy [Artist], 1984 (1985), 1988 (1989).
GORDON, Ruth. Oscar [Actress], 1968.
GORODISCHER, Angelica. Más Allá [Novel], 1983 (1984). Gilgamés [Fantasy Short Story], 1985 (1986).
GOTLIEB, Phyllis. Casper [Lifetime Achievement], 1982.
GOTO, Keisuke. Seiun Taisho [Artist], 1988 (1989).
GOTTFREDSON, Floyd. Inkpot, 1983.
GOUDRIAN, Roulof. Karel [Harrison], 1985 (1986).
GOULART, Ron. SFWA Vice President, 1969-1970.
GOULD, Chester. Inkpot, 1978. Reuben, 1959, 1977.
GOULD, Robert. World Fantasy [Artist], 1986 (1987).
GOY, Philip. Grand Prix de la SF Française [Novelette], 1976 (1977).
GRAHAM, Ron. Ditmar [Professional Magazine], 1969 (1970); [Special], 1970 (1971).
GRAIS, Mark. Saturn [Horror Film], 1982 (1983).
GRANT, Alan. Inkpot, 1992.
GRANT, Charles L.
  British Fantasy [Special], 1986 (1987).
  Nebula [Short Story], 1976 (1977); [Novelette], 1978 (1979).
  World Fantasy [Single Author Collection/Anthology], 1978 (1979), 1982 (1983); [Novella], 1982 (1983).
  GoH World Fantasy Convention, 1986.
  HWA President, 1988-1989; *President of Trustees*, 1989-1992.
GRANT, Donald M. First Fandom, 1989. World Fantasy [Special (Professional)], 1975 (1976), 1979 (1980), 1982 (1983); [Special], 1983 (1984).
GRANT, Richard. Arthur C. Clarke [3rd], 1988 (1989). Philip K. Dick Memorial [2nd], 1985 (1986).
GRANT, Rob. BSFA [Media Presentation], 1989 (1990).

GRAUE, Dave. Inkpot, 1981.
GRAY, Charles. Count Dracula Society [Special], 1979 (1980).
GRAY, Erin. Saturn [TV Actress], 1979 (1980).
GRAY, Louis. E. E. Evans/Paul Frehafer, 1979.
GRECHKO, Georgii. Aëlita [Yefremov], 1988 (1989).
GREEN, Michael. L. Ron Hubbard's Writers of the Future [4th Quarter, 1st Place], 1987 (1988).
GREEN, Roland. SFWA Vice President, 1984-1986.
GREENBERG, Martin H. Milford, 1989. GoH World Fantasy Convention, 1992. GoH World SF Convention, 1991.
GREENBERG, Stanley. Nebula [Dramatic Presentation], 1973 (1974). Premios Cometa d'Argento [Film], 1973 (1974). Saturn [SF Film], 1973/74 (1975).
GREENE, Eric. Count Dracula Society [Television], 1979 (1980). Saturn [Television Performance], 1978 (1979).
GREENE, Gloria. Count Dracula Society [Fauria], 1979 (1980).
GREENE, Jeff. Count Dracula Society [Fauria], 1979 (1980).
GREENLAND, Colin. Arthur C. Clarke [Winner], 1990 (1991). BSFA [Novel], 1990 (1991). J. Lloyd Eaton Memorial, 1983 (1985).
GRELL, Mike. Inkpot, 1982.
GRENIER, Christian. Grand Prix de la SF Française [Juvenile], 1987 (1988).
GRIFFIN, Rick. Inkpot, 1976.
GRIFFIN, Suzanna. Chesley [Unpublished Monochrome], 1984 (1985).
GRIFFITH, Bill. Inkpot, 1992.
GRIMAUD, Michel. Grand Prix de la SF Française [Juvenile], 1981 (1982).
GRIMWOOD, Ken. World Fantasy [Novel], 1987 (1988).
GROENING, Matt. Inkpot, 1988.
GROSS, Darick. Manning, 1991.
GROSS, S. Inkpot, 1980.
GROSSMAN, Michael. L. Ron Hubbard's Illustrators of the Future [2nd Quarter], 1990 (1991).
GROTH, Gary. Inkpot, 1988.
GRUNDKOWSKI, Jerzy. Fantastyka [New Author], 1983 (1984).
GRUSKOFF, Michael. Saturn [George Pal Memorial], 1981 (1982).
GRYGLASZEWSKA, Helina. Festival Internazionale del Film [Silver Asteroid—Actress], 1975 (1976).
GUARINO, Bettyann. Chesley [Special Award], 1990 (1991).
GUARNIERI, Annarita. Karel, 1986 (1987). Premios Italiano di Fantascienza [Translator], 1990 (1991), 1991 (1992).
GUCCHIONE, Bob. Balrog [Professional Publication], 1981 (1982).
GUERINGER, Frank. Saturn [Outstanding Service], 1987 (1988).
GUERRINI, Remo. Premios Italiano di Fantascienza [Critical Work], 1976 (1977).
GUINESS, Sir Alec. Saturn [Supporting Actor], 1977 (1978).
GUITARD, Agnes. Prix Boréal [Short Story], 1986 (1987).
GUNN, Ian. Ditmar [Fan Artist], 1988 (1989); [Fan Artist], 1990 (1991).
GUNN, James. Hugo [Nonfiction], 1982 (1983). J. Lloyd Eaton Memorial [Special Lifetime Achievement], 1990 (1992). Locus [Associational Item], 1975 (1976). Pilgrim, 1976. SFRA President, 1981-1983. SFWA President, 1971-1972.
GUREVICH, Georgi. Aëlita [Yefremov], 1986 (1987).
GURNEY, James. Chesley [Cover Illustration (Hardback)], 1987 (1988); [Unpublished Color], 1988 (1989); [Artistic Achievement], 1991 (1992).
GUTHKE, Karl S. J. Lloyd Eaton Memorial, 1990 (1992).
GUY, Gordon R. Count Dracula Society [Special], 1967 (1968).
HAEFS, Gisbert. Kurd Lasswitz [Short Story], 1989 (1990).
HAGGARD, Piers. Festival Internazionale del Film [Special], 1979 (1980).
HAGIO, Moto. Seiun Taisho [Comics], 1982 (1983), 1984 (1985).
HAGMAN, Larry. Festival Internazionale del Film [Special], 1971 (1972).
HAGUE, Michael. FGoH World Fantasy Convention, 1985.
HAHN, Ronald M. Kurd Lasswitz [Short Story], 1980 (1981), 1981 (1982); [Special], 1980 (1981), 1982 (1983); [Novella], 1985 (1986).
HALDEMAN, Joe.

Ditmar [International Fiction], 1975 (1976).
Hugo [Novel], 1975 (1976); [Novella], 1990 (1991), [Short Story], 1976 (1977).
Inkpot, 1991.
Lazar Komarcic [Foreign Novel], 1986 (1987).
Locus [Novel], 1975 (1976); [Short Story], 1976 (1977).
Nebula [Novel], 1975 (1976); [Novella], 1990 (1991).
Phoenix, 1982 (1983).
Rhysling [Long Poem], 1983 (1984), 1990 (1991).
U.S. Air Force Academy Special Achievement, 1989.
SFWA President, 1992- .
SFWA Treasurer, 1970-1973.
GoH World SF Convention, 1990.

HALL, Brian. N3F [3rd], 1990 (1991).
HALL, David. Count Dracula Society [Fauria], 1975 (1976).
HALL, Hal W. J. Lloyd Eaton Memorial, 1989 (1991).
HAMBLY, Barbara. Locus [Horror Novel], 1988 (1989). Science Fiction Book Club [3rd], 1988 (1989).
HAMILL, Mark. Saturn [Actor], 1980 (1981).
HAMILTON, Bruce. Inkpot, 1982.
HAMILTON, David F. SF Writers of Earth [3rd], 1987 (1988).
HAMILTON, Edmond. Alkor [Translated Novel], 1989 (1990). GoH World SF Convention, 1964.
HAMILTON, George. Count Dracula Society [Cinema], 1978 (1979). Saturn [Actor], 1979 (1980).
HAMILTON, Linda. Saturn [TV Actress], 1988 (1989); [Actress], 1991 (1992).
HAMILTON, Margaret. Saturn [Special], 1978 (1979).
HAMILTON, Todd Cameron. Chesley [Interior Illustration], 1989 (1990). Davis Readers (Analog) [Cover Artist], 1989 (1990).
HAMMELL, Tim. Readercon [Fantasy Artist], 1979 (1980).
HAMPSHIRE, Susan. Festival Internazional del Film [Silver Asteroid—Actress], 1972 (1973).
HANCOCK, D. Larry. Aurora [Fan Achievement (Fanzine)], 1991 (1992).
HANDFIELD, Carey. Ditmar [Special], 1986 (1987).
HANKE-WOODS, Joan. Hugo [Fan Artist], 1985 (1986).
HANKS, Tom. Saturn [Actor], 1988 (1989).
HANMURA, Ryo. Nihon SF Taisho, 1987 (1988).
HANNAH, Daryl. Saturn [Actress], 1984 (1985).
HARDESTY, William H. III. SFRA Secretary, 1982-1987; President, 1987-1989.
HARDING, Lee. Ditmar [Australian Fiction], 1969 (1970), 1971 (1972).
HARFST, Betsy. SFRA Newsletter Editor, 1990-1992.
HARJU, Kaj. Alvar Appletofft Memorial, 1982 (1983).
HARLAND, Paul. King Kong, 1990.
HARLINE, Leigh. Oscar [Original Music Score], 1940.
HARMETZ, Richard. Count Dracula Society [Fauria], 1971 (1972).
HARMON, Jim. Inkpot, 1977.
HARRINGTON, Curtis. Count Dracula Society [Cinema], 1967 (1968).
HARRIS, Anthony. Festival Internazional del Film [Special], 1971 (1972).
HARRIS, Dell. Chesley [Interior Illustration], 1984 (1985), 1986 (1987). Jack Gaughan Memorial, 1989.
HARRIS, Jonathan. Saturn [Television Performance], 1977 (1978).
HARRIS, Natalie. Count Dracula Society [Fauria], 1975 (1976). Saturn [Outstanding Service], 1980 (1981).
HARRIS, Raymond. Philip K. Dick Memorial [2nd], 1990 (1991).
HARRIS, Thomas. Bram Stoker [Novel], 1988 (1989).
HARRISON, Harry.
Alkor [Translated Short Story], 1989 (1990).
Locus [Original Anthology/Collection], 1973 (1974).
Nebula [Dramatic Presentation], 1973 (1974).
Premios Cometa d'Argento [Chronicles of Tomorrow], 1973 (1974).
Prix Jules Verne, 1980.

SFWA Vice President, 1968-1969.
GoH World SF Convention, 1990.
HARRISON, Mark. BSFA [Artist], 1991 (1992).
HARRISON, Philip. Saturn [Art Decoration], 1975 (1976).
HARRISON, William. Saturn [SF Film], 1975 (1976).
HARRYHAUSEN, Ray.
Count Dracula Society [Special], 1970 (1971); [Cunningham], 1977 (1978).
Inkpot, 1992.
Saturn [Stop Motion Animation], 1973/74 (1975), 1977 (1978); [Life Career], 1981 (1982); [Special Award], 1989/90 (1991); [Special Lifetime Achievement], 1991 (1992).
HART, Johnny. Inkpot, 1976. Reuben, 1968.
HARTLEY, Al. Inkpot, 1980.
HARTLEY, Mariette. Emmy [Actress in Drama], 1979.
HARTWELL, David G.
Gilgamés [Horror Collection/Anthology], 1989 (1990).
Locus [Publisher], 1981 (1982).
Milford, 1990.
Readercon [Review/Criticism Magazine], 1988 (1989); [Nonfiction Magazine], 1990 (1991).
SF Chronicle [Book Editor], 1983 (1984), 1986 (1987), 1987 (1988), 1988 (1989); [Most Attractive Male Editor], 1983 (1984).
World Fantasy [Special (Professional)], 1987 (1988).
HARVEY, Edwina. Robbie [Fan Writer], 1988 (1989).
HARVIA, Teddy. Hugo [Fan Artist], 1990 (1991). SF Chronicle [Fan Artist], 1989 (1990), 1990 (1991).
HAS, Wojonisch J. Festival Internazional del Film [Golden Asteroid], 1973 (1974).
HASELTINE, Susan J. E. E. Evans/Paul Frehafer, 1985.
HASSELBLATT, Dieter. Kurd Lasswitz [Special], 1985 (1986); [Radio Play], 1989 (1990).
HASSLER, Donald M. SFRA Treasurer, 1983-1985; President, 1985-1987.
HATHAWAY, Noah. Saturn [Juvenile Actor], 1984 (1985).
HAUSEROVA, Eva. Karel Capek [Mlok], 1987 (1988).
HAUTALA, Rick. HWA Vice President, 1991-1992.
HAW, Mark D. L. Ron Hubbard's Writers of the Future [2nd Quarter, 3rd Place], 1987 (1988).
HAYDEN, Patrick. SF Chronicle [Fanzine], 1987 (1988).
HAYDEN, Teresa Nielsen. SF Chronicle [Fanzine], 1987 (1988); [Fan Writer], 1987 (1988).
HAYES, Gary Kim. SF Writers of Earth [3rd], 1989 (1990).
HAYES, Martin. Aisling Gheal [2nd], 1978 (1979).
HAZELTON, Gene. Inkpot, 1979.
HEGSTED, Derek J. L. Ron Hubbard's Illustrators of the Future [2nd Quarter], 1989 (1990); [Gold], 1989 (1990).
HEIDEMAN, Eric M. L. Ron Hubbard's Writers of the Future [1st Quarter, 1st Place], 1986 (1987).
HEINLEIN, Robert A.
Clampett, 1985.
Forry, 1980.
Hugo [Novel], 1955 (1956), 1959 (1960), 1961 (1962), 1966 (1967).
Inkpot, 1977.
Locus [All-Time Author], 1976 (1977), 1987 (1988); [Fantasy Novel], 1984 (1985); [Nonfiction], 1989 (1990).
Nebula [Grand Master], 1974 (1975).
Prometheus Hall of Fame, 1983, 1987.
SF Book Club, [2nd], 1990 (1991).
GoH World SF Convention, 1941, 1961, 1976.
HEINLEIN, Virginia. Locus [Nonfiction], 1989 (1990).
HEMPEL, Marc. Inkpot, 1992.
HENDERICKX, Guido. Festival Internazional del Film [Golden Seal], 1971 (1972).

HENDERSON, Gene. Inkpot, 1977.
HENDERSON, Mary. Inkpot, 1981.
HENDRIX, Howard. L. Ron Hubbard's Writers of the Future [3rd Quarter, 1st Place], 1985 (1986).
HENNESY, Dale. Oscar [Art Direction], 1966. Saturn [Set Decoration], 1975 (1976); [Art Decoration], 1976 (1977).
HENRIKSEN, Hap. Balrog [Outstanding Professional Achievement], 1984 (1985). Chesley [3-D Art], 1984 (1985).
HENRY, John. Rebel, 1983.
HENSON, Jim. Balrog [Fantasy Film Hall of Fame], 1982 (1983). Inkpot, 1990. Saturn [Fantasy Film], 1982 (1983).
HEPING, Wang. China SF Constellation, 1990 (1991).
HEPPNER, Vaughn. L. Ron Hubbard's Writers of the Future [2nd Quarter, 2nd Place], 1992 (1993).
HERBERT, Frank.
Hugo [Novel], 1965 (1966).
Locus [All-Time Novel], 1974 (1975).
Nebula [Novel], 1965 (1966).
Premios Cometa d'Argento [Fiction], 1973 (1974).
Prix Apollo, 1977 (1978).
Prix Cosmos 2000, 1985 (1986).
HERBERT, James. Festival Internazional del Film [Golden Asteroid], 1981 (1982). GoH World Fantasy Convention, 1988.
HERBLOCK. Reuben, 1956.
HERHOLZ, Ulf. Kurd Lasswitz [Artist], 1982 (1983).
HERMAN, Ira. L. Ron Hubbard's Writers of the Future [3rd Quarter; 2nd Place], 1984 (1985)
HERMAN, Jack R. Ditmar [Atheling], 1979 (1980).
HERMANN, Bernard. Oscar [Music Score for a Dramatic or Comedy Picture], 1941.
HERNANDEZ, Gilbert. Inkpot, 1986.
HERNANDEZ, Jaime. Inkpot, 1986.
HERRMANN, Bernard. Saturn [Music], 1973/74 (1975).
HERSHEY, Allison. L. Ron Hubbard's Illustrators of the Future [1st Quarter], 1989 (1990).
HESCOX, Richard. Jack Gaughan Memorial, 1990.
HESTON, Charlton. Saturn [Special], 1973/74 (1975).
HEVELIN, Rusty. Big Heart, 1986. FGoH World SF Convention, 1981.
HEY, Richard. Kurd Lasswitz [Novel], 1982 (1983).
HEYER, Carol. Boomerang [Artist], 1989 (1990).
HICKMAN, Lin. Rebel, 1983.
HICKMAN, Stephen. Chesley [Cover Illustration (Paperback)], 1989 (1990). Jack Gaughan Memorial, 1986.
HICKMAN, Tracy. DASA [Fantasy Novel], 1990 (1991).
HICKS, Catherine. Saturn [Actress], 1988 (1989).
HILDEBRANDT, Tim. Balrog [Artist], 1982 (1983). World Fantasy [Artist], 1991 (1992).
HILLEGAS, Mark R. Pilgrim, 1992.
HILTON, Craig. Ditmar [Australian Artist], 1986 (1987).
HINZ, Christopher. Crook/Tall, 1987 (1988).
HIRSCH, Paul. Oscar [Film Editing], 1977. Saturn [Editing], 1977 (1978).
HITCHCOCK, Alfred. Count Dracula Society [Television], 1964 (1965). Grimmy, 19?? Oscar [Thalberg], 1967.
HLAVICKA, Jan. Karel Capek [Antiwar Story], 1985 (1986); [Short Story], 1987 (1988); [Mlok], 1988 (1989).
HOBAN, Russell. Ditmar [International Fiction], 1982 (1983). John W. Campbell, Jr. Memorial, 1981 (1982). Whitbread [Children's Literature], 1974.
HOBANA, Ion. Karel [Harrison], 1983 (1984).
HOBBS, Bob E. L. Ron Hubbard's Illustrators of the Future [1st Quarter], 1991 (1992).
HOBERG, Rick. Inkpot, 1984.
HOFFMAN, Eric. Inkpot, 1974. Saturn [Film Critic], 1978 (1979).
HOFFMAN, Lee. Rebel, 1987. FGoH World SF Convention, 1982.

HOFFMAN, Nina Kiriki. L. Ron Hubbard's Writers of the Future [1st Quarter; 3rd Place], 1984 (1985).
HOGAN, James P. Prometheus, 1982 (1983). Seiun Taisho [Foreign Novel], 1980 (1981), 1981 (1982).
HOGARTH, Burne. Inkpot, 1978.
HOLDER, Nancy. Bram Stoker [Short Story], 1991 (1992).
HOLDRIDGE, Lee. Emmy [Outstanding Achievment in Music and Lyrics], 1989.
HOLDRIDGE, Melanie. Emmy [Outstanding Achievment in Music and Lyrics], 1989.
HOLDSTOCK, Robert. BSFA [Short Fiction], 1981 (1982); [Novel], 1984 (1985). Gilgamés [Fantasy Novel], 1989 (1990). World Fantasy [Novel], 1984 (1985); [Novella], 1991 (1992).
HOLDYS, Boleslaw. Fantastyka [Nonfiction], 1985 (1986).
HOLICKI, Irene. Kurd Lasswitz [Translator], 1989 (1990).
HOLIDAY, Polly. Saturn [Supporting Actress], 1984 (1985).
HOLITZKA, Klaus. Kurd Lasswitz [Artist], 1986 (1987); [Artist], 1987 (1988).
HOLLANCK, Adam. Karel [Special President's], 1986 (1987).
HOLLINGER, Veronica. IAFA [Graduate Scholarship], 1986 (1987). Pioneer, 1990.
HOLLY, Joan Hunter. SFWA Treasurer, 1976-1979.
HONECK, Butch. Chesley [3-D Art], 1986 (1987).
HONECK, Susan. Chesley [3-D Art], 1986 (1987).
HOOPER, Jeanette M. Readercon [Nonfiction Writer], 1987 (1988).
HOPKINS, Harry. Saturn [Actor], 1991 (1992).
HOPKINS, Kevin. L. Ron Hubbard's Illustrators of the Future [4th Quarter], 1989 (1990).
HORI, Akira. Seiun Taisho [Novel], 1988 (1989).
HORNIG, Charles D. First Fandom, 1988.
HORRAKH, Livio. Premios Italiano di Fantascienza [Short Fiction], 1971 (1972).
HORSTING, Jessie. Readercon [Magazine Design], 1988 (1989).
HOUSSIN, Joël. Grand Prix de la SF Française [Novel], 1984 (1985). Prix Apollo, 1989 (1990).
HOWARD, Robert E. Gilgamés [Fantasy Short Story], 1983 (1984).
HUBBARD, L. Ron. Nova [Special], 1988 (1989). Prix Cosmos 2000, 1988 (1989).
HUBENTHAL, Karl. Inkpot, 1981.
HUBERT, Jean-Pierre. Grand Prix de la SF Française [Novel], 1982 (1983). Prix Rosny-Aîné [Novel], 1984, 1986; [Novelette], 1985, 1988.
HUDEC, Goran. Lazar Komarcic [Short Story], 1981 (1982).
HUDSON, Rock. Count Dracula Society [Special], 1972 (1973).
HUFF, Tanya. *Prisoners of Gravity* Reality 1 [Horror Novel], 1991 (1992).
HUGHART, Barry. Mythopoeic [Fantasy], 1985 (1986). World Fantasy [Novel], 1984 (1985).
HULL, E. Mayne. GoH World SF Convention, 1946.
HULL, Elizabeth Anne. Karel [Dedicated Service], 1982 (1983). SFRA Newsletter Editor, 1982-1984; President, 1989-1991.
HUME, Cyril. Balrog [SF Film Hall of Fame], 1981 (1982).
HUME, Kathryn. IAFA [Distinguished Scholarship], 1987 (1988). J. Lloyd Eaton Memorial, 1984 (1986).
HUNT, J. J. Davis Readers (IASFM) [Poem], 1987 (1988).
HUNTINGTON, John. J. Lloyd Eaton Memorial, 1982 (1984).
HURD, Gale Anne. Saturn [Writing], 1984 (1985); [SF Film], 1984 (1985).
HURLEY, Donal. Aisling Gheal [2nd], 1979 (1980).
HUTTAR, Charles A. Mythopoeic [Scholarship for Inklings Studies], 1991 (1992).
HUXLEY, Aldous. Alkor [Translated Novel], 1989 (1990). Award of Merit Medal, 1959. James Tait Black Memorial Prize [Fiction], 1940.
HYAMS, Peter. SF Chronicle [Dramatic Presentation], 1984 (1985).
HYMNS, Richard. Oscar [Sound Effects Editing], 1989.
IKEDA, Kensho. Seiun Taisho [Nonfiction], 1985 (1986).
IKIN, Van. A. Bertram Chandler, 1992. Ditmar [Australian Fanzine], 1977 (1978), 1987 (1988); [Australian Editor], 1982 (1983), 1983 (1984); [Atheling], 1987 (1988).
INGPEN, Robert. Ditmar [Australian Fiction], 1979 (1980).
INOUYE, Jon. Readercon [SF Writer], 1979 (1980).
ISHIHARA, Fujio. Seiun Taisho [Nonfiction], 1984 (1985), 1986 (1987).

ITO, Norio. Karel, 1981 (1982).
IVKOV, Slobodan. Lazar Komarcic [Short Story], 1989/1990 (1991).
JA YOUNG, Parris. L. Ron Hubbard's Writers of the Future [4th Quarter, 2nd Place], 1985 (1986).
JACKSON, Charles Lee II. E. E. Evans/Paul Frehafer, 1988.
JAINSCHIGG, Nicholas. Dell Readers (Analog) [Cover Artist], 1991 (1992).
JAKSIC, Zoran. Lazar Komarcic [Translator], 1986 (1987); [Novel], (as **David G. Strorm**), 1987 (1988); [Novella], 1988 (1989).
JAKUBOWSKI, Maxim. Karel, 1983 (1984).
JAMES, L. Dean. SF Writers of Earth [3rd], 1985 (1986).
JAMES, Richard D. Emmy [Outstanding Art Direction for a Series], 1990.
JANZUROVA, Iva. Festival Internazional del Film [Silver Asteroid—Actress], 1970 (1971).
JARVA, Risto. Festival Internazional del Film [Special], 1968 (1969).
JEDLINSKY, Pĕtr. Karel Capek [Short Story by Juvenile], 1981 (1982).
JEIN, Greg. Inkpot, 1984. Oscar [Visual Effects Special Achievement], 1977.
JENNINGS, Jor. L. Ron Hubbard's Writers of the Future [2nd Quarter; 1st Place], 1984 (1985).
JENSSEN, Elois. Saturn [Costumes], 1982 (1983).
JESCHKE, Wolfgang. Kurd Lasswitz [Special], 1980 (1981), 1981 (1982), 1987 (1988); [Novel], 1981 (1982), 1989 (1990); [Novella], 1981 (1982), 1982 (1983), 1984 (1985); [Radio Play], 1988 (1989). Karel [Harrison], 1986 (1987). GoH World SF Convention, 1990.
JESSUP, Harley. Oscar [Visual Effects], 1987.
JETER, K. W. John W. Campbell Jr. Memorial [2nd], 1989 (1990).
JEUDÉ, Samanda. Big Heart, 1994.
JEUNET. Grand Prix de la SF Française [Special], 1981 (1982). Prix Apollo, 1982 (1983).
JEURY, Michel. Grand Prix de la SF Française [Novel], 1973 (1974). Prix Cosmos 2000, 1982 (1983). Prix Julia Verlanger, 1985 (1986). Prix Rosny-Aîné [Novel], 1980, 1981.
JEZKOVA, Barbara. Karel Capek [Short Story], 1986 (1987).
JIANZHONG, Guo. Karel, 1990 (1991).
JIN, Zhang. China SF Milky Way/Forest Cup [3rd], 1990 (1991).
JINSONG, Zhang. China SF Constellation, 1990 (1991).
JITTLOV, Mike. Saturn [President's], 1987 (1988).
JOHNSON, Arte. Saturn [Supporting Actor], 1979 (1980).
JOHNSON, Brian. Oscar [Special Achievement (Visual Effects)], 1980. Saturn [Special Effects], 1980 (1981).
JOHNSON, Calvin W. L. Ron Hubbard's Writers of the Future [3rd Quarter, 2nd Place], 1988 (1989).
JOHNSON, Diane. Saturn [Fantasy Film], 1980 (1981).
JOHNSON, Don. Count Dracula Society [Special], 1975 (1976). Saturn [Actor], 1975 (1976).
JOHNSON, George Clayton. Balrog [Short Fiction], 1982 (1983). Inkpot, 1976. Saturn [SF Film], 1976 (1977).
JOHNSON, Kent. SF Writers of Earth [1st], 1991 (1992).
JOHNSON, Leanne. HWA Executive Secretary, 1990-1992.
JOHNSON, Ollie. Inkpot, 1984.
JOHNSON, Robin. Ditmar [Special], 1982 (1983).
JOHNSON, Toby. Lambda Literary [Gay SF/Fantasy], 1990 (1991).
JOHNSTON, Colin. Ken McIntyre, 1990 (1991).
JOHNSTON, Joe. Oscar [Visual Effects], 1981.
JOHNSTON, Lynn. Inkpot, 1991.
JONES, Charles M. Saturn [Animation], 1976 (1977).
JONES, Chuck. Atlanta Fantasy Faire, 1983. Inkpot, 1974.
JONES, Eddie. FGoH World SF Convention, 1969.
JONES, Edward. Oscar [Visual Effects], 1988.
JONES, Evan. Festival Internazional del Film [Golden Asteroid], 1963 (1964).
JONES, Gwyneth. James Tiptree Jr. Memorial [1st], 1991 (1992).
JONES, Jeff. World Fantasy [Artist], 1985 (1986). AGoH World Fantasy Convention, 1984.

JONES, L. Q. Hugo [Dramatic Presentation], 1975 (1976).
JONES, Malcolm III. Will Eisner Comic Industry [Graphic Album (Reprint)], 1990 (1991).
JONES, Neil R. First Fandom, 1988.
JONES, Peter. BSFA [Artist], 1980 (1981).
JONES, Sam J. Saturn [New Star], 1980 (1981).
JONES, Stephen.
Bram Stoker [Nonfiction], 1989 (1990), 1991 (1992).
British Fantasy [Small Press Magazine], 1978 (1979), 1979 (1980), 1980 (1981), 1981 (1982), 1982 (1983), 1984 (1985), 1986 (1987); [Anthology/Collection], 1990 (1991).
World Fantasy [Anthology], 1990 (1991); [Special (Nonprofessional)], 1983 (1984).
JORDAN, Louis. Count Dracula Society [Television], 1977 (1978).
JORON, Andrew. Rhysling [Short Poem], 1977 (1978); [Long Poem], 1979 (1980), 1985 (1986).
JOUANNE, Emmanuel. Grand Prix de la SF Française [Short Fiction], 1986 (1987). Prix Rosny-Aîné [Novel], 1983, 1985.
JULIAN, A. Grand Prix de la SF Française [Special], 1982 (1983).
JULIAN, Astrid. L. Ron Hubbard's Writers of the Future [2nd Quarter, 2nd Place], 1991 (1992).
JUTRISA, Vladimir. Festival Internazionale del Film [Silver Seal], 1966 (1967).
KADLECKOVA, Vilma. Karel Capek [Juvenile Writer], 1986 (1987).
KAFKA, Franz. Alkor [Translated Novel], 1989 (1990).
KAGAN, Janet. Davis Readers (IASFM) [Novelette], 1989 (1990), 1990 (1991).
KAGARLITSKI, Julius. Pilgrim, 1972.
KAI, Tan. China SF Milky Way/Forest Cup [1st], 1990 (1991).
KALE, Bonita. Boomerang [Poem], 1988 (1989).
KALISH, Carol. Inkpot, 1991.
KALUTA, Michael William. British Fantasy [Artist], 1976 (1977). Inkpot, 1977. Readercon [Interior Illustrator], 1988 (1989).
KAMBAYASHI, Chohei. Seiun Taisho [Novelette], 1982 (1983), 1983 (1984); [Novel], 1983 (1984), 1984 (1985), 1986 (1987).
KANBEI, Musashi. Nihon SF Taisho, 1984 (1985).
KANE, Bob. Inkpot, 1978.
KANE, Gil. Inkpot, 1975.
KANTOR, Vojtech. Karel Capek [Special], 1982 (1983). Ludvik Soucek [Novel], 1983 (1984).
KAPLAN, Stephen. Count Dracula Society [Summers], 1976 (1977).
KARLOFF, Boris. Count Dracula Society [Cinema], 1962 (1963); [Special], 1968 (1969). Festival Internazionale del Film [Gold Medal-President], 1967 (1968). Grimmy, 19??
KARLSSON, Lars-Arne. Alvar Appletofft Memorial, 1985 (1986).
KARNS, Robert. Saturn [Outstanding Service], 1982 (1983).
KASDAN, Lawrence.
Balrog [SF Film Hall of Fame], 1980 (1981).
British Fantasy [Film], 1980 (1981), 1981 (1982).
Hugo [Dramatic Presentation], 1980 (1981), 1981 (1982), 1983 (1984).
Saturn [Hall of Fame], 1979 (1980); [SF Film], 1980 (1981); [Writing], 1981 (1982); [Fantasy Film], 1981 (1982).
SF Chronicle [Dramatic Presentation], 1981 (1982).
KASTEN, Jeffrey. N3F [2nd], 1991 (1992).
KATHENOR, Sansoucy. L. Ron Hubbard's Writers of the Future [2nd Quarter, 3rd Place], 1985 (1986).
KATO, Hiroyuki. Seiun Taisho [Artist], 1988 (1989).
KATZ, Jack. Inkpot, 1982.
KAUFMAN, Philip. Saturn [Director], 1978 (1979).
KAWAI, Yasuo. Seiun Taisho [Shibano], 1990 (1991).
KAWAMATA, Chiaki. Nihon SF Taisho, 1983 (1984).
KAY, Guy Gavriel. Casper [Novel], 1986 (1987); [English Long Form], 1990 (1991).
KAYE, Richard. Saturn [President's], 1987 (1988).
KAYE, Simon. Oscar [Sound], 1982.

KAZAKOV, Vadim. SocCon [Fanzine], 1988 (1989).
KAZANJIAN, Howard. Inkpot, 1982.
KAZANTSEV, A. Aëlita, 1980 (1981).
KEANE, Bil. Inkpot, 1981.
KEARNS, Richard. Theodore Sturgeon Memorial [3rd], 1986 (1987).
KEARNS, Virginia. Emmy [Outstanding Achievement in Hairstyling], 1989.
KELLEHER, Victor. Ditmar [Long Australian Fiction], 1984 (1985).
KELLER, Janet. Turner Tomorrow [Hon. Mention], 1991.
KELLER, Katherine Stubergh. Count Dracula Society [Special], 1969 (1970).
KELLY, James Patrick. Davis Readers (IASFM) [Novelette], 1986 (1987); [Novella], 1990 (1991); [Poem], 1990 (1991).
KELLY, Richard. Chesley [Special], 1991 (1992).
KELLY, Walt. Inkpot, 1989. Reuben, 1951.
KELSO, Vicky. Inkpot, 1976.
KEMP, Earl. Hugo [Amateur Magazine], 1960 (1961).
KENDALL, Carol. Mythopoeic [Fantasy], 1982 (1983).
KENIN, Millea. Readercon [Large Circ. Magazine], 1983 (1984).
KEOWN, Dale. Will Eisner Comic Industry [Writer/Artist Team], 1991 (1992).
KEPPLER, Werner. Emmy [Outstanding Achievement in Makeup], 1988.
KERNAGHAN, Eileen. Casper [Novel], 1984 (1985); [English Short Form], 1989 (1990)
KERR, Noel. Ditmar [Australian Fanzine], 1970 (1971).
KERSHNER, Irvin. Saturn [Director], 1980 (1981).
KESSEL, John. John W. Campbell Jr. Memorial [3rd], 1989 (1990). Locus [Short Story], 1991 (1992). Nebula [Novella], 1981 (1982). Theodore Sturgeon Memorial [Winner], 1991 (1992).
KETCHAM, Hank. Inkpot, 1982. Reuben, 1952.
KEYES, Daniel. Hugo [Short Fiction], 1959 (1960). Kurd Lasswitz [Foreign Novel], 1985 (1986). Lazar Komarcic [Foreign Short Story], 1985 (1986). Nebula [Novel], 1966 (1967).
KHAMBATTA, Persis. Saturn [Special], 1979 (1980).
KIDD, Tom. Chesley [Unpublished Color], 1989 (1990). Davis Readers (Analog) [Cover Artist], 1986 (1987).
KIDDER, Margot. Saturn [Actress], 1978 (1979).
KIEL, Richard. Count Dracula Society [Special], 1979 (1980).
KILLOUGH, Lee. SFWA Secretary, 1986-1988.
KILWORTH, Gerry. World Fantasy [Novella], 1991 (1992).
KIMBALL, Ward. Inkpot, 1987.
KING, Frank. Reuben, 1958.
KING, Maureen. IAFA [Graduate Scholarship], 1991 (1992).
KING, Stephen.
  Alkor [Translated Novel], (twice) 1989 (1990); [Translated Short Story], 1989 (1990).
  Balrog [Collection/Anthology], 1979 (1980).
  Bram Stoker [Novel], 1987 (1988); [Collection], 1990 (1991).
  British Fantasy [Special], 1980 (1981); [August Derleth], 1981 (1982), 1986 (1987); [Short Story], 1982 (1983).
  Chronic Rift Roundtable [Novel], 1990 (1991).
  Collectors [Most Collectible Book], 1989 (1990), 1990 (1991); [Most Collectible Author], 1990 (1991).
  Daedalus [Horror Novel], 1986 (1987).
  Hugo [Nonfiction], 1981 (1982).
  Locus [Nonfiction], 1981 (1982); [Collection], 1985 (1986).
  Saturn [TV Horror Film], 1979 (1980); [Horror Film], 1980 (1981).
  Twilight Dimension [Novel], 1984 (1985).
  World Fantasy [Short Story], 1981 (1982).
  Zauber Zeit [SF Novel], 1990 (1991).
  GoH World Fantasy Convention, 1979.
KINGSBURY, Donald. Crook/Tall, 1982 (1983). Locus [First Novel], 1982 (1983). Saturn [New Writer], 1982 (1983).
KIRBY, Jack. Inkpot, 1974.

KIRK, Russell. Count Dracula Society [Literature], 1963 (1964). Gilgamés [Horror Short Story], 1985 (1986). World Fantasy [Short Fiction], 1976 (1977).
KIRK, Tim. Balrog [Artist], 1978 (1979). Hugo [Fan Artist], 1969 (1970), 1971 (1972), 1972 (1973), 1973 (1974), 1975 (1976). Locus [Fan Artist], 1972 (1973), 1973 (1974), 1974 (1975).
KISSINGER, Tess. SF Chronicle [Most Attractive Female Fan], 1983 (1984).
KITCHEN, Denis. Inkpot, 1986.
KIVINEN, S. Albert. Atorox, 1987 (1988)
KIWERSKI, Krzysztof. Festival Internazional del Film [Golden Seal], 1975 (1976).
KLEIN, Gérard. Grand Prix de la SF Française [Novelette], 1973 (1974); [Short Fiction], 1985 (1986). Prix Rosny-Aîné [Novelette], 1987.
KLEIN, J. K. Big Heart, 1990. FGoH World SF Convention, 1974.
KLEIN, T. E. D. British Fantasy [August Derleth], 1984 (1985). World Fantasy [Novella], 1985 (1986).
KLIBAN, B. Inkpot, 1980.
KLUSCJANTSEV, Pyotr. Festival Internazional del Film [Golden Seal], 1966 (1967).
KMINEK, Ivan. Karel Capek [Mlok], 1982 (1983), 1983 (1984).
KNAPP, Doug. Saturn [Special Effects], 1975 (1976).
KNEZEVIC, Boban. Lazar Komarcic [Long Fiction], 1984 (1985), 1985 (1986); [Short Story], 1988 (1989).
KNIGHT, Arthur. Saturn [Film Critic], 1976 (1977).
KNIGHT, Damon. Hugo [Critic], 1955 (1956). Jupiter [Short Story], 1976 (1977). Pilgrim, 1975. SFWA President, 1965-1967. GoH World SF Convention, 1980.
KNUDSON, Robert. Oscar [Sound], 1973, 1982.
KOBAYASHI, Yoshito. Seiun Taisho [Fanzine], 1984 (1985).
KOCH, Norma. Oscar [Costume Design (Black & White)], 1962.
KOCIS, Pavel. Karel Capek [Juvenile Writer], 1985 (1986).
KOENIG, Laird. Saturn [Horror Film], 1977 (1978).
KOENIG, Raymond. Saturn [Horror Film], 1972 (1973).
KOENIG, Walter. Inkpot, 1982.
KOHLER, Gilles. Saturn [Special], 1978 (1979).
KOJA, Kathe. Bram Stoker [First Novel], 1991 (1992). Locus [First Novel], 1991 (1992).
KOKOL, Cleo. Andre Norton Fantasy/SF Short Story [2nd], 1991 (1992).
KOLODYNSKI, Andrzej. Fantastyka [Nonfiction], 1986/1987 (1988).
KOLUPAYEV, Viktor. Aëlita, 1987 (1988).
KOMAN, Victor. Prometheus, 1986 (1987), 1989 (1990).
KOMATSU, Sakyo. Nihon SF Taisho, 1985 (1986). Seiun Taisho [Novel], 1982 (1983).
KOONTZ, Dean R. Collectors, 1988 (1989). HWA President, 1987-1988.
KOPOZYNSKI, Jerzy. Festival Internazional del Film [Golden Seal], 1972 (1973).
KORABEL'NIKOV, Oleg. Aëlita, 1989 (1990).
KORB, Liliane. Grand Prix de la SF Française [Juvenile], 1989 (1990).
KÖRBER, Joachim. Kurd Lasswitz [Special], 1984 (1985).
KORDEJ, Igor. Lazar Komarcic [Artist], 1987 (1988).
KORIAN, Chuck. Emmy [Outstanding Set Decoration for a Series], 1988.
KORNBLUTH, C. M. Hugo [Short Story], 1972 (1973). International Fantasy [2nd Fiction], 1952 (1953). Prometheus Hall of Fame, 1986.
KOSZOWSKI, Allen. L. Ron Hubbard's Illustrators of the Future [2nd Quarter], 1991 (1992). Readercon [Horror Artist], 1979 (1980), 1983 (1984); [Overall Artistic Achievement], 1983 (1984); [Artist], 1986 (1987), 1987 (1988).
KOTZWINKLE, William. World Fantasy [Novel], 1976 (1977).
KOWALSKI, Maroslaw. Polish SF & Fantasy Achievement [Publisher], 1987 (1988).
KRAPIVIN, Vladislav. Aëlita, 1981 (1982).
KREJCI, Natasa. Karel Capek [New Author], 1984 (1985); [Juvenile Author], 1984 (1985).
KRENKEL, Roy G. Hugo [Professional Artist], 1962 (1963). World Fantasy [Special], 1981 (1982).
KRESOVIC-BUNETA, Seka. Lazar Komarcic [Artist], 1989/1990 (1991).
KRESS, Nancy. Dell Readers (Analog) [Novella], 1991 (1992). Hugo [Novella], 1991 (1992). Nebula [Short Story], 1985 (1986); [Novella], 1991 (1992).
KRINARD, Sue. Prix Boréal [Artist], 1986 (1987).

KROMANOV, Grigori. Festival Internazional del Film [Special], 1979 (1980).
KRUEGER, Ken. Inkpot, 1978.
KRUKARCZYK, Grzegorz. Polish SF & Fantasy Achievement [Short Story], 1985 (1986).
KUBERT, Adam. Will Eisner Comic Industry [Inker], 1991 (1992).
KUBERT, Joe. Inkpot, 1977.
KUBIAK, Michael. Kurd Lasswitz [Translator], 1982 (1983).
KUBIC, Ladislav. Karel Capek [Mlok], 1981 (1982).
KUBRICK, Stanley. Balrog [SF Film], 1979 (1980). Hugo [Dramatic Presentation], 1964 (1965), 1968 (1969), 1971 (1972). Oscar [Special Visual Effects], 1968. Saturn [Fantasy Film], 1980 (1981).
KUCZKA, Peter. Karel, 1981 (1982); [Special President's], 1986 (1987).
KUIPERS, Jan J. B. King Kong, 1987.
KURAN, Peter. Saturn [Special Effects], 1987 (1988).
KURI, Emile. Oscar [Set Decoration], 1954.
KURTIS, Leonid. SocCon [Special], 1988 (1989).
KURTZ, Gary. British Fantasy [Film], 1980 (1981).
KURTZ, Katherine. Balrog [Novel], 1981 (1982).
KURTZMAN, Harvey. Inkpot, 1977. Will Eisner Comic Industry [Hall of Fame Inductee], 1988 (1989); [Comics-Related Book], 1991 (1992).
KUSAGAMI, Jin. Seiun Taisho [Short Fiction], 1988 (1989).
KUSHNER, Ellen. Mythopoeic [Fantasy Novel], 1990 (1991). World Fantasy [Novel], 1990 (1991).
KUTTNER, Henry. Gernsback [Short Fiction], 1946 (1983).
KYLE, David A. BSFA [Special], 1976 (1977). First Fandom, 1988. FGoH World SF Convention, 1983.
KYLE, Richard. Inkpot, 1982.
L'ENGLE, Madeleine. American Book [Children's Paperback], 1979 (1980). Empire State Award, 1992. Newbery Medal, 1963.
LACEY, Catherine. Festival Internazional del Film [Silver Asteroid—Actress], 1967 (1968).
LACIGNE, Bruno. Grand Prix de la SF Française [Novelette], 1980 (1981).
LACKEY, Mercedes. Lambda Literary [Gay SF/Fantasy], 1990 (1991).
LAEMMLE, Carl Jr. Saturn [Life Career], 1977 (1978).
LAFFERTY, Marcy. Saturn [Special], 1979 (1980).
LAFFERTY, R. A. Hugo [Short Story], 1972 (1973). Theodore Sturgeon Memorial [2nd], 1990 (1991). World Fantasy [Lifetime Achievement], 1989 (1990).
LAINE, Sylvie. Prix Rosny-Aîné [Novelette], 1986.
LAIRD, Peter. Inkpot, 1989.
LAKE, David. Ditmar [Australian Fiction], 1976 (1977); [Australian Novel], 1981 (1982).
LAKEY, Laura. Davis Readers (IASFM) [Interior Artist], 1988 (1989). Dell Readers (IASFM) [Cover Artist], 1991 (1992).
LALANDA, Javier Martin. Gilgamés [Special], 1984 (1985).
LALOUX, René. Festival Internazional del Film [Silver Seal], 1965 (1966); [Special], 1972 (1973).
LALOUX, Topor. Festival Internazional del Film [Silver Seal], 1965 (1966).
LAMB, Janie. Big Heart, 1967.
LAMBE, Dean R. SFWA Vice President, 1989-.
LANCE, Henri. Festival Internazional del Film [Gold Medal-Gruppo], 1967 (1968).
LANCHESTER, Elsa. Count Dracula Society [Cunningham], 1973 (1974). Saturn [President's], 1982 (1983).
LANDAKER, Gregg. Oscar [Sound], 1980, 1981.
LANDIS, Geoffrey A. Dell Readers (IASFM) [Short Story], 1991 (1992). Hugo [Short Story], 1991 (1992). Nebula [Short Story], 1989 (1990).
LANDIS, John. Festival Internazional del Film [Golden Asteroid], 1972 (1973). IAM [Short Story], 1990 (1991). Saturn [Horror Film], 1981 (1982).
LANDWEBER, Michael T. L. Ron Hubbard's Writers of the Future [1st Quarter, 2nd Place], 1989 (1990).
LANE, Barbara. Saturn [Costumes], 1988 (1989).
LANE, Timothy. SF Chronicle [Fanzine], 1988 (1989).

LANG, Fritz. Count Dracula Society [Cinema], 1969 (1970). Saturn [Life Career], 1975 (1976).
LANGE, Hope. Emmy [Actress in Comedy], 1969, 1970.
LANGELLA, Frank. Count Dracula Society [Walpole Medal], 1977 (1978); [Special], 1978 (1979).
LANGFORD, Dave.
  BSFA [Short Fiction], 1985 (1986).
  Hugo [Fan Writer], 1984 (1985), 1986 (1987), 1988 (1989), 1989 (1990), 1990 (1991), 1991 (1992); [Fanzine], 1986 (1987).
  SF Chronicle [Fan Writer], 1986 (1987), 1989 (1990), 1990 (1991); [Fanzine], 1986 (1987).
  FGoH World SF Convention, 1987.
LANGLEY, Noel. Balrog [Fantasy Film Hall of Fame], 1980 (1981).
LANSDALE, Joe R. Bram Stoker [Short Story], 1988 (1989); [Novella/Novelette], 1989 (1990). British Fantasy [Short Story], 1989 (1990). Readercon [Nonfiction Writer], 1986 (1987). HWA Vice President, 1989-1990; Treasurer, 1987-1988.
LANSKY, Bernie. Inkpot, 1978.
LAPERROUSAZ, Jerome. Festival Internazionale del Film [Golden Asteroid], 1975 (1976).
LA PORTE, Steve. Oscar [Makeup], 1988. Saturn [Makeup], 1988 (1989).
LARDREAU, Guy. Grand Prix de la SF Française [Nonfiction], 1987 (1988).
LARIONOVA, Olga. Aëlita, 1986 (1987). Alkor [Novel], 1989 (1990).
LARKING, David. World Fantasy [Special (Professional)], 1983 (1984).
LARSEN, Jeanne. IAFA [Crawford], 1989 (1990).
LARSEN, Milt. Count Dracula Society [Special], 1965 (1966).
LASKOWSKI, George. Hugo [Fanzine], 1985 (1986), 1990 (1991). SF Chronicle [Fanzine], 1989 (1990), 1990 (1991).
LASSWELL, Fred. Reuben, 1963.
LASZLO, Ernest. Saturn [Cinematography], 1976 (1977).
LATHAM, Rob. IAFA [Graduate Scholarship], 1990 (1991).
LATORRE, José María. Gilgamés [Special], 1988 (1989).
LAVREK, Andrija. Lazar Komarcic [Short Fiction], 1984 (1985).
LAZARUS, Mell. Inkpot, 1976.
LAZOVIC, Vladimir. Lazar Komarcic [Novella], 1987 (1988).
LE BLANC, Thomas. Deutscher Fantasy, 1990 (1991).
LE GUIN, Ursula K.
  Alkor [Translated Short Story], 1989 (1990).
  American Book [Children's Literature], 1973 (1974).
  Boston Globe Horn Book, 1969.
  Ditmar [International Fiction], 1985 (1986).
  Forry, 1988.
  Gilgamés [SF Novel], 1983 (1984); [Fantasy Novel], 1983 (1984), 1987 (1988); [SF Collection], 1985 (1986).
  Harold D. Vursell Memorial, 1990 (1991).
  Hugo [Novel], 1969 (1970), 1974 (1975); [Novella], 1972 (1973); [Short Story], 1973 (1974); [Gandalf Grand Master], 1978 (1979); [Novelette], 1987 (1988).
  Jupiter [Novel], 1974 (1975); [Short Story], 1974 (1975); [Novelette], 1976 (1977).
  Locus [Novel], 1971 (1972), 1974 (1975); [Short Story], 1974 (1975), 1982 (1983); [Novelette], 1975 (1976); [Collection], 1975 (1976), 1982 (1983); [Fantasy Novel], 1990 (1991).
  Nebula [Novel], 1969 (1970), 1974 (1975), 1990 (1991); [Short Story], 1974 (1975).
  Pilgrim, 1989.
  Premios Cometa d'Argento [Novel], 1976 (1977).
  Prix Jules Verne, 1976.
  Rhysling [Long Poem], 1981 (1982).
  Theodore Sturgeon Memorial [2nd], 1987 (1988).
  World Fantasy [Novella], 1987 (1988).
  GoH World Fantasy Convention, 1989; World SF Convention, 1975.
LEDERER, Francis. Count Dracula Society [Television], 1971 (1972).
LEDGERWOOD, Jo Etta. L. Ron Hubbard's Writers of the Future [2nd Quarter, 2nd Place], 1989 (1990).

LEE, Alan. Chesley [Interior Illustration], 1988 (1989).
LEE, Christopher. Count Dracula Society [Cinema], 1966 (1967); [Walpole Medal], 1971 (1972), 1978 (1979); [Cunningham], 1976 (1977). Saturn [Life Career], 1978 (1979); [World SF Film Favorite], 1979 (1980).
LEE, Danny. Oscar [Special Visual Effects], 1971.
LEE, Jim. Inkpot, 1992.
LEE, Jody. Chesley [Cover Illustration (Paperback)], 1988 (1989). Jack Gaughan Memorial, 1992.
LEE, Stan. Atlanta Fantasy Faire, 1986. Inkpot, 1974.
LEE, Tanith.
  British Fantasy [August Derleth], 1979 (1980).
  Gilgamés [Fantasy Novel], 1985 (1986), 1986 (1987).
  SF Chronicle [Most Attractive Female Writer], 1983 (1984).
  World Fantasy [Short Story], 1982 (1983), 1983 (1984).
  GoH World Fantasy Convention, 1984.
LEE, Terry. Chesley [Cover Illustration (Magazine)], 1987 (1988).
LEE, Walt. Hugo [Special Plaque], 1974 (1975).
LEIALOHA, Steve. Inkpot, 1986.
LEIBER, Fritz.
  Alkor [Translated Short Story], 1989 (1990).
  Balrog [Special], 1980 (1981).
  Bram Stoker [Life Achievement], 1987 (1988).
  British Fantasy [Short Story], 1979 (1980).
  Count Dracula Society [Literature], 1969 (1970).
  Forry, 1967.
  Gilgamés [Fantasy Collection], 1985 (1986), 1986 (1987), 1987 (1988); [Fantasy Short Story], 1985 (1986), 1986 (1987), 1987 (1988), 1989 (1990); [Horror Novel], 1989 (1990); [Fantasy Collection/Anthology], 1989 (1990).
  Hugo [Novel], 1957 (1958), 1964 (1965); [Novelette], 1967 (1968); [Novella], 1969 (1970), 1970 (1971); [Gandalf Grand Master], 1974 (1975); [Short Story], 1975 (1976).
  Locus [Collection], 1984 (1985).
  Nebula [Novelette], 1967 (1968); [Novella], 1970 (1971); [Short Story], 1975 (1976); [Grand Master], 1980 (1981).
  World Fantasy [Short Fiction], 1975 (1976); [Lifetime Achievement], 1975 (1976); [Novel], 1977 (1978).
  GoH World Fantasy Convention, 1978; World SF Convention, 1951, 1979.
LEIGH, Kari Llewellyn. Early Universe, 1983.
LEINSTER, Murray. Gernsback [Novel], 1936 (1983). Hugo [Novelette], 1955 (1956). GoH World SF Convention, 1963.
LEKIEWICZ, Z. Polish SF & Fantasy Achievement [Golden Meteor], 1985 (1986).
LEM, Stanislaw. Aëlita [Fan—Translation], 1988 (1989). Alkor [Translated Novel], 1988 (1989), (twice) 1989 (1990); [Translated Short Story], 1989 (1990). Eurocon [Author], 1990 (1991). Polish SF & Fantasy Achievement [Author], 1987 (1988).
LENNING, Arthur. Count Dracula Society [Literature], 1974 (1975).
LERNER, Fred. SFRA Newsletter Editor, 1971-1974.
LESSING, Doris. Medicis Prize, 1976. GoH World SF Convention, 1987.
LETHEM, Jonathan. Theodore Sturgeon Memorial [3rd], 1991 (1992).
LEVIGNE, Michelle L. L. Ron Hubbard's Writers of the Future [4th Quarter, 1st Place], 1990 (1991).
LEVRERO, Mario. Más Alla [Short Fiction], 1983 (1984), 1984 (1985).
LEWIS, Al. E. E. Evans/Paul Frehafer, 1959.
LEWIS, C. S. Carnegie Medal, 1956.
LEWIS, Arthur O. SFRA President, 1977-1979.
LEWIS, W. S. Count Dracula Society [Walpole Medal], 1973 (1974).
LEY, Willy. Hugo [Excellence in Fact Articles], 1952 (1953); [Feature Writer], 1955 (1956). International Fantasy [Nonfiction], 1949/1950 (1951), 1952 (1953); [2nd Nonfiction], 1951 (1952). GoH World SF Convention, 1953.
LI, Tan. China SF Milky Way/Forest Cup [1st], 1990 (1991).
LIANG, Kong. China SF Constellation/Galaxy, 1985 (1986).

LIEBSCHER, Walt. Big Heart, 1981.
LIGHT, Alan. Inkpot, 1975.
LIGHTMAN, Alan P. Rhysling [Short Poem], 1982 (1983).
LIN, Qi. China SF Constellation, 1990 (1991).
LINAWEAVER, Brad. Prometheus, 1988 (1989).
LINDAHN, Val Lakey. Chesley [Interior Illustration], 1990 (1991). Jack Gaughan Memorial, 1987.
LINDHOLM, Margaret. Readercon [SF Writer], 1983 (1984).
LINDHOLM, Megan. Davis Readers (IASFM) [Novella], 1989 (1990). Theodore Sturgeon Memorial [2nd], 1989 (1990).
LINDSEY, Donald. Count Dracula Society [Fauria], 1976 (1977).
LINZER, Gordon. Readercon [Small Circ. Magazine], 1979 (1980), 1983 (1984).
LIPPINCOTT, Charles. Saturn [Advertisement/Publicity/Public Relations], 1977 (1978).
LISLE, Holly. Boomerang [Poem], 1990 (1991).
LISLE, Janet Taylor. Newbery Medal, 1990.
LITTLE, Bentley. Bram Stoker [First Novel], 1990 (1991).
LoBRUTTO, Pat. World Fantasy [Special (Professional)], 1985 (1986).
LOFFICIER, Jean-Marc. Inkpot, 1990.
LOFFICIER, Randi. Inkpot, 1990.
LOGGIA, Robert. Saturn [Supporting Actor], 1988 (1989).
LONG, Frank Belknap. Bram Stoker [Life Achievement], 1987 (1988). World Fantasy [Lifetime Achievement], 1977 (1978). GoH World Fantasy Convention, 1979.
LONGENDORFER, John. Chesley [3-D Art], 1987 (1988).
LONGYEAR, Barry B. Hugo [Novella], 1979 (1980); [Campbell], 1979 (1980). Locus [Novella], 1979 (1980). Nebula [Novella], 1979 (1980).
LOREN, E. Alkor [Translated Short Story], 1989 (1990).
LORNE, Marion. Emmy [Supporting Actress in Comedy], 1968.
LORRE, Peter. Count Dracula Society [Cinema], 1963 (1964).
LORREY, Rayson. L. Ron Hubbard's Writers of the Future [2nd Quarter, 2nd Place], 1987 (1988).
LOSEY, Joseph. Festival Internazional del Film [Golden Asteroid], 1963 (1964).
LOUBARIE, Claude. Festival Internazional del Film [Special], 1970 (1971).
LOUBERT, Deni. Inkpot, 1987.
LOUIE, Gary. E. E. Evans/Paul Frehafer, 1990.
LOWENTROUT, Peter. SFRA President, 1991-1993.
LOWNDES, Robert A. W. "Doc." First Fandom, 1991.
LUCAS, George.
  Balrog [SF Film], 1979 (1980); [Outstanding Professional Achievement], 1980 (1981), 1981 (1982); [SF Film Hall of Fame], 1980 (1981).
  British Fantasy [Film], 1980 (1981), 1981 (1982), 1989 (1990).
  Hugo [Special Plaque], 1976 (1977); [Dramatic Presentation], 1977 (1978), 1980 (1981), 1983 (1984), 1989 (1990).
  Inkpot, 1977.
  Nebula [Special Plaque], 1977 (1978).
  Saturn [SF Film], 1976 (1977), 1980 (1981); [Director], 1977 (1978); [Writing], 1977 (1978); [Hall of Fame], 1979 (1980).
LUCAS, Marcia. Oscar [Film Editing], 1977. Saturn [Editing], 1977 (1978).
LUCZAK, Jerzy. Polish SF & Fantasy Achievement [Publisher], 1984 (1985).
LUMLEY, Brian. British Fantasy [Short Story], 1988 (1989). Fear Fiction [Established Author], 1989 (1990). TM World Horror Convention, 1992.
LUMLEY, Dorothy. British Fantasy [Special], 1990 (1991).
LUND, Bill. Inkpot, 1974.
LUNDGREN, Carl. Chesley [Cover Illustration (Paperback)], 1984 (1985); [Artistic Achievement], 1984 (1985).
LUNDGREN, Michele. Chesley [Special], 1984 (1985).
LUNDWALL, Sam J. Karel, 1989 (1990); [Harrison], 1982 (1983).
LUPINO, Ida. Count Dracula Society [Cinema], 1976 (1977). Saturn [Supporting Actress], 1975 (1976).
LUPOFF, Richard. Hugo [Amateur Magazine], 1962 (1963).
LUSKE, Hamilton. Oscar [Special Visual Effects], 1964.

LYCETT, Eustace. Oscar [Special Visual Effects], 1964, 1971.
LYNCH, David. BSFA [Media Presentation], 1990 (1991).
LYNCH, Dick. Hugo [Fanzine], 1991 (1992).
LYNCH, Nicki. Hugo [Fanzine], 1991 (1992).
LYNCH, Richard. Saturn [Supporting Actor], 1982 (1983).
LYNDE, Stan. Inkpot, 1977.
LYNN, Elizabeth A. World Fantasy [Novel], 1979 (1980); [Short Fiction], 1979 (1980).
MacAVOY, R. A. Hugo [Campbell], 1983 (1984). Locus [First Novel], 1983 (1984). Philip K. Dick Memorial [2nd], 1983 (1984).
MacDONALD, Ian. Philip K. Dick [1st], 1991 (1992).
MacDOUGLASS, Don. Oscar [Sound], 1977. Saturn [Sound], 1977 (1978).
MACEK, Carl. Inkpot, 1979.
MacEWEN, Pat. L. Ron Hubbard's Writers of the Future [1st Quarter, 3rd Place], 1987 (1988).
MACHULSKI, Juliusz. Polish SF & Fantasy Achievement [Author], 1983 (1984).
MACIA, Cristine. Gilgamés [Special], 1989 (1990).
MacINTYRE, Christine. Count Dracula Society [Fauria], 1977 (1978).
MACKIE, Andrew W. N3F [1st], 1991 (1992).
MacLEAN, Katherine. Nebula [Novella], 1971 (1972).
MADDERN, Philippa. Ditmar [Special], 1976 (1977).
MADLE, Robert. First Fandom, 1990. FGoH World SF Convention, 1977.
MAGUIRE, Kevin. Manning, 1988.
MAHDAVI, Seid. Count Dracula Society [Fauria], 1975 (1976). Saturn [Outstanding Service], 1978 (1979).
MAILANDER, Jane. L. Ron Hubbard's Writers of the Future [1st Quarter, 1st Place], 1987 (1988).
MAITZ, Don.
  Chesley [Cover Illustration (Paperback)], 1987 (1988), 1990 (1991); [Unpublished Color], 1987 (1988); [Cover Illustration (Hardback)], 1988 (1989); [Artistic Achievement], 1988 (1989), 1989 (1990).
  Hugo [Professional Artist], 1989 (1990); [Special], 1989 (1990).
  Inkpot, 1991.
  Locus [Nonfiction], 1988 (1989).
  Readercon [Jacket Illustrator], 1988 (1989).
  SF Chronicle [Most Attractive Male Artist], 1983 (1984); [Artist], 1988 (1989).
  World Fantasy [Artist], 1979 (1980).
  AGoH World Fantasy Convention, 1982.
MAKI, Shinji. Seiun Taisho [Shibano], 1989 (1990).
MAKOWSKI, Maciej. Polish SF & Fantasy Achievement [Special], 1985 (1986).
MALEY, Alan. Oscar [Special Visual Effects], 1971.
MALLETT, Daryl F. SFRA Newsletter Editor, 1992- .
MALY. Grand Prix de la SF Française [Special], 1987 (1988).
MALZBERG, Barry N. John W. Campbell, Jr. Memorial, 1972 (1973). Locus [Nonfiction], 1982 (1983).
MAMOULIAN, Rouben. Count Dracula Society [Walpole Medal], 1969 (1970). Saturn [Special], 1980 (1981).
MANARA, Milo. Inkpot, 1992.
MANLOVE, Colin. IAFA [Distinguished Scholarship], 1988 (1989).
MANNING, Russ. Inkpot, 1974.
MANSBRIDGE, John. Emmy [Outstanding Art Direction for a Series], 1988.
MANSFIELD, John. Aurora [Fan Achievement (Organizational)], 1991 (1992).
MANULI, Guido. Festival Internazional del Film [Golden Seal], 1976 (1977), 1978 (1979).
MARAFANTE, Virginio. Premios Italiano di Fantascienza [Short Fiction], 1976 (1977); [Novel], 1979 (1980).
MARCH, Fredric. Oscar [Actor], 1931/1932.
MARKER, Chris. Festival Internazional del Film [Golden Asteroid], 1962 (1963).
MARKS, Aleksandr. Festival Internazional del Film [Silver Seal], 1966 (1967), 1969 (1970).
MARRS, Lee. Inkpot, 1982.
MARSHALL, E. G. Count Dracula Society [Special], 1974 (1975).

MARSHALL, Frank. Inkpot, 1982.
MARSHALL, William. Count Dracula Society [Special], 1972 (1973); [Cinema], 1973 (1974).
MARSOL, Marek. Karel, 1985 (1986).
MARTENSSON, Bertil. Svenska SF Priset [Short Story], 1985 (1986).
MARTIN, Barbara. Andre Norton Fantasy/SF Short Story [1st], 1991 (1992).
MARTIN, George R. R.
Balrog [Novel], 1983 (1984).
Bram Stoker [Novelette], 1987 (1988).
Gilgamés [Horror Novel], 1983 (1984); [Horror Collection], 1986 (1987); [SF Novel], 1988 (1989).
Hugo [Novella], 1974 (1975); [Novelette], 1979 (1980); [Short Story], 1979 (1980).
Inkpot, 1988.
Locus [Novella], 1975 (1976), 1980 (1981); [Collection], 1976 (1977), 1981 (1982); [Novelette], 1979 (1980), 1981 (1982), 1983 (1984); [Short Story], 1979 (1980).
Nebula [Novelette], 1979 (1980), 1985 (1986).
SF Chronicle [Short Story], 1985 (1986).
Seiun Taisho [Foreign Novelette], 1982 (1983).
World Fantasy [Novella], 1988 (1989).
Writers Guild of America TV/Radio [Dramatic/Episodic Script], 1986.
MARTIN, James Michael. Count Dracula Society [Special], 1967 (1968).
MARTIN, Michel. Prix Boréal [Short Story], 1988 (1989).
MARTYNEC, Denis. L. Ron Hubbard's Illustrators of the Future [1st Quarter], 1992 (1993).
MAS, Miguel. Gilgamés [Fanzine], 1983 (1984), 1986 (1987), 1987 (1988), 1988 (1989).
MASLOW, Steve. Oscar [Sound], 1980, 1981.
MASON, Sue. Eastcon [Artist], 1989 (1990).
MASS, Joseph R. Count Dracula Society [Fauria], 1974 (1975).
MASSIE, Elizabeth. Bram Stoker [Novella/Novelette], 1990 (1991).
MASTERTON, Graham. Prix Julia Verlanger, 1987 (1988).
MATHESON, Richard.
Bram Stoker [Collection], 1989 (1990); [Life Achievement], 1990 (1991).
Count Dracula Society [Special], 1971 (1972); [Television], 1973 (1974).
Gilgamés [Fantasy Short Story], 1989 (1990).
Hugo [Motion Picture], 1957 (1958).
Playboy Writing [Fiction Short Story], 1958.
Readercon [Collection], 1989 (1990).
Saturn [Fantasy Film], 1980 (1981).
World Fantasy [Novel], 1975 (1976); [Lifetime Achievement], 1983 (1984); [Collection], 1989 (1990).
Writers Guild of America TV/Radio [Adapted Anthology], 1972; [Dramatic/Episodic Script], 1986.
GoH World Fantasy Convention, 1977
GoH World Horror Convention, 1992.
GoH World SF Convention, 1958.
MATHESON, Richard Christian. MGoH World Horror Convention, 1992.
MATHISON, Melissa. Balrog [SF Film Hall of Fame], 1984 (1985). Saturn [Screenplay], 1982 (1983); [SF Film], 1982 (1983).
MATSUMIYA, Shizuo. Seiun Taisho [Shibano], 1989 (1990).
MATTINGLY, David. Chesley [Cover Illustration (Magazine)], 1991 (1992). AGoH World Fantasy Convention, 1990.
MATZ, J. Marc. L. Ron Hubbard's Writers of the Future [4th Quarter, 2nd Place], 1988 (1989).
MAULDIN, Bill. Reuben, 1961.
MAURER, Norman. Inkpot, 1983.
MAURICIO, Jadwiga. Gilgamés [Special], 1983 (1984).
MAXWELL, Lisa. L. Ron Hubbard's Writers of the Future [1st Quarter, 1st Place], 1992 (1993).
MAY, Elaine. Saturn [Writing], 1978 (1979); [Fantasy Film], 1978 (1979).
MAY, Julian. Locus [SF Novel], 1981 (1982).

MAY, Paula. L. Ron Hubbard's Writers of the Future [2nd Quarter, 3rd Place], 1988 (1989).
MAYER, Frederick J. Balrog [Poet], 1981 (1982), 1982 (1983), 1983 (1984).
MAYER, Mercer. Balrog [Special], 1983 (1984).
MAYER, Sheldon. Inkpot, 1976.
MAYHAR, Ardath. Balrog [Poet], 1984 (1985).
MAZURANIC, Krsto. Karel, 1981 (1982); [Harrison], 1982 (1983).
MAZURKI, Mike. Count Dracula Society [Special], 1978 (1979).
McALLISTER, Michael. Emmy [Outstanding Achievement in Special Visual Effects], 1986. Oscar [Visual Effects], 1984.
McCAFFERY, Larry. Readercon [Nonfiction], 1990 (1991).
McCAFFREY, Anne.
Balrog [Novel], 1979 (1980); [Outstanding Professional Achievement], 1979 (1980).
Ditmar [International Fiction], 1978 (1979).
Hugo [Novella], 1967 (1968); [Gandalf—Fantasy Novel], 1978 (1979).
John W. Campbell Jr. Memorial [3rd], 1988 (1989).
Nebula [Novella], 1968 (1969).
SF Book Club, [Winner], 1986 (1987), 1989 (1990), 1990 (1991), [3rd], 1990 (1991).
Skylark, 1976.
SFWA Secretary/Treasurer, 1968-1970.
GoH World Fantasy Convention, 1992.
GoH World SF Convention, 1993.
McCAMMON, Robert. Bram Stoker [Novel], 1987 (1988), 1990 (1991), 1991 (1992); [Short Story], 1987 (1988), 1989 (1990). World Fantasy [Novel], 1991 (1992). GoH World Fantasy Convention, 1989.
McCANN, Edson—SEE: POHL, Frederik & DEL REY, Lester.
McCARTHY, Gerry. Aisling Gheal [3rd], 1978 (1979).
McCARTHY, John. Aisling Gheal [1st], 1978 (1979).
McCARTHY, Shawna. Hugo [Professional Editor], 1983 (1984). Locus [Anthology], 1988 (1989); [Magazine], 1988 (1989). SF Chronicle [Magazine Editor], 1985 (1986).
McCAULEY, Kirby. Balrog [Special], 1982 (1983). World Fantasy [Single Author Collection/Anthology], 1976 (1977), 1980 (1981); [Special], 1978 (1979).
McCAULEY, Paul J. Arthur C. Clarke [2nd], 1991 (1992). Philip K. Dick Memorial [2nd], 1988 (1989).
McCLOUD, Scott. Inkpot, 1992. Manning, 1985.
McCOMAS, J. Francis. Invisible Little Man, 1968.
McCUNE, Grant. Oscar [Visual Effects], 1977.
McDANIEL, Catherine. L. Ron Hubbard's Writers of the Future [4th Quarter, 3rd Place], 1986 (1987).
McDEVITT, Jack. Locus [First Novel], 1986 (1987). Philip K. Dick Memorial [2nd], 1986 (1987).
McDONALD, Ian. Arthur C. Clarke [3rd], 1989 (1990). Locus [First Novel], 1988 (1989). Philip K. Dick Memorial [1st], 1991 (1992).
McDOWELL, Roddy. Count Dracula Society [Special], 1970 (1971).
McFARLANE, Todd. Inkpot, 1992.
McFERRAN, David. British Fantasy [Small Press Magazine], 1980 (1981).
McGARRY, Terry. Boomerang [Poem], 1989 (1990).
McGAVIN, Darren. Count Dracula Society [Television], 1974 (1975).
McGOVERN, Tim. Oscar [Special Achievement (Visual Effects)], 1990.
McINTYRE, Vonda N. Hugo [Novel], 1978 (1979). Locus [Novel], 1978 (1979). Nebula [Novelette], 1973 (1974); [Novel], 1978 (1979).
McKEAN, Dave. World Fantasy [Artist], 1990 (1991).
McKEE, Erin. Chesley [Special Award], 1990 (1991).
McKENNA, Bridget. L. Ron Hubbard's Writers of the Future [4th Quarter, 1st Place], 1985 (1986).
McKENNA, Richard. Nebula [Short Story], 1966 (1967).
McKILLIP, Patricia. Balrog [Short Fiction], 1984 (1985). Locus [Fantasy Novel], 1979 (1980). World Fantasy [Novel], 1973/1974 (1975).
McKINLEY, Robin. World Fantasy [Anthology/Collection], 1985 (1986).
McKINNON, Patrick. Rhysling [Long Poem], 1989 (1990).

McMAHAN, Jeffrey N. Lambda Literary [Gay SF/Fantasy], 1989 (1990).
McLAUGHLIN, Dean. Dell Readers (Analog) [Novel], 1991 (1992).
McMULLEN, Sean. Ditmar [Australian Short Story], 1990 (1991).
McMURRIAN, Jody C. L. Ron Hubbard's Illustrators of the Future [2nd Quarter], 1992 (1993).
McNELLY, Raymond. Count Dracula Society [Walpole Medal], 1972 (1973); [Summers], 1974 (1975); [Literature], 1978 (1979).
McQUARRIE, Ralph. Oscar [Visual Effects], 1985.
McQUAY, Mike. Philip K. Dick Memorial [2nd], 1987 (1988).
MEACHAM, Beth. SF Chronicle [Book Editor], 1989 (1990).
MEAD, David G. SFRA President, 1993- ; Secretary, 1989-1992.
MEAD, Syd. Inkpot, 1989.
MEDDINGS, Derek. Oscar [Special Achievement (Visual Effects)], 1978.
MEEHAN, John. Oscar [Art Direction], 1954.
MEES, James J. Emmy [Outstanding Set Decoration for a Series], 1990.
MELCHIOR, Ib J. Saturn [Writing], 1975 (1976).
MELKONYAN, Agop. Graviton [Writer], 1989 (1990).
MEL'NIKOV, Gennadij. Boris Strugatsky [Fiction by a New Writer], 1986-1990 (1991).
MELTZER, Michael Paul. L. Ron Hubbard's Writers of the Future [1st Quarter, 1st Place], 1991 (1992).
MELVILLE, Pauline. Manchester Guardian, 1991.
MEMMOTT, David. Rhysling [Short Poem], 1990 (1991).
MEYNARD, Yves—SEE: FRÉMION, Yves.
MENGHINI, Luigi. Premios Italiano di Fantascienza [Novel], 1977 (1978).
MEREDITH, Burgess. Saturn [Supporting Actor], 1978 (1979), 1981 (1982).
MEREDITH, Jerry T. L. Ron Hubbard's Writers of the Future [1st Quarter; 3rd Place], 1985 (1986)
MERKEN, Alan. Oscar [Original Music Score], 1988.
MERLE, Robert. John W. Campbell, Jr. Memorial,1973 (1974).
MERRIL, Judith. Casper [Lifetime Achievement], 1983; [Special], 1985 (1986). Milford, 1991.
MESKYS, Ed. Hugo [Amateur Magazine], 1966 (1967).
MESSICK, Dale. Inkpot, 1976.
MESSNER-LOEBS, Bill. Inkpot, 1987.
METALNICOV, Budimir. Festival Internazionale del Film [Special], 1973 (1974).
METIOLKINA, Elena. Festival Internazionale del Film [Silver Asteroid—Actress], 1981 (1982).
METZGER, Robert A. Boomerang [Short Story], 1989 (1990).
MEYER, Nicholas. Count Dracula Society [Literature], 1979 (1980). Saturn [Writing], 1979 (1980); [Director], 1982 (1983).
MICHELUCCI, Robert V. Saturn [Special], 1979 (1980).
MICHIHARA, Katsumi. Seiun Taisho [Artist], 1989 (1990).
MIDDLEMISS, Perry. Ditmar [Australian Fan Writer], 1987 (1988).
MIELKE, Thomas R. P. Kurd Lasswitz [Novel], 1983 (1984).
MIKHALIKOV, Vladimir. Aëlita [Great Ring], 1982 (1983). Alkor [Short Story], 1989 (1990).
MILAN, Victor. Prometheus, 1985 (1986).
MILÉSI, Raymond. Grand Prix de la SF Française [Short Fiction], 1989 (1990).
MILIOTI, Victor. Festival Internazionale del Film [Special], 1977 (1978).
MILL, Virginia. E. E. Evans/Paul Frehafer, 1962.
MILLAND, Ray. Count Dracula Society [Special], 1971 (1972).
MILLER, Ann. Andre Norton Fantasy/SF Short Story [1st], 1990 (1991).
MILLER, Craig. E. E. Evans/Paul Frehafer, 1976.
MILLER, Frank. Inkpot, 1981. Will Eisner Comic Industry [Finite Series], 1990 (1991); [Graphic Album (New)], 1990 (1991); [Writer/Artist Team], 1990 (1991).
MILLER, Ian. BSFA [Artist], 1990 (1991).
MILLER, Michael D. L. Ron Hubbard's Writers of the Future [3rd Quarter; 3rd Place], 1984 (1985).
MILLER, P. Schuyler. Hugo [Special Plaque], 1962 (1963). Locus [Fan Critic], 1974 (1975).

MILLER, Richard. SFRA Newsletter Editor, 1984-1988.
MILLER, Walter M., Jr. Hugo [Novel], 1960 (1961), [Novelette], 1954 (1955).
MILLHAUSER, Steven. World Fantasy [Short Fiction], 1989 (1990).
MILLS, Robert P. Hugo [Professional Magazine], 1958 (1959), 1959 (1960), 1962 (1963).
MINER, Michael. Saturn [Writing], 1987 (1988).
MINKLER, Bob. Oscar [Sound], 1977.
MISAKI, Norihiro. Seiun Taisho [Shibano], 1990 (1991).
MISHA. Readercon [Novel], 1990 (1991).
MITCHELL, Betsy. Locus [Anthology], 1991 (1992).
MIUSHI. China SF Constellation/Galaxy, 1985 (1986).
MIYAZAKI, Hayao. Seiun Taisho [Media], 1988 (1989).
MOEBIUS. Grand Prix de la SF Française [Special], 1979 (1980). Inkpot, 1986. Will Eisner Comic Industry [Single Issue or Story], 1990 (1991).
MOENCH, Doug. Inkpot, 1981.
MOFFETT, Judith. Eunice Tietjens Memorial, 1973. Hugo [Campbell], 1987 (1988). Levinson Prize, 1976. Theodore Sturgeon Memorial [Winner], 1986 (1987).
MOLDOFF, Sheldon. Inkpot, 1991.
MOLLO, John. Oscar [Costume Design], 1977. Saturn [Costumes], 1977 (1978).
MONASH, Paul. Saturn [Horror TV Film], 1979 (1980).
MONDOLONI, Jacques. Grand Prix de la SF Française [Novelette], 1981 (1982).
MONTANARI, Gianni. Premios Italiano di Fantascienza [Critical Book], 1977 (1978).
MONTELEONE, Thomas. SF Chronicle [Most Attractive Male Writer], 1983 (1984). SFWA Secretary, 1975-1978. HWA Vice President, 1988-1989.
MONTPETIT, Charles. Casper [French Long Form], 1988 (1989).
MOON, Elizabeth. Crook/Tall, 1988 (1989).
MOORCOCK, Michael.
 British Fantasy [August Derleth], 1972 (1973), 1973 (1974), 1975 (1976).
 Gilgamés [Fantasy Novel], 1986 (1987).
 John W. Campbell, Jr. Memorial, 1978 (1979).
 Nebula [Novella], 1967 (1968).
 Seiun Taisho [Foreign Novel], 1985 (1986).
 World Fantasy [Novel], 1978 (1979).
 GoH World Fantasy Convention, 1976.
MOORE, Alan.
 Hugo [in Other Forms], 1987 (1988).
 Locus [Nonfiction], 1987 (1988).
 Will Eisner Comic Industry [Writer], 1987 (1988), 1988 (1989); [Writer/Artist Team], 1987 (1988); [Graphic Album], 1987 (1988), 1988 (1989); [Finite Series], 1987 (1988).
MOORE, C. L.
 Count Dracula Society [Literature], 1977 (1978).
 Forry, 1973.
 Gernsback [Short Fiction], 1946 (1983).
 Hugo [Gandalf Grand Master], 1980 (1981).
 World Fantasy [Lifetime Achievement], 1980 (1981).
 GoH World Fantasy Convention, 1976; World SF Convention, 1981.
MOORE, Clayburn. Chesley [3-D Art], 1991 (1992).
MOORE, Roger. Saturn [Most Popular International Performer], 1979 (1980).
MOORES, Dick. Inkpot, 1975. Reuben, 1974.
MORGAN, Don. Saturn [Advertisement/Publicity/Public Relations], 1976 (1977).
MORHEIM, George. Saturn [Fantasy Film], 1975 (1976).
MORLEY, Lewis. Ditmar [Australian Fan Artist], 1987 (1988).
MORRELL, David. Bram Stoker [Novelette], 1988 (1989), 1991 (1992).
MORRESSY, John. Balrog [Short Fiction], 1983 (1984).
MORRILL, Rowena. British Fantasy [Artist], 1983 (1984). Inkpot, 1992. AGoH World Fantasy Convention, 1983.
MORRIS, Harry O. AGoH World Horror Convention, 1992.
MORRISON, Grant. Inkpot, 1990.
MORRISON, John A. Chesley [3-D Art], 1988 (1989).
MORRISSEY, Dean. Chesley [Unpublished Color], 1990 (1991).

MORROW, Gray. Inkpot, 1978.
MORROW, James. John W. Campbell Jr. Memorial [2nd], 1986 (1987); [3rd], 1990 (1991). Nebula [Short Story], 1988 (1989). *Prisoners of Gravity* Reality 1 [Horror Novel], 1991 (1992). World Fantasy [Novel], 1990 (1991).
MORSE, Donald E. IAFA [Collins], 1990 (1991).
MOSCOSO, Victor. Inkpot, 1979.
MOSKOWITZ, Sam. Hugo [Special Plaque], 1954 (1955). Pilgrim, 1981.
MUELLER, Harald. Kurd Lasswitz [Radio Play], 1986 (1987).
MUELLER, Pat. Hugo [Fanzine], 1987 (1988).
MULLER, Jerry. Inkpot, 1980.
MULLIGAN, George. E. E. Evans/Paul Frehafer, 1991.
MULLIN, Willard. Reuben, 1954.
MUNN, H. Warner. Balrog [Poet], 1979 (1980), 1980 (1981).
MUNSON, Don. Chesley [Art Direction], 1990 (1991).
MUREN, Dennis. Oscar [Special Achievement (Visual Effects)], 1980, 1983; [Visual Effects], 1982, 1984, 1987, 1989. Saturn [Special Effects], 1982 (1983).
MURPHY, Pat.
  Arthur C. Clarke [3rd], 1990 (1991).
  Davis Readers (IASFM) [Novelette], 1987 (1988).
  Locus [Novelette], 1987 (1988).
  Nebula [Novel], 1987 (1988); [Novelette], 1987 (1988).
  Philip K. Dick Memorial [1st], 1990 (1991).
  Theodore Sturgeon Memorial [Winner], 1987 (1988).
  World Fantasy [Novella], 1990 (1991).
MURRAY, E. B. Count Dracula Society [Summers], 1973 (1974).
MUSA, Gilda. Premios Italiano di Fantascienza [Novel], 1975 (1976); [Short Fiction], 1977 (1978).
MUSGRAVE, Real. Balrog [Artist], 1981 (1982), 1983 (1984).
MYDLOWSKI, Gene. SF Chronicle [Covers (Books)], 1983 (1984).
MYERS, Julian F. Saturn [Advertisement/Publicity/Public Relations], 1978 (1979).
MYERS, Russell. Inkpot, 1974.
NABOKOV, Vladimir. Arts and Letters, 1951. Award of Merit Medal, 1969. Jack I. and Lillian L. Poses Brandeis University Creative Arts [Medal], 1964. Playboy Writing [Fiction Short Story], 1966, 1969.
NACIMENTO, R. C. Nova [Fanzine], 1988 (1989).
NADAUD, Alain. Prix Rotary, 1985 (1986).
NADRAMIA, Peggy. Readercon [Magazine], 1986 (1987); [Editor], 1986 (1987), 1987 (1988). World Fantasy [Special (Nonprofessional)], 1989 (1990).
NAKAI, Norio. Seiun Taisho [Novelette], 1987 (1988).
NASH, Clarence. Inkpot, 1978.
NASIR, Jamil E. L. Ron Hubbard's Writers of the Future [1st Quarter, 1st Place], 1988 (1989).
NASSTRADINOVA, Velitchka. Graviton [Writer], 1990 (1991).
NATWICK, Grim. Inkpot, 1978.
NAYLOR, Doug. BSFA [Media Presentation], 1989 (1990).
NEARY, Paul. Will Eisner Comic Industry [Art Team], 1988 (1989).
NEDELKOVICH, Alexander B. Lazar Komarcic [Translator], 1984 (1985), 1985 (1986), 1987 (1988).
NEFF, Ondrej. Karel Capek [Special—Professional], 1986 (1987). Ludvik Soucek [Short Story], 1985 (1986); [Golem], 1985 (1986); [Special], 1985 (1986).
NEILL, Ve. Oscar [Makeup], 1988. Saturn [Makeup], 1988 (1989).
NELSON, F. Ray. Philip K. Dick Memorial [2nd], 1982 (1983).
NESKOVIC, Zoran. Lazar Komarcic [Short Story], 1988 (1989).
NESSLE, David. Alvar Appletofft Memorial, 1980 (1981).
NESVADBA, Josef. Karel [President's], 1982 (1983). Karel Capek [Special—Professional], 1985 (1986). Ludvik Soucek [Life Achievement], 1985 (1986).
NEUMIER, Ed. Saturn [Writing], 1987 (1988).
NEVILLE, Kris. Forry, 1975.
NEW, David W. Aurora [Fan Achievement (Other)], 1991 (1992).
NEWLAND, John. Count Dracula Society [Special], 1973 (1974).

NEWMAN, Chris. Oscar [Sound], 1973.
NEWMAN, David. Hugo [Dramatic Presentation], 1978 (1979). Saturn [SF Film], 1978 (1979), 1981 (1982).
NEWMAN, Kim. Bram Stoker [Nonfiction], 1989 (1990). BSFA [Short Fiction], 1990 (1991).
NEWMAN, Leslie. Hugo [Dramatic Presentation], 1978 (1979). Saturn [SF Film], 1978 (1979), 1981 (1982).
NICASTRO, Monica. Gilgamés [Fanzine], 1987 (1988), 1988 (1989), 1989 (1990); [Special], 1986 (1987).
NICHOLLS, Peter. Hugo [Nonfiction], 1979 (1980). Locus [Nonfiction], 1979 (1980). Pilgrim, 1980.
NICHOLSON, Bruce. Oscar [Special Achievement (Visual Effects)], 1980; [Visual Effects], 1981.
NICHOLSON, Jack. Saturn [Actor], 1987 (1988).
NICHOLSON, Marjorie Hope. Pilgrim, 1971. Zabel, 1973.
NICOLAZZINI, Piergiorgio. Premios Italiano di Fantascienza [Editor], 1990 (1991); 1991 (1992).
NICOLLET. Grand Prix de la SF Française [Special], 1989 (1990).
NIELSEN, Marianne O. Casper [English Work (Other)], 1989 (1990); 1990 (1991).
NIKOLAEV, Andrej. Fond Fantastiki [Fiction Fanzine], 1990 (1991).
NIKOLAYEV, Mitia. Festival Internazional del Film [Silver Asteroid—Actor], 1971 (1972).
NIKOLIC, Dobrilo. Lazar Komarcic [Artist], 1989/1990 (1991).
NINO, Alex. Inkpot, 1976.
NIVEN, Larry.
  Alkor [Translated Short Story], 1989 (1990).
  Ditmar [International Fiction], 1971 (1972), 1974 (1975).
  Forry, 1969.
  Hugo [Short Story], 1966 (1967), 1971 (1972), 1974 (1975); [Novel], 1970 (1971); [Novelette], 1975 (1976).
  Inkpot, 1979.
  Locus [Novel], 1970 (1971); [Collection], 1979 (1980); [SF Novel], 1984 (1985).
  Nebula [Novel], 1970 (1971).
  Seiun Taisho [Foreign Novelette], 1980 (1981); [Foreign Novel], 1988 (1989).
  Skylark, 1973.
  GoH World SF Convention, 1993.
NIVEN, Marilyn "Fuzzy Pink". E. E. Evans/Paul Frehafer, 1982.
NODA, Masahiro. Seiun Taisho [Novelette], 1985 (1986); [Nonfiction], 1988 (1989).
NODELL, Marty. Inkpot, 1986.
NOEL, Scot. L. Ron Hubbard's Writers of the Future [3rd Quarter, 2nd Place], 1989 (1990).**NOLAN, William F.** Edgar Allen Poe [Special], 1971. Saturn [SF Film], 1976 (1977); [Horror Film], 1976 (1977).
NOOMIN, Diane. Inkpot, 1992.
NOREASCON. Locus [Convention], 1971 (1972).
NORTH, Edmund. Balrog [SF Film Hall of Fame], 1982 (1983).
NORTON, Andre.
  Balrog [Judges' Choice], 1978 (1979).\
  Big Heart, 1988.
  Daedalus [Life Achievement], 1986 (1987).
  Forry, 1989.
  Gray Mouser, 1983.
  Hugo [Gandalf Grand Master], 1976 (1977).
  Inkpot, 1989.
  Invisible Little Man, 1963.
  Jules Verne [Life Achievement in SF], 1983 (1984).
  Nebula [Grand Master], 1983 (1984).
  Norton, 1978.
  Skylark, 1983.
  World Fantasy [Special], 1986 (1987).
  GoH World SF Convention, 1989.

NORTON, Rosanna. Saturn [Costumes], 1982 (1983).
NOURI, Michael. Count Dracula Society [Television], 1978 (1979).
NOURSE, Alan E. SFWA President, 1968-1969.
NOVOTNY, Frantisek. Karel, 1984 (1985). Karel Capek [Mlok], 1984 (1985); [Short Story], 1984 (1985), 1985 (1986).
NUEVA DIMENSION. Hugo [Special Plaque], 1971 (1972).
NULL, Bob. E. E. Evans/Paul Frehafer, 1981.
NYREN, Ron A. SF Writers of Earth [1st], 1987 (1988).
O'BANNON, Dan. British Fantasy [Film], 1979 (1980). Hugo [Dramatic Presentation], 1979 (1980). Inkpot, 1985. Saturn [Special Effects], 1975 (1976); [SF Film], 1979 (1980).
O'BRIEN, Richard. Saturn [Hall of Fame], 1979 (1980).
O'BRIEN, Robert C. Newbery Medal, 1972. William Allen White Children's Book, 1974.
O'CALLAGHAN, Maxine. HWA Treasurer, 1988-1989.
O'DOINN, G. R. L. Ron Hubbard's Writers of the Future [4th Quarter, 2nd Place], 1986 (1987).
O'DONNELL, Kevin. Mannesmann-Tally, 1985 (1986).
O'DONNELL, Lawrence—SEE: KUTTNER, Henry and Moore, C. L.
O'DONNOL, Dion. Count Dracula Society [Fauria], 1966 (1967).
O'KEEFE, Claudia. HWA Secretary, 1992- .
O'NEIL, Dennis. Inkpot, 1981.
O'NEILL, Dan. Inkpot, 1979.
OATES, Joyce Carol. Gilgamés [Horror Short Story], 1989 (1990).
ODELL, David. Balrog [Fantasy Film Hall of Fame], 1982 (1983). Saturn [Fantasy Film], 1982 (1983).
offutt, andrew j. SFWA Treasurer, 1973-1976; President, 1976-1978.
OHARA, Mariko. Seiun Taisho [Novel], 1990 (1991); [Short Fiction], 1989 (1990).
OHASHI, Koichi. Seiun Taisho [Shibano], 1990 (1991).
OKOMOTO, Mike. Manning, 1992.
OLANDER, Thomas D. Karel [Special President's], 1986 (1987); [President's], 1987 (1988).
OLIFF, Steve. Inkpot, 1991. Will Eisner Comic Industry [Colorist], 1991 (1992).
OLIPHANT, Pat. Reuben, 1968, 1972.
OLIVER, Chad. Spur, 1967.
OLSA, Jaroslav Jr. Karel [Special Award], 1990 (1991). Ludvik Soucek [Fanzine], 1985 (1986).
OLSHEVSKY, George. Inkpot, 1980.
OLTION, Jerry. Davis Readers (Analog) [Short Story], 1987 (1988).
OMAN, Daniel S. L. Ron Hubbard's Illustrators of the Future [3rd Quarter], 1989 (1990).
OOTOMO, Katsuhiro. Seiun Taisho [Comics], 1983 (1984).
OPPER, Don. British Science Fiction [Film], 1983 (1984).
ORAMUS, Marek. Fantastyka [Nonfiction], 1983 (1984). Polish SF & Fantasy Achievement [Novel], 1985 (1986).
ORLANDO, Joe. Inkpot, 1980.
ORTIZ, Juan Manuel. Gilgamés [Fanzine], 1983 (1984), 1986 (1987), 1987 (1988), 1988 (1989).
ORTLIEB, Marc. Ditmar [Australian Fan Writer], 1978 (1979), 1980 (1981), 1981 (1982), 1982 (1983); [Australian Fanzine], 1980 (1981), 1981 (1982), 1982 (1983).
ORUILLET, Philippe. Grand Prix de la SF Française [Special], 1975 (1976).
ORWELL, George. Alkor [Translated Novel], 1989 (1990). Premios Cometa d'Argento [Film], 1973 (1974). Prometheus Hall of Fame, 1984.
ORZECHOWSKI, Tome. Inkpot, 1985.
OSWALD, Hélène. Grand Prix de la SF Française [Nonfiction], 1989 (1990).
OUTLA, Dagmara. Karel Capek [New Author], 1983 (1984).
OVERSTREET, Bob. Inkpot, 1990.
OWENS, Gary. Inkpot, 1981.
PACKER, John. Ditmar [Australian Cartoonist], 1982 (1983), 1983 (1984).
PAGETTI, Carlo. Karel [Harrison], 1986 (1987). Premios Italiano di Fantascienza [Reference Work], 1971 (1972).

Reginald's Science Fiction & Fantasy Awards, Third Edition

PAL, George. *Count Dracula Society* [Special], 1967 (1968); [Walpole Medal], 1970 (1971); [Cinema], 1977 (1978).
Inkpot, 1975.
Invisible Little Man, 1951.
Nebula [Special Plaque], 1975 (1976).
Saturn [Special], 1973/74 (1975); [Fantasy Film], 1975 (1976); [Hall of Fame Inductee], 1977 (1978).
PALANCE, Jack. Count Dracula Society [Television], 1973 (1974).
PALCZEWSKI, Juliusz K. Fantastyka [Nonfiction], 1985 (1986).
PALIN, Michael. British Science Fiction [Film], 1981 (1982).
PALMER, David. Crook/Tall, 1984 (1985).
PALWICK, Susan. Rhysling [Short Poem], 1985 (1986). Theodore Sturgeon Memorial [2nd], 1986 (1987).
PANCHYK, Dave. Casper [Fan Achievement (Organizational)], 1990 (1991).
PANEK, Zeljko. Lazar Komarcic [Artist], 1984 (1985).
PANGBORN, Edgar. International Fantasy [Fiction], 1954 (1955).
PANIC, Borislav. Lazar Komarcic [Novel], 1985 (1986).
PANIC, Nikola. Lazar Komarcic [Novel], 1984 (1985).
PANSHIN, Alexei. Hugo [Fan Writer], 1966 (1967); [Nonfiction], 1989 (1990). Nebula [Novel], 1968 (1969).
PANSHIN, Cory. Hugo [Nonfiction], 1989 (1990).
PAPIC, Krsto. Festival Internazional del Film [Golden Asteroid], 1976 (1977).
PAPIERKOWSKI, Krzysztof. Polish SF & Fantasy Achievement [Fan], 1987 (1988).
PARDOE, Rosemary. British Fantasy [Small Press Magazine], 1983 (1984).
PARKER, Brant. Inkpot, 1984.
PARKINSON, Keith. Chesley [Cover Illustration (Hardback)], 1989 (1990), 1990 (1991). Davis Readers (IASFM) [Cover Artist], 1989 (1990). Jack Gaughan Memorial, 1991.
PARNOV, Eremei. Karel [President's], 1987 (1988).
PARRINDER, Patrick. Karel [President's], 1986 (1987).
PARTCH, Virgil. Inkpot, 1979.
PASQUA, Mike. Inkpot, 1988.
PATTEN, Fred. E. E. Evans/Paul Frehafer, 1965. Inkpot, 1980.
PAUL, Frank R. Gernsback [Artist], 1936 (1983). GoH World SF Convention, 1939.
PAULS, Ted. Locus [Fan Critic], 1970 (1971).
PAUSEWANG, Gudrun. Kurd Lasswitz [Novel], 1987 (1988).
PAV, Zdenek. Karel Capek [Short Story], 1988 (1989).
PAVLAT, Peggy Rae. Big Heart, 1983.
PAVLOV, Sergei. Aëlita, 1983 (1984).
PAYACK, Peter. Rhysling [Short Poem], 1979 (1980).
PAYNE, Francis. Ditmar [Australian Short Fiction], 1977 (1978).
PAYNE, Michael H. L. Ron Hubbard's Writers of the Future [4th Quarter, 3rd Place], 1990 (1991).
PEAKE, Mervyn. Heinemann, 1951.
PEARCE, Alice. Emmy [Supporting Actress in Comedy], 1966.
PEARL, Dorothy. Saturn [Makeup], 1982 (1983).
PECINOVSKY, Josef. Karel Capek [Mlok], 1985 (1986), 1986 (1987).
PECK, Gregory. Saturn [Actor], 1976 (1977).
PEKAR, Harvey. Inkpot, 1986.
PELOT, Pierre. Grand Prix de la SF Française [Novel], 1977 (1978).
PELZ, Bruce. E. E. Evans/Paul Frehafer, 1966, 1969. FGoH World SF Convention, 1980.
PELZ, Elayne. E. E. Evans/Paul Frehafer, 1980.
PENDLETON, Michaelene. SF Writers of Earth [2nd], 1985 (1986).
PENDRAGON Gallery. Balrog [Outstanding Professional Achievement], 1983 (1984).
PENEV, Boyan. Graviton [Illustrator], 1990 (1991).
PENNINGTON, Bruce. BSFA [Artist], 1981 (1982); [Artist], 1983 (1984).
PEOPLES, David. British Fantasy [Film], 1982 (1983). British Science Fiction [Film], 1982 (1983). Hugo [Dramatic Presentation], 1982 (1983).
PERESLAGIN, Sergey. Boris Strugatsky [Critical Study], 1986-1990 (1991).

PEREZ, George. Atlanta Fantasy Faire, 1989. Inkpot, 1983.
PERISIC, Zoran. Oscar [Special Achievement (Visual Effects)], 1978.
PERKINS, Roger. Doc Weir, 1990.
PERUCHO, Juan. Gilgamés [Special], 1984 (1985).
PESTARINI, Luis M. Gilgamés [Fanzine], 1987 (1988), 1988 (1989), 1989 (1990); [Special], 1986 (1987).
PETERS, Mike. Inkpot, 1987.
PETERSON, Chris. Davis Readers (Analog) [Science Fact Article], 1987 (1988).
PETERSON, Lorne. Oscar [Visual Effects], 1984.
PETOLO, Tauno. Karel, 1988 (1989).
PETROVSKI, Slobodan. Lazar Komarcic [Short Fiction], 1985 (1986).
PFANNHOLZ, Maria J. SFCD [Novel], 1990 (1991).
PHELPS, Don. Inkpot, 1980.
PIESTRAK, Marek. Festival Internazional del Film [Golden Asteroid], 1978 (1979).
PIMPLE, Dennis J. L. Ron Hubbard's Writers of the Future [1st Quarter; 1st Place], 1984 (1985).
PINCKARD, Terri. Count Dracula Society [Special], 1970 (1971).
PINCKARD, Tom. Count Dracula Society [Special], 1970 (1971).
PINDAL, Kaj. Festival Internazional del Film [Silver Seal], 1966 (1967).
PING, Jin. China SF Milky Way/Forest Cup [3rd], 1990 (1991).
PINI, Richard. Balrog [Artist], 1984 (1985). Inkpot, 1980.
PINI, Wendy. Balrog [Artist], 1984 (1985). Inkpot, 1980.
PITTS, Jim. British Fantasy [Artist], 1991 (1992).
PLATT, Charles. John W. Campbell Jr. Memorial [3rd], 1991 (1992). Locus [Nonfiction], 1983 (1984).
PLAUGER, P. J. Hugo [Campbell], 1974 (1975).
PLEASANCE, Donald. Saturn [Special (Career)], 1979 (1980).
PLIEGER, Connie Maria. L. Ron Hubbard's Writers of the Future [1st Quarter, 3rd Place], 1991 (1992).
POE, Edgar Allen. Hall of Fame Colonnade Inductee, 1910.
POHL, Frederik.
  Alkor [Translated Short Story], 1989 (1990).
  American Book [Hardcover Science Fiction Novel], 1979 (1980).
  First Fandom, 1989.
  Galaxy SF Novel, 1955.
  Hugo [Professional Magazine], 1965 (1966), 1966 (1967), 1967 (1968); [Short Story], 1972 (1973), 1985 (1986); [Novel], 1977 (1978).
  IAM [Novella], 1990 (1991).
  Invisible Little Man, 1964.
  John W. Campbell, Jr. Memorial, 1977 (1978); 1984 (1985).
  Lazar Komarcic [Foreign Novel], 1984 (1985).
  Locus [Novella], 1972 (1973); [SF Novel], 1977 (1978).
  Nebula [Novel], 1976 (1977), 1977 (1978).
  Prix Apollo, 1978 (1979).
  Skylark, 1966.
  SFWA President, 1974-1976.
  GoH World SF Convention, 1972.
POLACK, Indrik. Festival Internazional del Film [Golden Asteroid], 1962 (1963).
POLLACK, Rachel. Arthur C. Clarke [Winner], 1988 (1989).
POLONIATO, Miriam. Premios Italiano di Fantascienza [Short Fiction (Professional)], 1990 (1991).
POMERLEAU, Luc. Aurora [French Work (Other)], 1990 (1991), 1991 (1992). Casper [French Work (Other)], 1988 (1989), 1989 (1990). Prix Boréal [Critical Work], 1988 (1989).
PORRUA, Francisco. Gilgamés [Special], 1987 (1988). Karel, 1985 (1986).
PORTER, Andrew.
  Hugo [Fanzine], 1973 (1974).
  SF Chronicle [Fanzine], 1981 (1982); [Semiprozine], 1982 (1983), 1983 (1984), 1984 (1985), 1985 (1986), 1986 (1987), 1987 (1988), 1988 (1989), 1989 (1990), 1990 (1991); [Special Award], 1990 (1991).

FGoH *World SF Convention*, 1990.
PORTER, Jim. Ken McIntyre, 1989 (1990).
POSPISIL, John. Oscar [Special Achievement (Special Effects Editing)], 1987.
POST, Jonathan V. Rhysling [Short Poem], 1986 (1987).
POTTER, J. K.
British Fantasy [Artist], 1984 (1985), 1986 (1987), 1987 (1988).
Davis Readers (IASFM) [Interior Artist], 1987 (1988).
Readercon [Jacket Illustration], 1989 (1990).
World Fantasy [Artist], 1987 (1988).
AGoH World Fantasy Convention, 1986.
AGoH World Horror Convention, 1993.
POUND, John. Inkpot, 1982.
POURNELLE, Jerry. E. E. Evans/Paul Frehafer, 1977. Forry, 1979. Hugo [Campbell], 1972 (1973); [Chocolate Hugo], 1983 (1984). Inkpot, 1979. SFWA President, 1973-1974.
POWERS, Richard. AGoH World SF Convention, 1991.
POWERS, Tim.
Gilgamés [Fantasy Novel], 1988 (1989).
Mythopoeic [Fantasy], 1989 (1990).
Philip K. Dick Memorial [1st], 1983 (1984), 1985 (1986).
Prix Apollo, 1986 (1987).
SF Chronicle [Novel], 1983 (1984).
POWYS, T. F. Gilgamés [Fantasy Novel], 1988 (1989).
POYARKOV, Sergey V. L. Ron Hubbard's Illustrators of the Future [4th Quarter], 1990 (1991); [Gold], 1990 (1991).
POYSER, Victoria. Hugo [Fan Artist], 1980 (1981), 1981 (1982). SF Chronicle [Fan Artist (Conventions)], 1981 (1982). AGoH World Fantasy Convention, 1985.
PRATCHETT, Terry. BSFA [Novel], 1989 (1990). Gilgamés [Fantasy Novel], 1989 (1990). *Prisoners of Gravity* Reality 1 [Fantasy Novel], 1991 (1992).
PRATT, Fletcher. International Fantasy [3rd Nonfiction], 1951 (1952).
PREISS, Byron. Inkpot, 1977.
PRICE, E. Hoffmann. World Fantasy [Lifetime Achievement], 1983 (1984).
PRICE, Jeffrey. Hugo [Dramatic Presentation], 1988 (1989). Saturn [Fantasy Film], 1988 (1989). SF Chronicle [Dramatic Presentation], 1988 (1989).
PRICE, Vincent. Count Dracula Society [Cinema], 1964 (1965); [Walpole Medal], 1968 (1969). Grimmy, 19??
PRICHARD, Michael. Saturn [Outstanding Service], 1979 (1980).
PRIDE, Marilyn. Ditmar [Australian Fan Artist], 1979 (1980), 1980 (1981), 1981 (1982), 1982 (1983).
PRIEST, Christopher. BSFA [Short Fiction], 1979 (1980). Ditmar [International Fiction], 1976 (1977), 1981 (1982). Kurd Lasswitz [Foreign Novel], 1987 (1988). Svenska SF Priset [Foreign Novel], 1985 (1986).
PRIETO, Frank. Hugo [Amateur Magazine], 1956 (1957).
PRINGLE, David. Eurocon [Magazine], 1990 (1991). Readercon [Fiction/Poetry Magazine], 1988 (1989); [Fiction Magazine], 1989 (1990).
PROCHAZHA, Pavel. Festival Internazional del Film [Golden Seal], 1963 (1964).
PROKOP, Gert. SFCD [Short Fiction], 1990 (1991).
PROSPERI, Pierfrancesco. Premios Italiano di Fantascienza [Novel], 1971 (1972).
PUKALLUS, Horst. Kurd Lasswitz [Translator], 1980 (1981), 1981 (1982), 1983 (1984), 1984 (1985).
PUNCH, Monkey. Inkpot, 1981.
PURDOM, Tom. SFWA Vice President, 1970-1972.
PUZO, Mario. Hugo [Dramatic Presentation], 1978 (1979). Saturn [SF Film], 1978 (1979), 1981 (1982).
QUARRY, Robert. Count Dracula Society [Cinema], 1971 (1972).
QUINN, Daniel. Turner Tomorrow [Grand Prize], 1991.
QUIST, Gerald. Emmy [Outstanding Achievement in Makeup], 1988.
RAIOLA, Tony. Inkpot, 1982.
RAKSIN, David. Saturn [Music], 1976 (1977).

RALSTON, Ken. Oscar [Special Achievement (Visual Effects)], 1983; [Visual Effects], 1985, 1988. Saturn [Special Effects], 1988 (1989).
RAMBALDI, Carlo. Oscar [Special Achievement (Visual Effects)], 1976; [Visual Effects], 1979, 1982. Saturn [Special Effects], 1982 (1983).
RAMBELLI, Roberta. Karel, 1981 (1982).
RAMEY, Stephen V. SF Writers of Earth [2nd], 1986 (1987); [2nd], 1990 (1991).
RAMIS, Harold. Saturn [Fantasy Film], 1984 (1985).
RAMSEY, Anne. Saturn [Supporting Actress], 1987 (1988).
RAMSEY, Clark. Saturn [Advertisement/Publicity/Public Relations], 1975 (1976).
RAMSEY, Louis. Saturn [Outstanding Service], 1982 (1983).
RAND, Ayn. Prometheus Hall of Fame, 1983, 1987.
RANDAL, John W. L. Ron Hubbard's Writers of the Future [2nd Quarter, 1st Place], 1989 (1990).
RANDALL, Marta. SFWA Vice President, 1981-1982; President 1982-1984.
RANDOLPH, Joe. Karel, 1985 (1986).
RANSOM, Peggy. L. Ron Hubbard's Illustrators of the Future [4th Quarter], 1989 (1990).
RAOS, Predrag. Lazar Komarcic [Novel], 1985 (1986), 1989/1990 (1991).
RAPARELLI, Reginald. Festival Internazional del Film [Special], 1972 (1973).
RASKIN, David. Inkpot, 1980.
RATHBONE, Wendy. L. Ron Hubbard's Writers of the Future [4th Quarter, 2nd Place], 1991 (1992).
RAYMOND, Alex. Reuben, 1949.
RAYNER, Richard Piers. Manning, 1989.
RAYYAN, Omar. L. Ron Hubbard's Illustrators of the Future [4th Quarter], 1991 (1992).
REAMY, Tom. Balrog [Novel], 1978 (1979). Hugo [Campbell], 1975 (1976). Nebula [Novelette], 1975 (1976).
REDONDO, Nestor. Inkpot, 1979.
REECE, Jim. L. Ron Hubbard's Illustrators of the Future [1st Quarter], 1990 (1991).
REED, Donald A. Count Dracula Society [Literature], 1963 (1964); [Walpole Medal], 1967 (1968); [Summers], 1968 (1969); [Television], 1977 (1978); [Fauria], 1978 (1979). Saturn [Special], 1977 (1978).
REEVES, Michael. Festival Internazional del Film [Golden Asteroid], 1967 (1968).
REEVES-STEVENS, Garfield. *Prisoners of Gravity* Reality 1 [Horror Novel], 1991 (1992).
REGINA, Ivan Carlos. Nova [Short Story], 1988 (1989).
REID, Kate. Festival Internazional del Film [Silver Asteroid—Actress], 1976 (1977).
REIGLE, James. British Science Fiction [Film], 1983 (1984).
REISS, Stuart A. Oscar [Set Decoration], 1966.
REITZ, Jean. L. Ron Hubbard's Writers of the Future [3rd Quarter, 3rd Place], 1986 (1987).
REMEC, Miha. Lazar Komarcic [Novel], 1981 (1982).
REMINGTON, Thomas J. SFRA Treasurer, 1989-1991.
RÉMY, Ada. Grand Prix de la SF Française [Novel], 1978 (1979).
RÉMY, Yves. Grand Prix de la SF Française [Novel], 1978 (1979).
RENARD, Christine. Prix Rosny-Aîné [Novelette], 1982.
RENDELL, Pam. Robbie [Fanzine], 1988 (1989).
RESNICK, Mike. HOMer [Novelette], 1990 (1991). Hugo [Novelette], 1990 (1991); [Short Story], 1988 (1989). SF Chronicle [Novella], 1990 (1991); [Novelette], 1989 (1990), 1990 (1991); [Short Story], 1988 (1989).
REYNANTE, Mary. Inkpot, 1990.
REYNOLDS, Barry H. L. Ron Hubbard's Writers of the Future [2nd Quarter, 1st Place], 1990 (1991).
REYNOLDS, Norman. Oscar [Art Direction], 1977, 1981. Saturn [Art Decoration], 1977 (1978).
REZMERSKI, John Calvin. Rhysling [Short Poem], 1986 (1987).
RHODES, Mark. SF Writers of Earth [1st], 1984 (1985).
RICE, Anne. Locus [Horror/Dark Fantasy Novel], 1990 (1991). *Prisoners of Gravity* Reality 1 [Horror Novel], 1991 (1992).
RICHARDSON, Darrell. Big Heart, 1982.
RICHARDSON, John. Oscar [Visual Effects], 1986.

RICHTER, Marjorie. SF Writers of Earth [1st], 1990 (1991).
RICO, Don. Inkpot, 1976.
RIGLEY, Karen. Andre Norton Fantasy/SF Short Story [1st], 1990 (1991).
RILEY, Frank. Hugo [Novel], 1954 (1955).
RINGWOOD, Bob. Saturn [Costumes], 1984 (1985).
ROBBINS, Trina. Inkpot, 1977.
ROBERTS, Keith. British Fantasy [Short Story], 1985 (1986); [Artist], 1985 (1986). BSFA [Short Fiction], 1982 (1983), 1986 (1987); [Artist], 1986 (1987); [Novel], 1987 (1988).
ROBERTSON, Robbie. Oscar [Special Visual Effects], 1969.
ROBINS, Arlin. AGoH World Fantasy Convention, 1991.
ROBINSON, Glen. Oscar [Visual Effects Special Achievement], twice in 1976.
ROBINSON, Jay. Count Dracula Society [Cinema], 1975 (1976); [Television], 1976 (1977). Saturn [Supporting Actor], 1976 (1977).
ROBINSON, Jeanne. Hugo [Novella], 1977 (1978). Locus [Novella], 1977 (1978). Nebula [Novella], 1977 (1978).
ROBINSON, Jerry. Inkpot, 1989.
ROBINSON, Kim Stanley.
Davis Readers (IASFM) [Novella], 1987 (1988).
John W. Campbell, Jr. Memorial [Winner], 1990 (1991); [2nd], 1988 (1989).
Locus [First Novel], 1984 (1985); [Novella], 1990 (1991).
Nebula [Novella], 1987 (1988).
Philip K. Dick Memorial [2nd], 1984 (1985).
SF Chronicle [Novelette], 1983 (1984).
World Fantasy [Novella], 1983 (1984).
ROBINSON, Roger. Doc Weir, 1992.
ROBINSON, Spider.
Hugo [Campbell], 1973 (1974); [Novella], 1976 (1977), 1977 (1978); [Short Story], 1982 (1983).
Locus [Fan Critic], 1976 (1977); [Novella], 1977 (1978).
Nebula [Novella], 1977 (1978).
Skylark, 1978.
TM World SF Convention, 1992.
ROCHE, Therese. Grand Prix de la SF Française [Juvenile], 1982 (1983).
ROCHELLE, Warren. N3F [1st], 1990 (1991).
ROCHESTER, Art. Saturn [Sound], 1978 (1979).
ROCHON, Esther. Grand Prix Logidec, 1991. Prix Boréal [Novel], 1986 (1987).
ROCKWELL, Richard. Inkpot, 1981.
RODDENBERRY, Gene.
Chronic Rift Roundtable [Hall of Fame Inductee], 1991 (1992).
Count Dracula Society [Television], 1966 (1967), 1975 (1976).
Hugo [Dramatic Presentation], 1966 (1967); [Special Plaque], 1967 (1968).
Saturn [Executive Achievement], 1976 (1977); [TV Show (Past Achievement)], 1978 (1979); [Life Career], 1979 (1980); [TV Series], 1988 (1989); [George Pal Memorial], 1989/90 (1991), 1991 (1992).
RODEK, Jacek. Polish SF & Fantasy Achievement [Publisher], 1983 (1984).
RODIGAN, David. Festival Internazional del Film [Silver Asteroid—Actor], 1976 (1977).
RODGERS, Alan. Bram Stoker [Novelette], 1987 (1988).
ROESSNER-HERMAN, Michaela. Hugo [Campbell], 1988 (1989). IAFA [Crawford], 1988 (1989).
ROGERS, Bruce Holland. L. Ron Hubbard's Writers of the Future [3rd Quarter, 1st Place], 1989 (1990).
ROGERS, John. Inkpot, 1985.
ROGERS, Marshall. Inkpot, 1979.
ROHAN, Michael Scott. IAFA [Crawford], 1990 (1991).
ROLFE, Felice. Hugo [Amateur Magazine], 1966 (1967).
ROLOFF, Julie. Inkpot, 1991.
ROMITA, John Sr. Inkpot, 1979.
ROSATTI, Renato. Nova [Fanzine], 1990 (1991).
ROSE, Mark. J. Lloyd Eaton Memorial, 1981 (1982).

ROSE, Ruth. Balrog [Fantasy Film Hall of Fame], 1981 (1982).
ROSENBLUM, Mary. SF Writers of Earth [2nd], 1987 (1988).
ROSIPALOVA, Jana. Karel Capek [Short Story by Juvenile], 1982 (1983).
ROSS, Gary. Saturn [Writing], 1988 (1989).
ROSS, Katherine. Saturn [Actress], 1975 (1976).
ROSS, Stanley Ralph. Inkpot, 1977.
ROSZA, Miklos. Saturn [Music], 1975 (1976), 1979 (1980).
ROTRECKI, Theodor. Karel, 1984 (1985). Karel Capek [Special], 1984 (1985).
ROTSLER, William. Big Heart, 1978. Hugo [Fan Artist], 1974 (1975), 1978 (1979). Inkpot, 1978. Locus [Fan Artist], 1970 (1971), 1971 (1972). FGoH World SF Convention, 1973.
ROTTENSTEINER, Franz. Fantastyka [Special], 1986/1987 (1988).
ROTTENSTEINER, Hanna. Fantastyka [Special], 1986/1987 (1988).
ROTTERMUND, Dieter. Kurd Lasswitz [Artist], 1989 (1990).
ROUELLAN, A. Alkor [Translated Novel], 1989 (1990).
ROVANO, Marcelaine. IAFA [Graduate Scholarship], 1991 (1992).
ROWLEY, Christopher. Crook/Tall, 1983 (1984).
ROYER, Mike. Inkpot, 1978.
ROYLE, Nicholas. British Fantasy [Collection/Anthology], 1991 (1992).
ROZYCKI, Andrzej. Fantastyka [New Author], 1986/1987 (1988).
RUBINO, Ralph. SF Chronicle [Covers (Magazines)], 1983 (1984).
ROBBINS, Arlin. Chesley [3-D Art], 1989 (1990).
RUBIN, Bruce Joel. Oscar [Writing (Original Screenplay)], 1990.
RUBINSTEIN, Zelda. Saturn [Supporting Actress], 1982 (1983).
RUCKER, Rudy. Philip K. Dick Memorial [1st], 1982 (1983), 1988 (1989).
RUDE, Steve. Inkpot, 1988. Manning, 1984. Will Eisner Comic Industry [Artist], 1987 (1988), 1990 (1991); [Art Team], 1987 (1988).
RUELLAN, André. Grand Prix de la SF Française [Novel], 1983 (1984).
RUFF, Matt. Readercon [Novel], 1988 (1989).
RUMPH, Jim. Count Dracula Society [Special], 1974 (1975), 1975 (1976).
RUNTE, Robert. Casper [Fan Achievement (Other)], 1988 (1989), 1989 (1990). FGoH World SF Convention, 1994.
RUSCH, Kristine Kathryn. Hugo [Campbell], 1989 (1990). Locus [Novella], 1991 (1992); [Nonfiction], 1990 (1991). World Fantasy [Special (Nonprofessional)], 1988 (1989).
RUSCONI Editore. Premios Cometa d'Argento [Special], 1973 (1974).
RUSHDIE, Salman. Collectors [Most Collectible Author], 1989 (1990). Gilgamés [Special], 1985 (1986). Mythopoeic [Children's Literature], 1991 (1992).
RUSS, Joanna. Hugo [Novella], 1982 (1983). Locus [Novella], 1982 (1983). Nebula [Short Story], 1972 (1973). Pilgrim, 1988. SF Chronicle [Novella], 1982 (1983).
RUSSELL, Eric Frank. Hugo [Short Story], 1954 (1955). Prometheus Hall of Fame, 1985.
RUSSELL, Ray. World Fantasy [Lifetime Achievement], 1990 (1991).
RUSSO, Richard Paul. Philip K. Dick Memorial [1st], 1989 (1990).
RUTLEDGE, Robert. Oscar [Sound Effects Editing], 1985.
RYAN, Alan. World Fantasy [Short Story], 1984 (1985).
RYAN, Dave. Southpaw [Artist], 1982 (1983).
RYAN, John. Festival Internazional del Film [Silver Asteroid—Actor], 1973 (1974).
RYBAKOV, Vyacheslav. Boris Strugatsky [Fiction], 1986-1990 (1991).
RYMAN, Geoff. Arthur C. Clarke [Winner], 1989 (1990). BSFA [Short Fiction], 1984 (1985), 1987 (1988). John W. Campbell, Jr. Memorial [Winner], 1989 (1990); [3rd], 1987 (1988). World Fantasy [Novella], 1984 (1985).
RZHANOV, Yevgeny. L. Ron Hubbard's Illustrators of the Future [4th Quarter], 1991 (1992).
SABA, Arn. Inkpot, 1983.
SABIN, Eleanora Rose. Andre Norton Fantasy/SF Short Story [1st], 1988 (1989); [3rd], 1991 (1992). Gryphon, 1991 (1992). SF Writers of Earth [1st], 1988 (1989); [Author of the '80s—1st], 1990 (1991).
SADOUL, Jacques. Premios Cometa d'Argento [Critical Work], 1974 (1975).

SAGAN, Carl. Hugo [Nonfiction], 1980 (1981). John W. Campbell, Jr. Memorial [Special], 1973 (1974). Locus [First Novel], 1985 (1986).
SAKAI, Stan. Inkpot, 1991.
SAKAMI, Kenichi. Japan Fantasy Novel, 1988 (1989).
SAKERS, Don. Dell Readers (Analog) [Short Story], 1991 (1992).
SAKHAROFF, Gary. Saturn [Special], 1981 (1982).
SALETRI, Frank R. Count Dracula Society [Cunningham], 1975 (1976). Saturn [Outstanding Service], 1978 (1979).
SALMONSON, Jessica Amanda. Lambda Literary [Lesbian SF/Fantasy], 1989 (1990). Readercon [Anthology], 1989 (1990). World Fantasy [Single Author Collection/Anthology], 1979 (1980).
SALTER, Hans. Saturn [Special], 1981 (1982).
SANCHEZ, Susana Alicia. SF Writers of Earth [3rd], 1991 (1992).
SANDRELLI, Sandro. Karel, 1984 (1985).
SANFORD, Rob. L. Ron Hubbard's Illustrators of the Future [3rd Quarter], 1990 (1991).
SANGSTER, Jimmy. Saturn [Writing], 1976 (1977).
SAPIRO, Leland. E. E. Evans/Paul Frehafer, 1963.
SAPLAK, Charles Michael. L. Ron Hubbard's Writers of the Future [2nd Quarter, 3rd Place], 1992 (1993).
SAUDEK, Kaja. Eurocon [Artist], 1990 (1991). Karel Capek [Special—Professional], 1987 (1988).
SAUNDERS, Allen. Inkpot, 1981.
SAUNDERS, Charles R. Readercon [Fantasy Writer], 1979 (1980); [Nonfiction Writer], 1979 (1980).
SAUNDERS, Elizabeth. Readercon [Anthology], 1990 (1991).
SAVAGE, Fred. Saturn [Juvenile Actor], 1988 (1989).
SAVCHENKO, Vladimir. Chumatski Shlyah, 1988 (1989).
SAVILLE, Philip. Festival Internazonal del Film [Golden Seal], 1966 (1967).
SAVINI, Tom. Atlanta Fantasy Faire, 1987.
SAWYER, Robert J. Aurora [English Long Form], 1991 (1992). HOMer [First Novel], 1990 (1991).
SAXON, John. Saturn [Special (Career)], 1979 (1980).
SAYER, George. Mythopoeic [Scholarship], 1990 (1991).
SAYRE, Chris Curry—SEE: CURRY, Chris.
SCAGLIA, Franco. Premios Italiano di Fantascienza [Critical Article], 1977 (1978).
SCHAKEL, Peter J. Mythopoeic [Scholarship for Inklings Studies], 1991 (1992).
SCANLON, Michael L. L. Ron Hubbard's Writers of the Future [4th Quarter, 2nd Place], 1989 (1990).
SCARBOROUGH, Elizabeth Ann. Nebula [Novel], 1989 (1990).
SCHAMI, Rafik. Wetzlar, 1990 (1991).
SCHANES, Bill. Inkpot, 1987.
SCHANES, Steve. Inkpot, 1987.
SCHIFF, Stuart David. Readercon [Large Circ. Magazine], 1979 (1980). World Fantasy [Special (Nonprofessional)], 1973/1974 (1975), 1976 (1977), 1982 (1983), 1984 (1985).
SCHIMA, Roberto. Jeronimo Montiero [1st], 1990 (1991). Nova [Fan Illustrator], 1989 (1990), 1990 (1991).
SCHLOBIN, Roger C. IAFA [Collins], 1985 (1986).
SCHMOLL, Fritz. SFCD [Novel], 1988 (1989).
SCHNEEMAN, Charles. Invisible Little Man, 1967.
SCHOENHERR, John. Hugo [Professional Artist], 1964 (1965).
SCHOMBURG, Alex. Chesley [Artistic Achievement], 1986 (1987). First Fandom, 1990. Hugo [Special], 1988 (1989). Inkpot, 1985.
SCHOW, David J. Twilight Dimension [Short Story], 1984 (1985). World Fantasy [Short Story], 1986 (1987).
SCHRECK, Bob. Inkpot, 1990.
SCHULMAN, J. Neil. Prometheus, 1983 (1984); [Hall of Fame], 1989.
SCHULTZ, Mark. Will Eisner Comic Industry [B&W Series], 1990 (1991).
SCHULZ, Charles. Inkpot, 1974. Reuben, 1955, 1964.
SCHULZE, Kenneth. L. Ron Hubbard's Writers of the Future [2nd Quarter, 2nd Place], 1985 (1986).

SCHUTZ, Diana. Inkpot, 1989.
SCHWARTZ, Julius. Atlanta Fantasy Faire, 1988. Big Heart, 1991. First Fandom, 1986. Forry, 1984. Inkpot, 1981. Jules Verne [Life Achievement in Comics], 1983 (1984).
SCHWARZNEGGER, Arnold. Saturn [Life Career], 1989/90 (1991), 1991 (1992).
SCHWEITZER, Darrell. World Fantasy [Special (Professional)], 1991 (1992).
SCHWEITZER, Mikhail. Festival Internazional del Film [Special], 1976 (1977).
SCITHERS, George. Hugo [Amateur Magazine], 1963 (1964), 1967 (1968); [Professional Editor], 1977 (1978), 1979 (1980). World Fantasy [Special (Professional)], 1991 (1992).
SCOTT, Bill. Inkpot, 1977.
SCOTT, Melissa. Hugo [Campbell], 1985 (1986).
SCOTT, Ridley. Saturn [Director], 1979 (1980).
SCOTT, Walter M. Oscar [Set Decoration], 1966.
SCROGGY, David. Inkpot, 1977.
SEAMAN, Peter S. Hugo [Dramatic Presentation], 1988 (1989). Saturn [Fantasy Film], 1988 (1989). SF Chronicle [Dramatic Presentation], 1988 (1989).
SEARLE, Ronald. Reuben, 1960.
SEGAL, Boris. Festival Internazional del Film [Golden Asteroid], 1970 (1971).
SEKOWSKY, Mike. Inkpot, 1981.
SELLERS, Peter. Saturn [Special TV], 1979 (1980).
SELTZER, David. British Fantasy [Film], 1976 (1977).
SEMITJOV, Eugen. Prix Jules Verne, 1975.
SERLING, Robert J. AWA Writing [Books (Nonfiction)], 1964, 1970, 1975; [Books (Fiction)], 1967. James J. Strebig, 1964.
SERLING, Rod. Count Dracula Society [Television], 1967 (1968); [Walpole Medal], 1971 (1972). Hugo [Dramatic Presentation], 1959 (1960), 1960 (1961), 1961 (1962). Inkpot, 1975. Saturn [Special TV], 1979 (1980). Laurel, 1976.
SERMINE, Daniel. Casper [Short Fiction], 1984 (1985).
SERVA, Frederic. Grand Prix de la SF Française [Short Fiction], 1986 (1987).
SEULING, Phil. Inkpot, 1974.
SEUSS, Dr. Inkpot, 1991.
SEVERANCE, Carol. Crook/Tall, 1991 (1992).
SEVERIN, John. Inkpot, 1988.
SEVERIN, Marie. Inkpot, 1988.
SEVERSON, Merritt. L. Ron Hubbard's Writers of the Future [4th Quarter, 2nd Place], 1990 (1991).
SEWELL, Brocard. Count Dracula Society [Special], 1964 (1965).
SEYRIG, Delphine. Count Dracula Society [Cunningham], 1978 (1979).
SHAARA, Michael. Pulitzer Prize [Fiction], 1975.
SHAFFER, Anthony. Saturn [Writing], 1978 (1979); [Horror Film], 1978 (1979).
SHANOWER, Eric. Manning, 1987.
SHAPIRO, Arnold. Saturn [Special], 1978 (1979).
SHARMAN, Jim. Saturn [Hall of Fame], 1979 (1980).
SHARP, George. World Fantasy [Special (Professional)], 1983 (1984).
SHARPE, Don. Oscar [Sound Effects Editing], 1986.
SHATNER, William. Saturn [TV Performer (Past Achievement)], 1978 (1979); [Life Career], 1979 (1980); [Actor], 1982 (1983).
SHAYNE, Robert. Inkpot, 1984. Saturn [President's Award], 1989/90 (1991).
SHAW, Bob.
  British Fantasy [August Derleth], 1985 (1986).
  BSFA [Novel], 1974 (1975), 1986 (1987).
  Clark Darlton Prize, 1983 (1984).
  Eastcon [Long Text], 1989 (1990); [Short Text], 1989 (1990).
  Hugo [Fan Writer], 1978 (1979), 1979 (1980).
  Premios Italiano di Fantascienza [Special], 1974 (1975).
SHAW, Larry. Hugo [Special], 1983 (1984).
SHAW, Sam. Saturn [Sound], 1977 (1978).
SHAW, Scott. Inkpot, 1980.
SHEA, Michael. World Fantasy [Novel], 1982 (1983).
SHEA, Robert. Prometheus Hall of Fame, 1986.

SHECKLEY, Robert. Alkor [Translated Novel], 1989 (1990); [Translated Short Story], 1989 (1990). Jupiter [Short Story], 1973 (1974).
SHEFFIELD, Charles. Dell Readers (Analog) [Fact Article], 1991 (1992). SFWA President, 1984-1986; Vice President, 1982-1984.
SHELDON, Racoona—SEE: **TIPTREE, James Jr.**
SHELTON, Gilbert. Inkpot, 1978.
SHELUKHIN, Vladimir. Boris Strugatsky [Fan Article], 1986-1990 (1991).
SHEPARD, Lucius.
  Clarion [1st], 1984.
  Hugo [Campbell], 1984 (1985).
  Kurd Lasswitz [Foreign Novel], 1989 (1990).
  Locus [Short Story], 1984 (1985); [Novella], 1986 (1987), 1988 (1989), 1989 (1990); [Collection], 1987 (1988).
  Nebula [Novella], 1986 (1987).
  Rhysling [Long Poem], 1987 (1988).
  SF Chronicle [Short Story], 1984 (1985); [Novella], 1986 (1987); [Novelette], 1986 (1987).
  World Fantasy [Anthology/Collection], 1987 (1988); [Collection], 1991 (1992).
SHERIDAN, Dave. Inkpot, 1978.
SHERMAN, Josepha. Crook/Tall, 1989 (1990).
SHERTOBYTOV, Eugenii. Festival Internazionale del Film [Special], 1967 (1968).
SHIBANO, Takumi. Karel, 1990 (1991); [President's], 1983 (1984).
SHIFFMAN, Stu. Hugo [Fan Artist], 1989 (1990).
SHIINA, Makoto. Nihon SF Taisho, 1989 (1990).
SHIPPEY, Thomas A. Mythopoeic [Scholarship], 1983 (1984).
SHIREEN, Gayna. Saturn [Special], 1978 (1979).
SHIRO, Masamune. Seiun Taisho [Comics], 1985 (1986).
SHOCKLEY, Gary W. Clarion [2nd], 1984. L. Ron Hubbard's Writers of the Future [2nd Quarter, 1st Place], 1988 (1989); [Gold], 1988 (1989).
SHOOTER, Jim. Inkpot, 1980.
SHORT, Robert. Oscar [Makeup], 1988. Saturn [Makeup], 1988 (1989).
SHORTER, Elliot K. FGoH World SF Convention, 1970.
SHTERN, Boris. Aëlita [Start], 1988 (1989); [Fan—Short Story], 1988 (1989). Alkor [Short Story], 1988 (1989). Chumatski Shlyah, 1988 (1989).
SHUSETT, Ronald. British Fantasy [Film], 1979 (1980). Hugo [Dramatic Presentation], 1979 (1980). Saturn [SF Film], 1979 (1980).
SHUSTER, Joe. Inkpot, 1975. Will Eisner Comic Industry [Hall of Fame Inductee], 1991 (1992).
SHWARTZ, Susan. U. S. Air Force Academy Special Achievement, 1989.
SICKLES, Noel. Inkpot, 1976.
SIEGEL, Jerry. Inkpot, 1975. Will Eisner Comic Industry [Hall of Fame Inductee], 1991 (1992).
SIENKIEWICZ, Bill. Inkpot, 1981.
SILLIPHANT, Stirling. Oscar [Writing (Screenplay Based on Material from Another Medium)], 1967; [Best Story of the Year], 1967.
SILVA, David B. Balrog [Outstanding Amateur Achievement], 1984 (1985). Bram Stoker [Short Story], 1990 (1991). Readercon [Dale Donaldson Memorial], 1986 (1987), 1987 (1988). World Fantasy [Special (Nonprofessional)], 1987 (1988).
SILVERBERG, Robert.
  Alkor [Translated Short Story], 1989 (1990).
  Forry, 1985.
  Gilgamés [Fantasy Short Story], 1985 (1986); [SF Novel], 1987 (1988).
  Hugo [New Author], 1955 (1956); [Novella], 1968 (1969), 1986 (1987); [Novelette], 1989 (1990).
  Inkpot, 1987.
  Jupiter [Novella], 1973 (1974).
  Lazar Komarcic [Foreign Short Story], 1986 (1987), 1988 (1989), 1989/1990 (1991); [Foreign Novel], 1987 (1988), 1989/1990 (1991).
  Locus [Anthology/Collection], 1970 (1971); [Novella], 1974 (1975), 1987 (1988); [Anthology], 1975 (1976); [Fantasy Novel], 1980 (1981).

Milford, 1981.
Nebula [Short Story], 1969 (1970), 1971 (1972); [Novel], 1971 (1972); [Novella], 1974 (1975), 1985 (1986).
Premios Cometa d'Argento [Novel], 1974 (1975).
Prix Apollo, 1975 (1976).
Prix Cosmos 2000, 1981 (1982).
SF Chronicle [Novella], 1986 (1987).
Skylark, 1984.
SFWA President, 1967-1968.
GoH World SF Convention, 1970.
SILVESTRI, Alan. Saturn [Music], 1987 (1988).
SIM, Dave. Inkpot, 1981.
SIMAK, Clifford D.
Alkor [Translated Short Story], (twice) 1989 (1990).
Bram Stoker [Life Achievement], 1987 (1988).
Hugo [Novelette], 1958 (1959); [Novel], 1963 (1964); [Short Story], 1980 (1981).
International Fantasy [Fiction], 1952 (1953).
Jupiter [Novel], 1977 (1978).
Locus [Short Story], 1980 (1981).
Nebula [Grand Master], 1976 (1977); [Short Story], 1980 (1981).
GoH World SF Convention, 1971, 1981.
SIMMONS, Dan.
Arthur C. Clarke [3rd], 1991 (1992).
Bram Stoker [Novel], 1989 (1990); [Collection], 1991 (1992).
British Fantasy [August Derleth], 1989 (1990).
BSFA [Novel], 1991 (1992).
Collectors [Most Collectible Author], 1991 (1992).
Hugo [Novel], 1989 (1990).
Locus [SF Novel], 1989 (1990), 1990 (1991); [Horror Novel], 1989 (1990), 1991 (1992); [Novelette], 1990 (1991), 1991 (1992).
Readercon [Short Work], 1990 (1991).
SF Chronicle [Novel], 1990 (1991).
World Fantasy [Novel], 1985 (1986).
SIMON, Erik. Karel, 1988 (1989).
SIMON, Marge. Readercon [Comics], 1987 (1988).
SIMONAY, Bernard. Prix Cosmos 2000, 1986 (1987). Prix Julia Verlanger, 1986 (1987).
SIMONSON, Louise. Inkpot, 1992.
SIMONSON, Walt. Inkpot, 1985.
SIMONTON Family. Count Dracula Society [Special], 1972 (1973).
SIMPSON, Rick. Oscar [Set Decoration], 1990.
SIMS, Roger. FGoH World SF Convention, 1988.
SINISALO, Johanna. Atorox, 1984 (1985); 1988 (1989).
SIODMAK, Curt. Festival Internazional del Film [Golden Asteroid], 1970 (1971). Forry, 1991. Gernsback [Special Pioneer], 1926 (1983).
SIROIS, Guy. Prix Boréal [Short Story], 1988 (1989).
SIUDMAK. Grand Prix de la SF Française [Special], 1978 (1979).
SKEET, Michael. Aurora [English Short Form], 1991 (1992). Casper [Special], 1987 (1988); [Fan Achievement (Fanzine)], 1988 (1989), 1989 (1990).
SKINNER, Cortney. Boomerang [Artist], 1988 (1989).
SKODLAR, Ort. Festival Internazional del Film [Golden Seal], 1967 (1968).
SKOTAK, Dennis. Oscar [Visual Effects], 1989.
SKOTAK, Robert. Oscar [Visual Effects], 1986.
SKOWRONSKI, J. Polish SF & Fantasy Achievement [Golden Meteor], 1985 (1986).
SLADEK, John. BSFA [Novel], 1983 (1984). John W. Campbell Jr. Memorial [3rd], 1983 (1984). University of Texas/Carl Hertzog, 1990 (1991).
SLATER, Joyce. FGoH World SF Convention, 1987.
SLATER, Ken. FGoH World SF Convention, 1987.
SLOCA, Sue Ellen. SF Writers of Earth [3rd], 1988 (1989).
SLOCOMBE, Douglas. Saturn [Cinematography], 1975 (1976).
SLONCZEWSKI, Jean. John W. Campbell, Jr. Memorial [Winner], 1986 (1987).

SLUSSER, George E. Pilgrim, 1986.
SMIRL, Dennis E. L. Ron Hubbard's Writers of the Future [1st Quarter; 3rd Place], 1985 (1986).
SMITH, Allen J. M. L. Ron Hubbard's Writers of the Future [2nd Quarter, 3rd Place], 1990 (1991).
SMITH, Cordwainer. Invisible Little Man, 1966. Seiun Taisho [Foreign Novel], 1987 (1988); [Foreign Short Story], 1989 (1990).
SMITH, David Alexander. SFWA Treasurer, 1987-1990.
SMITH, Dean Wesley. Locus [Nonfiction], 1990 (1991). World Fantasy [Special (Nonprofessional)], 1988 (1989).
SMITH, Dick. Saturn [Makeup], 1973/74 (1975), 1980 (1981).
SMITH, E. E. "Doc." First Fandom, 1964. GoH World SF Convention, 1940.
SMITH, George O. First Fandom, 1980. Gernsback [Novel], 1946 (1983).
SMITH, Jack Martin. Oscar [Art Direction], 1966.
SMITH, Kenneth F. Oscar [Visual Effects], 1982, 1987.
SMITH, L. Neil. Prometheus, 1979 (1980).
SMITH, Michael Marshall. British Fantasy [Short Fiction], 1990 (1991), 1991 (1992); [Icarus], 1990 (1991).
SMITH, Paul J. Oscar [Original Music Score], 1940.
SMITH, Ron. Hugo [Amateur Magazine], 1955 (1956).
SNEARY, Rick. E. E. Evans/Paul Frehafer, 1960.
SNEGOV, Sergei. Aëlita, 1984 (1985).
SNELL, Richard. Emmy [Outstanding Achievement in Makeup], 1990.
SNYDER, Zilpha K. William Allen White Children's Book, 1974.
SOGLOW, Otto. Reuben, 1966.
SOLE, Albert. Gilgamés [Special], 1986 (1987).
SOLO, Robert H. Saturn [Special], 1978 (1979).
SOMERS, Ron. Count Dracula Society [Fauria], 1972 (1973), 1975 (1976).
SOMTOW, S. P.—SEE: SUCHARITKUL, Somtow.
SOTHART, Herbert. Oscar [Original Music Score], 1939.
SOUKUP, Martha. L. Ron Hubbard's Writers of the Future [3rd Quarter, 1st Place], 1986 (1987). SFWA Secretary, 1989-.
SOUL, David. Saturn [TV Performer (Past Achievement)], 1979 (1980).
SOUTHWORTH, Scott. N3F [2nd], 1990 (1991).
SOUTO, Marcial. Karel, 1983 (1984).
SPANG, Laurette. Saturn [TV Actress], 1978 (1979).
SPARK, Muriel. Bram Stoker [Nonfiction], 1987 (1988).
SPEHNER, Norbert. Grand Prix de la SF Française [Nonfiction], 1987 (1988).
SPENCER, Garth—SEE: FRÉMION, Yves.
SPICER, Bill. Inkpot, 1979.
SPIEGEL, Dan. Inkpot, 1983.
SPIEGELMAN, Art. Inkpot, 1987. Will Eisner Comic Industry [Graphic Album (Reprint)], 1991 (1992).
SPIELBERG, Anne. Balrog [SF Film Hall of Fame], 1984 (1985). British Fantasy [Film], 1978 (1979). Saturn [Writing], 1988 (1989).
SPIELBERG, Steven. Balrog [Outstanding Professional Achievement], 1981 (1982). British Fantasy [Film], 1981 (1982). Inkpot, 1982. Oscar [Thalberg], 1986. Saturn [Director], 1977 (1978), 1981 (1982); [SF Film], 1982 (1983); [Horror Film], 1982 (1983).
SPINRAD, Norman. Jupiter [Novella], 1974 (1975). Prix Apollo, 1973 (1974). SFWA Vice President, 1972-1974; President, 1980-1982.
SPRANG, Dick. Inkpot, 1992.
SPRINGETT, Martin. Aurora [Artistic Achievement], 1991 (1992).
ST. CLAIR, William. NCR Book for Nonfiction, 1990.
ST. JAMES, Susan. Count Dracula Society [Cinema], 1979 (1980).
STABLEFORD, Brian M. Arthur C. Clarke [2nd], 1988 (1989). IAFA [Distinguished Scholarship], 1986 (1987). J. Lloyd Eaton Memorial, 1985 (1987).
STADLER, Mark. Inkpot, 1986.
STAMP, Terrence. Festival Internazional del Film [Silver Asteroid—Actor], 1975 (1976).

STANDISH, Timothy. L. Ron Hubbard's Illustrators of the Future [1st Quarter], 1989 (1990).
STANLEY, John. Inkpot, 1980.
STARLIN, Jim. Clampett, 1986. Inkpot, 1975.
STARR, Leonard. Inkpot, 1982. Reuben, 1965.
STATHOPOULOS, Nick. Ditmar [Australian Artist], 1983 (1984), 1984 (1985), 1985 (1986)
STATON, Joe. Inkpot, 1983.
STEACY, Ken. Inkpot, 1990. Will Eisner Comic Industry [Art Team], 1987 (1988).
STEADMAN, Ralph. W. H. Smith Illustration [1st], 1986 (1987).
STEARS, John. Oscar [Special Visual Effects], 1965; [Visual Effects], 1977. Saturn [Special Effects], 1977 (1978).
STEELE, Allen. Locus [First Novel], 1989 (1990).
STEELE, Barbara. Count Dracula Society [Walpole Medal], 1970 (1971).
STEENBURGEN, Mary. Saturn [Actress], 1979 (1980).
STEFFAN, Daniel J. Pong [Fan Artist], 1982 (1983); [#1 Fan Face], 1982 (1983). Readercon [Criticism Magazine], 1989 (1990); [Magazine Design], 1989 (1990).
STEFKO, Joe. Collectors [Most Collectible Book], 1991 (1992).
STEINER, John. Festival Internazionale del Film [Silver Asteroid—Actor], 1972 (1973).
STERANKO, Jim. Inkpot, 1975.
STERLING, Bruce. John W. Campbell, Jr. Memorial [Winner], 1988 (1989); [2nd], 1991 (1992). SF Chronicle [Short Story], 1989 (1990). Theodore Sturgeon Memorial [3rd], 1989 (1990).
STERNBACH, Rick. Emmy, 1981. Hugo [Professional Artist], 1976 (1977), 1977 (1978). Inkpot, 1990. Locus [Professional Artist], 1975 (1976), 1976 (1977).
STERNBERG, Scott. Saturn [Special], 1978 (1979).
STERNHAGEN, Frances. Saturn [Supporting Actress], 1981 (1982).
STEVENS, Dave. Inkpot, 1986. Manning, 1982.
STEVENS, Milt. E. E. Evans/Paul Frehafer, 1971.
STEWART, George R. International Fantasy [Fiction], 1949/1950 (1951). Western Heritage, 1963.
STEWART, Patrick. Saturn [TV Actor], 1988 (1989).
STEWART, W. Gregory. Rhysling [Long Poem], 1986 (1987).
STITH, John E. HOMer [SF Novel], 1990 (1991); [Novella], 1990 (1991). Top Hands [Original Adult Fiction Paperback], 1989.
STÖBE, Norbert. Kurd Lasswitz [Novel], 1988 (1989).
STOCKS, Del. Ditmar [Australian Fanzine], 1974 (1975).
STOCKS, Dennis. Ditmar [Australian Fanzine], 1974 (1975).
STOFF, Ondrej. Fantastyka [Nonfiction], 1983 (1984).
STOKES, T. J. L. Ron Hubbard's Writers of the Future [3rd Quarter, 2nd Place], 1986 (1987).
STOLYAROV(WON), A(ndry). Aëlita [New Author], 1989 (1990). Alkor [Short Story], 1989 (1990).
STOPA, Jon. FGoH World SF Convention, 1991.
STOPA, Joni. FGoH World SF Convention, 1991.
STORCHI, Franco. Premios Italiano di Fantascienza [Artist], 1977 (1978), 1979 (1980).
STORK, Matthew. L. Ron Hubbard's Illustrators of the Future [3rd Quarter], 1991 (1992).
STOUT, Amy. Locus [Anthology], 1991 (1992).
STOUT, Bil. Inkpot, 1978.
STRADLEY, Randy. Will Eisner Comic Industry [Anthology], 1991 (1992).
STRANDBERG, Lars-Olov. Prix Jules Verne, 1975.
STRANGE, Glenn. Count Dracula Society [Special], 1971 (1972).
STRASSL, Lore. Kurd Lasswitz [Translator], 1985 (1986), 1986 (1987), 1987 (1988).
STRATTON, Rick. Emmy [Outstanding Achievement in Makeup], 1990.
STRAUB, Joseph. Andre Norton Fantasy/SF Short Story [1st], 1989 (1990); [2nd], 1988 (1989).
STRAUB, Peter. British Fantasy [August Derleth], 1983 (1984). Twilight Dimension [Novel], 1984 (1985). World Fantasy [Novel], 1988 (1989). GoH World Fantasy Convention, 1982. GoH World Horror Convention, 1993.

STRIZHENOV, Oleg. Festival Internazional del Film [Silver Asteroid—Actor], 1967 (1968).
STRORM, David G.—SEE: **JAKSIC, Zoran.**
STRUGATSKY, Arkady. Aëlita, 1980 (1981); [Fan—Novel], 1988 (1989). Alkor [Novel], 1988 (1989), (twice) 1989 (1990). Karel [President's], 1986 (1987). Prix Jules Verne, 1979.
STRUGATSKY, Boris. Aëlita, 1980 (1981); [Fan—Novel], 1988 (1989). Alkor [Novel], 1988 (1989), (twice) 1989 (1990). Karel [President's], 1986 (1987). Prix Jules Verne, 1979.
STURGEON, Theodore.
Forry, 1971.
Hugo [Short Story], 1970 (1971).
Inkpot, 1975.
International Fantasy [Fiction], 1953 (1954).
Nebula [Novelette], 1970 (1971).
World Fantasy [Lifetime Achievement], 1984 (1985).
GoH World SF Convention, 1962.
SUCHARITKUL, Somtow. Daedalus [Fantasy Novel], 1986 (1987). HOMer [Horror/Dark Fantasy Novel], 1990 (1991). Hugo [Campbell], 1980 (1981). Locus [First Novel], 1981 (1982). SFWA Secretary, 1980-1982. GoH World Fantasy Convention, 1989.
SUDRIA, Stefano. Premios Italiano di Fantascienza [Short Fiction], 1975 (1976).
SUEMI, Jun. Seiun Taisho [Artist], 1987 (1988).
SULLIVAN, Tim. Daedalus [SF Short Story], 1986 (1987).
SULLIVAN, Tom. Readercon [Interior Illustration], 1989 (1990).
SUMMERS, Ian. Locus [Art Book], 1979 (1980).
SUMNER, M. C. L. Ron Hubbard's Writers of the Future [3rd Quarter, 1st Place], 1991 (1992).
SURMACZ, Rafal. Polish SF & Fantasy Achievement [Fan], 1984 (1985).
SUSKIND, Patrick. World Fantasy [Novel], 1986 (1987).
SUSSAN, René. Grand Prix de la SF Française [Short Fiction], 1983 (1984).
SUSSEX, Lucy. Ditmar [Australian Short Fiction], 1988 (1989).
SUTTON, David. British Fantasy [Small Press Magazine], 1978 (1979), 1979 (1980), 1980 (1981), 1981 (1982), 1982 (1983), 1984 (1985), 1986 (1987). World Fantasy [Special (Nonprofessional)], 1983 (1984).
SUTTON, Peter. Oscar [Sound], 1980.
SUVIN, Darko. Pilgrim, 1979. SFRA Vice President, 1977-1978.
SVENSSON, Michael. Alvar Appletofft Memorial, 1986 (1987).
SWAIN, Dwight V. Oklahoma Professional Writers Hall of Fame Inductee, 1991.
SWAN, Curt. Inkpot, 1984.
SWANSON, Gloria. Saturn [Special], 1973/74 (1975).
SWANWICK, Michael. Boomerang [Short Story], 1990 (1991). Davis Readers (IASFM) [Short Story], 1988 (1989). John W. Campbell Jr. Memorial [3rd], 1991 (1992). Nebula [Novel], 1991 (1992). SF Chronicle [Novelette], 1981 (1982). Theodore Sturgeon Memorial [Winner], 1989 (1990).
SWOPE, Mike E. L. Ron Hubbard's Writers of the Future [4th Quarter, 3rd Place], 1991 (1992).
SYDNEY, Sylvia. Saturn [Supporting Actress], 1988 (1989).
SYLBERT, Richard. Oscar [Art Direction], 1990.
SZABO, Peter. Karel [Dedicated Service], 1985 (1986).
SZAFRAN, Gene. Locus [Paperback Artist], 1971 (1972).
SZASZ, Eva. Festival Internazional del Film [Golden Seal], 1968 (1969).
SZMIDT, Robert. Polish SF & Fantasy Achievement [Fan], 1985 (1986).
SZULKIN, Piotr. Festival Internazional del Film [Golden Seal], 1977 (1978).
TABAKOW, Lou. Big Heart, 1980. Hugo [Unpublished Story], 1954 (1955).
TAIT, Janet. Inkpot, 1989.
TAKACHIHO, Haruka. Seiun Taisho [Novel], 1985 (1986).
TAKAHASHI, Rumiko. Seiun Taisho [Comics], 1986 (1987), 1988 (1989).
TAN, Shaun C. Y. L. Ron Hubbard's Illustrators of the Future [3rd Quarter], 1991 (1992).
TANAKA, Yoshiki. Seiun Taisho [Novel], 1987 (1988).

TANDY, Jessica. Saturn [Actress], 1987 (1988).
TANI, Kosyu. Seiun Taisho [Novelette], 1986 (1987).
TARASSOV, V. Festival Internazional del Film [Special], 1978 (1979).
TARR, Judith. IAFA [Crawford], 1986 (1987). Mary Lyons, 1989.
TATSUMI, Takayuki. American Studies Book Prize, 1988 (1989). Seiun Taisho [Shibano], 1983 (1984).
TAURASI, James V. Hugo [Amateur Magazine], 1954 (1955), 1956 (1957).
TAVARES, Braulio. Nova [Novel], 1990 (1991); [Short Story], 1990 (1991).
TAVERNIER, Bertrand. Festival Internazional del Film [Golden Asteroid], 1979 (1980).
TAYLOR, B. K. Inkpot, 1980.
TAYLOR, Bill. Saturn [Special Effects], 1975 (1976).
TAYLOR, Gilbert. Saturn [Cinematography], 1977 (1978).
TAYLOR, Keith. Ditmar [Australian Short Fiction], 1981 (1982); [Australian Novel], 1986 (1987).
TAYLOR, Lucy. Andre Norton Fantasy/SF Short Story [3rd], 1988 (1989).
TEM, Melanie. Bram Stoker [First Novel], 1991 (1992). British Fantasy [Icarus], 1991 (1992).
TEM, Steve Rasnic. British Fantasy [Short Story], 1987 (1988). Daedalus [Horror Short Story], 1986 (1987).
TEMESVARI, Ferenc Temil. L. Ron Hubbard's Illustrators of the Future [3rd Quarter], 1990 (1991).
TEMPLETON, William. Premios Cometa d'Argenta [Film], 1973 (1974).
TENHOVAARA, Mika Henry. Alvar Appletofft Memorial, 1981 (1982).
TENN, William—SEE: KLASS, Philip J.
TENTORI, F. Premios Italiano di Fantascienza [Book Length Essay], 1990 (1991).
TEPPER, Sheri S. *Chronic Rift* Roundtable [Novel], 1991 (1992). Locus [Fantasy Novel], 1991 (1992).
TERREL, Denise. Karel [Harrison], 1985 (1986).
TERVONEN, Ari. Atorox, 1989 (1990).
TEZUKA, Osamu. Inkpot, 1980. Seiun Taisho [Special], 1988 (1989).
THEISS, William Ware. Emmy [Outstanding Costume Design for a Series], 1988.
THOLE, Karel. Premios Cometa d'Argento [SF Artist], 1974 (1975); [Fantasy Artist], 1974 (1975). Premios Italiano di Fantascienza [Artist], 1971 (1972), 1974 (1975), 1975 (1976), 1976 (1977), 1978 (1979).
THOMAS, Bill. Saturn [Costumes], 1976 (1977).
THOMAS, Elizabeth Marshall. IAFA [Crawford], 1987 (1988).
THOMAS, Evan T. L. Ron Hubbard's Illustrators of the Future [Gold], 1991 (1992); [2nd Quarter], 1991 (1992).
THOMAS, Frank. Inkpot, 1984.
THOMAS, Kevin. Saturn [Film Critic], 1977 (1978).
THOMAS, Louis-Vincent. Grand Prix de la SF Française [Special], 1979 (1980).
THOMAS, Roy. British Fantasy [Comics], 1978 (1979). Inkpot, 1974.
THOMAS, Thomas T.—SEE: WREN, Thomas.
THOMPSON, Arthur "ATom". SF Chronicle [Fan Artist], 1987 (1988).
THOMPSON, Don. Inkpot, 1976. Will Eisner Comic Industry [Comics-Related Periodical], 1991 (1992).
THOMPSON, Maggie. Inkpot, 1975. Will Eisner Comic Industry [Comics-Related Periodical], 1991 (1992).
THOMPSON, Ruth. Chesley [Unpublished Monochrome], 1989 (1990). L. Ron Hubbard's Illustrators of the Future [2nd Quarter], 1989 (1990).
THOMPSON, W. R. Davis Readers (Analog) [Short Story], 1990 (1991).
THORNE, Frank. Inkpot, 1978.
THROWER, B. J. N3F [Hon. Mention], 1991 (1992).
TICHY, Zdenek. Karel Capek [Short Story by Student], 1985 (1986).
TIPPETT, Phil. Oscar [Special Achievement (Visual Effects)], 1983.
TIPTREE, James Jr.
Hugo [Novella], 1973 (1974), 1976 (1977).
Jupiter [Novella], 1976 (1977).
Locus [Short Story], 1983 (1984); [Novella], 1985 (1986).

Nebula [Short Story], 1973 (1974); [Novella], 1976 (1977); [Novelette (as Racoona Sheldon)], 1977 (1978).
SF Chronicle [Novella], 1985 (1986).
Seiun Taisho [Foreign Novelette], 1987 (1988).
World Fantasy [Anthology/Collection], 1986 (1987).
TODD, Justin. W. H. Smith Illustration [2nd], 1986 (1987).
TOLKIEN, J. R. R.
Balrog [Collection/Anthology], 1980 (1981).
Benson Medal, 1966.
Ditmar [International Fiction], 1977 (1978).
Gilgamés [Fantasy Novel], 1984 (1985).
Hugo [Gandalf—Grand Master], 1973 (1974); [Gandalf—Fantasy Novel], 1977 (1978).
International Fantasy [Fiction], 1956 (1957).
Locus [Fantasy Novel], 1977 (1978).
Mythopoeic [Scholarship], 1989 (1990).
Zauber Zeit [Fantasy Novel], 1986 (1987).
TONANI, Dario. Premios Italiano di Fantascienza [Short Fiction (Professional)], 1991 (1992).
TORRES, Joan. Saturn [Horror Film], 1972 (1973).
TOTH, Alex. Inkpot, 1981. Will Eisner Comic Industry [Hall of Fame Inductee], 1990 (1991).
TOUZALIN, Robert. L. Ron Hubbard's Writers of the Future [2nd Quarter, 1st Place], 1985 (1986); [Gold], 1985 (1986).
TREMAINE, F. Orlin. Gernsback [Editor], 1936 (1983).
TRIMBLE, Bjo. Inkpot, 1974
TRIMBLE, John. E. E. Evans/Paul Frehafer, 1961.
TRIMBLE, Terri. L. Ron Hubbard's Writers of the Future [2nd Quarter, 2nd Place], 1990 (1991).
TRIPP, Galen. E. E. Evans/Paul Frehafer, 1987.
TRNKA, Jiri. Festival Internazional del Film [Golden Seal], 1962 (1963). Hans Christian Anderson International Medal, 1968.
TROUT, Kilgore—SEE: FARMER, Philip José.
TRUMBULL, Douglas. Festival Internazional del Film [Golden Asteroid], 1971 (1972). Oscar [Visual Effects Special Achievement], 1977. Saturn [Special Effects], 1979 (1980); [George Pal Memorial], 1984 (1985).
TRUSCOTT, Gerry. Casper [English Work (Other)], 1988 (1989).
TRYON, Thomas. Count Dracula Society [Literature], 1973 (1974).
TSERJENTJEV, Kanancey. Festival Internazional del Film [Silver Asteroid], 1962 (1963).
TUBB, E. C. GoH World SF Convention, 1970.
TUCK, Donald H. Hugo [Special Plaque], 1961 (1962); [Nonfiction], 1983 (1984). World Fantasy [Special (Nonprofessional)], 1978 (1979). GoH World SF Convention, 1975.
TUCKER, Wilson. First Fandom, 1985. Hugo [Fan Writer], 1969 (1970). John W. Campbell, Jr. Memorial [Special], 1975 (1976). Skylark, 1986. FGoH World SF Convention, 1967.
TUREK, Leslie. Hugo [Fanzine], 1989 (1990).
TURNER, George. Arthur C. Clarke, 1987 (1988). Ditmar [Atheling], 1975 (1976), 1976 (1977), 1980 (1981), 1984 (1985), 1985 (1986); [Australian Fiction], 1978 (1979); [Long Australian Fiction], 1983 (1984). John W. Campbell, Jr. Memorial [2nd], 1987 (1988).
TURNER, Morrie. Inkpot, 1981.
TURNER, Paul. E. E. Evans/Paul Frehafer, 1964.
TURNER, Ron. Inkpot, 1989.
TURTLEDOVE, Harry. HOMer [Short Story], 1990 (1991). SFWA Treasurer, 1986-1987.
TURZILLO, Mary A. L. Ron Hubbard's Writers of the Future [1st Quarter, 2nd Place], 1987 (1988).
TUTTLE, Lisa. BSFA [Short Fiction], 1989 (1990). Hugo [Campbell], 1973 (1974). Locus [Novella], 1975 (1976). Nebula [Short Story (refused)], 1981 (1982).
TUTTLE, William. Oscar [Makeup Achievement], 1964. Saturn [Makeup], 1975 (1976), 1976 (1977), 1978 (1979), 1979 (1980).

TWAIN, Mark. Hall of Fame Colonnade Inductee, 1920. DGoH World SF Convention, 1993.
TWEET, Roald. SFRA Newsletter Editor, 1978-1981.
TYMN, Marshall B. IAFA [Collins], 1988 (1989). Karel [Special President's], 1986 (1987). Pilgrim, 1990. SFRA Treasurer, 1977-1978; Vice President, 1979-1980.
TYRELL, Susan. Saturn [Supporting Actress], 1977 (1978).
URDIALES, Richard. L. Ron Hubbard's Writers of the Future [3rd Quarter, 3rd Place], 1987 (1988).
VALCOUR, Paul. Casper [Fan Achievement (Organizational)], 1988 (1989).
VALENTINO, Jim. Inkpot, 1984.
VALÉRY, Francis. Prix Rosny-Aîné [Novelette], 1989.
VALLEJO, Boris. British Fantasy [Artist], 1978 (1979). Inkpot, 1978. AGoH World Fantasy Convention, 1980.
VAN ALLSBURG, Chris. World Fantasy [Special (Professional)], 1984 (1985).
VAN DER VEER, Frank. Oscar [Visual Effects Special Achievement], 1976.
VAN EIOYCK, Annemarie. Karel, 1981 (1982); [Special], 1983 (1984).
VAN HISE, James. Inkpot, 1983.
VAN HOUTEN, Ray. Hugo [Amateur Magazine], 1954 (1955), 1956 (1957).
VAN TOORN, Kees. Eurocon [Promoter], 1990 (1991).
VAN ULSEN, Henk. Festival Internazional del Film [Silver Asteroid—Actor], 1974 (1975).
VAN VOGT, A. E.
  Casper [Lifetime Achievement], 1980.
  Count Dracula Society [Literature], 1967 (1968).
  Forry, 1972.
  Jules Verne [Life Achievement in SF], 1982 (1983).
  Premios Italiano di Fantascienza [Special], 1980 (1981).
  Saturn [Literature], 1978 (1979).
  GoH World SF Convention, 1946.
VANCE, Jack.
  Edgar Allen Poe, 1961.
  Gilgamés [Fantasy Novel], 1987 (1988); [SF Novel], 1988 (1989).
  Hugo [Short Fiction], 1962 (1963); [Novelette], 1966 (1967).
  Jupiter [Novelette], 1974 (1975).
  Nebula [Novella], 1966 (1967).
  World Fantasy [Lifetime Achievement], 1983 (1984); [Novel], 1989 (1990).
  GoH World Fantasy Convention, 1980.
  GoH World SF Convention, 1992.
VANDERMEER, Jeff. Fear Fiction [Established Author], 1990 (1991).
VARLEY, John.
  Gilgamés [SF Collection], 1984 (1985); [SF Anthology/Collection], 1988 (1989); [SF Short Story], 1988 (1989).
  Hugo [Novella], 1978 (1979), 1984 (1985); [Short Story], 1981 (1982).
  Jupiter [Novella], 1977 (1978).
  Locus [Special], 1976 (1977); [Novella], 1978 (1979), 1981 (1982), 1984 (1985); [Novelette], 1978 (1979); [SF Novel], 1979 (1980); [Collection], 1980 (1981), 1986 (1987); [Short Story], 1981 (1982).
  Nebula [Novella], 1978 (1979), 1984 (1985).
  SF Chronicle [Short Story], 1981 (1982); [Novella], 1984 (1985).
  Seiun Taisho [Foreign Novelette], 1986 (1987).
VARLEY, Lynn. Will Eisner Comic Industry [Graphic Album (New)], 1990 (1991).
VARMA, Devendra P. Count Dracula Society [Special], 1967 (1968); [Walpole Medal], 1969 (1970), 1974 (1975), 1976 (1977); [Summers], 1970 (1971). Saturn [Literature], 1977 (1978).
VARNEY, Bill. Oscar [Sound], 1980, 1981.
VAS, Judit. Festival Internazional del Film [Golden Seal], 1969 (1970).
VASIL'EV, Vladimir. Boris Strugatsky [Essay], 1986-1990 (1991).
VEPSA, Ritva. Festival Internazional del Film [Silver Asteroid—Actress], 1968 (1969).
VERHOEVEN, Paul. Saturn [Director], 1987 (1988).
VERNAY, Jean-Pierre. Grand Prix de la SF Française [Short Fiction], 1986 (1987).

VEROUTERE, Marcel. Saturn [Special Effects], 1973/74 (1975).
VERSINS, Pierre. Hugo [Special Plaque], 1972 (1973). Karel [President's], 1985 (1986). Pilgrim, 1991.
VESS, Charles. Inkpot, 1990. Will Eisner Comic Industry [Single Issue or Story], 1990 (1991). World Fantasy [Short Fiction], 1990 (1991).
VEVERKA, Vladimir. Karel Capek [Antiwar Story], 1984 (1985).
VICTOR, Michael. Saturn [Horror Film], 1982 (1983).
VIKTOROV, Rikiard. Festival Internazional del Film [Special], 1974 (1975), 1975 (1976).
VINCENT, Larry "Seymour." Count Dracula Society [Special], 1974 (1975). Inkpot, 1975.
VINGE, Joan D. Hugo [Novelette], 1977 (1978); [Novel], 1980 (1981). Locus [SF Novel], 1980 (1981).
VINGE, Vernor. Hamilton/Brackett Memorial, 1986. Inkpot, 1992. Prometheus, 1986 (1987).
VOLODINE, Antoine. Grand Prix de la SF Française [Novel], 1985 (1986); [Short Fiction], 1986 (1987).
VONARBURG, Elisabeth.
Aurora [French Long Form], 1991 (1992).
Casper [Short Fiction], 1986 (1987); [Special], 1986 (1987); [French Short Form], 1989 (1990), 1990 (1991); [French Long Form], 1990 (1991).
Prix Rosny-Aîné [Novel], 1982.
VONNEGUT, Kurt Jr. Alkor [Translated Novel], 1989 (1990). Arts and Letters, 1970. Hugo [Dramatic Presentation], 1972 (1973). International Fantasy [3rd Fiction], 1952 (1953). Playboy Writing [Fiction Short Story], 1976.
VORLICEK, Vaclav. Festival Internazional del Film [Golden Asteroid], 1965 (1966); [Special], 1971 (1972).
VOSBURGH, Kris. Count Dracula Society [Fauria], 1973 (1974).
VOSBURGH, Linda. Count Dracula Society [Fauria], 1973 (1974).
VOSK, D. M. Readercon [Poet], 1986 (1987).
VUKOTIC, Dusan. Lazar Komarcic [Film], 1981 (1982).
WAGNER, Karl Edward. British Fantasy [Short Story], 1974 (1975), 1976 (1977), 1983 (1984); [Special], 1982 (1983). Phoenix, 1977 (1978). World Fantasy [Novella], 1982 (1983).
WAGNER, Lindsay. Emmy [Actress in Drama], 1977.
WAGNER, Matt. Inkpot, 1988.
WAGNER, Roland C. Prix Rosny-Aîné [Novelette], 1983; [Novel], 1988, 1989.
WAGNER, Roy H. Emmy [Outstanding Cinematography for a Series], 1988, 1989.
WAHL, Sharon. L. Ron Hubbard's Writers of the Future [4th Quarter, 3rd Place], 1989 (1990).
WIATER, Stanley. Bram Stoker [Nonfiction], 1990 (1991). GoH World Horror Convention, 1993.
WAKATSUKI, Megumi. Seiun Taisho [Comics], 1989 (1990).
WALAS, Chris. Saturn [Special Effects], 1984 (1985).
WALDROP, Howard. Locus [Collection], 1991 (1992). Nebula [Novelette], 1980 (1981). Readercon [Short Work], 1989 (1990). Theodore Sturgeon Memorial [2nd], 1988 (1989). World Fantasy [Short Fiction], 1980 (1981).
WALKER, Jane. L. Ron Hubbard's Illustrators of the Future [2nd Quarter], 1991 (1992).
WALKER, Mort. Inkpot, 1979. Reuben, 1953.
WALKER, Sansoucy—SEE: KATHENOR, Sansoucy.
WALLACE, Edgar. Balrog [Fantasy Film Hall of Fame], 1981 (1982).
WALLACE, Oliver. Oscar [Music Score of a Musical Picture], 1941.
WALSTON, Ray. Saturn [Life Career], 1988 (1989).
WALTER, Tracey. Saturn [Supporting Actor], 1984 (1985).
WALTERS, Bob. Chesley [Cover Illustration (Magazine)] 1984 (1985); [Interior Illustration], 1986 (1987), 1991 (1992).
WALTHER, Daniel. Grand Prix de la SF Française [Novel], 1979 (1980).
WALTON, Evangeline. World Fantasy [Special], 1984 (1985); [Lifetime Achievement], 1988 (1989). GoH World Fantasy Convention, 1985.
WANDREI, Donald. First Fandom, 1986. World Fantasy [Lifetime Achievement], 1983 (1984).

WANG, Fengzhen. Karel [Long Distance], 1982 (1983).
WANGERIN, Walter Jr. American Book [Paperback Science Fiction Novel], 1979 (1980).
WARD, Jay. Inkpot, 1977.
WARNER, Frank. Oscar [Special Achievement (Sound Effects Editing)], 1977.
WARNER, Harry Jr. Hugo [Fan Writer], 1968 (1969), 1971 (1972). Locus [Fan Writer], 1970 (1971). FGoH World SF Convention, 1971.
WARREN, Bill. E. E. Evans/Paul Frehafer, 1973.
WARRICK, Patricia. SFRA President, 1983-1985.
WASHINGTON, Ned. Oscar [Original Music Score], 1940.
WATERS, Elisabeth. Gryphon, 1988 (1989).
WATKINS, Michael. Emmy [Outstanding Cinematography for a Series], 1990.
WATKINS, Peter. Festival Internazional del Film [Golden Asteroid], 1969 (1970).
WATSON, Andy. Readercon [Fiction Magazine], 1990 (1991); [Magazine Design], 1990 (1991).
WATSON, Ian. BSFA [Novel], 1977 (1978). Prix Apollo, 1974 (1975).
WATT-EVANS, Lawrence. Davis Readers (IASFM) [Short Story], 1987 (1988), 1989 (1990). Hugo [Short Story], 1987 (1988).
WATTERSON, Bill. Will Eisner Comic Industry [Comic Strip Collection], 1991 (1992).
WATTS, Peter. Aurora [English Short Form], 1991 (1992).
WDOWIAK, Longin Albert. Karel Capek [Juvenile Writer], 1987 (1988).
WEBB, Sharon. Phoenix, 1984 (1985).
WEBBER, Colin. Gollancz/BBC Radio 4 *Bookshelf* First Fantasy Novel [2nd], 1990 (1991).
WEDDALL, Roger. Ditmar [Australian Fanzine], 1986 (1987); [Fannish Cat], 1990 (1991).
WEIN, Elizabeth. L. Ron Hubbard's Writers of the Future [1st Quarter, 2nd Place], 1992 (1993).
WEIN, Len. Inkpot, 1977.
WEINBERG, Robert. World Fantasy [Special (Nonprofessional)], 1977 (1978); [Special (Professional)], 1988 (1989).
WEINSTEIN, Elst. Hugo [Special Award], 1990 (1991).
WEIS, Margaret. DASA [Fantasy Novel], 1990 (1991).
WEISINGER, Mort. Inkpot, 1978.
WELLER, Tom. Hugo [Nonfiction], 1985 (1986).
WELLMAN, Manly Wade. British Fantasy [Special], 1985 (1986). World Fantasy [Single Author Collection/Anthology], 1973/1974 (1975); [Lifetime Achievement], 1979 (1980). GoH World Fantasy Convention, 1983.
WELTMAN, Manuel. Count Dracula Society [Walpole Medal], 1973 (1974).
WENSKE, Helmut. Kurd Lasswitz [Artist], 1983 (1984), 1984 (1985), 1985 (1986), 1988 (1989).
WENTWORTH, K. D. L. Ron Hubbard's Writers of the Future [4th Quarter, 3rd Place], 1988 (1989). SF Writers of Earth [2nd], 1988 (1989); [Author of the '80s—2nd], 1990 (1991).
WENTWORTH, Kathy D.—SEE: WENTWORTH, K. D.
WEST, Adam. Inkpot, 1980.
WEST, D. Pong [Fan Writer], 1982 (1983).
WEST, Kit. Oscar [Visual Effects], 1981.
WEST, Ray. Oscar [Sound], 1977.
WESTFALL, Norman. Oscar [Sound Effects], 1964.
WESTMORE, Michael. Emmy [Outstanding Achievement in Makeup], 1988.
WESTON, Peter. Locus [Special], 1976 (1977).
WHEATLEY, Mark. Inkpot, 1992.
WHEELER, William. Karel, 1988 (1989).
WHELAN, Michael.
    Balrog [Artist], 1979 (1980).
    Chesley [Cover Illustration (Hardback)], 1984 (1985), 1991 (1992); [Cover Illustration (Paperback)], 1986 (1987), 1990 (1991); [Unpublished Color], 1986 (1987); [Unpublished Monochrome], 1991 (1992); [Artistic Achievement], 1990 (1991).
    Davis Readers (IASFM) [Cover Artist], 1990 (1991).
    Golden Lion, 1981.

Hugo [Professional Artist], 1979 (1980), 1980 (1981), 1981 (1982), 1982 (1983), 1983 (1984), 1984 (1985), 1985 (1986), 1987 (1988), 1988 (1989), 1990 (1991), 1991 (1992); [Nonfiction], 1987 (1988); [Original Artwork], 1991 (1992).
Locus [Professional Artist], 1979 (1980), 1980 (1981), 1981 (1982), 1982 (1983), 1983 (1984), 1984 (1985), 1985 (1986), 1986 (1987), 1987 (1988), 1988 (1989), 1989 (1990), 1990 (1991), 1991 (1992).
Saturn [Book Cover Artist], 1982 (1983).
SF Chronicle [Artist], 1981 (1982), 1982 (1983), 1983 (1984), 1984 (1985), 1985 (1986), 1986 (1987), 1987 (1988), 1990 (1991).
World Fantasy [Artist], 1980 (1981), 1981 (1982), 1982 (1983).
AGoH World Fantasy Convention, 1979.
WHITBORN, John. Gollancz/BBC Radio 4 *Bookshelf* First Fantasy Novel [1st], 1990 (1991).
WHITE, Alan. Count Dracula Society [Fauria], 1970 (1971).
WHITE, James. Davis Readers (Analog) [Novelette], 1988 (1989).
WHITE, Lori Ann. L. Ron Hubbard's Writers of the Future [2nd Quarter, 3rd Place], 1986 (1987).
WHITE, T. H. Gilgamés [Horror Short Story], 1989 (1990).
WHITE, Ted. Hugo [Fan Artist], 1967 (1968). FGoH World SF Convention, 1985.
WHITE, Tim. BSFA [Artist], 1982 (1983).
WHITMORE, Andrew. Ditmar [Atheling], 1977 (1978); [Short Australian Fiction], 1983 (1984).
WHITTAKER, Thomas. L. Ron Hubbard's Illustrators of the Future [4th Quarter], 1991 (1992).
WIDNER, Arthur L. Jr. Big Heart, 1989.
WILDEO, Kelley. Bram Stoker [First Novel], 1988 (1989).
WILDER, Cherry. Ditmar [Austrlian Novel], 1977 (1978).
WILDER, Gene. Hugo [Dramatic Presentation], 1974 (1975). Nebula [Dramatic Presentation], 1975 (1976).
WILHELM, Kate.
Hugo [Novel], 1976 (1977).
Jupiter [Novel], 1976 (1977).
Locus [Novel], 1976 (1977).
Nebula [Short Story], 1968 (1969), 1987 (1988); [Novelette], 1986 (1987).
Prix Apollo, 1980 (1981).
GoH World SF Convention, 1980.
WILLARD, Nancy. IAFA [Crawford], 1985 (1986).
WILLIAMS, John. Oscar [Original Music Score for a Motion Picture (Not a Musical)], 1977; [Original Music Score], 1982. Saturn [Music], 1977 (1978), 1978 (1979), 1981 (1982), 1982 (1983).
WILLIAMS, Lawrence Allen. L. Ron Hubbard's Illustrators of the Future [3rd Quarter], 1990 (1991).
WILLIAMS, Paul O. Hugo [Campbell], 1982 (1983).
WILLIAMS, Richard. Festival Internazionale del Film [Silver Seal], 1962 (1963). Oscar [Special Achievement (Animation Direction)], 1988; [Visual Effects], 1988. Saturn [Special Effects], 1988 (1989).
WILLIAMS, Robert. Inkpot, 1982.
WILLIAMS, Sean. L. Ron Hubbard's Writers of the Future [1st Quarter, 3rd Place], 1992 (1993).
WILLIAMS, Tad. Science Fiction Book Club [2nd], 1989 (1990).
WILLIAMS, Walter Jon. Rhysling [Long Poem], 1988 (1989).
WILLIAMSON, Al. Inkpot, 1984. Jules Verne [Life Achievement in Comics], 1982 (1983). Will Eisner Comic Industry [Inker], 1990 (1991).
WILLIAMSON, Chet. HWA Vice President, 1990-1991.
WILLIAMSON, J. N. Balrog [Professional Publication], 1984 (1985). HWA Secretary, 1987-1988.
WILLIAMSON, Jack.
First Fandom, 1968.
Forry, 1986.
Hugo [Nonfiction], 1984 (1985).

L. *Ron Hubbard's Writers of the Future* [Special Golden Age], 1988 (1989).
Nebula [Grand Master], 1975 (1976).
Pilgrim, 1973.
Skylark, 1985.
SFWA President, 1978-1980.
GoH World SF Convention, 1977.
WILLIS, Connie.
Davis Readers (IASFM) [Novella], 1986 (1987), 1988 (1989).
Hugo [Novelette], 1982 (1983); [Novella], 1988 (1989).
John W. Campbell, Jr. Memorial [Winner], 1987 (1988).
Nebula [Novelette], 1982 (1983), 1989 (1990); [Short Story], 1982 (1983); [Novella], 1988 (1989).
SF Chronicle [Novella], 1988 (1989); [Novelette], 1982 (1983).
WILLIS, Matthew. L. Ron Hubbard's Writers of the Future [2nd Quarter, 3rd Place], 1989 (1990).
WILLIS, Walter A. Ditmar [Pat Terry], 1980 (1981). Hugo [Most Outstanding Actifan], 1957 (1958). FGoH World SF Convention, 1992.
WILLS, Mary. Oscar [Costume Design (Color)], 1962.
WILSON, A. N. NCR Book for Nonfiction, 1990.
WILSON, Dawn. Chesley [Unpublished Color], 1984 (1985); [Unpublished Monochrome], 1987 (1988). SF Chronicle [Most Attractive Female Artist], 1983 (1984).
WILSON, F. Paul. Prometheus, 1978 (1979); [Hall of Fame], 1990, 1991. GoH World Fantasy Convention, 1990.
WILSON, Gahan. Bram Stoker [Life Achievement], 1991 (1992). Inkpot, 1989. World Fantasy [Special], 1980 (1981).
WILSON, Red. Emmy [Outstanding Achievement in Makeup], 1986.
WILSON, Richard. Nebula [Novelette], 1968 (1969).
WILSON, Robert Anton. Prometheus Hall of Fame, 1986.
WILSON, Sam. L. Ron Hubbard's Writers of the Future [3rd Quarter, 3rd Place], 1991 (1992).
WILSON, William G. Jr. Saturn [Special], 1979 (1980).
WIMMER, Heinrich. Kurd Lasswitz [Special], 1983 (1984).
WINDLING, Terri. World Fantasy [Anthology/Collection], 1981 (1982) [Anthology], 1988 (1989), 1989 (1990), 1991 (1992); [Special (Professional)], 1988 (1989).
WINKLER, Timothy. L. Ron Hubbard's Illustrators of the Future [3rd Quarter], 1989 (1990).
WINOGURA, Dale. Saturn [Film Critic], 1975 (1976).
WINSOR-SMITH, Barry. Inkpot, 1975.
WINSTON, Stan. Oscar [Visual Effects], 1986. Saturn [Makeup], 1984 (1985).
WINTER, Douglas E. SF Chronicle [Buns], 1983 (1984). World Fantasy [Special (Nonprofessional)], 1985 (1986).
WINTREBERT, Joëlle. Grand Prix de la SF Française [Novel], 1987 (1988). Prix Rosny-Aîné [Novelette], 1980; [Novel], 1988.
WISE, Robert. Count Dracula Society [Cinema], 1972 (1973).
WISKES, Andrew. Saturn [Sound], 1978 (1979).
WOGGON, Bill. Inkpot, 1981.
WOGGON, Elmer. Inkpot, 1978.
WOHLGEMUTH, Tim. Saturn [Outstanding Service], 1979 (1980).
WOJCIK, Andrzej. Polish SF & Fantasy Achievement [Special], 1985 (1986).
WOLF, Eric Carl. SF Writers of Earth [1st], 1986 (1987).
WOLF, Leonard. Count Dracula Society [Literature], 1975 (1976), 1978 (1979).
WOLFE, Gary K. J. Lloyd Eaton Memorial, 1979 (1981). Pilgrim, 1987.
WOLFE, Gene.
British Fantasy [August Derleth], 1982 (1983).
BSFA [Novel], 1981 (1982).
Gilgamés [SF Novel], 1989 (1990).
John W. Campbell, Jr. Memorial [Winner], 1983 (1984).
Locus [Novella], 1973 (1974); [Fantasy Novel], 1981 (1982), 1982 (1983), 1986 (1987).
Nebula [Novella], 1973 (1974); [Novel], 1981 (1982).
Prix Apollo, 1984 (1985).

Rhysling [Long Poem], 1977 (1978).
SF Chronicle [Novel], 1981 (1982), 1982 (1983), 1987 (1988).
Skylark, 1989.
World Fantasy [Novel], 1980 (1981); [Collection], 1988 (1989).
GoH World Fantasy Convention, 1983; World SF Convention, 1985.
WOLFMAN, Marv. Inkpot, 1979.
WOLLHEIM, Betsy. Chesley [Art Direction], 1989 (1990), 1991 (1992).
WOLLHEIM, Donald A.
British Fantasy [Special], 1983 (1984).
Forry, 1987.
Golden Lion, 1983.
Hugo [Publisher], 1963 (1964); [Special Plaque], 1974 (1975).
Karel [President's], 1983 (1984).
Locus [Reprint Anthology/Collection], 1971 (1972).
Milford, 1980.
World Fantasy [Special (Professional)], 1980 (1981); [Special], 1985 (1986).
GoH World SF Convention, 1988.
WOLLHEIM, Elsie. British Fantasy [Special], 1983 (1984).
WOLVERTON, Dave. L. Ron Hubbard's Writers of the Future [4th Quarter, 1st Place], 1986 (1987); [Gold], 1986 (1987). Philip K. Dick Memorial [2nd], 1989 (1990).
WOOD, Susan. Ditmar [Atheling], 1978 (1979). Casper [Lifetime Achievement], 1981. Hugo [Fan Writer], 1973 (1974), 1976 (1977), 1980 (1981), [Fanzine], 1972 (1973) (as Susan Glicksohn).
WOOD, Wally. Inkpot, 1980. Will Eisner Comic Industry [Hall of Fame Inductee], 1991 (1992).
WOODS, Jack. Festival Internazional del Film [Special], 1971 (1972).
WOODWORTH, Stephen. L. Ron Hubbard's Writers of the Future [4th Quarter, 1st Place], 1991 (1992).
WRAY, Fay. Count Dracula Society [Cunningham], 1972 (1973). Saturn [Special], 1973/74 (1975).
WREN, Thomas. Crook/Tall, 1986 (1987).
WRIGHTSON, Berni. Clampett, 1986. Inkpot, 1987.
WU, Diana G. Gallagher—SEE: GALLAGHER, Diana G.
WUL, Stephen. Prix Julia Verlanger [Lifetime Achievement], 1985 (1986).
WURTS, Janny. HOMer [Fantasy Novel], 1990 (1991).
WYNDHAM, John. International Fantasy [2nd Fiction], 1951 (1952).
XIANKUI, Wu. China SF Constellation/Galaxy, 1985 (1986).
XINGSHI, Liu. China SF Constellation/Galaxy, 1985 (1986); 1990 (1991). China SF Milky Way/Forest Cup [2nd], 1990 (1991).
YAHUA, Wei. China SF Constellation/Galaxy, 1985 (1986).
YAMAOKA, Ken. Seiun Taisho [Shibano], 1986 (1987).
YAN, Wu. China SF Constellation/Galaxy, 1985 (1986), 1990 (1991). China SF Milky Way/Forest Cup [3rd], 1990 (1991).
YANG, Xiao. Karel [Long Distance], 1988 (1989); [Special Award], 1990 (1991).
YANO, Tetsu. Karel, 1984 (1985). Seiun Taisho [Shibano], 1983 (1984); [Nonfiction], 1987 (1988).
YAP, Johnson. Festival Internazional del Film [Silver Asteroid—Actor], 1978 (1979).
YARBRO, Chelsea Quinn. SFWA Secretary, 1970-1972. HWA President, 1989-1990; President of Trustees, 1992- .
YASUDA, Hisaki. Davis Readers (IASFM) [Cover Artist], 1988 (1989).
YEATMAN, Hoyt. Oscar [Visual Effects], 1989.
YEH, Phil. Clampett, 1989.
YEP, Lawrence. Boston Globe Horn Book, 1977. Children's Book, 1976.
YOKOTA, Junya. Nihon SF Taisho, 1987 (1988).
YOKOYAMA, Eiji. Seiun Taisho [Artist], 1990 (1991); [Comics], 1990 (1991).
YOLEN, Jane.
Catholic Library Association Regina Medal, 1992.
Daedalus [Fantasy Short Story], 1986 (1987).
Dell Readers (IASFM) [Poem], 1991 (1992).
Skylark, 1990.

World Fantasy [Special (Professional)], 1986 (1987).
SFWA President, 1986-1988.
GoH World Fantasy Convention, 1984.
YORK, J. Steven. L. Ron Hubbard's Writers of the Future [3rd Quarter, 3rd Place], 1988 (1989).
YOUNG, Bramwell. Count Dracula Society [Summers], 1978 (1979).
YOUNG, Chic. Reuben, 1948.
YOUNG, Christopher. Saturn [Music], 1988 (1989).
YOUNG, Peter. Oscar [Set Decoration], 1989.
YOUNT, Rena. Clarion [3rd], 1984.
YRONWODE, Cat. Inkpot, 1983.
YULSMAN, Jerry. Kurd Lasswitz [Foreign Novel], 1986 (1987).
YUMEMAKURA, Baku. Nihon SF Taisho, 1988 (1989). Seiun Taisho [Novel], 1989 (1990); [Short Story], 1990 (1991).
YUNSHEN, Jiang. China SF Milky Way/Forest Cup [2nd], 1990 (1991).
YURICICH, Matthew. Oscar [Visual Effects Special Achievement], 1976, 1977.
YURICICH, Richard. Oscar [Visual Effects Special Achievement], 1977. Saturn [Special Effects], 1979 (1980).
YURIEV, Zinovi. Aëlita, 1982 (1983).
ZAGRIAJSKI, Boris. Festival Internazional del Film [Golden Seal], 1974 (1975).
ZAHN, Timothy. Hugo [Novella], 1983 (1984).
ZAJDEL, Janusz A. Fantastyka [Grand Master], 1984 (1985). Polish SF & Fantasy Achievement [Author], 1984 (1985); [Polish Fandom], 1984 (1985).
ZAKHARCHENKO, Vasily. Karel, 1983 (1984).
ZAMBRENO, Mary Frances. L. Ron Hubbard's Writers of the Future [2nd Quarter, 2nd Place], 1984 (1985).
ZAUNER, Georg. Kurd Lasswitz [Novel], 1980 (1981).
ZAVGORODNY, Boris. Karel [Long Distance], 1988 (1989).
ZDINAK, Richard S. Saturn [Special], 1979 (1980).
ZELAZNY, Roger.
  Alkor [Translated Novel], 1989 (1990).
  Balrog [Short Fiction], 1979 (1980); [Collection/Anthology], 1983 (1984).
  Hugo [Novel], 1965 (1966), 1967 (1968); [Novella], 1975 (1976), 1985 (1986); [Novelette], 1981 (1982), 1986 (1987).
  Lazar Komarcic [Foreign Novel], 1985 (1986).
  Locus [Collection], 1983 (1984); [Fantasy Novel], 1985 (1986).
  Nebula [Novella], 1965 (1966), 1975 (1976); [Novelette], 1965 (1966).
  Prix Apollo, 1971 (1972).
  Seiun Taisho [Foreign Novelette], 1983 (1984).
  SFWA Secretary/Treasurer, 1967-1968.
  GoH World SF Convention, 1974.
ZELEZNY, Ivo. Karel Capek [Special], 1983 (1984). Ludvik Soucek [Anthology], 1983 (1984).
ZEMECKIS, Robert. Saturn [Director], 1988 (1989). SF Chronicle [Dramatic Presentation], 1985 (1986).
ZHU, Jianjiong. IAFA [Graduate Scholarship], 1989 (1990).
ZIEGLER, Thomas. Kurd Lasswitz [Novella], 1980 (1981), 1983 (1984).
ZIEMIANSKI, Andrzej. Polish SF & Fantasy Achievement [Novel], 1987 (1988).
ZIESING, Mark V. Readercon [Reprinted Item], 1989 (1990); [Value in Bookcraft], 1990 (1991); [Fiction Magazine], 1990 (1991); [Magazine Design], 1990 (1991). World Fantasy [Special (Professional)], 1989 (1990).
ZILLIG, Werner. Kurd Lasswitz [Novelette], 1989 (1990).
ZINDELL, David. L. Ron Hubbard's Writers of the Future [1st Place], 1984 (1985).
ZIPES, Jack. IAFA [Distinguished Scholarship], 1991 (1992).
ZIVKOVIC, Bob. Lazar Komarcic [Artist], 1986 (1987), 1988 (1989).
ZONE, Ray. Inkpot, 1987.
ZSIGMOND, Wilmos. Oscar [Cinematography], 1977.
ZUDDAS, Gianluigi. Premios Italiano di Fantascienza [Novel], 1978 (1979).

INDEX TO AWARD NAMES

A. Bertram Chandler, 14
Academy of Family Films & Family TV, 142
Ackerman, 51-52
A.D.E.-M.L.A. Distinguished Teaching, 142
Aëlita, 14
Aerospace Communications, 142
Aisling Gheal, 14-15
Alkor Poll Awards, 15
Alvar Appletofft Memorial, 16
American Book, 142
American Mystery, 143
American Studies Book Prize, 143
Andre Norton, 16
Andre Norton Fantasy/SF Short Story, 16-17
Ann Radcliffe, 44-48
Antonius Prize of Danish Society, 143
Apollo, 109-110
Arthur C. Clarke, 17-18
Arts and Letters, 143
Atheling, 39-43
Athenaeum Literary, 143
Atlanta Fantasy Faire, 18
Atorox, 18
August Derleth, 22-25
Aurora, 27-28
Avery Hopwood Drama, 160
AWA Writing, 143-144
Award of Merit Medal, 144
Balrog, 18-20
BBC Radio 4 *Bookshelf* First Fantasy, 54
Benson Medal, 144
Bertram Chandler, 15
Bess Hokin Prize, 144
Big Heart, 60-61
Boomerang, 20-21
Boréal, 110
Boris Strugatsky Prize, 21
Boston Globe Horn Book, 144
Brackett/Hamilton Memorial, 63
Bram Stoker, 21-22
Brandeis University Creative Arts, 149
Bright Vision, 16
British Critics, 144
British Fantasy, 22-25
British SF Association, 25-27
Brown University, 145
Buenos Aires City Hall Literary Prize, 145
Caldecott Medal, 145

California Writers, 145
Campbell Jr., 58-67
Campbell Jr. Memorial, 73-75
Canadian SF&F Achievement, 33-35
Capek (Cena Karla Capka), 77-78
Capek (Karels), 76-77
Carl Hertzog/University of Texas, 160
Carnegie Medal, 145
Casper, 27-28
Catholic Library Assoc. Regina Medal, 145
Chandler, 15
Chesley, 28-30
Children's Book, 145
China SF Constellation/Galaxy, 30-31
China SF Milky Way/Forest Cup, 31
The Chronic Rift Roundtable, 31
Chumatski Shlyah, 31
Clampett Humanitarian, 32
Clarion, 32
Clark Darlton Prize, 32
Clarke, 17-18
Cleveland Critics, 146
Collectors, 32-33
Collins, 69-70
Cometa d'Argento, 103-104
Compton N. Crook/Stephen Tall, 33
Cosmos 2000, 110
Count Dracula Society, 34-37
Crawford Memorial, 69-70
Crook/Stephen Tall Memorial, 33
Cunningham International Cinema, 34-37
Daedalus, 37
Daroff Memorial Fiction, 146
DASA, 37
Davies, 214
Davis Readers, 37-39
Dell Readers, 37-39
Derleth, 26-29
Deutscher Fantasy Preis, 39
Dick, 131-132
Distinguished Scholarship, 69-70
Ditmar, 39-43
Doc Weir, 43
Donaldson Memorial, 140-141
Dracula, 34-37
Dracula Society, 34-37
Duodecimal Society, 146
Dwight V. Swain, 160
E. E. Evans/Paul Frehafer, 43-44
E. Everett Evans "Big Heart," 44
Early Universe, 45

245

Eastcon, 45
Eaton Memorial, 71-72
Edgar (Allan Poe), 146
Edmond Hamilton/Leigh Brackett, 45
Edward E. "Doc" Smith Memorial, 132-133
Eisner Comic Industry, 135-136
Emmy, 146-148
Empire State Award, Excellence in Lit., 148
Eunice Tietjens Memorial, 148
Eurocon, 45-46
Evans "Big Heart," 44
Evans/Paul Frehafer, 43-44
Fandom Hall of Fame, 65
Fantastyka, 46
Fantasy Faire, 19
Fantasy Film Hall of Fame, 20-22
Fauria, 34-37
Fear Fiction, 47
Festival Fantastique d'Avoriaz, 47
Festival Internazionale del Film, 47-51
First Fandom Hall of Fame, 51
Fond Fantastiki Prize, 51
Forest Cup/China SF Milky Way, 31
Forry (Ackerman), 51-52
Frank R. Cunningham Cinema, 44-48
Frank R. Paul, 52
Freedom Foundation at Valley Forge, 148
Frehafer/E. E. Evans, 43-44
Galaxy/China SF Constellation, 30-31
Galaxy/Dell SF Novel Contest, 52
Gandalf, 58-67
Gaughan Memorial, 72
George Pal Memorial, 118-124
Georges Méliès, 53
Gernsback, 53
Gilgamés, 104-107
Gold, 107-112
Golden Asteroid, 47-51
Golden Duck, 53-54
Golden Globe, 148
Golden Lion, 54
Golden Meteor, 102-103
Golden Seal of the City of Trieste, 47-51
Golem, 92-93
Gollancz/BBC Radio 4 *Bookshelf*, 54
Governor General's Literary, 148
Graduate Scholarship, 69-70
Grand Prix de la SF Française, 54-56
Grand Prix Logidec, 56
Graviton, 56
Gray Mouser, 56-57
Great Ring, 14
Grimmy, 57
Gryphon, 57
Hall of Fame Colonnade, 148
Hamilton/Leigh Brackett Memorial, 45
Hans Christian Andersen Medal, 149

Harold D. Vursell Memorial, 149
Harrison, 76-77
Harry Harrison, 76-77
Heinemann, 149
HOMer, 57
Horace Walpole Medal, 34-37
Horror Hall of Fame, 57
Howard, 136-139
Hubbard's Illustrators of the Future, 81-85
Hubbard's Writers of the Future, 81-85
Hugo, 58-67
IAM Readers Contest, 67
Icarus, 22-25
Illustrators of the Future, 107-112
Image, 149
Inez & Virgil Fauria, 44-48
Inkpot, 67-68
International Association for the Fantastic in the Arts, 69-70
International Fantasy Award, 70
International Forum for Neurological Organization, 149
Invisible Little Man, 71
Isaac Asimov's SF Magazine, 50-52
Italiano di Fantascienza, 107-109
Ivan Yefremov, 14
J. Lloyd Eaton Memorial, 71-72
Jack Gaughan Memorial, 72
Jack I. & Lillian L. Poses, 149
James J. Strebig, 150
James Tait Black Memorial Prize, 150
James Tiptree Jr. Memorial, 72
Janusz A. Zajdel, 102-103
Japan Fantasy Novel, 72
Jerónimo Montiero Contest, 73
Jerry Oltion Really Good Story, 73
Jerusalem Prize, 150
John Llewelyn Rhys Memorial Prize, 150
John Masefield, 150
John W. Campbell Jr., 58-67
John W. Campbell Jr. Memorial, 73-75
Jules Verne, 75
Jules Verne (Prix), 111
Julia Verlanger, 111
Jupiter, 75-76
Karel, 76-77
Karel Capek, 77-78
Ken McIntyre, 78-79
King Kong, 79
Knighthood of Mark Twain, 150
Komarcic, 86-87
Kurd Lasswitz, 79-81
L. Ron Hubbard's Illustrators, 81-85
L. Ron Hubbard's Writers, 81-85
Lambda Literary, 85
Lasswitz, 79-81
Lazar Komarcic, 86-87

Leigh Brackett/Edmond Hamilton Memorial, 45
Lenin Peace Prize, 151
Levinson Prize, 151
Locus, 87-92
Long Distance, 76-77
Ludvik Soucek, 92-93
Macmillan Cock Robin, 151
Manchester Guardian Fiction Prize, 151
Mannesmann-Tally, 93
Manning, 117-118
Mary Lyons, 151
Más Allá, 93
McIntyre, 78-79
Medicis Prize, 151
Méliès, 53
Melville Cane, 151
Milford, 94
Minnesota Fantasy, 94
Mlok, 77-78
Montague Summers, 34-37
Montiero Contest, 73
Morton Dauwen Zabel, 152
Mythopoeic Society Fantasy, 94-95
N3F Amateur Short Story Contest, 95-96
NASA Headquarters Exceptional Performance, 152
NCR Book Award for Nonfiction, 152
National Book, 142
Nebula, 96-99
New York Critics, 152
Newbery Medal, 152
Nihon Science Fiction Taisho, 99
Nobel Prize, 152
Norton Fantasy/SF Short Story, 17
Nova, 100
Oklahoma Professional Writers Hall of Fame, 152
Oltion Really Good Story, 73
Oscar, 153-156
Pal, 118-124
Pat Terry, 39-43
Patsy, 156-157
Paul, Frank R., 52
Paul Frehafer/E. E. Evans, 43-44
Peabody, 157
Philip K. Dick Memorial, 100-101
Phoenix, 101
Pilgrim, 101-102
Pioneer, 101-102
Playboy Writing, 157
Polish SF&F Achievement, 102-103
Pong, 103
Premios Cometa d'Argento, 103-104
Premios Gilgamés, 104-107
Premios Italiano di Fantascienza, 107-109
Presidential Medal of Freedom, 157
President's Award (Count Dracula), 34-37

President's Award (Karels), 76-77
President's Hall of Fame, 138-139
Prisoners of Gravity Reality 1, 109
Prix Apollo, 109-110
Prix Boréal, 110
Prix Cosmos 2000, 110
Prix du Meilleur Roman Etranger, 157
Prix Jules Verne, 111
Prix Julia Verlanger, 111
Prix Rosny-Aîné, 111-112
Prix Rotary, 112
Prix Sylla Monsegur, 157
Prometheus, 112-113
Prometheus Hall of Fame, 112-113
Pulitzer Prize, 158
Pyramid Books/*F&SF*/Kent SF Novel Contest, 113
Radcliffe, 44-48
Radio 4 *Bookshelf* First Fantasy Novel, 54
Readercon Small Press, 113-115
Reality 1 Commendation, 109
Rebel, 101
Reuben, 115-116
Rhysling, 116-117
R1ckie, 109
Robbie, 117
Robert A. Collins, 69-70
Robert S. Ball Memorial, 158
Rosny-Aîné, 111-112
Rotary, 112
Russ Manning, 117-118
Saturn (film), 118-124
Saturn (literary), 124
Science Fiction & Fantasy Workshop, 125
Science Fiction Book Club, 125
Science Fiction Chronicle, 125-128
Science Fiction Club Deutschland, 128
Science Fiction Games of the Year, 129
Science Fiction Film Hall of Fame, 20-22
Science Fiction Writers of Earth, 129-130
Seiun Taisho, 130-132
SFinks, 102-103
Shasta Publishers/Pocket Books Contest, 132
Shibano, 130-132
Sidney Howard Memorial, 158
Silver Asteroid, 47-51
Silver Seal of the City of Trieste, 47-51
Skylark, 132-133
Smith Memorial, 132-133
Soccon, 133
Somerset Maugham, 158
Soucek, 92-93
Southpaw, 133
Southwest Book, 158
Spur, 158
Start, 14

Stephen Tall/Compton N. Crook Memorial, 33
Stoker, 24-25
Strugatsky Prize, 21
Sturgeon Memorial, 73-75
Summers Memorial, 34-37
Svenska SF Priset, 133-134
Tall/Compton N. Crook Memorial, 43
Terry, 39-43
Theodore Sturgeon Memorial, 73-75
Theresa Holburn Memorial, 159
Tiptree Jr. Memorial, 72
Top Hands, 159
Turner Tomorrow, 134
Twilight Dimension, 134
U.S. Air Force Academy Special Achievement, 159
U.S. Industrial Film and Video Festival, 159
U.S.S.R. Writers' Union, 159
Union League Arts and Civic Foundation Poetry Prize, 159
University of Chicago Professional Achievement, 160
University of Michigan/Avery Hopwood Drama, 160
University of Texas/Carl Hertzog, 160
Verlanger, 111
Verne, 75
Verne (Prix), 111
ViRA, 160
Virgil & Inez Fauria, 44-48
W. H. Smith Illustration, 160
Waldo, 161
Walpole Gold Medal, 34-37
Weir, 43
Western Heritage, 161
Wetzlar Fantastik Preis, 134
Whitbread Prize, 161
Will Eisner Comic Industry, 135-136
William Allen White Children's Book, 161
William Atheling Jr., 39-43
William L. Crawford Memorial, 69-70
World Fantasy, 136-139
Writers Guild, 161-162
Writers of the Future, 107-112
Writers of the Past, 140
Yefremov, 14
Zajdel, 102-103
Zauber Zeit, 140
Zeus, 37